Black Book

February 2024 [Episodes #2819-2847]

Dre Baldwin & Work On Your Game Inc.

Copyright

Contents

A Note About How The Black Book is Created

All the material in the Black Book references an episode of Dre Baldwin's **Work On Your Game MasterClass** (Podcast).

You can find ALL the episodes to listen along to at http://WorkOnYourGamePodcast.com. We release the Black Book the month *after* the episodes are published (so, the episodes listed in this issue were published last month).

We created the Black Book by using auto-transcription of Dre's recorded voice. So, there ~~may~~ will be some "typos" and mis-transcribed words!

The transcription is accurate enough, however, that the main message is maintained in the process. Over time, these (along with technology) will improve.

If you'd like, the best thing we recommend is listening to the audio episodes and seeing the video (all episodes are at http://WorkOnYourGamePodcast.com and full episode pages are at http://www.DreAllDay.com/blog) along with reading the Black Book to get the exact wording of what Dre is saying.

Enjoy!

#2819: Say NO To Drugs

Let's get into this topic, which is to say no to drugs. Now if you are on my email list, which if you are not, I would suggest you get on it, it is free. I write a lot and almost as frequently as I put the show out I write.

So go to work on my game.com, work on my game.com. That's how you can get on my email list. It is free. I do a lot of stuff for free. If you didn't know, I wrote an article about this in late December, 2023, about the time where this happened, where what happened is I unknowingly took some gummies that were unknowingly very strongly infused with Delta eight. Those of you don't know what Delta eight is. In short, it is a synthetic form of THC. You don't know what THC is. THC is the ingredient that is high in marijuana. So when people smoke marijuana and they get high, THC is the ingredient that makes them get high. So Delta eight is basically a laboratory created version of THC, which often means it is much stronger than the natural version, which it is. That's what Delta eight is.

So if you think of right now on my desk, I have a bag of Skittles. The sugar in Skittles is not natural sugar. It's not the same. The sugar that you would get from a banana or an orange, I got a banana on my desk as well. So the sugar and Skittles, which I'm looking at this, let's see, corn syrup, hydrogenated palm kernel oil, modified corn starts, natural and artificial flavors, colors like red, 40 lake, yellow five, lake blue, five lake, all this shit is a bunch of chemical garbage and yes, I'm eating them anyway. Alright, candy is probably my personal vice. If you just look through my whole life and follow me around with a hidden camera. My vice is eating candy so I know it's garbage and I still eat it. So the sugar that is in candy is not natural. The same way that the delta ate is not the natural thing to get you high.

Again, if you ate an orange, you can get sugar from an orange but is not nearly as potent as the sugar that is in candy. This is why nobody sits around and eats oranges all day and they're addicted to oranges. But people will sit around and eat candy and candy bars and Skittles and Twizzlers all day to get addicted to this stuff because the laboratory may be designed to do that. So this is what happened and the way that I ended up taking these gummies, I told you I unknowingly took them and mistakenly took them. How do you magically just eat something? It doesn't make any sense. Well, let me make sense of it. So I appear on a lot of other people's podcasts, other people's platforms, and when I appear on other people's platforms, I would say about 30% of the shows I appear on, I appear on somewhere between 50 and 150 shows per year.

About 30% of them will send me some type of physical care package as a thank you gift after my appearance, maybe 25%. And this one particular show I was on, I'm not going to say the name of the show because I don't want people to get a negative impression of their product. I think their product did exactly what it was supposed to do. So I was on this person's show and this person, I will say it was a man, this person owns a company that makes Delta eight products, basically CBD based products. Don't ask me what CBD based means. You can look it up, it's easily Googleable. So he sent me a care package and in his package what his company did was a hat, a thank you note, thanks for being on the show and all of that. And then it was like three sample packs of his CBD gummies and these are gummies, they're like little gumdrops.

And there were two pieces in each pack. It was two of them that were like a nighttime version, ones that I guess you take at night to go to sleep. And it was one of 'em that was like a regular, I guess daytime version. So I'm not that stupid. I wasn't just going to take these because I don't normally take any type of, I don't even take over the counter drugs. I don't go to the pharmacy and buy, I don't take Advil or Tylenol. So let alone am I going to just put some gummies into my body just because no, I wouldn't do that. So before I did it, I reached out to a friend of mine who does engage in drug use and I asked this friend, Hey, this is what I got. I sent my friend a picture of the sample package that I had with the label and all of that.

Are these safe to take? How much would this affect somebody like me? Alright. And this person knows me well. They know that I don't take drugs, I don't put anything foreign in my body and I'm an athlete. They know all this stuff. And they said, oh well you'll be cool. And then they said, wait a minute, is that Delta eight? They said, no, Delta eight will really get you fucked up high. And then they came back and said, oh no, no, no, no, no, you're good. I just looked it up. No, you're good. You can take it. It is something that, and this person was saying, I knew somebody who was kind of old and they were arthritic and they took it and it was just for relaxing your muscles and stuff like that. So if you have any muscle or joint pain, it'll help you for that.

But other than that, you'll be completely fine. Now, I don't have any muscle or joint pain and they said I'll be fine. I said, all right, well let me try it. What's the worst thing that can happen? Let me just try this and let me just see what all the buzz is about when it comes to CBD products and Delta eight and all this stuff. Last time I consumed any form of this type of drug was the last time I smoked twice in my entire life. The last time I smoked was the summer after my freshman year, before my sophomore year of college. That was the last time I smoked and I didn't even get high. So it was probably some shitty weed that I had smoked and I only hid it one time, literally one time. So that's my experience when it comes to taking in this type of stuff.

So I took the gummies at about, and again, you can read the article about this by the way it's called because I got High, because I got high. So you can find that on@dreallday.com or anywhere else that you follow me. You'll find that article or in your inbox if you're in my email list. Now, when I took this stuff at about 3:45 PM on a Sunday and by four o'clock I could start to feel a little bit like a little buzz in my head, yeah, this is starting to do something and within about an hour, about 4 30, 4 40 5:00 PM that Sunday, no later than that, I would say about five o'clock, about five to five 30, that shit hit hard and I was high if that's what high is, I was high, yes, I hope that was what it was. It was strong. So strong that, and again, you can read the article where I went into more detail on this.

I'm not going to do it all here, but it was like my conscious brain was registering everything that happened about 15 seconds after it occurred and time felt like it was passing either extremely slowly or extremely quickly, but it wasn't happening in normal time. So I would walk, I was outside taking my son on a walk and yes, I did this while I was high and I would take 10 steps and in my conscious mind finding registered, how did I get from here? How did I get here 10 steps ago? I looked back 10 steps ago and it felt like it was like three days ago that I was there, or it felt like it was two seconds ago, but it wasn't either one because that's how it kind of bended my brain or mixed up my brain. I don't know what you called this.

I guess you just called high. Alright, that's what it was. I was high in this situation. And again, go to DRE all day.com/blog and you can read the article yourself. And this high lasted. So the interesting thing about the high, actually let me add this, is that I was doing all the right things. I didn't do anything crazy or stupid. I didn't say anything crazy or stupid. My subconscious mind was controlling everything. The good thing is I have very good habits. I'm a disciplined individual. So my subconscious mind took over. I did everything normally. My son didn't get in any type of trouble. I didn't get in any trouble. We were never in danger. I walked around the park and it was completely fine. I was out with my son for an hour, came home and it was still, my brain was all boggled. It was all boggled.

I couldn't do anything. So I went to sleep at seven o'clock that night and tried to sleep off the high and I could still feel it, I could still kind of feel it in my chest through the nights Next day I woke up, went to the gym, tried to workout, couldn't really do a workout, my brain was not connecting to my body. So I went back home, tried to work out, didn't do anything, and went back home. I was going to do a live stream. It was a Monday now, I didn't do my live stream, went back to sleep, slept, and I woke up at four o'clock in the morning. So this was about eight o'clock, I was going to do a live stream, but didn't do the live stream. Laid back down in bed around 8 39 o'clock, slept till 12 noon that day. And then by Monday afternoon I was starting to feel back to normal.

By Tuesday I was 100% back to myself. This high lasted for about a day. No, it wasn't even, it was less than a day. It was about 12 hours, not 12 hours or so. Alright, if you want to read the story, read the story where I gave you, I will go into much more detail today, what I'm going to do in a funny but serious way. At the same time, I'm going to explain to you why drugs are not good for your system. And let me be clear before I go further here, because this episode is not designed for me to convince you to not partake. If you are already an active drug user or if you are, I'm not even trying to convince you to not try it. If you are drug curious, you've never done it before and you're thinking about taking some drugs or you got a friend offering you some drugs right now while you're listening to me talk, I'm not trying to tell you not to do it, but as always, this is what I do here on the show.

For those of you who do not know, I'm going to present to you what I know to be true. I'm going to use some personal experiences, which I just explained to you as supporting points, not necessarily evidence because personal experiences are not proof of a position, but they can support a position and I'm going to show you what I know to be true along with some personal opinions in mind, which you will know their opinions and you can make your own decisions. Alright? Does that all sound good? Great point. Number one, topic once again is say no to drugs. Number one, know what you're putting in your body and that's known as in KNOW. Know what you're putting in your body.

Never ever, ever be ignorant as to what you're putting in your body. This is the mistake that I made. My mistake was my own ignorance of not knowing exactly what Delta eight was and I put it in my body anyway. Now, yes, I did ask a friend, my friend said It's okay, I should have gotten a second opinion and figured it out myself, what exactly is this before I put this in my body? Because what if I had something serious to do that day or the next morning? Then I would've completely blown that opportunity or I would've had to postpone it. I probably would've been able to postpone it. But that

Was a bad decision by me due to my own laziness. I could have got the information very easily. It's not like the information was hard to find. I could have easily just Googled delta eight and I could have triangulated. And by triangulate what I mean is get three different, get feedback from three different sources on the same question and find the commonalities at least three, maybe five, maybe 10, and see what the commonalities are. And that's where I can start to find a consensus as to what is agreed upon between these people. And I would trust the commonalities that I found. I could have done that, but I was too lazy to do it. I just want to take the damn gummies at the gummies. This is a bad idea. Know what you're putting in your body, alright? Don't take anyone's word for it. Even if you trust that person, you don't have to trust what they said on that thing because guess what?

Is it your body that's going to be affected, not theirs? So even though they gave you something and told you something, it's not their responsibility if they end up being wrong. Because when I went to the same friend, the friend who I asked who said it was okay and I told them like, yo, this shit got me high as hell. They kind of laughed. It was funny, it was a funny thing. So again, this episode is kind of tongue in cheek and serious at the same time. They kind of laughed and they said, oh my bad. Because I was looking at one thing and when you told me about it, I went and looked up this and I said, no, that's not the one that I took. And it was a miscommunication, but it's not their fault, it's my fault. It's my responsibility because I'm the one who was asking the question.

I'm the one who needed the information and I'm the one whose body was affected by it, not theirs. So again, you should not take anyone's word for anything that's going in your body. I don't care what it is and I don't care who the person is. I don't care if they're a doctor, a dentist, I don't care if you trust them. Your whole life, if you love them, is your body that's going to be affected. You need to know what is going on in your body. If you don't know what something is, do not put it in your body. I don't care who is giving it to you. Everybody got me. This is not just referring to drugs, this is referring to what you drink. It's referring to the foods that you eat and anything else that you take into your physical person through any other orifice.

Make sure you know what it is, know what it's not, and use your best judgment or the best judgment of someone you trust fully before you make decisions about putting anything inside of yourself. This includes when it's coming from someone who, as we talked about yesterday, is an expert. Just because someone's an expert does not mean that they may not be incentivized to get you to do something that may not be in your personal best interest. I told you about this when we talked about the medical industry, the medical industry in the United States. The reason that it's not privatized is that the United States has plenty of money or at least the United States has access to plenty of money. Let's put it that way. Those of you listening to this, who are Americans? Most of you in the United States have access to plenty of money, not much money We've sent to Ukraine over there.

Conflict with Russia. A lot is enough that it could provide some free doctor and dental visits for a bunch of us here. Americans enough that it could pay some bills for some Americans enough that some homeless people would no longer be homeless. It is that much money. Alright, look it up and you can see it yourself. I'm bringing that up to say this. The United States doesn't have privatized healthcare. All of our healthcare, I mean excuse me, doesn't have publicly available or public service healthcare. We have privatized healthcare. So let me backup. Our healthcare is privatized. Meaning when something is privatized, for those who don't understand that lingo, it just means that private businesses can basically sell their services, which means it's going to cost you money to get that service.

So an example of something that is public and is not privatized would be something like garbage collection. Do any of you pay a bill? You may pay a bill if you live in a condominium or something for the garbage. No collection, like a little small percentage for the whole building. But if you live in a house, for example, you don't pay money to a particular company and you don't have a choice of six companies to choose from when it comes to who picks up your trash every Thursday, put the trash out, they take the trash, alright? There's no bill that comes to you for that. That's something that's, it's a municipal thing. You pay taxes and it goes to that, alright? But it's a government thing in a simplified way, okay? The healthcare system is not that. The healthcare system is privatized, meaning if you break your leg, it's going to cost you money to get it fixed.

Everybody got me. If you have a virus and you end up going to the doctor, it is going to cost you. Now some of you say, well I have insurance. Well, you pay for insurance, don't you? Okay? And the insurance company pays the doctor based on whatever your services are. You may have a little copay of 10 bucks or 50 bucks or whatever it is, but most of the costs go to the insurance company if you have insurance. If you don't have insurance, you have to pay it out of your pocket. The point being that the medical industry is privatized and it is based on profit from the United States medical industry because of these truths. The United States medical industry is a scam. It's a scam. What is a scam? Scam is a dishonest process and the medical industry is a scam because doctors and physicians and nurses are financially incentivized through the companies that they work for to put you on medications and interventions and operations that you may not necessarily need because the more of them they get you to take or do, the more money they make is a profit motive and something that is supposed to be based on health and helping you mix it with profit.

It's just natural. I mean, think about this, and this is something that I told you all yesterday. Just think about this with your own knowledge, whatever knowledge base you have, think about this. If you incentivize people to do a certain thing, do you agree that people are probably going to do that thing more often? That they're incentivized to do it? Incentive just means they get a reward for doing it. If you reward people for doing a certain thing, are they probably going to do it more often than if you did not reward them? Does everybody agree with that? Okay, that's the medical industry in the United States, you're a doctor, your nurse, your physician is financially incentivized to get you on prescriptions, to get you to take drugs, to get you to get operations, to put jabs in your body because every time they get you to say yes to that and they perform it or they get you on that thing, they make money.

And if they don't perform it or you say no and they don't get you on that thing, they don't give you that jab. Guess how much money they make? Less the money that they didn't make because you didn't accept the operation or the intervention or the suggestion. This is the medical industry in America and if anybody believes that I'm wrong, factually is impossible. You could believe I'm wrong factually because that is literally how the system works. If I'm wrong, somebody will let me know, but I'm not wrong. So nobody should be letting me know shit. That is the medical system in the United States. It is designed to get you on stuff. So any of you ladies or a gentleman who has a wife, child's mother, whatever, who's had a c-section, the number of C-section operations that happen, cesarean sections that happen to give birth to babies in America is way higher than the number that actually needs to happen.

Doctors aren't incentivized to scare you if they need to get that c-section, which is a major operation. That is a major surgery, a c-section. They scare you into doing that because they're incentivized to do it. Why are they incentivized to do it? Well, first of all, the charge for the actual operations. Secondly, the faster they get you out of that hospital bed, the faster they can get the next person in and do the same thing to them. More people, more money is called hospital bed turnover. That's the same way that the restaurant wants to turn over the table, they want you to come in, eat, pay the bill leave so they can put somebody else at the table, they can get them to eat, pay the bill leave. They want to turn that bed over. I mean they want to turn that table over. Same way the hospital wants to turn the bed over. Now, I'm not going to go too deep into this. If you want to hear me go deeper on trashing the medical industry in the United States, I have good news for you. I did that already. That was in episode number 2338.

We're still on point number. What point are we on here? We're still on point number one here in today's episode. Do not trust anybody's word on what to do with or put into your body. You need to know who this person is or who this thing is, what this thing is that you're putting in your body, what it's about, what's inside of it before you we, anything inside of you. And that includes people. Everybody got me, everybody got me. Alright. It includes people. You're going to put a person inside of you ladies because, well, I guess men too. Hey, are you going to put something inside of yourself? You need to know who they are, what they're about, and what's in them before you let them inside of you. Okay? 20 years ago, roughly many baseball players, major league baseball players got caught up in I guess what we can call a scandal over athletes taking performance enhancing drugs.

Some of you who are old enough, you follow sports. You remember this. It was like multiple scandals, but the whole thing was just the peds. Also performance enhancing drills, also known as peds and baseball. And many of the initially who were called out, defended themselves by saying that they took some supplement that they thought was just like a muscle relaxer or something to recover or some kind of energy drink or they thought it was just something that wasn't going to do anything. Just something benign that they were just taking for just normal things that they could get away with taking and they would claim that they didn't know that there was anything illegal in the stuff that they were taking. This defense that many baseball players offered at that time was mostly rejected by the powers that be and also was rejected in the court of public opinion.

The reason being is that for professional athletes, the general idea of a professional athlete is that they're very meticulous about what they do with and put into their bodies, which is generally true. Not every athlete is, I've been a professional athlete and there's some athletes who really don't pay any attention to that stuff. But the accepted public perspective is that pro athletes are very meticulous about their bodies because pro athletes make their money based on their bodies. So how could you make money based on your body? You're not paying attention to your body. Well, there is a way if someone's talented enough, but different conversation for a different day. It was generally rejected when these players tried to claim ignorance, whether players were telling the truth or not. Ignorance is not an excuse when it comes to what you put in your body. So this applies to all you the same way it applied to a pro baseball player 20 years ago in 2013 when I first decided to start paying attention to my eating habits for example, and I initially went vegan.

A friend of mine gave me some simple ideas to keep in mind, and I still remember them to this day. She said, anything you're going to eat, look at the label on the food. She said, if anything you eat has more than five ingredients in it, it probably has some synthetic materials that are not real and not natural. In other words, they are chemically created laboratory made stuff that is in your food that is not natural and it probably is not going to help you physically to eat it if it has more than five ingredients. If any of you start applying that you probably have to throw out half of your kitchen right now. And I'm not telling you not to do it, I'm just letting you know what I was told and that made perfect sense to me. You tell me if it makes sense to you.

Another of the things she said, she said, if there are ingredients in something that you cannot pronounce or you cannot explain what they are, like the ingredients in these skittles that I have on my desk right here, you are putting lab created chemicals in your body. That's usually not a good thing. The human body was not made for laboratory chemicals to go inside of it. So some of these chemicals again, may ultimately be harmless. I've been eating Skittles since as long as I can remember since I was in fifth grade and I'm still alive, right? So maybe the chemicals are not that bad. Maybe they're only killing me very slowly instead of quickly. But some of them, maybe your body can withstand those chemicals, but that doesn't mean it's not using some resources to fight against these foreign agents that you are putting inside of you and you are ultimately responsible for whatever happens as a result.

Now, why would you eat something if you didn't know what it was? Well, all human beings do this because generally we are lazy and we like what we like and this stuff is chemically created to make us want more of it. So if you were to adopt this mindset for again, even 25% of what you eat, it would drastically change many of your eating lifestyles who are listening to me right now and your drinking lifestyles. And again, as I said, you would have to throw half of your kitchen in the trash right now if you actually started applying this directly. And again, I'm not telling you you should do it. I'm not telling you not to. I'm just letting you know what point number two is. Today's topic, once again, is to say no to drugs. Point number two, the better the shape of your end, the better your body can deal with foreign agents.

This is important because this is why I've done multiple episodes on this show about health and fitness and nutrition because these matter just as much as how you run your business and how you make your money, protecting your mindset, how you make your money and how you protect your mindset. Because a business can be shut down and replaced with a job you can get fired from and get another one. Your mindset can be in a dumpster, you can raise it back up your body if destroyed does not come back the same way. Your career, your business, your money, your mindset, all those could be in a really bad space and you can bring them back even stronger than before. You mess it up. It doesn't come back the same way.

The good thing about being in great physical shape is that when you make a mistake like I did and you take a drug or you take in some foreign agent that makes you sick or whatever the situation is, the better the shape you're already in, the more easily you can recover from the mistake. Alright, and keep in mind something folks, let's be clear. The human body is ingesting all types of germs and bacterias all day, every day, every time you breathe and every time you breathe in air, you are taking in random agents from the air particles that are around you. Unless you are in some type of sterile lab environment where no other humans can come in and everybody's in those white suits and nothing can touch anything and there's no dust possibly in the room unless you're in an environment like that, you are taken in foreign agents all the time.

Now you have a window open in your home. Have you been around another human being? Have you shooken anybody's hand today? Have you got an elevator? You walk up some steps, have you been outside? Then there are germs and bacteria floating around the air that you can't even see and you're breathing it in all the time. Every single breath you take, you're breathing this stuff in. So why are you not sick and dead right now? Why are you not dropping dead right now at the moment? Because your immune system is aware of these things. It has seen these things before and it can easily fight and destroy them so that you don't get sick and don't feel ill when you take the stuff in. However, the weaker your immune system is, the more susceptible you become to those germs making you sick. This is the reason why people tend to get sick more often in the winter than they do in the summer.

And as again, I'm being very, very, very simplistic with this. In the winter it is colder outside and because it's colder outside, your immune system is doing more to keep your body's resources in your body. Let's not even just say the immune system. Your body overall is doing more just to keep your temperature regulated so damn cold and you're just trying to keep yourself from getting too cold. And while it's doing all that now, it is not putting its attention and focus, let's say humanizing it towards fighting the germs as much so then a germ can get through. Now there's an opening for a germ to get through simply because the body has to do more work to just keep you warm. This is why if you go outside in the wintertime and you don't have a coat on, well the body has to work extra hard because you're not doing anything to help keep it warm yourself.

So the body has to do more to do what you didn't do for yourself. Put on a coat and hat and gloves and then while I was doing all that, it's distracted and now the germ can get in and now you can get sick again. I'm being very, very, very simplistic with that point. So medics out there, don't get mad at me and attack me for the simplification of that point. So also with the immune system, the more it has to fight against outside stuff, especially stuff that you put in there voluntarily, the less resources it has to fight against the other stuff. In other words, the more you do to weaken your immune system by taking drugs and alcohol and not sleeping and not taking care of your body and not taking care of your health and not breathing in good air and not being in a positive state of energy and not doing all of these things, all the stuff that you do to voluntarily weaken your immune system, you don't even realize that you're doing it.

That makes it that much harder for the immune system to have resources left over to do all the other work. You get it? So if you're out of shape right now, if you're 50 pounds overweight right now, your body has to do extra work just to make sure your heart keeps working to pump blood through your 50 pound overweight body. And the resources used to do that are resources that it can't use to fight against those germs that you just breathed in the last three days. And now you're more susceptible to getting sick because there are only so many resources. This is a universe of abundance, but there are limitations on certain things as well. Everybody following where I'm coming from here. So the weaker your immune system is, the more susceptible you are to getting sick because your immune system, again, can only do so much.

So you want to give your immune system less work to do. So when it really needs to do a job, it's ready to go, but you don't want to as resources spread thin all over the place. Healthy people don't require as many interventions as less healthy people require because they're taking care of their bodies. And again, the more you take care of your body, the stronger your immune system is, the more easily it can defeat stuff. So it's basically a self-perpetuating system. Stronger your immune system, the better you fight off stuff, the weaker your immune system, the more sick you get. So the richer you get, richer the poor get poor. Point number three, today's topic once again is say no to drugs. Number three, mental acuity is the most valuable personal asset you can possess. Mental acuity. Well, let's say the most valuable state that you can be in is a better way of saying it.

I would say the best asset is discipline, but mental acuity is the best state that you can be in. You're just mentally sharp, you're on point, you're focused. And as I told you and a little bit of a story that I told you to frame this episode when I was high that day, I was completely not focused. I was not sharp, I was not on point. I didn't even know what the hell was happening. I was watching myself. It was like watching a movie of myself walking around. That's what it felt like. Drugs kill brain cells. That's what happened that day when I got high, my brain cells, some brain cells got killed off that day because of the drug that I had taken. Although it was ultimately a funny story and I got some content out of it, I wrote an article about it.

I'm doing this episode right here. The worst part of getting high on accident was that I didn't have full control of my mental faculties for a good three hours from about four o'clock to seven o'clock. I could not think straight. And the only reason that it was only three hours is that I went to sleep. And then the next morning again, I felt a little bit better, but I still couldn't do what I wanted to do. It didn't do my livestream, couldn't really work out, had to go back to sleep. It wasn't until 12 o'clock the next day that I was awake and kind of feeling normal again. So do the math on that. It was like a day and eight hours.

So I was doing stuff during those three hours that I was really high and awake and doing them the right way, but I wasn't consciously processing anything that was taking place. And I can only realize again, something happened about 15 seconds after it occurred. Now I'm guessing somebody can let me know is that the normal experience when people get high and people actually go into this space on purpose, people do this, they want to. And I got a few responses when I put the article out via email. So some people said yes, that's the experience that I've had, Dre. And yeah, some people said that to me. If that's something that people do on purpose, I will never get high again. I'm not interested in that. Doesn't sound doesn't seem fun to me. And it was not fun when I did it. Maybe you get used to it, you do it often enough.

But no, not for me. I'm not a fan of this mental state. I like being mentally sharp. I like being focused. I like being on point at all times. I don't ever want to be disconnected from conscious reality unless I'm sleeping. And whether you agree with that or not, here's something that you can't agree with. Drugs, kill brain cells, you take drugs, you are killing cells in your body, specifically your brain. And I don't think there are any positive benefits to killing brain cells unless you're just a really stupid person and you want to clear the slate and start all over again. Other than that, there's no positive to killing brain cells. So I'm not a fan of that. So with all that said, let's recap today's class, which says no to drugs. And again, you can read that article called because I Got High if you want to read it@dreallday.com slash blog.

B oog number one, know what you're putting in your body. Do not take anyone's word for it. I don't care who they are, I don't care what level of expertise they are. The person who has to live with the result of what goes in your body is you. It is not them regardless of who they are or what they are. And if you allow another person into your body, you better know who they are, what they're about and where they've been and what's in them before you let them in you. Because whatever is in them may end up in you. Everybody understands exactly what I mean when I say that. Number two, the better you shape your end, the better your body will deal with foreign agents. Alright? This is why I've done many episodes about health and fitness and nutrition. Alright? Your business can get shut down. You can open a new one, you can lose the job, get another one. You can be in a terrible state mentally and come back. If your body gets into a bad state, it never comes back the exact same way. It doesn't mean you're going to die immediately, but it doesn't come back the same way that it

Was before. Alright? So do not destroy your body. You only get one and understand that you have an immune system. The stronger your immune system is that is supported by you drinking water, exercising daily, breathing in good air thinking, positive thoughts, being around positive people, putting the right stuff in your body, stronger your immune system is the better it can fight the foreign agents that you're taking in every day, every single time you breathe. Number three, mental acuity is the most valuable mental state that you can be in. And your drugs, any drug you take kills brain cells. It puts you in a worse state mentally because you are literally killing the brain cells and causing the brain to not function the way that they're supposed to. And again, I guess there are people who like going into that state for whatever reason. I personally am not a fan of that. So any of you who are drug curious, I'm telling you what it's like, what it feels like for someone who doesn't take drugs. If this sounds appealing to you, hey, do what you got to do. Do what you want to do, but don't say nobody didn't give you any information.

#2820: Identifying & Embracing Your Unique Ability

Let's get into this topic, which is identifying and embracing your unique ability. Now this is a topic of unique ability that I have touched on in a few episodes recently where when I've talked about building your brand, when I talk about putting your material out there in different formats, and I want to make sure people understand unique ability is not the same as just a skill or a talent.

Being very good at something is not your unique ability, and I'm going to explain well, something like a job or a role or being in a particular industry. That's not what a unique ability is. So today I'm going to talk about this subject in a very specific way. I'm going to help you understand exactly what it means. I just told you what it doesn't mean because a lot of people think when they hear the phrase unique ability often think that it means one thing, but it actually means something completely different from that. What I'm going to do today here is explain that and I'm going to help you understand it. So let's get into it. Point number one, the topic once again is identifying and embracing your unique ability. Number one, as I said, your unique ability is not a job specific skill. This is important.

You need to understand this in order to understand everything else I'm going to give you here today. This point right here, your unique ability is not a job specific skill. So if you are a teacher, an author, a speaker, a professional athlete, a ditch digger, a web coder, and you are great at them, you may be the best there is at those things. None of those is a unique ability, none of them. Maybe you are very good at it. Again, maybe the best there is is still not a unique ability. When I have conversations with people on X, that's the app known as Twitter, where I do actually engage with people in the comments. I don't do that anywhere else, but for some reason people seem to, and as often I talk to people who are in educational space, maybe it's just recently the topics that I've been engaging on, but there's people in this educational space and I often notice that they will talk about their position in education.

These academics folks talk about their position as if that's what makes them somebody. They'll say, well, I'm an authority on this subject because I teach at a college on said subject, whatever that subject happens to be. My son just crashed into my office while I'm recording my show. And they talk about the subject like, Hey, I am an expert on this subject, which makes them some type of expert on that topic and that means that I'm supposed to listen to them. Or they'll say something like, well, I'm not going to listen to this person who I'm recommending or maybe this book that I recommend.

All right, just lock the door so my son can't come back in or they won't read this book that I'm recommending because it's quote unquote not written by an expert. Or they'll challenge me and say, well, you are not an expert on whatever subject we may be opening on sharing our opinions on as if the position that you hold is what makes you someone who should be listened to. I 100% reject this idea and I'm someone who has enough of a resume that I could use this the same way that these people I'm referring to the same way that they use it kind of as an offensive weapon. I could easily use this against other people, but I don't do that because again, I don't believe in this. This is why I'm saying what I'm saying here in this first point, and I did an entire episode on this concept already, but these people who I'm referring to, they don't understand the concept of unique ability.

And if you're listening to this and you have found yourself using this framing, you don't understand the concept of unique ability. And that's okay if you don't understand it because maybe you never even considered it, but that's why I did this episode. So now you can understand it given these people's career choices, these people who say, well, I'm an expert at X, Y, Z, and they're saying they're an expert at it because they have a job doing it, having a job, doing something, and even if you consider yourself an expert, again, that's not your unique ability and I'm going to help you understand why your unique ability matters as well because maybe you do have a job doing something and maybe some people consider you to be an expert or let's just say that all these things are true. It's not a unique ability. Unique ability is more important than your job or your expertise.

And I suppose that these people, they don't have to understand their unique ability because maybe they just stay in that space, they stay in that bubble, they can just stay there forever and they'll be fine. But you entrepreneur and I make this show with the entrepreneur in mind, this episode is made with the entrepreneur in mind. If you are an entrepreneur, you must understand your unique ability. Now, someone who's working on some campus somewhere or they're an electrician or a plumber or they're making sandwiches at the local grocery store, maybe they never need to understand us. You need to understand and embrace us. We're playing a different game than them. Unique ability is not related to what you do as a job. It is not in ot, not related to what you do as a job. It is not related to your career or however you make money.

It is not related to that. Unique ability is about what you personally bring to the things that you do and your way of doing them. Your unique ability is about your style and your energy and what you bring to the table as you do the things that you do that's unique ability, which means it doesn't really matter what you are doing because your unique ability travels with you and it'll be obvious to others who observe you doing what you're doing wherever you choose to take it. We're going to get more into that as we move into the next point. So point number two, today's topic once again is identifying and embracing your unique ability. So everyone understands the first point here, right? What you do for a living, your job title, whatever is printed on your business card, whatever office building you have, whatever building in which you have an office is not your unique ability. It doesn't mean that thing doesn't matter, doesn't mean you don't get paid, doesn't mean you're not great at what you do, whatever. That is not a unique ability. I'm making sure you all understand what unique ability is not so I can tell you what it is as we go deeper. Number two, your unique ability is transferable between jobs and industries because it belongs to you personally. It does not belong to the task or the job.

I shall repeat. Your unique ability is transferable between jobs and between industries because your unique ability belongs to you. That's why it's called a unique ability. It belongs to you personally. It does not belong to the task or the job. This is the key of what unique ability is about. And again, this is why I said these people who I'm referring to that for some reason I found myself talking to people in the academic space probably because I was commenting on some academic things in the news. These people don't understand the concept of unique ability and as long as they stay in the academic bubble, they never need to understand this because they'll always be in the same spot. And those of you who think that the spot that you're in right now is the spot you're going to be in for the rest of your life, perhaps you may not need to understand unique ability either, but I would suggest that you learn it because even if you're going to stay in the same spot, you probably want to grow and advance and be better in that spot, provide more value in that spot and hopefully produce more returns for yourself while in that spot.

And the thing that's going to move you forward is not necessarily that you are better subjectively based on, I don't know who's doing the measuring, but you're embracing your unique ability because the more unique it is and the more valuable it is, then the more the higher the returns you can command from the marketplace. That's why this matters. So when I ask people what it is, for example, I'll give you an example using myself, what is it about my delivery or approach or my skill or my game, whatever, I ask them, what is it that makes me valuable to you? Nobody tells me. It's because I have this framework around discipline, confidence, mental toughness, and personal initiative. Even though I do have those things nobody says because dre, you're good at breaking down mindset and strategies and systems and accountability even though I do actually do those things. They are valuable things and I do them and I do them at a high level and I believe I'm up there. You may not consider me the best in the world, but I'm in the conversation in those areas. But that's not the point.

The thing that you, when I ask people this question, and I get this from people who ask correctly, I mean I ask directly is the fact that Dre, I like the fact that you get straight to the point that you are no bs, that you don't have fluff in your conversation that I like. You keep it real. You're directing your delivery that even when you make a point on something that I may not necessarily see eye to eye, I still understand exactly where you're coming from and why you're saying what you're saying. That is my unique ability. It's the way that I deliver when I'm delivering. So for those of you who have just come around, let's say if you come around the work on your game world anytime in the last eight to nine years, then I'm going to give you another, I'm going to give you a further example to help you understand why this is my unique ability.

I can take this ability, what I just described to you. I can take this anywhere I want to take it. I can talk about any subject that I want, that ability comes with me. It doesn't matter the topic. Now my background is in basketball, before I was talking about this kind of stuff that y'all here on this show every day I was talking about basketball every single day from 2005 to 2015, I was putting out basketball material every single day for 10 years straight. Now, about half of that time starting about halfway through that, that's when I started also adding in mindset stuff. And that became the segue between the basketball audience and you all who are in this audience right now. Some of you have been in both audiences because you have evolved as well, but when I was making basketball material, everyone in my audience, again, a hundred percent of my audience, the first five years I was putting on material was all basketball players.

These are people who are looking to play college ball or looking to play professional ball, maybe even high school ball. Some of them, even that young, many of you listening to me today do not play basketball and many of you have never played a single minute of basketball and even those of you who have played, you may no longer be an aspiring basketball player. You're not trying to make it to the NBA right now. Maybe you had a thought, a notion at one point that maybe you would, maybe you were trying to make the high school team or the college team or you were trying to play pro at some point, and maybe that's how you came across me, but right now, that's not your focus yet. You're still here in this audience. And I still have this very eclectic audience. I have people in my audience who are in the finance space.

I have people who are in the military. I have people who are running IT firms, they work in the tech space. I have people, of course athletes, athletes who have graduated from being the athlete to being the coach or the trainer or the analyst. I have people who are working in sports that I never even did before. Believe it or not, in my audience, I've had softball players and these are people who I've heard from softball players, wrestlers, combat sport people, MMA, fighters, boxers, equestrian, horseback riders. Believe it or not, I've had several horseback riders I've heard from over the years who listened to this show and other sports, football, of course baseball, hockey who are into this audience and these are things, all these things that I'm missing are things that I have never personally partaken in any of these things. Yeah, I still have these people in my audience.

And why is this? Because even though my subject matter has changed, my delivery and my approach have not because that's my unique ability. My delivery and approach is the same when a horseback rider consumes me that the basketball players back in 2009 were consuming is the exact same. That unique ability, the same thing that brings the horseback rider and the same thing that brought the basketball players in. It's the same thing that brings the entrepreneur in today because that's the unique ability. It doesn't matter what I'm talking about. Everyone understands where I'm coming from and I'm sharing all of this not to have you thinking about what it means for how it reflects on me. I need you to use me that I'm putting as an example here to think about how this reflects on you. What is your unique ability? And one way you can figure this out is to think back to other positions you've had, other roles that you've played in life before, the one that you're in now and what are some of the commonalities that made you valuable in your past job and the one before that or the one before that that also make you valuable in the role that you have right now.

And the more clearly you can zero in on that, the more strong of a grasp you will have on your unique ability. And then the more you can start leveraging your unique ability because now you're doing it consciously and intentionally and that will make you a higher level player because what you're doing is separating yourself from everybody else. You're not competing on, well, I'm just better at doing this thing, whereas a hundred other people are doing the same thing. You don't want to be in that kind of competition. You don't want to be in a better competition. You want to be in a uniqueness competition that only you can win because you're bringing something unique that people can only get by coming through you. And as long as you're offering something that people can only get through you, well guess what? Now all roads lead to you and now you get the people that you want because they're coming for the very thing that you bring to the table.

They're getting what they want. You get what you want. Everybody wants that process, alright? My delivery and my approach from back in the basketball days has not changed. I've delivered the same way. Now that I did then I'm probably not probably, I'm definitely more articulate now. I have more resources in terms of experience and knowledge to dig, to pull from now because I got 20 years of experience on my back that I didn't have back then. I have achieved things that put more, I guess we can say more shine on my resume, which brings more credibility to me, which we have to admit, brings more eyeballs and ears to me because of my status and the things that I've accomplished, but the delivery hasn't changed. This is the exact same delivery. You all watch my own videos from 2010 and listen to me now.

It's the same delivery, same style, same. Let's get to the point. No B us, I'm not going to bullshit you. I'm not going to walk around the topic. We want to talk about it exactly as it is. Whatever that thing happens to be hasn't changed at all. The people who are getting it have changed. The subject matter has changed. My unique ability has not changed. It's traveled with me from basketball to the internet before we were calling it social media to talking about mindset, to talking about business stuff, to talking entrepreneurship to what we have here at work on your game, which is again, very eclectic. It transferred into all of these spaces from basketball and entrepreneurship, personal development and business because the ability has nothing to do with the subject matter. Lemme say that again. The unique ability has nothing to do with the subject matter.

Pick a topic, it doesn't matter. It still can deliver on it. This is an important point that you must understand. And I'll tell you one thing that I was when I was first getting into entrepreneurship, this is the end of my basketball days, getting into professional, just entrepreneurship days, thought leadership, writing, speaking, coaching, things like that. I remember I was sitting with Donna St. Louis, she was one of my early mentors. She's a professional speaker. And Donna said, all right, here's what we're going to do. We're going to go through all the jobs that you've had in your life. And I've had a lot of jobs. I've told you I've had probably 15, 20 jobs before I got to the point that I became effectively unemployable where I will never have another, whatever that number of jobs I've had, it will never get attitudes, I'll never have another job in my life.

But neither here nor there. Donna was saying, let's go through all the jobs that you have had. And then she would ask me, okay, when you worked at that job, what was it that your bosses most valued about you? And as I started listing jobs and I said, well, y'all worked here from this time to this time and what they liked most was this, this, and this. And I was just jogging my memory, just going through these jobs that I had. And this is working at McDonald's, working at Rita's water ice, working at the movie theater. What was the thing that made you most valuable at these places? And I was coming up with whatever answers I could come up with. And as we went down the list of all these jobs, there were some commonalities that kept coming up and Donna said, do you see these commonalities?

The commonalities were that you were consistent. The bosses knew they could rely on you, that you were disciplined, that you were told to do a job. You did exactly, you were told and you would be punctual and you became just a dependable person, not necessarily in any of the jobs. Did somebody say you're just the best? There's a couple of jobs that somebody told me I was one of the best at, but for the most part, the most valuable thing about me was the consistency, the discipline, the punctuality that I know what I'm going to get from this person. And that was in, this is like 2014, 2015. We did this exercise almost 10 years ago. And do you notice again, those of you who weren't even following me didn't even know who I was nine or 10 years ago. Do you notice that those same things that I just told you are the same things that many of you know me for Now? That's what I mean when I say unique ability and I didn't even know what unique ability was at that time.

So again, the ability and delivery that I have now would be the same if I was talking about politics, if I was talking about celebrity gossip or if I went back to basketball right now, let's say I decided to open a training business, I would have the same style. My job does not make you unique, you make your unique ability and you bring it to the job. Point number three, today's topic once again is identifying and embracing your unique ability. Number three, once understood, this will shine through no matter what you do. Alright? This is what unique ability is about. Again, it comes with you and this is the thing that makes you unique, different, valuable and needed in any space that you walk into. So you just have to find a space that actually values your unique ability because it ain't everywhere. There are some places that my unique ability and my style of delivery probably wouldn't do too well.

Alright? So I mentioned earlier academics. I would not last a week in the academic space. I would not last a week working at a college campus because those are highly politicized environments and I don't do well in highly politicized environments because I'm not going to hold my tongue. I'm not going to not say something and I'm not going to have anybody talk to me in any kind of bounds simply because they got a certain status and I have a lesser status. And frankly, I would never put myself in that position anyway, but if I did, it wouldn't last long because I'm just not going to stand for it. So again, a unique ability doesn't necessarily make you better than other people. It means you need to find where this ability is most valuable and that's where you need to place yourself strategically. In the marketing world, we call this positioning and the good thing about unique ability and the world that we have today folks, is that it doesn't have to fit into any pre-made positions.

For example, what I do right now, there's no premade position for this. There was not a job board posting on careerbuilder.com that said we need somebody who used to play basketball who's now going to have a podcast and write books and do coaching and have a university who's a no bs, no fluff and get to the point brass tack kind of guy to go and start his own business. That wasn't a job posting. I created this. I created this on my own. That's the good thing. That's the good news for you. The good news for you is that you don't have to fit into anything that already exists. You can make your own thing, but you need to know what your unique ability is and you need to stand firm on it so that the people who need it can eventually find and discover you and they can gather around and now you have your own audience.

Don't have to go to something that somebody else already made for you. And that's what I did, and that's what I've been doing for the last two decades. What I just told you, that's it. And you can do the exact same thing or hey, you can step into a space that already exists. You can step into a role that needs to be filled. Maybe some of you, your unique ability works perfectly in the places where my unique ability would go terribly. I told you I couldn't be a politician. Politicians have to lie in order to win elections. I can't tell people lies. I got to tell you the objective truth, which means some of it you're going to like some of it you're not going to like or you can't win elections doing that. You want to win an election. You got to tell people all of the things that they want to hear and leave out the stuff they don't want to hear.

Even if the stuff they don't want to hear is actually true. You can't tell 'em that because if you tell 'em that they're not going to vote for you, you won't win. So I couldn't work in politics, but some of you, your unique ability is suited perfectly to do that. I couldn't do it, but that's why we ain't all the same. Every human being is unique. So you need to find your space. And again, academia, I cannot do well working in academia, especially at any type of liberal university. Please, I wouldn't even get called for a job interview, let alone could I work there and it wouldn't work because I'm not going to go along with the bullshit. I will call it out the first time I see it and the first person or how I see doing it, I'll call 'em out and that'd be the end of my career that fast.

I won't even make it to a paycheck. The whole point is I know what my unique abilities are and I know where they are valued. I also know where they are not valued and I stay out of the places that my unique abilities are not wanted. And I try to put myself as often as possible in the places where my unique abilities are valued. Everybody understands where I'm coming from here, and this is the same thing that you need to be doing. So I'm just using myself as an example here, but this is not about me. I'm telling you all these things so that you can get a good feel for how you can do it. I'm using me because you can get a tangible example of someone doing this in a space where again, I didn't have to fit in any box. There's nothing wrong with fitting in a box.

Some boxes are perfect fits for the right people. This is why it's called a unique ability. It is not about a job, it's about what makes sense for you. So as I mentioned in a previous point, I can go into a completely different space. My approach would be the same subject matter and content would be different. My approach would be the same. Now, would it be valued or not? I have to be strategic and think about that because I don't want to go to a place where it's not going to be valued. When you understand your unique ability, you increase the opportunities you have in life because now you understand that the thing that makes you special is not the job of the industry or subject. So now you're wide open. So I don't have to say, alright, I used to play basketball. Let me find something that is related to basketball so that I can fit into that box.

I don't have to do that. See, my unique ability has nothing to do with basketball. The fact that I used to play basketball can go on my resume, but I am not limited to or by basketball. Everyone understand where I'm coming from here? Remember when I was doing one of my first, it was the first TED Talk that I've done. I've done four TEDx talks. Remember the first TEDx talk I was going to do was in Broward County. What was the name of that school? I think it's called Broward High School. I think it's called Broward High School, west Broward High School, maybe West Broward High School. But anyway, the first TED Talk I was going to do, I remember one of the curators, the curators are just the people who organize the event. They basically choose the people who are going to give a talk and they basically coach you through getting ready for your TED Talk.

So as I'm getting ready for my TED Talk, this talk was called the third day. I actually did a TED talk on the third day before I wrote the book called The Third Day. And I remember the organizer, one of the curators, this black guy named Horace, he reached out to me and he said, well, Dre, me and the other curators have been talking about your talking. We love your subject and we're thinking about how you can best frame your presentation. And he said, when you come out on stage, here's what we're thinking. He said, how about you come out on stage holding a basketball and you give your speech while holding the basketball because that'll help people understand and connect that this whole concept of the third day came from you being a basketball player. And I immediately outright with no equivocation, rejected that idea.

I said, hell no, I'm not doing it. I'm not stepping on the stage holding a basketball. I'm not going to take a whole bunch of pictures wearing a suit and holding a basketball because personally, again, no knock on any of you, and no knock on horse if he's hearing this, that shit is corny to me. I don't need to hold a basketball, let you know I used to play basketball to get you to respect what I got to say about business. That's just me. Again, I'm not saying any of you is wrong if you choose to do it. I see athletes do it all the time. People who are connected to basketball in some way, then they put on their business clothes and then they hold a basketball and they take a picture with it. I see sports coaches do this all the time. They hold the basketball or the football or the boxing glove or the baseball bat and whatever, and they take the picture and then they're giving you the connection visually that yes, I'm in business, but hey, it is coming from this sport that I used to play personally.

That's just not me. I wasn't doing that. I said, I'm absolutely not doing that. I remember when I was talking to Donna, a Donna St. Louis person, I told you one of my early mentors when we first got into it, she was helping me just put together what became the skeleton of what is now work on your game. And I told her it was very important to me. I said, Dawn, it's very important to me that I don't want to be the basketball player business guy. I don't want to be that. I am much more than a basketball player. This is not more than an athlete that bullshit. People put on T-shirts. I said, I'm not that. I don't need to tell you that I'm more than a basketball player. I want my presentation to say it without me needing to say it. And I want my presentation to be the way that I put myself out there to stand on his own two feet without me even mentioning basketball.

The fact that I played basketball becomes a footnote in who I am. That was my vision in 2014. So here we are now, and I think I have self-actualized that, I mean, I'm not done. I still got a lot more to do, but I believe I self-actualized that because I never wanted the only reason that I'm on the stage or talking to someone or people listening to me, oh, he used to play basketball. So that's, listen to that. Fuck that. I was never into that. And again, I'll say for the third time, this is not a knock on any of you who does that. Maybe that works for you. Alright, that might make perfect sense for you. It does not make sense to me. And that's why when Horace, the guy from the TEDx talk said, Hey, maybe you should come out and hold a basketball while you give your speech.

I said, hell fucking no, I'm not doing that because you're not going to listen to me talk just because I got a basket. Oh, he's a basketball player. So now let's see what he has to say. No, fuck that. Just see what I got to say, period. The fact that I play basketball is a footnote to what I'm about to give you. Everybody understands where I'm coming from. And again, all of this is just my perspective for what works for me. You have to find out what works for you. This is the reason why we have worked on your game university. I help people do exactly this. We got to find what your angle is, what your approach is, what makes you unique, what makes you different, where you kind of fit in perfectly. What is your lane where it is? It just flows where you're doing hard work, but you make it look easy and it feels easy because it's perfect.

It's the perfect lane for you. Give you another example. When I did my second TEDx talk, a couple months later, this TEDx talk was in Miami here in Coconut Grove in Miami. And that talk was called Dear Dre, how to Be Confident When You're Not. I believe to this day, I haven't looked it up in a while, but I believe it's my most viewed TEDx talk. I remember when I did that talk and that talk was all about just literally what I said, how to be confident when you're not, how people can build confidence. And this is a big thing. Everybody's looking for confidence. Every human on the planet wants to be more confident. And I remember when I gave that talk, I used as source material a lot of comments and questions I've been getting on YouTube over the years because at that time, this was 2016, so I already had 10 years of basketball audiences asking me questions.

And I even used them in some of the slides during my TED Talk. I think that the only one of my four TEDx talks is the only one where I use slides because the curators of that event insisted that I use slides and they insisted that the slides would help aid the presentation. So that's the only time I use slides. And folks, I've been a professional speaker for almost a decade. I never, ever, ever use slides in my presentations. Not even to this day. Somebody could pay me $25,000 for a keynote. I'm not using slides. And I will tell them I do not use slides. This is the only talk I've ever given that I have used slides. This one in 2016. And by the way, you can see all my TED talks. If you go to work on your game.com/ted TD, work on your game.com/t.

You can see all my TED talks. So I remember giving that talk. The video came out and I sent the link to the video to my early mentor Donna, and I sent it to her. I said, Hey, my TED talk came out, you want to see it? She said, yeah, lemme see it. So I sent it to her and the TED talk was only like 14, 15 minutes and she watched it and she sent me a text message back and she said, Dre, I didn't know how, I didn't realize it when all this time we've been talking and you've been telling me about yourself and we've been working on stuff. I didn't even realize it, but I just realized it by watching your TED talk. She said, Dre, you need to be talking about mental toughness. It's so obvious to me now, now that I watch that TED talk, it's clear you need to be talking about mental toughness.

That is your lane, that is your zone, that's your space. And she was 100% correct, but she just needed to hear me talk about it. See, so once she heard me talk about it and she saw kind of the way that it flowed, the way it came out of me naturally, the way it kind of just was like, this guy is in his zone talking about this subject. He said, that's your zone. That's it. And here we are. And the thing that I want you to get from that is this is 2016. I've been putting out contests since 2005. So over 10 years of putting out material before I realized this is the zone, this is the space that I really can give the most value to, where it makes the most sense for me and it comes the most easily to me. And that means for you when it comes to figuring out your unique ability, you gotta get out there and you got to try stuff.

You got to do stuff, you got to try. Lemme try this approach. Lemme try this angle. Lemme try this style. And again, you may know the topic and don't know the style. Maybe you know the style, but you don't know the topic. But you have to try different things to find what makes the most sense for you. So again, it's not the job, it's not the industry, it's not the subject. It's you and your way of doing things that no one else can replicate. Remember that unique ability is about what you bring to the table that no one else is bringing to the table. That's why it's unique. People can learn your subject matter and regurgitate your material to other people in their own audiences. So if somebody can read your book, then go say what you said in your book to their audience. They probably won't do it as well as you, but the information is not the thing.

People can understand your process. Do it the same way that you do it. You can teach a process to somebody. I've had staff who worked for me, I taught them a process. They quit working for me, got hired away by other companies, stopped working for those companies and started their own business doing the same thing that I taught them in my process. That's happened. And again, that's not a unique ability. It can be transferred. Somebody else can learn that. Somebody else can do it the same way, but your way and your energy and your style, those things can never be replicated. And those are the things that you really need to focus the most on. So that said, let's recap. Today's classes are identifying and embracing your unique ability. Again, I've touched on this a few times, but I hadn't done a full episode on it.

So here it is. Number one, your unique ability is not a job specific skill. Even if you're great at your skill, even the best in the world at your skill, that's not what makes it a unique ability. Okay? So you as an entrepreneur specifically, if you're an entrepreneur, you must understand your unique ability because you're not stepping into a box that someone else has built. You are building your own box and you need to be clear what makes you unique so that people, when they see you, they understand why you instead of the other 500 options that they have out there. Number two, unique ability is transferable between jobs and industries because it belongs to you, not the task. It doesn't matter what specifically you are doing. Your unique ability goes with you. I used to make basketball videos every single day for five years.

The only content I ever put out was basketball. Even when I started talking about mindset. It was once a week. Basketball was the other six days a week. And that style that I had then is the same style that I have now. Even though basketball's being completely eliminated from the equation as far as what I talk about. Why? Because my unique ability is not basketball. My unique ability is my style and my delivery and my approach. It does not matter the topic. And number three, once understood, your unique ability will shine through no matter what you do, no matter where you go. Again, I can go into a completely different space. I can talk about celebrity gossip or politics. My delivery and style are not going to change. And that's the thing that makes me unique from my experiences and from the feedback that I've gotten from people who have really connected with my approach.

And again, many of them come from worlds that are not the worlds that I'm from. I played basketball, I played professional basketball, I got on social media and then I started business. Many of the people who I work with and work in your game, university clients, come from completely different backgrounds and have done things that I have never done before. Yet I can still serve them and work with them and they still connect with me even though they are not trying to do the same thing that I'm doing. They don't come from the same world that I come from and they're not trying to go to the same places that I've gone because my unique ability is what makes me valuable to them. It is not that we do the same thing or have a specific skill. I got some skills, but that's not the main thing. Main thing is the unique ability. The skills are secondary.

#2821: Everything You Believe About Marketing Is WRONG [Part 1 of 7]

Now, I'm not going to say that they're scammers because some of these people are not intentionally misleading you. A scam has to be intentional. So I wouldn't say that these people are scammers, but they also don't know what they're doing. That's what I'll say about them. You can come up with a name for that if you wish. I don't know what you call that, unintentional scammers. These people, we'll just call 'em idiots because they don't know what they're doing. They don't understand marketing. They're trying to sell somebody a marketing plan or some type of marketing service and they don't even know how marketing works. The challenge folks are not them. The challenge is if you don't know how marketing works, you may end up falling for that bullshit and buying from them and they aren't even going to do what you need them to do because again, you're asking the wrong questions because you have the wrong information.

So this is why I'm making this series to help you out. Point number two, today's topic once again is what you think about marketing is all wrong. Number two, social media attention equals instant success. False social media attention or increased social media attention or any amount of social media attention equals instant success. First of all, let's define this word success. What I tell you is success is for an entrepreneur, you are in the business of generating revenue. That is what an entrepreneur's mandate is to generate revenue. So I'm going to preface this point. Well, I already got into it, but I'll say that I'm prefacing this point by saying that this is all based on how you're defining success. As I said, you're in the business of collecting money when you're an entrepreneur and that's not optional. If you're running a business, you are in the business of collecting money, period.

So more money collected means more success in terms of entrepreneurs. So when I say success for an entrepreneur, that's what I mean by collecting more money. Again, this is a principle non opinion. This is related to the first point. Very strong false belief because many people believe this, many people think this and they think more eyeballs means more people following on social media and that means more money. Getting a lot of attention on social media does not necessarily mean you're going to make more money or necessarily you're making any money whatsoever. Yes, you heard me correctly. Getting attention on social media does not mean more money. It sometimes doesn't mean any money at all. In episode 1690, explain, I helped you understand through my explanation the game that social media is playing in the game that meta, that's Facebook and Instagram or Snapchat or X or LinkedIn or TikTok or YouTube.

The games that those companies are playing to make their money is not the same as the game that you are playing to make your money, and this is the thing that a lot of entrepreneurs do not understand. This is how a lot of people end up using too much of their resources on social media, trying to get attention on social media. That does not turn into a return on investment of dollars collected because not because they're doing anything necessarily wrong is because you strategically do not understand the game that you're in. Don't understand what business you're in. Social media knows what business is in. Alright? You know how much money meta makes every year? It's a lot. Look it up. They put it out there. They're a public company so you can find out how much money they make. X, LinkedIn, TikTok, Snapchat, Google who owns YouTube.

You know how much money these companies make every year. You know why they make that money is because they know what game they're in. They know exactly what game they're trying to play and what they do is let you who may not know what you're doing, they let you think you know what you're doing by collecting your money and collecting your money in the process. They're winning, you're losing not because you're doing anything wrong, not because they're doing anything wrong, but simply because you don't know what game you're in and it's not their job to educate you. It's your job to educate yourself. That's why you're listening to this show. Episode 1690 will help you understand the social media hustle, what their business is, their business and your business ain't the same. In other words, you shouldn't do everything that they want you to do because that ain't the business model that works for you.

That's what works for them. I'm not saying that they're always lying to you, but they have a certain business model. You got a certain business model, you got to know what yours is and you should know what theirs is. You're going to do business with another person. You should know what their business is so that you don't get caught out there. Let's just say again, episode 1690. Also in episode 1114, I talked about the value of social media in your business and whether or not you even need to be on social media for your business. Just because social media exists doesn't mean you have to be there for your business. Again, it depends on your business. Now, I know many entrepreneurs, many of whom pay very little attention to social media when it comes to generating dollars and there's a commonality amongst them. You don't know what it is.

There's a commonality amongst them. They all understand the same thing that I'm about to tell you, okay? You want to know what it is? Common thing that I know is a whole bunch of entrepreneurs who pay very little attention to social media. Here's the thing, there are a whole bunch of social media influencers out there who have a lot of attention. I mean, they got a bunch of followers, they got engagement, they got likes, comments, numbers, all of that stuff that makes many people, some of you listen to this, look up to them and admire them because of their vanity metrics. That's what we call those vanity metrics. Numbers that make you look good and serve your ego, but don't actually contribute to the bottom line of collecting money that these influencers, many of them have a lot less money than they have followers. Lemme take a sip of water while you absorb that. There are many influencers out there who have a lot less money than they have followers, Ike's comments, subscribers, whatever the data is. Many everyday people falsely believe that the amount of attention and followers a person generates on social media is commensurate with the amount of money that person is generating. This

The false number of followers someone has on social media says very little about how much money they're making, very little. Now, that doesn't mean that someone with a lot of followers isn't necessarily making a lot of money and it doesn't mean that someone with a little bit of money doesn't necessarily have a few followers, but there are people with a lot of followers and no money, people with a few followers and a lot of money. Social media is not indicative of what's going on in someone's actual business. Especially when you take into consideration how much that person is actually using or caring about or investing in. Even generating social media metrics, sometimes they're not even paying attention. I know people who earn a healthy six figures a year and you would be hard pressed to even find them on social media, let alone do they have interesting follower numbers.

So social media followers are not directly correlated to sales receipts or money collected. If you didn't read between the lines there, remember that many of your social media followers are merely social media freeloaders. Alright, so next time you see the word followers, it's substituted with freeloaders. That's who most of your social media followers are. They're freeloaders, they're loading up on all the free stuff you put out and they have no intention or maybe even ability or desire to give you money. That's just what it is. They're just consuming your free stuff and that's what it's, that's the deal. The deal with social media is you put free stuff out and people will follow you. You're putting out free stuff. That's it. That's the only agreement. No one's obligated to anything else. Alright? There's no other obligations. This is someone's following you on. Social does not mean they're obligated to give you money, and for the most part doesn't mean they will give you money most of the time in my experience. Moving on to point number three, today's topic once again is everything you think about marketing is wrong and it's a seven part series. We're on part number one. Number three, more platforms equals better false.

Now, this is a question I get often from entrepreneurs who are just getting their footing, getting themselves out there, getting known, and they wonder, they asked me because I am over here working your game, we are on every social media platform. So you name one, we are active on it and we're publishing there multiple times per day on every single social platform that exists. Or at least the one, the prominent ones. Lemme not say every one, all the prominent ones we're on, so let me name those prominent ones. X, Instagram, YouTube, TikTok Threads, Facebook, LinkedIn, and no, we don't do Snapchat anymore. So Snapchat, I demoted, they're not in that group, but all those others I just mentioned, we publish there every single day, morning once. So someone will look at me and say, well Dre, do I need to be on every platform like that?

The answer is no. You do not need to be on every platform because people think incorrectly. I mean logically, I can see how they get to this point, but it's incorrect. They think, well, if I get on every social media platform, then it helps maximize my exposure and that gives me the opportunity to possibly capture more attention to more places that I am, right? Logically I can see how someone can draw that line and make it make sense, but it's also not true. Based on what you heard in the first two points, you might be able to guess where I would end up on this. I already gave you where I'm at, but you might have been able to guess if you heard the first two points. While it can be beneficial to be on multiple platforms, I mean there's a reason why we are on every platform.

It can be beneficial to be on those platforms. My suggestion to any entrepreneur is that you focus on the platform, singular or platform's plural, where you are strongest, where you engage the most, where you feel most comfortable. That's what I would suggest you do, and that doesn't have to be all of 'em. If you are really comfortable and your strongest and you like engaging on X, also known as Twitter, used to be known as Twitter. If that's your thing, then just get on Twitter. Just get on Twitter and do that all day. Alright? If that's what works for you, do that all day. And again, I know very well funded, let's say entrepreneurs who really put all of their time and effort into one platform and you don't see them on any other platform. They literally don't have accounts, and even when they do, they're not even posting that much.

So from there, once you master one, then you can expand to other platforms if you so choose. And again, I know successful entrepreneurs who do all of their social media dealings in one, maybe two spaces and they ignore everything else. And I know successful entrepreneurs don't even have Instagram pages and I know some who don't use TikTok, they don't use X at all. I know some who are on everything all day every day, and there's no one right answer. I'm on every social media platform. I told you there's only one where I actually go back and forth and engage with people. Now on LinkedIn, for example, someone tags me in a post and something that I posted because I do a lot of media appearances and a lot of times they will post clips from their appearance and tag me and stuff like that. I wouldn't engage in that way, but when I say I don't engage in comments anywhere, what I mean is I do not get into comments of something that someone else posted that had nothing to do with me and just jumped into conversation.

X is the only app that I do that and that's the only one where I am active in that way. Instagram, I use the stories function everywhere else. I'm just publishing, I'm not reading, I'm not scrolling, I'm looking at other people's shit. I don't do any of that. And there are other people who do the exact opposite. They're on every app and they're just doing everything and doing all this stuff all day every day. And again, that works for them. You got to figure out what works for you and I just told you how to do it. Start with one, get comfortable with it, and then you can expand if you so choose. There's no one right answer, but as I just told you, directionally, you want to start with mastering one and then you expand. If you so choose, do not think that you need to be on every platform because that gives you more opportunities to make money.

Again, I can see how someone could logically think that, but it doesn't. No, don't do that. Okay? Just take my word. Don't do that. I just told you what the word is, why not to do it. All that said, let's recap. Today's topic, which is part one of seven, was going to be everything that you think about marketing is wrong. Number one, more traffic equals more sales. It's not necessarily true. It depends on what type of traffic and you need to be specific and strategic about drawing more traffic into what you do, because often more traffic means you're spending money to get that traffic. So you don't want just anybody coming into your world and then wondering why you're not getting the sales. You have to get the right type of people and if you're not spending money, you're spending time and effort.

All of those things are valuable resources. Number two, social media attention equals instant success. This is a false idea. Again, there are a lot of people on social media who have a lot more followers and likes and comments than they have actual dollars. If you're an entrepreneur, you're in the business of collecting dollars, not in the business of collecting followers, do not get fooled. And again, social media platforms are incentivized to make you think. Getting more followers and likes is the game. That's their game. That is not your game. Alright, number three, more platforms equals better. No, this is not true. And again, there are people who are on every platform like I am. It doesn't mean you need to be on every platform. It depends on who you are. It depends on who your audience is and also depends on your resources. Do you have the resources to be on every platform every day?

If not, don't try to do it. Focus on where you're strongest, where you're most comfortable, and where you can find your ideal people. That's what you need to focus on. And again, I know successful entrepreneurs, healthy six figure and seven figure entrepreneurs who only focus on one social platform. I know some who aren't on any of them. Alright? Okay, so you don't need to do it any one way just because you saw somebody else doing it. It has to make sense for you. Speaking of such work on your game university.com, that is the place where you can work with me directly. We could talk about where you're at, where you want to go, what you're doing, who you want to serve, and we will get clear on a clear plan for what you're going to do marketing wise, what you're going to do as far as your strategy, as far as your systems for getting your name and your work and your materials out there so that you can reach your ideal people, make the money that you want to make, live the life you want to live through. Mindset, strategy, systems and accountability.

#2822: Everything You Believe About Marketing Is WRONG [Part 2 of 7]

We can just pick this up right where we left off. I don't need to get more intro on this subject. You heard that in part one of this series. So we're picking up on point number four because we did the first three yesterday of everything you believe about marketing is wrong. Number four, more leads equals more sales. This is false. Now this point is headed more in the right direction than the idea that we talked about in the previous entry to this series, which is that more eyeballs equals more success. And we know success means collecting money, right?

So you're better at getting leads than just getting eyeballs. Now what's the difference between an eyeball and a lead? Let me explain. So leads are by definition people who are or could become interested in giving you money for your business, not for buying your business, but to actually give your business money because they want to buy your products and services. So an eyeball could be, for example, if you give you a real life example. If I'm running a sneaker store, let's say I run a sneaker store in my neighborhood, eyeballs will be me just putting a store on a block where more people are going to walk past it and see it. So all these people are walking past and seeing it. Those are eyeballs. A lead on the other hand is a person who walks in the store and they start picking his shoes up off the shelves and looking at them and asking if they could try shoes on a certain size.

That's a lead because that person has demonstrated that they are interested in possibly giving me money. Just the fact they walk in the store and makes them a lead. And eyeball is the fact they walk past the store. A lead is a person who not only walks past the store, but they stop and actually come into the store. So the lead is the person who is showing you that they are interested in business. You want to be gathering as many leads as possible and usually the people we gather as leads, we call these a list. We call it a list. The group of people that we gather who have shown some interest in us and whatever it is that we're offering. And in order to become a lead, usually what people do is they share with you some contact information of theirs in which they are giving you permission to contact them and market them.

Usually an email address or phone number or even a physical address. Those are all ways of people offering you their contact information and sometimes they don't even have to offer it. You can reach out to them legally in ways even if they didn't actually give you the information. For example, how many of you receive physical mail that you do not ask for but you receive it because maybe the building you live in or neighborhoods you're in, you get mail just because maybe you're on some type of list. Maybe you were on a different list and that list was shared with some other people. And this is the thing that happens in business that people will go get that list and they'll want to market to those people. So to give you an example, if you own a high-end luxury vehicle like a Rolls Royce or a Ferrari or something along those lines, the company from which you bought that car has your contact information, right?

They have your name, your address, your phone number, your email address, they know all that stuff. You are on their list. Now another company, let's say I was a company who was selling, let's say I was selling timeshares. Let's say I was selling timeshares that are within a hundred miles from where you live, where you bought that Ferrari or that Rolls-Royce. What I might do is reach out to the local Ferrari and Rolls-Royce dealerships and say, Hey, Mr. Rolls-Royce dealership owner, I have a timeshare business and I think some of your customers who bought Rolls-Royces also have enough disposable income to invest in the timeshare. So here's what I'll do. I'll offer you X amount of dollars to allow me to contact the people on your customer list so that I can sell them my timeshares. And here's what we can do. Mr Rolls-Royce dealership owner, I can either give you a percentage of all the money that I make or I can just offer you a lump sum just to give me access to your list and whatever I make, I make you don't participate in the upside, but you get paid because you let me access the list.

So if I make no money, you still get paid. Or if you want to do a kind of a split, then you get a percentage of everything I sell. Or we could do a hybrid, I give you a lump sum to give me access to the list and you get a percentage. I probably wouldn't offer that upfront, maybe I would. But this is the kind of thing that I'm giving you all that as a hypothetical, but these things actually happen in business. So any of you ever wonder how the hell did this company get my phone number? How did these people get my email address? How did this person get my physical address to be mailing me something? This is how it happens. You get on one list and that list information gets shared with other people because other companies will go and they will literally do this.

So if I was starting a timeshare business for example, this is something that I would do. I would say all who buy timeshares, usually people with disposable income, people who are not check to check type individuals. These are people who have disposable income and they are willing to spend more because they want to have more. So what I'm going to do is look for a zip code where the houses are higher priced. I may look for a zip code where I know demographically that people have more money or the net worths are higher. I may look for, again, I can go to a business that sells high-end stuff. I might go to a place that sells high-end jewelry and I'll try to get access to their list because people don't buy high-end jewelry when they're broke most of the time.

Or I'll go to a high-end car dealership because people don't buy those when they ain't got any money. So again, I want to reach these people because if they buy that high-end thing, they might buy my high-end thing as well. And these are luxury items that I'm selling. So I'm looking for what other luxuries these people buy and I'm going to go and try to get access to them. The whole point is that's what a lead is. So you can become a lead for someone even if you don't even know that they exist. That's the reason I'm explaining leads. So all of you understand. So a lead is anyone who could be interested in giving you money in business. So you can go acquire a lead. You don't necessarily have to, the person doesn't necessarily have to know that you exist and the internet world gives you an example of a lead.

A lead can be someone who just comes to your website and looks at your stuff and hopefully you can what we call capture the lead. Capturing the lead means giving that person an opportunity to give you their information so that you know that they actually were interested in your thing. That's what we call capturing the lead. This is why when you go to websites these days, often people are looking for a way to let you give them your information and they usually offer you some type of enticement in order to do so. Hey, give me your phone number so I can give you daily motivation every day. That is an example of capturing a lead. When you give me your number to get the daily motivation or the weekly motivation text, I'm capturing your information. Now I know that you exist, I know you're there and I know you're interested.

And guess what I'm going to do? I'm going to market to you in some way, shape or form. When you come to a website, I may say, Hey, get my emails for free every single day, which I do offer and go to work on my game.com. When you put your email address in, now you become a lead. You are now part of my list and now when I send emails out, you shall receive them. That is a way of capturing a lead. So you will notice if you didn't understand this already, this is what companies do all the time. You notice how many times over the course of a day you are asked, Hey, give me your email address, give me your phone number. Notice this happens in businesses these days a lot nowadays as well. And again, companies will do something like, what's the last business I was at?

I was at Nordstrom for example, and I'm talking about physical businesses online. You have to give them some kind of contact information when you buy because they have to have a way of contacting you after you make the sale, after you make the purchase, right? Jewelry, buy some jewelry for someone else or for myself, they need to contact info so they can let me know, Hey, your order has shipped or whatever situation. When you go into a physical store and go to Nordstrom for example, they say they ask for your phone number. Why do they want your phone number? Because they can connect it to your purchases. That's a way that they can also pull your receipts. That gives you some convenience. They can put you into their no rewards club. You get points for every dollar you spend, you get a point and after $500, you get a $20 gift certificate or something like that.

And why do they do that? They offer you those enticements because they want you to give them their contact information, your contact information because now you are on their list and you're a customer. They want the customers, they want to know who all the customers are because now they can market to you. Again, if I bought something from you before, guess what? I might buy something from you again, but if you don't market to me, I might forget that you exist. So companies want to do this on purpose and there are some businesses that I can think of right here in Miami that I go to frequently physically show up to their places and they never ask me for my contact information. They might have it because I've ordered online or something, but they don't do anything with the information. There are many businesses that I've gone to consistently spend money on and they don't do anything with the fact that they have my information.

They don't offer me like, Hey, when's your birthday? Or we'll offer you a $20 gift card for your birthday. Well guess what I'm going to do? I'm going to come buy something on my birthday. There's a customer, I might bring people with me. So these are things that businesses could do, but a lot of businesses have a lot of money falling through their fingers. They're not doing these things. But I'm going on a tangent here on this subject, but what we're talking about here is again, the false belief that more leads equals sales. So leads are a good thing, but just because you have more leads does not necessarily mean more sales. And now let me finally get to explaining why, because getting leads is better than just getting random people, but you must qualify what a good lead is for you. A good lead for one person is not necessarily a good lead for another person.

As I told you, if I'm selling timeshares, which is an extra home away from home that a person can have access to or they own it completely, usually that person is going to have some disposable income. So I'm probably not going to go to what's a bargain basement car. I'm not going to go to that dealership and ask for the leads from those people because the quality of those leads is not equivalent to the quality of the leads from the Rolls-Royce dealership because the Rolls-Royce people probably all have disposable income, whereas the people at the Kia dealership may not. Maybe there are some, but most of them, probably not Everybody following what I'm saying here. So the quality of the lead matters and that is not just a lead as a lead, that is not true. The quality of the lead matters depends on who the person is.

If you're a sports coach right now you're a basketball coach, you tell me if you walk into a gym and there's a bunch of guys who are a 6, 8, 6 9 and six 10 running up and down the court playing basketball, that's one quality of lead. You walk into a different gym, you walk into the gym down the hall and there's a bunch of guys who are 5, 5, 5 6 and five seven playing basketball. They're all leads. They all want to play college basketball. They all want to come play for your college coach. But are they the same quality of lead? Hell no. Alright. And it doesn't even matter. I didn't even say anything about their skills, whether they could dribble, shoot or pass. Just the fact that one group is 6 8, 6 9 and six 10, the other one's 5, 5, 5 6, and five seven is a big fucking difference. That's what I mean when I say leads.

The quality of the lead matters. So it's not just if they're interested, are you interested? Because you got to be just as interested as they are. So it's not the same for all of us. So a good lead for a smart car is not the same as a good lead for a Ferrari. A good lead for if you're selling a product that costs $5, that is not the same as a lead when you're selling a product that costs $10,000 because the $5 customer may not be willing nor able to come up to the $10,000 price point. So the leads are not equal. So when you are gathering leads, you must note their qualification based on what you are selling. And this is completely dependent on again, what you're selling and who is for. And these are things that again, I will work with you in when we get to strategizing for your business and work on your game university.

All leads are not equal. Remember I went into a suit supply store here in Miami. This is a story that I told in writing. I may have talked about it on this show. There's a store called Suit Supply and they do exactly what the title says. They sell suits. And I went in there one day and I remember I was dressed in basketball shorts, a white T-shirt and

Jordan sneakers. This is a weekend, usually I'm in a suit, but this weekend I was in casual clothing and there's a bunch of salespeople there. There's about eight salespeople in the store. Not one of them really paid any attention to me. I mean, they might've said hi when I walked in. They said bye when I walked out. But nobody really tried. Nobody tried to engage me, nobody even walked up to me and asked me anything.

And I assumed that they probably judged me as a low quality lead for purchasing a suit. And why? Because they looked at what I was wearing that day, which was not a suit. And they probably figured, all right, this guy's not a suit buyer nor a suit wearer, so I'm not going to waste time talking to 'em. That was a mistake by them because guess what? I guess what had made me a possible weed for them was the fact that I walked into the store at all because the store was in a mall. I could walk into any store I want. I didn't have to walk into that store. The fact that I walked into the store, they should have treated me as a buyer even if they had no idea if I was a buyer or not. Why? Because they fucking salespeople, they had nothing else to do but sell stuff and it's not like they were inundated with customers and I just got overlooked because there was no one available.

They were all available. I went in the store when it first opened, there was nobody else in the store. All the only people they were talking to were wearing each other, alright? Any one of them could have sold me something. They probably would've sold me something had they tried, they didn't even try because they judged me as a low quality lead. So you need to have your parameters for how a lead is quality or not. It's not just lemme just look at the person and eyeball it. No, that is not a parameter, that's not a formula. You need to have a system for determining if someone is a quality lead or not. Let me tell you what your system is. If you work in a physical retail store, if someone opens the door and walks into the fucking store, they are a lead or you need to treat them like one suit supply.

Y'all missed out on sale because they just assumed and it was a bunch of salespeople. It wasn't like it was just one person, it was all of him. They just assumed. They looked at me and said, all right, he ain't a suit buyer. He ain't got on a suit, so I guess he ain't going to buy a suit. Now again, I'm assuming what they were assuming, but I was in the store, I walked around, I took stuff off the rack, I was looking at it, looking at the shoes, I was looking at the suits. I spent a few minutes in the store walking around just seeing, I was looking at the stuff number one, but number two I went to see is anybody going to walk up to me and just strike up a conversation with me? What brings you into the suit store, sir? Or do you normally wear suits? How often do you wear a suit? What's your suit size? They could ask me any one of those questions. My answer to that question would've let them know immediately that I was a suit wearer because I would've probably told them in the answer to the question and boom, they would've had a sale. But if you're not a good salesperson, you probably shouldn't be in sales because you don't want to go broke. You're not going to make any money anyway,

So this is another hint for you folks. You can't just look at surface level information to know if someone's a good lead or not. You need, again, a system to know how to judge whether a lead is quality or not? You have to come up with a system for this. Don't just eyeball it in no time. And again, in work at your game university, this is one of the things that we work with people on. More quality leads equals more sales, not just more leads, period. Point number five, today's topic once again is everything that you believe about marketing is wrong. Number five, marketing is expensive. False marketing is never expensive and there's no counterpoint to this. There's no caveat to this. This is 100% false, always. No flip side, marketing is never expensive because marketing is the only way that you can get to the next step with selling. If you don't do any marketing, you can't do any selling. It's impossible.

Everybody understands that if you don't do marketing, you can't sell. So it's impossible for marketing to be expensive because you can't sell and make money if you don't do any marketing. So in other words, your marketing is an investment that pays for itself. And nothing is an expensive investment because investments by definition pay you back. Sonos is an expensive one. They're just investments that may take longer to mature IE to pay you back. Maybe there are bad investments in good investments and notice that it is an expensive investment. It doesn't make sense. It's a misnomer.

Marketing is the only way you can get to selling. Selling is the place where the money is collected. So even when your marketing is costing you more money than is making you, let's say you're spending a thousand dollars a day on ads, but you're only making $500 a day back. So you're losing $500 a day. Is that advertising expensive? No, as long as you're doing it the right way, you will probably be getting closer and closer to getting into the black, which is you're making money instead of being in the red, which means you're losing money. So let's say I spent a thousand dollars a day on ads for five days and I only made $500 per day on each of those days. So I spent $5,000 total and I made $2,500 total. Everybody with me, okay, so I'm $2,500 in the red right now.

I'm down $2,500. Now you may be asking yourself, Dre, how the hell is that? Not expensive, that's expensive. $2,500, I just lost $2,500. Well, on the contrary, what happened over those five days is I learned what worked and what didn't because I know who bought it. When I made that $2,500 in sales, I figured out who the buyers were. I figured out who the non-buyers were. So guess what? On day six, when I run those ads, I can target, I can more specifically target who I'm advertising to. I'm going to make it lean more towards the type of people who said yes and bought from me and away from the people who said no, and it completely ignored me. And now I'm going to, instead of losing $500 a day, now the next day I might only lose $200 and the next day I might lose only $50 and the next day I break even and then after that I start making money.

And then once I nail in exactly what works, guess what? I'm making money every day to the point that that 2,500 that I lost the first day, I've completely eclipsed that because now I'm making a thousand dollars a day and now I can just keep doing it over and over again. Now, does advertising work that simply? No. There's adjustments and ongoing processes that had to be done. This is all part of your marketing. So advertising is a part of marketing just in case anybody, I don't want to get anybody confused with that. Advertising goes underneath, marketing is a way of marketing. It's not all of marketing, it's a way of marketing. So these are the things that you need to understand and you don't necessarily need to understand them in detail, but you need to have someone on your team or be working with someone who does understand 'em in detail because this is the way that you're going to get your name and your stuff out there.

So even when your marketing is not converting and converting just means you do some marketing and it produces the result that you want. Even when that's not happening, you're doing marketing and are not working right now as long as you are learning from the marketing and you have the right systems and processes in place in which to learn from it. In other words, you know what to look for and you know what metrics to pay attention to and what changes to make if necessary, then you are learning along the way. You eventually get to the point that your marketing is working. I have an ad campaign going on right now when I'm recording this. By the time you hear this, we'll probably have had a much better target than it is right now, but we're spending money every single day and it's not quite converting.

So right now, technically we are losing money on this, but we're not really losing money because this is an investment. We're basically paying to get education on what types of marketing works and what doesn't work. So every time we spend money and we don't get the result we want, we know that doesn't work. So all I'm doing is paying for an education. I'm paying to get them, I'm investing in my education on how this particular product, on this space with these people, with these parameters, how does this produce results or how does it not produce results I'm paying to learn. As long as we learn from what we're paying for, then it's an investment. Now, if you're not learning, then it is a cost, then it can become expensive. This is why you gotta know what you're doing, folks, is everybody's saying with me here, am I saying this too fast?

If so, rewind it and listen to it again. So what you want to do is get to the point where you eventually do have things working. So even when you lose money, again, all you're doing is educating yourself so you're not really losing money, losing money. I'm using air quotes that again, education works when you have the right knowledge. This all requires knowing what to look for, how to look for it, not just randomly doing stuff and hoping, which is what a lot of people do, and hoping that the right knowledge just hits you upside the head like an apple falling off the tree doesn't happen. So this is why I always tell marketers that if you're going to get into advertising, which means you're paying to get attention, you must have the right metrics in mind and know what you're doing because you can lose a lot of money very quickly when you have the wrong process or you have no process.

And I've seen this happen to too many entrepreneurs. They just didn't have a process. Moving on point number six, today's topic once again is part two of seven. Everything you believe about marketing is wrong. Number six, set it and forget it. False, set it and forget it is simply all you have to do is set up this process and set up this system and then you just push a button and everything just works on autopilot and the money just piles in. All you gotta do is collect and count the money. That's all you got to do. And you will hear many marketers basically promote their offerings as if this is how it works. This is a lie. It is not true. It's a little bit of puffery. It's a little bit of salesmanship that they're doing. They are lying. Many times they're lying by omission.

And so sometimes they are outright lying because of the way that they position and sometimes they're just selling. They're just kind of hyping it up and making it seem easy. You got to do that to market. You don't buy the way you sell. So I understand them. At the same time, I'm giving a word a warning that this is never, ever, ever the case. You never just set it and forget it because if it was just set it and forget it. Well, why the hell are they running ads? Think about that. So this is not a real thing, although many marketing against salespeople and they'll present themselves as being just setting and forget it. Get into my program. I make it so easy, I'm going to get 10 new clients in the next 24 hours. And this is the kind of stuff you hear people say, and I don't buy it. I don't like this, I don't like people market like that and I don't respond to that stuff.

But there are probably people who do respond to it. This is why you see so many people doing it. So they're not telling you the full truth. If you didn't catch that, no marketing is just set one time and left alone, no use. Productive marketing is set at one time and leaves it alone. That does not happen. If that is happening, the person who's doing that, they are losing money and they're not doing marketing in a smart nor success driven way. Only way marketing can be set and forget it is if you hire somebody else to do it and you set them in place to do the work and they ain't forgetting it. They're doing it all day every day. So maybe you personally don't have to do it, but somebody gotta be doing it. Alright? That's the way it works. So when it comes to advertising on my end for example, I don't like running ad campaigns.

I don't like setting up ad campaigns. I don't like monitoring ad campaigns. I like doing any of that. All I want to know is how much are we spending and how much are we making back so I get other people to do it. So the ad campaign I just referenced, I'm not running that ad campaign. I can log in, I can see what's happening, I can see, what do we call 'em, the ad sets and the ads that are being run, the campaigns. I can see how much money is spent, what the bill is, I can see all of that, but I'm not in charge of making all that stuff actually get set up the right way. I got somebody else responsible for that and that's the way that I want it to be. So am I setting it and forgetting it? Technically, personally, I am, but I have access and there is someone who is not forgetting it.

Again, they're working on it all the time. Any kind of marketing that matters that is productive is not setting to forget it. Somebody has to be looking at it. It doesn't have to be you, but somebody better be looking at it. Otherwise you're going to be losing money and time. So you hire somebody else to do it for you. They know what they're doing, okay? You can go ahead and forget it. Actually, don't forget it. You just need to watch it. You need to watch what they're doing and they need to give you a clear report as to what's happening. Somebody needs to be minding the business, okay? And marketing is your business. Somebody must be minding the business at all times. So I suggest you never forget about what's happening in your marketing. Even if you have the best expert in history doing your marketing for you, you should not forget about it because that marketing is driving your ability to collect dollars.

If you don't have someone with eyeballs on marketing and you're not paying attention to it, then your ability to collect dollars is being effective and you're asleep at the wheel. So again, when people do marketing for me, there are parameters that I need you to show me exactly what we're doing, how much is it costing, and what kind of results are being produced. I want to know those things and I know what questions to ask so I can know whether or not I'm going to keep doing this or not keep doing it. I make the ultimate decision because my business is my money. I don't care who the expert is. You could be some expert off TV who did ads for Oprah and Barack Obama and you're the most successful ad person in the world. It's my fucking money and it's my business.

I'm making the final call, alright? You need to have that same mindset because it is your business that matters. It's your business that is being run here, not theirs. I don't care who they are. So if you're going to pay attention to anything consistently in your business, it needs to be the marketing. Alright? Nothing else is more important than that. So this whole set it and forget it thing. What you need to do is forget that, alright? You need to wake up and forget that you're not setting and forgetting anything. All that said is recap. Today's points. We are on part two of a seven part series. Everything you believe about marketing is wrong. Number four, more leads equals more sales. Not necessarily a lead is better than an eyeball, but a lead, a person who's interested in your business needs to be the right type of lead and you need to be clear on who the right type of lead is.

That's why you gotta know who your customer is. Number five, marketing is expensive. No, it's never expensive. Marketing is an education and information you are getting based on what you are doing. And as long as you learn from all your marketing, even when it is not producing an ROI, it is not converting as we say, meaning you're spending money but not making it back. You are still learning in that process as long as you know how to learn, you know what to look for. If you don't know, then marketing can be expensive. You don't know what you're doing. So what is expensive is not actually the marketing. What's expensive is your ignorance. You not knowing something is costing you money. It's not the marketing itself. And number six, excuse me, set it and forget it. You don't ever want to set it and forget it when it comes to your marketing.

Marketing is the lifeblood of your business. You should always be paying attention to it. I don't care who's running it, I don't care how many people are in between. You should always know exactly how much money you're spending. You know exactly what's happening and exactly how much money you're making back, and you should know what questions to ask to figure these things out and what questions to ask. If you don't like what those numbers look like and you should know how to access all of that stuff, regardless of who's in charge of your marketing, you should have direct access to all of that stuff. If you don't, then you are making a mistake in your business.

#2823: Everything You Believe About Marketing Is WRONG [Part 3 of 7]

Let's pick up where we left off here and I'm just reading some messages. Somebody's messaging me here. Okay, so picking up where we left off, we are on the 21 things that you have been taught to believe about marketing that are actually not true. We're picking up on point number seven. Number seven, people hate hearing and seeing advertisements. This is false. Now some of you at some times and in certain places you may hear or see an advertisement and you do actually hate hearing and seeing it. You might think, well somebody's show, maybe this show has too many ads on it or I don't like having to look at ads every time I turn on a YouTube video or I don't like there being ads on. I opened my favorite magazine. Magazines like Vogue or GQ have more ads and have articles in them.

If you actually look through it, you will notice that it literally does have more advertisements than has articles, but this is one that is 100% false and it has no flip side. Even though there may be times that you don't like seeing ads. And let me explain to you why it's still 100% false even though I just said that there are times that you don't like seeing ads. There are times when I'm watching YouTube and I don't want to have to wait for the ad to end so I can finish watching the video that I'm watching, but it's still 100% false that people hate hearing and seeing ads. Lemme tell you why people these days have become fully accustomed, accustomed to seeing advertisements. We expect there to be ads. Anytime you're looking at something online or consuming something online, we expect ads to be there. I will go as far as to say people know that there's going to be an ad, they just don't know what the ads are going to be.

If I was to open YouTube right now, if you were to open YouTube right now, we both fully expect that an ad will play before we get to watch the video that we clicked on and usually YouTube fulfills that expectation. This is the normal experience of using the internet in the world that we live in today. And all of us have accepted this and we know we've grown again. We're used to it, we're accustomed to it. Ads have always existed offline. I think about Watson tv, there's commercials, right? There's commercial breaks on tv. Those are ads. The newspaper has ads in it all the time. Oh, go grab a newspaper off the newsstand and you will see their ads all through that newspaper. Open up a magazine like GQ or Vogue. Those magazines again have more ads than they have actual content and there's a reason for that and there's a reason why those magazines are still printing where many magazines have gone all digital because they're making the money from the ads.

Okay? We are used to ads, we expect ads and most of the ads we see our brains just unconsciously filter 'em out. We don't even realize that an ad just happened because our brain just completely ignores and deletes it. Now, while many of you may get some complaints here and there about your ads, I'm talking on the sales side when you're the person making the ads or you're the person who is offering the ads, it might not even be an ad for your stuff, but let's say you're advertising somebody else's stuff Here on this show I advertise Ag one and AquaTru filters and then I have some my books and working your game university. Now you may get some complaints from people who say, well, you got a lot of ads in whatever your video or your magazine or your newsletter or your podcast episode.

That does not mean you should stop running the ads. That would be a very, very bad idea and I'll tell you why that'd be a bad idea. The people who complain about your ads, they're telling you that the ad is not for them. Anybody complaining about an ad that you run on your material is telling you indirectly that whatever it is you are advertising is clearly not for them. They are not the customers for that thing. That's completely fine. That's excellent feedback for you because now you know that that person is not your customer, especially if it's an ad for your product. Alright? So if somebody's complaining about an ad that you're advertising somebody else's product, that's a different story. But if your ads are all your stuff and people complain about that, well that's probably not your customer. They're probably not your ad. Even the ads that are related to your stuff, they're probably not your customer.

They're complaining about it because people, if they like your material that you're putting out, and usually ads we find on free stuff, usually people don't put ads on paid stuff. Ads are usually on the free stuff. We put ads on the free stuff that is related to what we think or things that are what we think our ideal person, the consumer, would be interested in. It doesn't mean you're going to buy it, but we put ads that we believe you'd be interested in for whatever reason. So a person who complains about that is probably not your customer, and of course they're not the customer for the thing that you're advertising, which is completely fine. They're just letting you know that they're not your ideal person. That's all they're letting you know. That's excellent feedback for you and you can do with that information whatever you need to do.

See, the people who don't complain about your ads, they might be the ones who are clicking on those ads and actually buying the stuff that you're advertising. They may not announce it like the person who doesn't like the ads announces that they don't like the ads, but the people who are actually responding to the ads and doing stuff, they may not announce it, they just do stuff. Just go and click on the ad and they buy the stuff. So never allow yourself to be influenced and persuaded by a person who is complaining about the ads on your podcast, YouTube video or anything you create. Take it in as feedback that the person complaining is not the person you're targeting and not the person you should be targeting with that ad. Again, it could be good news, it could be good news, it could be bad news, it depends, but you should just take that as feedback and understand that ads help sell things and as an entrepreneur, you all know the mandate, your mandate as an entrepreneur is to generate revenue.

So if someone is complaining about you doing something that is going to generate revenue for your business, all they're letting you know is that they're not your ideal person. That is not something you need to react negatively to. Is it something that you can take in as feedback? Take a look at that person or those people and say, okay, what do these people have in common? What are some things I'm noticing about this person that might help me avoid attracting more people like them into my audience so that I'm not putting my ads in front of people who are just not customers, not the right people. That's how you should look at anyone complaining about your ads. But there's nothing wrong with running ads, people complaining about the ads. So what they really don't want you to have ads, guess what they can do? They can pull out their wallet and they can buy something. They can get into the stuff that's paid where there probably aren't any ads, and if they're not doing that, then you sometimes may have to take their feedback with a grain of salt. Point number eight, today's topic once again is everything that you believed about marketing is wrong. And again, we are on a series here, so we're on part three of the series. Number eight, marketing is about selling. This is not true.

Marketing is two different activities. Alright? So I want you all to understand the difference between the two marketing leads to selling marketing is the activities of you, the activities that encompass you, building a relationship and nurturing that relationship with your audience. And again, you could build and nurture a relationship with people who don't even know you and they can join into a relationship with you because of your marketing and selling is the act of you actually showing them, Hey, here's what I have, here's what it does, here's how it can help you and here's what you have to do to get it. That's selling. That's me saying, here's this car, here's what it does. It goes zero to 60 in five seconds and this is how it'll solve your problem because right now you're taking a bus and now you'll have a car to drive and costs $50,000 and you could put $10,000 down, it'll be $5,200 a month for the next four years, whatever.

That's the process of selling. That's selling. So marketing leads to selling. What marketing does is again, create and cultivate and nurture relationships, whether with a new person or someone who already knows you because you must maintain relationships with people who know you already and it sets the stage for selling. Selling is when you exchange your products and services for that person's money. Marketing is an ongoing process because I would expect that you as an entrepreneur want to have an ongoing process of money coming in, right? If you want money coming in consistently, you must nurture relationships consistently. Alright? So any amount of money you want coming in consistently, you need to be doing a commensurate amount of marketing consistently. So marketing is an ongoing process, which means you need to have an ongoing process of nurturing relationships. What can you do to continually nurture the relationships that you have?

It's a lot of different things that you can do. Putting out free content is one thing that you can do. Finding different ways of putting out free content. We have audio, we have visuals, we have written material. Those are three different methods of putting out content and you can use a lot of different ways to do that. Audio, you got a live stream audio like Clubhouse and Twitter spaces or X Spaces audio. You have a recorded audio like this that you're listening to right now. You have video, you have every app that has video now, Facebook, Instagram, TikTok, YouTube, what's the other one I'm missing? Twitter has video threads, has video, so you can put video on any one of these applications. Then written material. You can even do a written post these days on YouTube. I don't know if everybody knows that you can put a written post up on YouTube.

X has it, Facebook has it. Instagram, I mean you kind of can do a written post, but it's not really a written post. Threads has written posts. Facebook already said they have written posts. So there's a lot of different ways you can do this and you can do this offline as well. Those of you who are members that work at your game university, you know that I send out two physical mailings every month that are written material, the black book and the Bulletproof Bulletin. If you're watching this on video right now, you can see the Bulletproof Bulletin is right behind my head. I'm moving to the side so you can see it. That is the December issue, the title, the theme of that issue is why we are here. And then the black book right here behind my left shoulder, that is the October 20, 20, 23 issue.

I send both of those out every month. I print those and those are written material and those are ways of me staying in touch with my audience through written material. So again, you are only limited by your imagination, but this is all part of the ongoing process of nurturing the relationship and making sure that people remember that you exist. So it's not a, excuse me, it's not a stop and start thing when it comes to marketing is also not a one time thing. It's an all the time thing. Good marketing brings in quality leads who are already interested in participating in a sales conversation, which should make your sales conversations go more smoothly and easily and hopefully successfully, which means you're actually making sales. In other words, if your sales process has been challenging for lack of a better term, is your sales process not going as smoothly as you want it to go? What you need to look at is not changing up your sales presentation or firing your salespeople. What you need to look at is your marketing process and ask yourself, am I bringing in the right type of people into sales conversations so that the sales conversations can go much more smoothly? See, no wizard of a salesperson can fix the fact that you're doing bad marketing, bad marketing, which is bringing in bad leads. No salesperson can undo that.

It's like trying to shine up dog poop. You take some dog poop and you try to shine it up and make it look good. No matter how good of a shiner you are, it's hard to shine up dog poop. Now, if I gave you a brand new pair of leather shoes that cost a thousand dollars at the local department store, you can shine those up and make 'em look excellent, right? You only have to be that good of a shiny person to make those shoes look good because the shoes already came looking good. Everybody understands where I'm coming from? So this is why you're marketing and selling work together, but they are not the same thing. Your marketing needs to be better dialed in so that you are attracting more of the right type of people, which makes it easier for you to convert them into customers, clients, and overall just sales.

Okay, so good marketing brings in quality leads and makes selling much easier. So while marketing is not selling, it is the table setter for selling. Point number nine, today's topic once again, we are on a seven part series and we're on part three of seven. Everything you believe about marketing is wrong. Number nine, influencers guarantee success. And this could be any kind of connection that you have to or with an influencer. This could be you being the influencer does not guarantee that you are going to be successful as an entrepreneur and the success again means you are bringing in dollars.

Just because you're an influencer does not mean you're going to make money connecting with an influencer, meaning you have an influencer who's your friend or an influencer post about you and their story or they put a link up about your product or service, whatever it is that you're selling or they follow you and now everybody can see that they're following you.

Just being connected to an influencer or even being one yourself is not a guarantee of entrepreneurial success. And again, in entrepreneurship, the success is dollars collected. We have touched on this a bit already in this series, and this is another false idea that is completely not true. Now, in some cases it can be true, but it's not true for the reasons that most people think it is. See, the reason that most people think being an influencer creates entrepreneurial success are completely false, and let's get into that. Most people think that you will make more sales by either being one or engaging with an influencer simply because an influencer has by definition a bunch of eyeballs on their stuff or they will bring more eyeballs to your stuff. So if I got Kim Kardashian to post the link about the mirror of motivation, that guarantees that I'm going to make a bunch of money selling copies of the Mirror of motivation now. I can expect that a few people might click on the link and actually buy the book because Kim Kardashian posted about it.

I would say yes. Now we have to not juxtapose, but weigh that against what I had to invest in order to get Kim Kardashian to post that link? Well, I recoup my investment. You see, just because you got an influencer doesn't necessarily mean you're going to make money on a deal. You may lose money on a deal. Just because they have eyeballs does not mean it's going to help your stuff sell. As I've already told you, many of the eyeballs that you get on your stuff through an influencer or through influencing are people who are either not really that interested in you or what you're selling, not willing to buy you or what you're selling or not able to buy you or what you're selling. This is why your marketing matters so much because your marketing should filter out the people who are not interested, not willing and not able, and your marketing should only send through.

The only people who should get through the filter of your marketing are the people who are interested, willing and able to buy. And depending on what you are selling, that filter may be very, very detailed and you may not have so many leads, but you don't need so many depending on what you're selling and how much you're selling it for. These are all things you need to understand as foundational marketing concepts. These are foundational marketing understandings that you need to have if you're going to be in an entrepreneurial game. So eyeballs do not necessarily equal sales because again, just because somebody looked at something doesn't mean they want to buy it. It doesn't mean they can buy it, it doesn't mean they aren't even interested in buying it. So eyeballs can get you attention and they can serve your ego. So if I woke up tomorrow and I had 10 times the followers on every single social media app, that would make me feel good.

It would give me a very strong rush of dopamine to know that I have 10 times more followers in the morning than I had when I went to bed the night before. But does any of that make me any money? Not necessarily. So I say all that to say the right influencer who has the right audience of the right people and you have the right marketing message. That combination can help you make money. You can make money on that if you have the right influencer, the right offer and everything is dialed in the way that it's supposed to be, but it's like a combination lock there and it is not just let me just throw an influencer and let them throw my product out there and all of a sudden the money's going to come in. There are many people who have falsely believed this and have lost their shirts as they used to say back in the day, trying to do business just through influencing just because people saw yourself means nothing when it comes to collecting dollars, whether again that influencer is an outside person or you, the same thing has happened.

You have to ask the right questions. You got to know what information you need in order to discern who that influencer could be. In other words, which influencer would be best? If I'm going to find an influencer to help me sell the mirror of motivation, which influencer would best help me sell that? Probably not Kim Kardashian because to be honest, and not a dis to Kim, she happens to hear this. I don't think she's much of a book reader and I don't think she has an audience of book readers and I don't think even the people in her audience who do read books, I don't think they go look at her post because they're looking for a recommendation of a book to read. I don't think that's happening. So it'd probably be a bad idea for me. It'd be great for Kim because she makes some easy money and doesn't have to do much.

It would be a bad idea for me because I don't think she has the audience that is looking to read a book on how to be the best version of yourself so you can do what you need to do and have what you want to have in life. I don't think those are the people that she has attracted. Everybody understands. So that's on me because I'm the business owner, alright? She's just collecting the dollars. It ain't her business to tell me, Hey Dre, I don't think it's a good idea for you to pay me $50,000 to do a post about your book. All she gotta do is collect the bread. Alright? It's my job to ask myself, is this a good investment? And if I don't ask myself that question, then it is my responsibility, whatever happens from there. So you have to ask the right questions.

So it's not just looking at follower numbers of the person. Just because somebody has a certain number of followers does not mean any of those followers will buy any of your shit, okay? Not even the engagement numbers. That's another thing you hear people say, well, we are not looking at followers. Looking at engagement. Even if somebody has a lot of engagement, doesn't necessarily mean they want to engage with your stuff or just because they're engaging with that person on their stuff does not mean they want to engage with you on your stuff. So all of these things have to be considered, and this is where many people start and also where they stop or how many followers you got, what kind of engagement they got, and this is how people end up making mistakes because they're asking the wrong questions. All that out the way was to recap today's class which says, we are on part three of seven.

Everything you believe about marketing is wrong. Number seven, people hate hearing and seeing ads. This is not true. The right people love seeing ads because the ads are telling them about products that they actually want and will possibly buy. I remember Tim Ferriss, who has a very popular podcast. He once tried it as an experiment. He said, I'm going to stop running ads on my podcast and I'm going to let people become sponsors of the show. So basically what Patreon is now, that's what Tim Ferriss was doing I believe before Patreon was even a thing. And he took his ads down off his podcast for a while and he had a paid group of people, the people who paid to support his show and he would do a separate type of meeting gathering, get together just for those people who paid and that would be the special thing they got in exchange for the money.

In other words, exactly what Patreon does these days. Tim was doing this years ago, probably 2016 ish around this time he was doing this and he killed the experiment after about maybe a month or two, and he announced from the beginning that this wasn't the experiment was me. He would kill it if it wasn't working. And the reason that he killed it, you know how he killed it? Because a bunch of Tim's listeners, even the people who paid the money to support him, said, Tim, I actually like when you have ads on your show because I listen to your ads and I actually go and buy and try the products that you mentioned on your show. So I actually want you to have ads on the show because those ads give me good recommendations for things that I should go buy and try because I trust you in your word.

So understand folks that when you have the right audience and your audience is your ads are actually serving them, it is not annoying them. Number eight, marketing is about selling. No, it is not. Marketing leads to selling. Marketing sets the table for sales because your marketing is going to filter out the wrong people and it's going to bring in the people who are interested in what you are selling. They have a desire to have what you're selling and they have the ability to buy what you're selling. And that is not everybody. Just because somebody sees your stuff does not mean there are any of those three things. Your marketing should be finding people who are all of those three things. And number nine, influencers guarantee success. This is absolutely false. As I already told you, there are a bunch of influencers out there who are not making any money.

They have less money than they have followers. Influencers do not guarantee success. All they guarantee, possibly not. They don't guarantee this. Possibly they get you eyeballs, but do not be fooled by vanity metrics. You heard me talk about this many times. Do not be fooled by vanity metrics. As an entrepreneur, the only metric that truly matters is dollars collected vanity metrics like followers and likes and subscribers and comments and engagement. All of that bullshit is designed to dazzle you to shock and all you and to get you to give more of your most valuable resource was not your money but your time to the social media applications. That's what vanity metrics are for. They are not metrics for your business. The bottom line of your business has nothing to do with likes, comments, and followers. You can't pay bills with that. You cannot buy diapers for your children with that.

You cannot eat dinner likes, comments, and followers. Do not be full of vanity metrics. You need to be looking at hard metrics like IE dollars in the bank, okay? Never be fooled by influencer stats on and out the way.

#2824: Everything You Believe About Marketing Is WRONG [Part 4 of 7]

Let's pick up right where we left off on point number 10. Everything you believe about marketing is wrong. Number 10, short content is always better. Here's another one that is 100% false, but it has been widely accepted and it is widely believed unfortunately by too many entrepreneurs who simply don't know what they don't know. Alright? Many content creators these days have bought into this idea that you should create a bunch of short content and do so as much as possible because people have shorter attention spans.

It's not the concept of creating short content that is necessarily bad because I put out short content as well. I just had, I'm looking on my Instagram right now as my assistant handles these clips that we put out just today alone. What was the first one we put out today? That was today? That was today. And we put out a lot of content today. We put out a lot of stuff today. So today I put out one short clip, two short clips, three short clips, four short clips, five short clips, 6, 7, 8 short clips. We put out just today, it's four 30 in the afternoon when I'm recording this and we are probably going to put out one or two more before the end of the day. So putting out short clips is not necessarily a bad thing. It's the reasoning behind the short clips that is incorrect.

And when your reasoning for doing something is inaccurate, then your actions are going to end up inaccurate. It's kind of like if you have an airplane and you're flying from New York to LA, you could be headed west, but if you tilt the direction that the plane is going one or two degrees, you could end up in a completely different place. Even though directionally you may be going the right direction, you're still not going to end up in the right destination. So people putting out short content is a good idea just to put out content periods and to utilize short content because it is useful. But putting it out because you believe people have shorter attendance spans is the wrong reason to do it.

While short form content is useful, and again I partake, I just told you this very show is proof positive that longer form content still exists, it still matters and people still consume it. My own form content still matters and it still matters for a reason that makes it very different from short form content, which I'll explain in a moment and understand the most important part is not the content itself, it is what you are asking of the people in your audience through which you give them the content. So let me ask you a question. Well, do you know anything about marketing, selling entrepreneurship or not? You need not know anything about these spaces. To answer this question, I'm going to ask you a question as a consumer that says an everyday person. Alright, so everyone listens to this. I want you to answer this question in your head while I'm talking.

Which person are you more likely to give money to if you don't know anything else about them? I'm only going to give you a couple pieces of information and just based on that I want you to give me your answer. Which person are you more likely to be giving your money to? In other words, you are a customer or client of this person. Either A, the person to whom you have given 30 seconds of time, or B, the person to whom you're given one hour of time. Which person are you more likely to be a customer and or client of the person who you've given 30 seconds to or the person you've given an hour to. I'll take a sip of water. While you contemplate your answer, I want you to think of the reason why you're given the answer that you're given as well. Okay?

Time's up. Even if you know nothing about entrepreneurship or marketing or sales, the answer is the same for the same reason. It's the person to whom we've given the hour. Now why is this? Here's the important part. Why are you more likely to be a customer of a person you've given an hour to than a person you've given 30 seconds to? Because it is easier to make a second investment in something once we have already made the first investment. See, a one hour investment is a much bigger buy-in than a 32nd investment. In other words, if I'm looking for people who I believe will be serious about working with me, I'm not going to just ask you for 30 seconds of your time because that's not a big enough investment for me to know that you're serious about coming to the next step. Now, if I ask you for an hour of your time and you give me that hour, okay, now I know I'm talking to some serious people because whatever I said in that hour had your attention enough for you to actually consume it all.

Now, if I gave you 30 seconds and you consume that, that's not enough of a buy-in. I don't know if you really know. I don't know if that's enough. Which person are you more likely to be in a long-term relationship with? The person who you talk to for 30 seconds at the train station or the person who you've gone out on 30 dates with and spent 30 nights at their house and they spent 30 nights at your house? Of course the person you've given more time to because there's more of a relationship in that place because you spent more time there. That time matters in marketing everybody in an hour, for example, I can give 30 seconds of my time. Let's say I'm a consumer. Let's say I'm on the consumer side, so I'm thinking about buying something, but I don't know what I'm going to buy.

I can give 30 seconds of my attention to 120 different people over the course of an hour, 30 seconds, 120 different times over the course of an hour. Just divide the hour up into 32nd intervals. Now does that mean I'm going to buy from any or all of those 120 people? No, I probably won't buy anything from any of them. Why? Because I haven't had enough time to even digest or process what I consume or even think about whether or not I want it. I haven't invested at all. I'm not mentally invested in any of these people, but if I spend an hour in a conversation with a person, I'm at least considering what they're offering. Now, if I'm a consumer and you're selling me something, I spend an hour in a conversation with you, I'm at least considering what you got because otherwise I wouldn't have let the conversation even keep going if I wasn't even at least thinking about it.

Again, it doesn't guarantee that I'm going to buy, but I'm probably thinking hard about it because we spent an hour talking. Even if I don't buy, it's still in my mind that we had the conversation. Now, if I only gave you 30 seconds, I might forget that we even, I might forget that I even met you by the end of the day. If all I gave you was 30 seconds, see if I had paid attention to something for long enough, like an hour. Remember that focus is a force multiplier. We talked about focus in episode 1193. Then I know exactly what you're offering because in an hour you were able to explain it. I know exactly what it could do for me. Again, you've explained it and I have been already considering in my mind what it would look like because again, in an hour my mind is going in all different directions as you're telling me what it is that you're doing.

See, I can't do those things in 32nd bursts. Now, while I am a fan of thinking fast and making decisions fast, an hour to picture something versus 30 seconds to picture something is a big difference. So as a content creator, you need to be making long form content as well as your short stuff with the understanding that not as many people are going to consume the long stuff necessarily, but that's a good thing. Why is it a good thing that not as many people may consume? The longer stuff that you do, people who do consume it are those who might be your best leads. See, if you ask people for 30 seconds, you don't know if they're serious or not, you ask people for 30 minutes and they give it to you, okay? That person is at least eligible to be serious. Even if they're not serious, they're at least eligible because at least they gave you the 30 minutes. Person won't give you the 30 minutes is not serious, and the reason why so many people get this wrong these days is because many people have been conditioned to seek out the dopamine hits that come with vanity metrics. IE how many clicks, how many views, how many likes, how many subscribers? Rather than the entrepreneurial benchmark of dollars collected and actually making money.

The social media apps want you to follow the benchmark of vanity metrics, likes, comments, followers, subscribers, et cetera. The entrepreneur wants you to follow the benchmark of action making money. Sometimes you will be able to do both. There'll be times where you have to choose and you cannot do both. That's why you need to understand these principles, what works, how it works and why so that you're not making mistakes. So understand this and tattoo this on your forehead. It does not matter how many followers or views you are getting if you are not collecting any money from those followers or viewers. Lemme say that again, for the influencers out there, it doesn't matter how many followers or viewers you get if you are not collecting money from those followers or viewers. Point number 11, we are talking here today about everything you believe about marketing is wrong.

We are on a series as part four. Number 11, marketing is only for big businesses. Now, I could have put this point earlier in the series because if you've been paying attention, you know that this is complete nonsense. So this one has already been knocked out indirectly through previous points. But let's talk about this point. Anyone who is doing any form of business, whether you are the head of Facebook or you're running a local lemonade stand or you're helping your daughter sell Girl Scout cookies, you must always be marketing. Marketing is not only for big businesses and marketing is not only for people who are official businesses, marketing is for anyone who wants to make money in the marketplace. Lemme say that again. Marketing is for anyone who wants to make money in the marketplace. It doesn't matter what your actual is, you must be marketing.

Marketing is for anyone who wants to do business, alright? It doesn't even matter what you're doing. Again, you don't even have to be an entrepreneur, alright? If you are in, I know I have a lot of coaches, sport coaches who listen to this show. If you were to get fired from your job that you coach at right now, coach and you need another job, would you be out there marketing yourself? Of course you would reach out to all your warm contacts, you go through your Rolodex of all the people that you know would look at all the job openings that are out there, at least the ones that you know about and see which ones maybe you could make yourself. I was before, what are you doing? Marketing. You would polish up your resume and you would try to figure out, okay, how can I best position myself to get my next opportunity?

Because the last one's over. What are you doing? You're marketing. When I was trying to get on playing professional basketball, I told you, some of you have heard me tell this story. That first thing I did was go to an exposure camp, which is a way to market myself. Exposure is a form of marketing because I was able to expose my game to some decision makers who could actually possibly help me move forward. Then when I came back from the exposure camp, I'm back home. I started cold calling basketball agents. What was I doing? Marketing myself. I wanted to get one of those agents on the phone so I could pitch them on the concept of representing me. I was trying to sell myself to them, but I had to market to them first in order to get the sale. I had the first market like here's who I am, here's what I got, here's what I can do.

Then I was sending out bubble mailed copies of a VHS film that had my best basketball footage on it. All of that was part of the marketing process and again, I'm bringing it up. I wasn't an entrepreneur at that time. I was trying to get a job, but I was marketing myself in order to get a job. So anyone who wants to make money in business in any way, shape or form, you must be marketing. If you are not marketing, then people can't know that you are there. Therefore, they can't come to you and they can't get what you're offering because they just are completely unaware of your presence. Every entrepreneur goes into this. Even if you are a solopreneur and you do everything on your own in your business, you must have a plan and a strategy for marketing you and or your stuff.

If you do not have a plan or strategy for marketing yourself, you are putting yourself in peril. When it comes to the mandate of generating revenue and collecting dollars, which is what a business owner must do, the only way your stuff's going to get sold is if someone is marketing and selling it. And this is why marketing is an ongoing thing that never ends in business. It is not a stop and start, it is not a one-time thing, it is not a set it and forget it thing. Number 12, we are today on part four of our series. Everything you believe about marketing is wrong. Number 12, negative attention is bad. This is false. Now, this point requires a bit of nuance, but the nuance is actually pretty simple. Negative attention can be very useful for you with the caveat that you need to have the internal fortitude, whether as a person or as an entity to weather the storm of negative feedback.

In other words, if you are going to do something that know may draw negative feedback or you do something and you're intentionally looking for negative feedback, as long as you have the intestinal fortitude to deal with the pushback when it comes, then yes, negative feedback is great for you because all it's doing is drawing attention to you. It is marketing and you can leverage that attention for your own purposes as long as you can deal with it. Now, if you're not ready to deal with that blow back, then don't get into the negative attention game. Now, if you get negative attention through no fault of your own, you weren't trying to, but it just happens. Now that's a different thing. But if you do something on purpose knowing you're going to get negative feedback, just be ready to deal with it. That's all. That's all I'm saying here.

So not everyone is built to deal with backlash coming from the public. And the public doesn't have to be all 300 million Americans or 8 billion people, period. Because there's very few things that all 8 billion people on the planet care about all at the same time. Backlash from the public could be 10 people sending you a negative DM all on the same day. Backlash from the public could be you getting three responses to an email you just sent out. And all three are people disagreeing with you and pushing back. So backlash from the public is relative to who you are and what your thresholds are for how much you can take before it starts to feel overwhelming. For some people, it's only one negative comment. For some people it's 10. For some people it was a thousand. Some people could take as many as you got and it doesn't bother 'em.

So we're all different, but you need to know who you are so you know what you can handle. And again, it is one thing when you're getting backlash from the public, especially another thing when you're getting it from people who you don't even know or there's a whole other thing when you're getting it from people who you do know. Maybe when you get negative feedback from people who you do know, maybe that bothers you more than when you get negative feedback from somebody who you've never heard of before. You can just dismiss some random nobody on social media in the comments. It's hard to dismiss somebody who you personally know who says something about you that they're not feeling what you did or they're not feeling something about something you said or something they have heard about you or whatever it may be. Some people fall apart under that type of heat, they melt under that heat.

Others, on the other hand, thrive on it. So the whole point is you got to know yourself and you got to know, and also if you run an organization, you need to know the temperature of your organization. What is the temperament of the organization as a whole? Can your organization stand up to that kind of negative feedback? Negative attention can be very useful as long as it doesn't cause you to crack and lose your presence of mind and forget about what the actual goal is, which is again, collecting money. Now your goal is collecting money. This negative attention can help you get closer to collecting the money. Then go ahead and deal and you can deal with the negative feedback. Now, if you can't deal with the negative feedback or it's not helping you get closer to collecting the money, either one, then you can do things a different way.

Alright? There are many business people and businesses who have capitalized strongly on negative attention. I'll give you some examples. Every presidential candidate, every single one you take, every presidential election we've had, I believe at this point we have 46. I believe Joe Biden is the 46th president in the history of the United States, if my math is correct, and every single one, so all 46 who won, and then the other 46 who they ran against and defeated all were those 80, 92, 92 presidential candidates. And some of them have been the same person more than once, but all 92 presidential candidates have dealt with negative feedback from a very, very large percentage of the population, a very large percentage of the population. Now, most of those 46 candidates who didn't win and the ones who didn't win were dealing with negative feedback coming from the traditional press and maybe people they were running into in person.

So that's newspaper, tv, and whoever they ran into in person now is a different animal. So we take this last, let's just go back to maybe 2000 and we'll say 2008 like the Obama first Obama campaign, I think from that one from 2008 and then 2012, 2016 and 2020, those four elections, those presidential candidates that are part of those four elections, they've dealt with even more blow back because now people can give their blowback from the comfort of their own homes through the internet and a whole lot more people can reach the same person with whatever message they want and they ain't got to do anything to get the message across. So it's not just tv, at least tv, you can turn the TV off, alright? You could put the newspaper down and technically you can put your phone down, but as a different animal when so many people on every app can say something about you to you, et cetera, they're dealing with a lot more negative attention, but they have found a way to deal with it.

You got to be able to deal with it because they couldn't deal with it. They wouldn't have won the election. Every president's candidate has dealt with it before winning anyway, even the winning ones, Conor McGregor and Floyd Mayweather, those are two people in combat sports who have capitalized on having, I would say anywhere from 50 to 60%, maybe even more of the paying public, let's say about 50, let's say roughly 50% that both of these guys became huge draws in their particular lines of work, especially later in their careers as they became more and more known and they continued to amass successes that they would do pay-per-view fights, and I would say about half the audience was showing up just from the opportunity to see them lose, not to see them win, but to see them lose and about half were cheering for them to win.

But that conflict between the people who wanted to see them lose and the people who wanted to see them win is entertaining, is fun, and it draws attention. And attention draws eyeballs. Eyeballs draw money, and they know how to monetize that money. Let's be clear. So just because you have eyeballs, you have to be able to monetize the attention once it comes. I talked about this in the episode, let me find out if I can find that episode. It was episode number 1920, how to turn attention into revenue. They know how to do it. So just because you have attention doesn't mean you're going to make money, but you have to have a process for turning all that attention into something that you can financially benefit from. Again, half the public paid to see them lose and then ultimately went home disappointed because they didn't lose, but then satisfied because they got to see the show, right?

And that's something I heard Bill Walton say this, Bill Walton's a former basketball player, hall of Fame, I believe he's in the Hall of Fame, and he talked about Michael Jordan. He said, no, Michael Jordan became so famous that no fans would come to the games when Michael Jordan would play on the road just so they could kind of, of course they would cheer against him because they wanted to see the home team win and Michael Jordan was on the road team and the fans would go home disappointed because Michael Jordan usually beat their team, but they were also satisfied because Michael Jordan always put on a show. Even in beating the home team, the fans said, all right, yeah, he beat us and I'm disappointed that he beat us, but damn that mofo is good. He put on a good show in the process of disappointing us so you can put on a show and disappoint and satisfy all at the same time.

Some more contemporary examples, the Paul Brothers, Jake, Paul, Logan Paul, these two brothers are capitalizing on, again, roughly 50% of the audience hating them and wanting to see them fail. I would say their numbers are actually even higher. I would say these two guys, if Floyd Mayweather and Conor McGregor had about half the audience wanting to see them lose, I think Jake Paul and Logan and Paul got about, I would go more up to about 70% of the audience want to see these guys lose because they don't have as many hardcore fans as McGregor and Floyd had, but they do have a ton of haters. But either way, if these two eyeballs and both of these guys, it appears they are comfortable dealing with public blowback and public backlash and just people in the public wanting to see them fail, and they're okay to keep going anyway.

Andrew Tate is another example. He's a guy who I would say about half the population doesn't like him and half are defending him. I did an episode where I was, I guess you could put me in the defending him Category category. That was in episode number 26 99. If you'd like to hear my thoughts on Andrew Tate. All of these people are successfully collecting money. I'm not asking you whether you think they're successful as people, period. There's a whole conversation we could have about that that we're not going to have because that's not what the show is about, but you can have it. They're all successfully collecting money, and what we're talking about here is marketing and entrepreneurship, and your number one mandate as an entrepreneur is to collect money. Now, I'm not saying that you should just do anything and everything to collect money and don't go against your own morals or principles to collect money if you don't want to.

However, I'm using these people as an example because they have dealt with a ton of negative backlash and most of them continue to deal with negative backlash, yet they're still collecting money and it seems that they're still standing and not falling apart under the weight of the negative backlash that they are receiving. And let me remind you, again, collecting money is the goal of being an entrepreneur. If you're not collecting money, you are not doing entrepreneurship. I don't know what you're doing, but it ain't entrepreneurship. Let's recap today's class, which is part four of seven. Everything you believe about marketing is wrong. Number 10, short content is always better. This is false. Short content is useful. I'm not saying don't do it, but understand you want to ask people for more of a time engagement. Those people are the filter. The longer the content you create, it is a filter for the type of people who you are looking for.

They won't give you their time to consume your longer content. They're probably not going to give you their money to buy whatever it is that you're selling. You understand this. And again, one person may be willing to give you two hours of time for something you put out where the next person might not be willing to give you two minutes. So it is not that each of us is willing to give all of our time to everybody who asked for it. We are willing to give time to people who we believe are useful for us, and we're not going to give time to people who we don't believe are useful for us. So you should ask for more time for people. And again, it's a great filter because the people who will give you the time are usually your best prospects. Those are the ones who are probably most likely and most eligible to give you anything other than time.

Point number 11, marketing is only for big businesses. This is not true at all. Marketing is for anyone who makes money, who wants to make money in the marketplace and wants to do business with entrepreneurs and non entrepreneurs. If you want to make money, you must be marketing, letting people know who you are, what you do, how it can help them, and what they have to do to get it. That is marketing. And number 12, negative attention is bad. It's a false idea. Negative attention is good as long as you have the fortitude to deal with the negative attention, and you have a way of converting that attention into money. And I did a whole episode explaining to you how to convert attention into money. So as long as you can stomach the negativity coming your way and you're going to have people being very negative, as negative they can possibly be, especially on the internet where there's no accountability for anything that anybody says.

As long as you can deal with that and you have a mechanism for converting that negativity into money, then I will convert. You should court as much negativity as you possibly can. Again, I gave you some examples of people who are doing that and have done it well.

#2825: Everything You Believe About Marketing Is WRONG [Part 5 of 7]

Let's get into this topic, which is that everything you believe about marketing is wrong. We're picking up on these false beliefs that people have. We're on number 13 in our series, so we have passed the halfway point. Number 13, marketing is all about new customers and new prospects. Not all the time, marketing is about new customers and new prospects. It's a false belief because this is not always true. Now, while you do want to bring in fresh, no fresh blood and new eyeballs to your stuff consistently, I'm not saying don't bring in new people. Marketing is not just about the new people. You can't forget about the people who are already on the inside with you and the fact that you must continually market to people who have already connected with you even after they have already shown interest.

Even if they have already given you money, you must still market to them. I cannot emphasize this point strongly enough. You must continue to market to people even after that you have already got them into your world. In the service business world, we call this servicing the account, you must service the account. Do any of you know why the United States of America is called the United States of America instead of the United States of Columbus? Because I mean, according to the textbooks that we used to have back in the day, we were always taught that Christopher Columbus discovered America. Now that didn't quite ever make sense because the stories also told us that when he got to America, there were already people here. So how did you discover something that already existed? But technically what Columbus did do was he brought the concepts or the idea, the belief that there was land over here.

He bought it to the Europeans who otherwise did not know that there was land here. So while there were Native Americans, they didn't really discover it either. Maybe if they were native, that means they just showed up there somehow some way Columbus discovered it for the rest of the world who otherwise didn't know that it existed. But that's not the point that I'm here to discuss. Why is it not called the United States of Columbus being that he was credited with discovering it for so long before people started coming up with other or putting out, let's say other versions of what happened. Why didn't they just name it Columbus? Shouldn't it be called the United States of Columbus since he's the one who found it? The reason why it didn't end up that way, and it was actually named after a guy by the name of America that Pucci, that's why it's called America, is named after this guy named Ergo, who was for the most part, a map maker and he created a map.

And his updated map now identified this country here that is now known as the United States of America or this land now known as America. And because he was the one who was most widely connected to having put it on the map, literally putting it on the map, they named it after him. So they called it America After America go, but why not after Columbus? Because Columbus failed after he discovered America, he failed to service the account. In other words, he didn't do a good enough job of buttoning up the sale, which is that's what we call it in the sales world, buttoning up the sale that maybe you get the agreement, but you gotta make sure you tie everything down, button everything down and don't let the deal come undone. Columbus allows the deal to come undone to the point that the country didn't get named after him.

Now, there are plenty of Columbus' out there, right? There's Columbus, Ohio, and there are small towns called Columbus Pride in every state in the United States, there are statues for Columbus, there are schools named after Columbus. All of these things, streets named after him and everything. And I know some people are trying to destroy those these days because they had this idea that he was just this bad guy and all that. But anyway, the whole point is country's not named after him because he didn't focus on the customers he already had. He was trying to focus on other stuff and he didn't tie down the sale in front of him. You need to do this in marketing. People who are already in your world must still be marketed to. Those of you who are on my email list, how often do you hear from me? And I know that a lot of people on my email list have heard from me before they bought from me before.

I'm still marketing to you. I'm not just out running around looking for the new people, I'm focused on the people who are already there. Because remember folks in business, the second dollar is the easiest dollar to acquire in business. First dollar is infinitely harder than the second dollar. The first dollar is getting someone who has never paid you money to pay you money. That's called the first dollar. Getting someone who has already paid you money to pay you more money is called the second dollar and it is infinitely easier than the first because that person, the second dollar person already knows you, likes you, trusts you, and has had an experience with you that was positive. That's why they're considering the second dollar. So you will make much more money focusing on dollar number two than you will focusing on dollar number one. And any of you who you do your business buy, you have a clear acquisition cost.

Here's how much money you have to spend on ads in order to acquire one customer. You can look at your own data and see that it costs a lot more money to acquire a new customer than it does to sell to a prior or already existing customer. Alright? So you have to make sure that your marketing is targeted not just towards the new folks, but also the old folks if you want to call 'em that. People who are already in, people who are already bought in. Do not neglect these people because then you're going to find yourself going after the most expensive customer you can get, which is the new one. You don't have any old ones anymore because they're coming and leaving. You don't want churn. You want them to stay, and you just keep expanding the people coming in and staying because you're serving the people who stay so well that they want to stay.

Okay? Just because someone bought from you last week does not mean they'll buy from you again this week or this year. I mean, think about it yourself as a consumer, how many different marketing messages do you get hit with every single day? Probably more than you can count. Now, how many different people do you buy from even when you have found something that you like? Don't you try other stuff? Don't. How many of you have bought more than one thing in the same genre from different companies and different people? So if you're in personal development, how many of you only read personal development books by one author and you don't read anything else by anybody else, only from that one person? Most of you don't do that. You will read what this guy has to say. Let's see what this woman has to say.

Let's see what they have to say. You'll try other things out. Just because you buy, and it doesn't mean you won't buy again from one person, but doesn't mean that's the only person you're going to buy from. Okay? So the client what a practitioner relationship or customer company relationship is not a monogamous relationship, alright? The company is selling to more than one person and the customer's buying from more than one person. This is the economy. This is the reason why we have an economy, because we have the circulation of the dollar. It's going around and around and around at different people at different times. So your clients and customers are doing the same thing that you're doing. So do not get complacent and assume that just because someone has already bought from you that they're going to buy from you again. They may keep buying from you, but only if you keep marketing to them because you understand that they have options and they can leave you just as easily as they found you. Point number 14, we're talking here today and we're on point number. I mean we're on part five of our what will be a seven part series. Everything you believe about marketing is wrong. Number 14, word of mouth happens naturally. This is a falsehood and many marketers and salespeople and entrepreneurs believe that word of mouth is just something that happens. And this is why many marketers and salespeople and entrepreneurs don't do anything

To generate word of mouth because they never considered that. There are things you can do to generate word of mouth and I'm going to help you out right now. Word of mouth folks can happen on its own. I'm not saying it's impossible. It is possible that if you have clients and customers and you get a great experience and they love the product and the outcomes they're getting from it, that they were on their own volition, go to one of their friends or family members and say, man, this person over here is great. You gotta go buy from them. You got to go sign up with them. Whatever it is that can happen manually, but I think we would all be happy when it does happen without you having to do anything right, that you would just sit around and people just spread the word about you and you don't have to do anything.

Your own customers are your best marketers. That would be great. However, you can manufacture word of mouth conversations about you by doing things that cause and force people to talk about you. Lemme say that again. You can manufacture word of mouth by doing things that cause and force people to talk about you. This is simple deductive reasoning. Let me explain what I mean. How do you get somebody to talk about you? If you wanted someone to talk about you, what would you do? You probably want to do something that makes them want to talk about you. Now, what could that be? We talked about this a little bit in the last entry of this series. Why did so many people show up to the Jake Paul fight or the Floyd Mayweather fight or the Conor McGregor fight to see them lose because those guys did things that stirred up the audience and got them excited in a negative way to see them lose and those people paid money for a ticket just to come to the fight just to watch them possibly get beat and often again left home, left disappointed.

So that's one thing you could do is stir up people's emotions, positive or negative will draw their attention. And when you have someone's attention, you are now eligible to get their money. Alright? So this is why you got to strategize in marketing. You have to do something that gets people talking about you. And this is why strategy matters because the answer to this question, how can I get people to talk about me, will help you do things that actually get people to talk about you. The keyword here, when I say generating conversation, keyword is generating, you have to generate the conversation. Generation is not a natural occurrence, alright? Things don't just naturally generate new stuff they generate because they're doing it on purpose. If you want to have more customers, more clients, more money in your business, you must be conscious and intentional about it.

Don't just hope that it's going to happen. You do this consciously and on purpose. That is what marketing is about. Point number 15, today we are talking on point number. We are part five rather of our what will be a seven part series. Everything you believe about marketing is wrong. Number 15, your marketing should get everyone's attention. Here's another one that could have benefited from being earlier in this series. I've already made clear that your marketing is about your target person or people, you know exactly who they are and focus on them to the exclusion of everyone else. That is what your marketing is. Who's your target person? Focus on them and ignore everybody else. So that right there debunks this false belief that your marketing should get everyone's attention because you don't want everyone's attention. You want the attention of the right people, especially if you are investing in your marketing.

If you're spending money on ads, you do not want your ads to be looked at and clicked on by a bunch of people who are not qualified to buy your product. You want that ad to only be shown to the right type of people so that you're not wasting any of your resources. IE your advertising budget on people who you don't even want to be talking to. You don't even want them buying your product even if they wanted it. So getting everyone's attention is not the goal and it is impossible to get everyone's attention at the same time anyway. Your goal is to get the attention of the right people at the right time in the right way with the right message. That's what you want to do and that's why there's a strategy behind this is not just throw stuff out there and hope that it works.

Now, while let's add this possibility, there may sometimes be times that you do things to get everybody's attention, even people who are not in your target market. Even if you do that, you better be careful of the resources that you use in order to get that attention and the resources that you use to respond or engage with the everyone whose attention you then get. Because if you get everybody's attention, you're going to get some feedback from everybody. Now, how much of your resources will you use, first of all to get all that attention? Secondly, to engage with all that attention, that time investment that you got to put into the responses, alright? That time you can't get back. So that's why you gotta be careful about what you're asking for. When you say everyone's attention, you don't want it all. You want the attention of the right people again, right time, right place, right message because the attention from person number three is not the same as the attention from person number 12.

See, this is one of the challenges of trying to get everyone to see you and paying attention to platforms like social media who promote the chasing of vanity metrics. You get a bunch of attention from a bunch of people who are worthless. That's what you don't want. Lemme say it again. A bunch of attention from a bunch of people who are effectively worthless. You don't want to be that person. And what happens is you end up giving these people your attention and you're not getting any ROI from the attention that you are giving up. You're paying but not getting anything back. That's why you need to be clear and you happen to have a clear strategy for your marketing. It should not be haphazard, it should not be random. So you're not out here doing what they call random acts of marketing and hoping that something works out and then being dumbfounded when things do not work out.

That said, let's recap these three points. Here we are on part five of 7 21. Things that you thought about marketing or that you believed about marketing are all wrong. Number 13, marketing is about new customers and new prospects. While some of marketing is about that, that's not what all of it is. And marketing, you also want to give just as much if not more of your resources to the people who are already in your world. They have already bought, they've already paid, they've already signed, sealed, delivered, and need to keep giving them attention because the second dollar is infinitely easier than the first dollar. Number 14, word of mouth happens naturally. Now, while word of mouth can happen naturally, most of the time it doesn't, not nearly as much as we would like it to when it comes to generating referrals for our businesses. So you need to actually think about a kind of reverse roadmap, strategize out how can I get more people talking about me?

So that word of mouth starts spreading even more naturally than it is right now. You want to generate this, you want to make this happen, you want to cause this to occur, alright? So don't just sit around hoping that people talk about your business. You want to figure out what can I do that would force them to talk about my business and forcing it and may have negative connotations that you're forcing. You're not manipulating these people. All you're doing is actually manipulating them, but not in a negative way. You're manipulating them to talk about you as opposed to talking about the weather or the local baseball team. And what's the difference? They're going to talk about something. They might as well talk about you and make you some money in the process. And if you're the one instigating all this even better, number 15, your marketing should get everyone's attention false.

This could have benefited from being earlier in the series. Remember that your marketing is about getting the right message to the right person at the right time. Who has the right need? And yeah, that's it. Let's just say that that's what marketing is. And it doesn't mean everybody, not everybody needs to hear what you have to say. Not everybody is a customer for tampons, right? Not everybody's a customer for the hair club, for men. Not everybody's a customer for some workout supplement that's going to help them have great big muscles in a six pack. Not everybody's a customer. So you need to make sure that your marketing is going to the right people, not just to all people. And you don't want to be throwing spaghetti at the wall as they say, and hoping that, hoping that it hits something that makes sense because you could use up a lot of your resources, specifically your advertising budget, marketing to the wrong people.

This is why you have to get around professionals and experts who know what they're doing in these spaces so you don't waste your resources in ways that you're not supposed to.

#2826: Everything You Believe About Marketing Is WRONG [Part 6 of 7]

Let's get right into this, which is again, we're picking up on our series here. This is part six of a seven part series. Everything you believe about marketing is wrong. Point number 16. So I'm telling you the thing that you believe that's not true and I'm going to tell you why it is not true and what actually is true.

Number 16, you should follow every marketing trend that you see or hear about. You should not do this. Now, this one is a softball. I'll admit it's an easy one, at least for me, and maybe for some of you that maybe you didn't already believe that you should follow every marketing trend, but I had to put this in there because there are people out there who I know and know of who follow anything that they see, any bright, shiny information slash object that they see when it comes to marketing, they go follow it because they believe that maybe they should just try that. Lemme try this. Lemme try this again. They have the intense span of a squirrel when it comes to just staying focused on what they have been focused on when it comes to their marketing. You should not follow every marketing trend.

As a matter of fact, none of us, no human listening to me right now has enough eyeballs, hands, brains or feet to follow. Every marketing trend is impossible for you to follow every marketing trend. There are too many of them for you to even process their existence, let alone to execute on them or even to understand that they are there. There are just too many of 'em. They're happening too often. So you can't do them all. Even if you had a team, you got a bunch of people working for or with you and you have the resources to implement 100 different things at the same time. Let's say you had enough resources to do that, you should not do that. Just because you can just do something does not mean you should do something. And this does not mean that you can't try a bunch of different things at the same time.

You could try 10 different marketing tactics at the same time. That's fine. Which one works and then we'll put all our resources into that one or two or three or five. And understand that anything that you do try, you should try it because you have a specific reason and you have a specific measurable goal that you are after in trying it. You need a baseline for measuring the outcome of the things that you try. So whether this is actually working or not, you shouldn't just be on your fingertip or just know how you feel about it. How do we know that this is working? How do we know that this one is better than this one? How do you know that idea number six is better than idea number 12? You need a measurable way of knowing this so that you're making logical, rational decisions when it comes to your marketing, not just going off of your feelings or emotions or just what side of the bed that you woke up on today.

That's not the way that you want to do your marketing. So don't do something just because it's a hot thing and everybody else is doing it. That's one of the worst reasons to do anything in life. It's because you see everybody else doing it. And if you're looking to stimulate your marketing, any of you who's looking to stimulate your marketing and a lot of business people need to stimulate their marketing, I do suggest that you try multiple things at the same time because as I just said, you can figure out which one works. But the things that you try, let's be clear, they need not be new. See, just because something's new doesn't mean it will necessarily be good for your business. Many of the things that many of us, all of us in all of our lives in business or not need to do or that we should try that could actually help us are not necessarily the new things that just came out six months ago is the old stuff that has been around for years.

Maybe you know about it, maybe you don't, maybe you have partaken in the past, maybe you haven't. But a lot of times one of the best things that we can do to put ourselves in a better position is utilize something that already exists, has always been around, yet we have not given enough of our attention and focus to it and energy to it to get the best ROI we could out of it or we haven't applied the right strategy or process to doing it to get the right ROI out of it. It's kind of like if someone wants to get in shape, let's say your goal for this year or this birthday year, let's say a birthday came around, you say, I want to get in shape this year before my next birthday. I want to get in shape this year on the calendar or this quarter or whatever the situation is.

It's not that you need to do the brand new workout thing that you just heard about three weeks ago. It might just mean you just need to go down to the gym, sign up for a membership and hire a personal trainer. Or are any of those things new? No gym's been around forever. Membership has been around forever and personal trainers have been around forever and that might be the best route that you could take to get to the outcome that you want to get to. It's not that you need to do any of the newer stuff that's coming out. And it's the same thing when it comes to your marketing and your business. The thing that could best help your marketing and business is you to look around at stuff that is already out that maybe you'll see somebody else using and say, well, why not just focus on just doing that and that'll be the thing that helps you.

So the thing that can help any of us achieve a breakthrough and get to the level that we want to get to and any aspect of life is not always, is often not the new bright shiny object. It's often the old rusty object and we will call it rusty, but it's not necessarily rusty because it's still sitting in the packaging. It hadn't rusted out yet because it hadn't even touched oxygen because it's still sitting in the shrink wrap because nobody's used it. You haven't actually applied it and used it in any way. So it's not rusty, but I'm just using that as a metaphor. Look at the stuff you haven't used, the stuff that you have not implemented, the stuff that you have not tried. The solution might be right there in front of your face. And the challenge with this, the solution is right in front of your face is that implementing it might be more work than you thought you were signing up for, might take a little bit more effort than you want to give, might require more discipline than you want to apply.

That's the thing that really stops people is not that people don't have the information. A lot of people use an alleged lack of information as an excuse for not taking action. That's not the thing that slows damn near anybody down. If you're listening to this show right now, you have access to more information than your grandparents had access to in their entire lives. You got more access in the next hour to more information they had access to in their lives. So it's not information that is your problem. The problem is implementing the information that would actually help you. And often we know exactly what it is or we are wary of what it is because we know what kind of work comes with it and we want to avoid the work because human beings are naturally lazy. So again, it doesn't mean anything wrong with you personally, just means you're human.

Human beings are naturally lazy and this is why most people are average and below you want to be different from them. You have to do something different from what other people do. So I suggest trying multiple things at once, but again, they don't have to be new things. They may be classic things that are basics, but the basics are the foundational pieces. Those are the fundamentals and every professional who's great at what they do has mastered the fundamentals of what they're doing. That's just a universal truth. And again, sometimes it might be something you were doing a long time ago but you stopped doing it and maybe because you got bored or you got again lured away by a new bright shiny object. But getting back to the basics might be exactly what you need for your success and it can be the key to your future growth. Point number 17, we're talking here today about the 21 things that you believe about marketing that are wrong. We broke this up into seven parts. This is part six. Number 17, marketing automation solves everything. No, this is wrong. Now this is a big one that I want to make sure all of you catch.

This is especially important for I would say solopreneurs, but it applies to entrepreneurs as well. You have a team, you have other people working with you or for you, this applies to everybody because a lot of people get distracted. Let's just say for lack of a better term, from their path by the bright shiny object of marketing automation. What does marketing automation mean? In simple terms, it means using software and coding and software is coded. So software and coding like AI or applications or some type of program that you basically put some inputs in and then it basically takes care of everything for you. So when I say marketing automation, it means stuff that does your marketing for you so that you only have to do the work one time. Then it basically does everything else on its own on autopilot and you don't have to pay any attention to it and it's hands off and you don't have to actually do anything or even look at it.

That's the general concept. When I say marketing automation, what I'm referring to. So you can just pay less attention to your marketing overall. That's the general idea of what marketing automation is selling on a high surface level, that's what marketing automation is selling and the app will tell you, we're going to take care of this and this so you don't have to worry about posting to X every day. You don't have to worry about making sure that your Facebook feed stays full with posts from your page. You don't have to remember to post on Instagram three times a day. We're going to take care of all of that for you. That's what marketing automation, the general concept of marketing automation, that's what it's saying. And again, automation doesn't have to be social media posting. It can be your emails, it can be your ads, it can be your follow-ups, all of those things.

That's marketing automation. And again, the concept here that I'm debunking is that marketing automation solves everything. I'm not saying that marketing automation does not work. I actually use marketing automation. If you didn't know, I do use marketing automation and we'll continue to use it and as it expands, I will use more of it, but marketing automation is not the solution to all of my marketing needs, nor do I abdicate my responsibility as a marketer just because I have marketing automation. That's the point that I want you to get. Let's talk about this a little bit more while I again don't have a problem with the concept of automation. You should never, ever abdicate your responsibility for paying attention to your marketing.

You should never abdicate your responsibility for paying attention to your marketing. Why should you never abdicate this responsibility? Because marketing is the lifeblood of your business. If you are not marketing actively, that means your sales processes will eventually slow up and dry up, which means the money will dry up, which means you are not doing your job as an entrepreneur, which is bringing in money. This is one of the good things about entrepreneurship and if you ever heard me talk about the juxtaposition between the sports world and the business world, the thing I like most about the sports world that I will never replicate in the business world is that the sports world is black and white. It has an objective, known as the scoreboard is an objective arbor and the sports game, you look at the scoreboard, the scoreboard tells the story.

Coaches in sports say you are your record. What that means is your team has played 10 games and you won two and lost eight then that's who we are. We are a two and eight team. We won 20% of our games and 80% of the time lost. That's our record. No matter how good you think you are, no matter what you thought could have happened in these three gains that make it different, you are the outcomes that you produce in the sports world. It is black and white straight up just like that. That's why sports is the ultimate meritocracy. The business world is not like this. The business world does not have a black and white scoreboard. And also in the business world, there's not like one game. Coca-Cola plays against Pepsi is not like that. We're out in the marketplace doing our thing. We do have competitors.

Often it's more than one. Sometimes the competitors we don't even know about, but it's not a black and white or this team won. This team is losing just because it's not like that. It's a little bit more slippery. So this is why as an entrepreneur, I like the concept of us understanding what our number one mandate is as business owners, which is to bring in money. That is your number one mandate. That's the closest thing that I can get to a parallel between the business world and the sports world is that in business, your job is to bring in money. Again, you're not comparing your money to another company's money necessarily, but what you should be doing is trying to bring in more money now than you were bringing in before as a business. So you're competing against yourself. Same goes for athletes, Kim, but again, we don't have the games the same way in business that we have in the sports world.

So as a marketer, and if you own a business, you are a marketer by default because if you're not marketing, your business is not going to do much. Just because you have marketing automation does not mean you stop marketing. It just means that the marketing automation can handle some stuff so that maybe you don't have to do those things manually as much anymore, but you are still very much hands on both hands on when it comes to marketing. Everybody understand what I just said there? Do not overlook this point. You are always hands-on as many hands as you have. You are always hands-on when it comes to your marketing automation just makes it so that it's easier for you to do even more work in your marketing, but not that you do less ever. Everybody heard what I said there, right? Okay. You need to know what your marketing is doing, where it's doing it, why it's doing it.

You need to know what results are being produced and you need to be actively involved in whatever changes need to be made. No app, no amount of artificial intelligence software or program should ever replace the human attention that is required When it comes to your marketing. I don't care what AI comes out, you never, ever, ever stop paying attention to an aspect of your marketing because you believe AI is taking care of it. Do not need to be paying attention. I remember when I was in college, I did my senior year internships. I have a business degree from Penn State University and we had to do an internship to get a business degree. It was a nine credit internship and I did an internship with this guy named Phil Sky who is, he's passed away now. He passed away maybe 6, 5, 6 years ago.

And Phil Sky was an entrepreneur, well-known entrepreneur in the city of Altoona, Pennsylvania was I went to the Penn State Altoona campus and my internship was basically working as his right hand person and he had some things that he was working on and he wanted me to kind of try to go and promote the products and things like that. And I got to spend a good amount of time with Phil Sky and he would tell me, he would just give me a few little business axioms that he had learned along the way. And one of the things that he said was, your staff doesn't do what you expect. They do what you inspect. That's one of the ones that I remember him saying, they don't do what you expect. They do what you inspect. And that's what I mean when it comes to your marketing automation.

Even though it's software and it generally does the same thing over and over again, unless a human interferes and messes it up, you still need to be looking at it. You still need to inspect what the software is doing because there may come a time when what the software is doing is no longer serving you. So you need to change the program that you're giving the software. So maybe it is doing the thing you're told to do, but the thing you're told to do is no longer relevant. So you need to change it. So don't think just because you have automation that you're done working, you're never done working. Marketing is the faucet that makes it possible for you to produce dollars. So somebody needs to be in control of the marketing at your business. Somebody needs to have responsibility for the marketing. So if it's not going to be you, it needs to be someone other than you, but there must be someone.

Okay? The last thing that you offload to software in your business is the money making stuff. Now, if you want to offload editing video, you want to offload coming up with responses to comments on social media. You want to offload the graphic design, good, offload all of that. The last thing you offload in a business is the money. Marketing is the money. Everybody understand what I'm saying here? Okay, so do not offload to software or even another human without your overlooking supervision and hands-on attention. Is there anyone unclear on what I just talked about in point 17?

It is vitally important to your business. Number 18, today we are talking, we are on part six of seven, the 21 things you believe about business that are not true. Number 18, all marketing happens online. This is false. A lot of you believe this. Millennials, I see you, I'm looking at you. A lot of you believe this, that all marketing happens online. If you just get a phone and you got a data plan or a wifi connection, you can just do all the marketing that needs to be done. In theory, this sounds good. And in theory for some people, this is all the marketing they do. They just do stuff online. Technically you could do all your marketing online if you're doing this. However, I would say you are costing yourself money. Let me explain to you why many people believe that all marketing happens online because many people use the internet all damn day, alright? Through your phones, your tablets and your computers. And yes, a lot of marketing does take place online these days, but at the same time, a lot of marketing happens offline. And those of you who don't do any offline marketing, this is why I said you are missing out on money. You don't even know that there's money being made out there and you're not partaking. People still do marketing through the mail. And when I say the mail, I don't mean email. I mean physical mail. The letters that you open and you're in your

Physical mailbox. Notice that the mailman comes to your house every day. Notice that Amazon sends packages, Amazon drivers, their packages drop off every day, alright? UPS every day, FedEx, every day, United States Postal Service every day, a lot of people are still sending things in the physical mail. Now you may be thinking to yourself, Dre Mail physical mail is for old people. Why the hell do I need to pay attention to that? I'll just stick to my email and dms and social media. What are you talking about here? Can you get to the next point? Let me tell you why you need to hear what I'm saying here. Do any of you ever get what most of us call junk mail in your physical mailbox and you got any junk mail? You probably got some junk mail within the last 24 hours. So last time you checked your mailbox, you probably had some junk mail in there and you got some junk mail. Okay? Junk mail has been coming to your physical mailboxes for how long? Since you were a kid and before we had email, people were sending that physical junk mail, right? It's been going on forever. Now think about this. Why do you think people still send that mail?

I'm taking a sip of water. Why do you think that? Why do you think people still send junk mail? Junk mail has been going on for a hundred years. I don't know, as long as mail's been around, as long as I've been around, there's been junk mail. Why do you think people were sending it back in the nineties and they're still sending it now why? Now I understand it costs money to send mail, right? And if you sent anything physically in the mail lately, did you send it for free? No, you got to pay, even if I write you a letter and say, Hey, this is Dre. Just wanted to say hello and I put that in the envelope, I got to put a stamp on it. The stamp costs money. The envelope costs money, the paper that I printed, the message on costs, money, all of those things cost money.

And when you're sending a lot of it, think about the junk mail that you get. Think of how many houses that mail got sent to understand how much money it costs to send that kind of stuff out. So sending junk mail costs a lot of money. It costs more money to send junk mail than it costs to send email. So here's the question. Here's the question, why aren't people still doing it? Being that you see it as junk mail, why would people still be doing this over the last 30, 40 years? Why do people keep doing it? Does anybody know the answer?

Here's the answer. The reason people still send junk mail is because it works. Now, what does work mean? It is a slippery term. A relative term works. I'm going to tell you what it means. It means that mail makes money. The reason people still send junk mail to this day is because junk mail converts and turns an investment into a profit. Yes, junk mail, it works. And when you just logically think about this, I told you one of the things that I do here at work on your game, you'll never be confused when you listen to an episode of this show. No one will be confused. You need not bring any prior knowledge of the subjects that I'm talking about and you will completely understand what I'm saying. Okay? A true expert always does this, and I am a true expert at the subjects that I choose to talk about.

Think about how a male costs money. All of you logically understand that it costs money to send mail, right? Everybody agrees with that, right? Okay. And that junk mail always comes right? And that a lot of mail you receive, you see it as junk. You also understand that every other house in town got that same mail, right? Or at least in your neighborhood or in your building, every other house got that same mail. So when you start multiplying how much money it costs to send that much mail, you understand that no smart business person would keep spending that much money to send that much mail if they weren't getting a return on their investment. Does that make sense? Of course it makes sense. It has no choice but to make sense, physical mail works people. That's my point. Now think about this. How many of you have an email inbox with at least 500 unread emails in it right now?

How many of you have an email inbox with at least 500 unread emails in it right now and you're not even planning, you don't actually have a plan in place to get that inbox down to zero. In other words, a bunch of those emails may never get opened. That's the point of me asking this question. How many of you have at least 500 emails in your inbox that may never get opened? Alright, I bet a bunch of you now think about this. How many of you have a physical mailbox of at least 500 pieces of mail that you haven't opened? The answer is zero. None of you have it. That when something comes in the physical mailbox, guess what happens? You look at every single thing that comes in your physical mailbox, but you just proved to me and to yourself, you don't look at every single thing that comes to your email inbox.

Oh, it's getting deep now. I think somebody just had a light bulb moment. You look at every single thing that comes to your physical mailbox, even if you look at it, just decide to throw it in the trash without opening it. You still look at it, you acknowledge it, you don't let it just sit in the physical mailbox and rot and until it goes away, you don't let that happen. You look at every single piece of mail you get in your physical mailbox, you don't look at every single email you get. Some of your email goes automatically through a spam filter and you don't even know that it got sent to you because it automatically went to spam. And you don't check your spam filter and your spam folder and your spam folder gets automatically deleted every 30 days. So it's a bunch of mail you've gotten digital deleted.

You never even knew you got it because it got spammed and filtered and trashed physical mail. That doesn't happen. So are y'all reading between the lines here? If not, let me read between the lines. For you. People who send quote unquote junk mail are making money and some of them are making much more money than people who always send email because email can get ignored or left to rot in an inbox that has 787 unopened emails. That never happens with physical mail. Nobody has 300 unopened physical letters, nobody. Everything that comes, we look at, so are y'all catching this? That's why junk mail has never gone away. It makes money for people. Now you might not know how to make money for it yourself, but it does make money. I have a book right here on the Bookshelf behind me, you can't see it. It's called Million Dollar Mailings.

Lemme pull this book up. Actually, this is a book that I haven't actually read yet, but I will be reading because I purchased this book with the intention of reading. I'm going to read it. It says, Million Dollar Mailings, the Art and Science of Creating Money Making Direct Mail, including Secrets of Using Direct Mail to Make Money on the Internet. So the principles for this book that was written based on sending physical mail, you can use it in the digital space. I would suggest using it in the physical space as well. I don't even know how much I paid for this book, how much was this book? But anyways, this book is called Million Dollar Mailings. And again, I haven't read it yet, so you can't ask me what I got from it. I haven't read it yet, but I will read it and I will be implementing it.

And I use these books kind of as textbooks. It's not like a book, you just sit and read for fun and pleasure. You read this so that you can do something physically with it. It was first published in 1992. Okay? So this book, this is before there was such a thing as the internet. Then they updated and expanded it and they have a ton of examples. Y'all can't see this, but there are a ton of examples in the book of things people sent in the physical mail that actually made the money. They even talk about business reply mail. So any of you remember back in the day when you would get mail, physical mail from magazines and stuff and they would say, all right, just take this letter, this self, what was it called? Self-addressed stamped envelope. And you didn't even have to put a stamp on it.

All you had to do was put your order form in there with your credit card number or a check or something like that and just drop it in the mailbox. They would pay the postage just for you to send them your order so that they could collect the money. Understand folks, there's money being made in the mail. I'm going through all this to help you all understand that if you are only focusing on the internet, you are missing out on some money, you're missing out on some opportunity and you're swimming in a very red ocean. Because a lot of people who only go to the internet, why? Because it's easier to use the internet. Physical mail takes a little bit more effort, a little bit more work and costs a little bit more money. And guess what? The returns are the same. The same meaning more.

When I say the same, they're the same as the effort. You can make more money through physical mail because it takes more effort to do physical mail. And so few people are doing it and there are fewer and fewer people doing it because the people who grew up doing it, they're dying out. So any of you who's in the younger generations, if you start picking up on this, you're going to have a blue ocean all to yourself that other people can see right in front of their Facebook and never even consider it. Anytime you see a marketing strategy being used over and over and over again by the same company is because it's making the money.

Anytime you see a marketing strategy being used over and over and over again by the same company, it is because that strategy is making them money, especially if they're doing something that you can deduce is costing them money. If you see junk mail coming in the mail all the time it is because sending junk mail in the mail makes money. No company's just going to keep throwing away money at something it is not actually producing. Everybody understand this? So what's something that you always get in the mail, let me tell you, let me just think of some things. I always get in the mail for junk mail. I always get some kind of credit card offer. There's always some kind of credit card offers from companies that I've even heard of. There's always those credit card offers. Any of you who have your name in any credit card company's database, you get these kinds of mailings all the time too.

Now, whether you respond to 'em or not is a different story, but you get them all the time, right? Why? Because credit card companies make money by sending those mailers. The local grocery store is always sending you the circular of what's on sale this week or this month. Why do they do this? Because it makes them money. Everybody following here and there are a bunch of other companies, those are the two that I'm thinking of off the top of my head that I get all the time. There's always some credit card company stuff and there's always some, the local grocery store and then any business that has your physical address, they often send you stuff, alright, work on your game. University. We send stuff. We send a bulletproof bulletin in a black book every month, physically to your mailbox when you're a member working at your game university. If you're a member of a company, send car companies.

If you have bought a car from a certain company or you currently have a car from a certain company, they're physically sending you mail all the time. If you have bought a car in the past from a company, they are sending you mail all the time. They want to bring you back. They want you to come in and be a customer again. So think about this, think about this folks. A lot of big department stores, Saks Fifth Avenue, JCPenney, Nordstrom, Bloomingdale's, these companies send physical mail all the time. Why? Because it brings you back into the store and makes them money. Okay? So anything you see over and over again, if you watch tv, you still see commercials on tv, right? Why do people run commercials? Because it makes money. When you drive on the highway, you see billboards. Why? Y'all can answer the question now it makes money. It's old, but it's not outdated. There's a difference between something being old and being outdated. Outdated means it's old and it doesn't work. If it's old and it still works, then that's more classic. Classic means it's old and it still works. And now if it's old and it doesn't work anymore, then you can call it outdated. But a lot of the stuff that people call outdated, they call it outdated because they're two ways to look into whether it could actually help them or not. I'm doing the work for you by telling you this today.

Again, there are people who do marketing through these methods who are making more money than people who are doing all their marketing online. Do not be fooled by the bright, shiny object of the internet into thinking that it's the only way to do business. It is not. Just because something is new and popular does not mean it will produce your desired outcome. And just because something is old and you haven't thought of it or none of your friends think of it or own your parents do it, it doesn't mean there isn't money there. Your parents might have more money than you got. You should think about that. The older people get, usually the more money they make, people usually go into their careers up until their sixties or their seventies, and most people's incomes increase as they age. So older people usually have more money than younger people.

Why? Because they've been in their careers longer. So they've been able to amass more career credibility, more status, and they've gotten better at what they do. And then you just get raises with people who are employed. So just because you see a bunch of old people, unquote old people like your parents' age doing something, don't dismiss that. Alright? The stuff that appeals to old people is stuff that appeals to people who have money. They got more than you got. Alright? Think about that. Okay? All that said, let's recap these points here. Part six, everything you believe about marketing is wrong. Number 16, follow every marketing trend. Do not do this. Don't follow every marketing trend. You do need to try new things in marketing, but you should try things strategically and have a clear way of measuring whether something is working or not. And you need to define what working means.

Number 17, marketing automation solves everything. No marketing automation will help you do things, but you must always pay attention to your marketing. You must always be hands-on with your marketing, both hands on your marketing because marketing is the lifeblood of your business. Never abdicate that to software or even to a human without your oversight. Number 18, all marketing happens online. This is completely false. Open your physical mailbox. Notice that you get mail every single day from people who you didn't even know have your address and you don't even know they know who you are, but they sent you something. Why? Because physical mail still makes money. And I just only use physical mail as an example here, but there are other ways that offline stuff can make money. And you need to know what these ways are and you should be taking advantage of them.

If you want to be serious in your business, and again, do not dismiss something because it's old. If something's old and it doesn't work anymore, you can call it outdated. But if it's old and it still works, then you call it a classic. And when something's a classic, that means you need to catch on to what it is because there are secrets in there and principles within that classic that could help you if you would just wake up, open your eyes to what's happening.

#2827: Everything You Believe About Marketing Is WRONG [Part 7 of 7]

Let's get into this topic here. Again, we are picking up where we left off. This is part seven of a seven part series. Everything you believe about marketing is wrong. Part number 19 point number 19, logo is branding. No, your logo is not branding. Your logo is part of your brand, but is not all of your brand. As a matter of fact, it is only a small part of your brand. It is not even as much of your brand as a lot of people think that it is given the amount of resources and amount of emphasis that people put on their logo, it has a, is not a, what's the word?

Let's just say no, I don't want to use that word. The amount of resources and energy that people put into their logos is not reflected in how much the logo actually matters to the brand. The logo does not matter that much. It matters a lot less than the amount of resources we put into it. That's what I want to say. Your brand is about the position and the image that you create in the mind of your audience. That's what your brand is. What do people think about and how do people feel when your name, your company name comes up, that's your brand and your brand is constantly evolving because every time you have an engagement with your audience, you are updating or adjusting or making some type of even if minute change to the image that they have in their mind about you. So your brand is always evolving.

Your brand is not just say, whoa, whoa. Logo is a stagnant object that can represent visually what you and your company or your brand are about. But the brand itself, the idea that the consumers have about you is more important than the logo itself. And now there is a point when that logo can become so big that it says everything about your brand just on its own. Just stand on its own two feet. So think of the Apple logo, think of the Nike logo. Those are companies who if you just see the logo, you already know what it means. You see the Amazon logo, as soon as you see it, you already know what it means and it gives you a certain thought or idea or feel in your mind. Your logo may not be at that level just yet and that's completely okay. Maybe one day it will get there.

But the point is you want to dominate the thought in the consumer's mind, the concept of who you are, what you're about, what you bring to the table and why they should care. That's what your brand is and your logo, again, can't do that. The logo can't do all of that. Now the logo again, it supports it even when you are a Nike. The Nike Swoosh supports the brand idea of Nike. But when I'm thinking about Nike, I'm thinking about, okay, those are athletic gear. If I want to get some workout clothes and need some new running sneakers, whatever it is, I'm going to look at Nike first because I like Nike's stuff. That's the position that they have occupied in my mind. I'm not even looking at other options. That's just me. I'm not saying everybody does that, but there's a lot of people who only do that.

That's why Nike is who they are. So again, your logo is just one piece of this game. So think of your logo as someone meeting you and you had on a certain outfit that day. Okay, that's your logo, is that outfit that you are wearing that day, the entirety of who you are and what you're about. Of course not the next day you'll be wearing different clothes and there's much more to you than the clothes that you wear, right? At least for most of us, it's the same thing when it comes to your business. And again, that's not a perfect example because the logo is with you all the time. I mean it represents you all the time, but the logo is a cool thing to have. However, it is far from the most important thing that you have in your marketing. It's a cool thing to have, but it is not the most important thing that you have.

When's the last time you went to a friend of yours to recommend a business or a product or service that they should buy and you told 'em that they should do it because the logo was great. Now you gotta go buy from this company. They have this amazing logo. Exactly. You never did that. Nobody has ever done that in the history of marketing or business or sales or word to mouth. Nobody does it. Nobody says you got to go buy from them. They have a great logo. If you recommend a friend go to a business and do business with that company, why are you recommending it? You're recommending it because of the product, because of the result, because of the service you got. Because something you think they're doing that can help your friend. That's why you're telling 'em what is all of that?

The brand you write, the product you write, the service you believe can help. It has already helped you. Thus all ideas that it is put into your mind that have been put into your mind by your experience and because you were so excited about that experience, you wanted to go tell somebody else about it. We call that word of mouth and that is all based on the experience that people have with you. That is your brand, the experience people have with you and the experience that people have of you. It may not even be with you because someone who is listening to this right now, you've never made yourself known to me. I don't know that you exist, but you are aware of this show and you consistently consume it and there are certain things that are happening through you. Well to you through what you're hearing here on this show, without me actually trying to make it happen to you personally, I don't know you personally, that's all part of the brand and you're getting a different perspective about me and who I am.

The more you listen to me talk, the more you consume my stuff. Assuming that I'm saying stuff that you haven't heard before, most of the time I know I am. Sometimes I repeat things because not everybody's listening. Sometimes I repeat 'em, they're good and I want to say 'em again. But there's an evolution of a relationship happening anytime people who already have a relationship aren't engaging with each other and communicating. So the reason that people recommend a product or a service is because of the experience, because of the brand. Your logo doesn't make you money. It is the engagements that people have with you and the results of what they got from you or through you and how they feel about you. That leads to them wanting to get into a position where they could give you money. In other words, it leads to them wanting to go, let me go save up this money so I can buy this.

So let me go have a conversation with these people over here so they can sell me something. That all only happens because your brand is doing the work of getting people to understand that you can solve a problem that they have. You can supply a thing that they need or are looking for. Point number 20, we're talking here today about part seven of our seven part framework. Everything you believe about marketing is wrong. Number 20, ignore all negative feedback. This is a false idea. You should not ignore all negative feedback and I'm going to tell you why You should embrace and engage with negative feedback, especially negative feedback about your business when it comes to your marketing. Now why is this? Why should you embrace negative feedback? And some of you are saying, Dre, I don't know about that one now I want to get involved.

Somebody's trolling and being negative or just saying bad stuff about me. I'd rather just block 'em and delete 'em and not deal with them at all. Why should I engage? So first of all, if the negative feedback you get is something from someone who has purchased from you, let's say you get negative feedback from a customer. Someone's bought something from you and they have something negative to say because of their experience with your product, with the service, whatever. Alright, remedying a situation can turn a disgruntled customer into a lifetime fan. Lemme say that your process for how you remedy a situation with a customer can turn a disgruntled angry customer into a lifelong fan and fanatic who will maybe be your best recruiter. You don't even have to pay them. That's the value of how you remedy a situation. You could take someone from being your enemy to being your friend based on how you deal with it.

Secondly, if it's someone who is just hating on you, let's just say you have a troll, somebody who's just talking shit about you and your business every day, every time you post something that's coming and saying negative stuff, depending on how you handle it, you can either turn the hater into a fan because they just have some issues going on maybe with themselves or maybe with you or what you represent. You can turn that hater into a fan and get them on your side or you could turn the hater away, but get your fans to become even more deeply entrenched with you and into who you are. So you basically can use the negative person who's talking bad about you as proof to the audience of people who talk good about you, that there's an us versus them dynamic here. Here's this guy who doesn't like me, but here's us, all of us out here doing our thing together.

So you can use that negative feedback that you get from someone else depending on how you handle it. Again, you turn a hater into a fan and turn a hater away, but get your fans more deeply ENT terms with you. Third, lemme tell you another thing you can do. The negative feedback that you may get from someone helps you to make the, again, us versus them dynamic a real thing. So I just stepped on this part, that dynamic matters, alright? When I say the us versus them dynamic, this dynamic matters because people like being a part of something that not everyone can be a part of. Human beings like being a part of exclusive groups, groups that not everyone can join no matter what they do. So that dynamic is a real thing. And again, people always want to be part of something that they can't be a part of and people like being a part of exclusive groups again somewhere that not everyone can get in, but negative feedback from the outside folks gives you the opportunity to create the inside and prove that it's real.

So you take someone like I go to Russell Brunson's ClickFunnels conference every year. It's called Funnel Hacking Live. And one of the things that he talks about are the entrepreneurs, the makers, the creators, the people who help society move forward. The entrepreneurs out there and he often has at his conferences. I don't normally take one, but he often has t-shirts for his company that talk about, Hey, here's who we are, here's the group that we are a part of, and here are the people. And he doesn't say in so many words, but by saying who they are, he's excluding who they aren't. And it's letting everyone know that there's an in-crowd here. If you want to be part of the in-crowd, these are the things that, these are the beliefs that we have when you're part of this in-crowd and here are the beliefs of everybody else out there.

What he's doing is creating that us versus them dynamic, which creates a stronger bond amongst the people who are part of us. Everybody understand? So this us versus them thing is a real thing and people again like to be part of a group that not everyone can be a part of. And negative feedback from the outsiders gives you the opportunity to create an inside and prove that it's real. So when negative people on the outside have stuff to say about you, all you gotta do is create an inside, a bubble within the bubble and that proves that it's real. It proves that this is a real thing and that people can join this. It's tangible. There's a group, there are other people, there's a community. People want to see that people like to be a part of something that not everybody else can be a part of, but at the same time they don't want to be a part of something that nobody is a part of. So there's a balance that you have to strike there in that process. Moving on to point number 21, we're talking here today about part seven of our series 21 things that You Believe about marketing that are not True. Number 21, marketing and sales are completely separated. False.

This one we touched on earlier and that marketing and sales, the one that said marketing and sales are the same thing. No, they're not the same thing at the same time, they are not completely separated. So I talked about both of these here. They support each other. Your marketing supports your sales. If you do marketing the right way, what happens is you're going to have a whole bunch of ideal prospects coming to you wanting to have a sales conversation, which means your sales percentages will go up. You can have fewer sales conversations, but you will make more money simply because you are using your time more consistently and you are using your resources specifically your time, but also your attention, energy and focus in a smarter way. You're helping the marketing supply, the sales and the sales also help the marketing. How is that? Because the sales process should be pretty smooth and easy when you're talking to a person who is marketed to properly, which means they come in knowing what to expect, knowing what they're going to get, knowing why they want it, and exactly how to get it.

That's all based on your marketing. Your marketing sets up the sales, the sales sets up the marketing. So they support each other. You have a marketing team and a sales team. They should be working in unison. If you have a marketing person and a salesperson, those two people should be communicating with each other every day. Now the question is why would a marketing person and a salesperson be having a conversation together? Because the sales team cannot be successful in selling unless the marketing team does a good job of connecting with and attracting the right type of leads who are interested, willing to buy and capable of buying what the sales team is selling.

Lemme say all that again because that was pretty fast. Your marketing and your sales department should be communicating consistently IE every day. Why? Because the sales team cannot be successful at selling unless the marketing team does a good job of connecting with and attracting the right type of leads who are actually interested in your thing, willing to buy your thing, and they're capable of buying what the sales team is selling. So just because someone is willing to buy your thing doesn't mean they're capable of buying it. So I might say, well, I want to buy that $250,000 Ferrari, but I'm not capable of buying it. Those are two different things. Willing to buy means If I had the money, I would be capable of buying it if I had the money, I would do it. And guess what? I had the money so I'm going to do it.

So they're not the same thing. Don't conflate these. Now, that's not even the main point that I'm making here. And point number is this. Point 21. Yeah, point 21. It's not even the main point that I'm making here, but you have to keep in mind that these two things, again, marketing and selling work together. I would think most of you who are entrepreneurs, want to sell, sell, sell as much of your stuff as possible. You want to make that easy. The selling part, all you gotta do is get your marketing down. That's it. You got to focus on your marketing. Your selling is a reflection of your marketing. Your selling is a reflection of your marketing. Your selling is not a reflection of your ability to sell. It's a reflection of your ability to market to the right people so that you get the right people coming to you and then it's easy for you to close the deal because they already know that the answer is yes.

So your marketing, again, supports selling, you're selling supports marketing for the first time. If you find yourself having a problem in sales, the first thing you need to look at is not your sales call process. Am I saying the right things that I forget online in the script? That's not the issue. First thing you need to look at is your marketing. First thing to look at anytime you're not getting the sales that you want is the marketing. Who are the people that we're getting in front of and why are these people getting in front of us? What type of leads are we bringing in right now and are those the right types of people? That's another question you gotta ask yourself. This is all assuming that you actually have a product or a service that is proven. This is all assuming that your product or service is proven. Then you start asking your question, asking these questions about marketing. You don't have a proven product or service. You may need to examine that piece as well. To be clear, you got the best sales presentation in the world, but if your marketing is off, that amazing sales presentation will not bring in any money. Everybody hears that?

You could have the best sales presentation in the world, but if your marketing is off, that amazing presentation will not bring in any money. Send the text real quick.

And it's not because there's something wrong with your sales presentation. Nothing wrong with the sales presentation. A lot of people think when they're not making sales, you're having sales conversations but nobody's buying or something's wrong with my salesperson. I got to get better at selling, I got to get better at closing. I got to get better at overcoming objections maybe. But also here's what also could be happening is that your marketing is off so that you are just bringing in people who are not the right clients, they're not the right prospects. So no matter how good of a seller you are, you ain't going to sell to these people because they're the wrong people. Your marketing is attracting the wrong prospects. When your marketing is dialed in and you're attracting more of the right prospects, you could be a very okay salesperson, you could be a below average salesperson and you're still going to make sales because the customers are the right people.

Give you an example here. When I was working, lemme see, I was working at this gym called Valley Total Fitness in Philadelphia. It was my last job that I had before I started my pro basketball career. So this is 2005 and I remember I was working at this one in the Cedarbrook Mall and the Cedarbrook Mall is still standing, but it's not a valley Total Fitness anymore, it's the LA Fitness. Now, the last time I checked, but at this location, this location was relatively new to the neighborhood when I started working there and I remember talking to some of the salespeople who had been there when the place actually opened. I wasn't there when it actually opened, but when it did, they told me that the selling process was extremely easy. It was a brand new gym. Everybody in the neighborhood came around because they wanted to get a membership to the gym.

So if you were a salesperson working at that time, it was easy to get really fat commission checks because all the customers were just walking in ready to buy. All you had to do is walk, bring 'em in, show 'em around the gym and sign 'em up. People were just signing up easily. No, you didn't really have to sell. They were just buying from you. You just were lucky. You were in the right place at the right time. You were just making sales without having to do anything. That's the kind of selling that you want to do. Now again, I'm not telling you to open a gym in a neighborhood in order to do this, but your marketing should do that job. Your marketing should be so good that the right people who know that they want it are coming in. All they're asking is, how much do I gotta pay?

I know I want this. That's when your marketing is on point. And again, your sales game doesn't have to be that great. Now, I'm not saying don't not show up mediocre just because you can get away with it. Your sales game may not need to be that great when your marketing is good and your marketing is just okay and your sales game needs to be amazing. Now, if your sales game is great and your marketing game is great, alright, that's when the money comes in, everybody follows. So you have to make sure you're bringing the right people in. And again, this is a marketing issue, not a sales issue. All that said, let's recap this last entry into the seven part series of everything you believe about marketing is wrong. Number 19, your logo is your brand. Your logo is part of your brand, but it is not all of your brand.

A logo is just a small piece of it. Your brand is the space that you occupy. The idea and the feeling that you occupy in the mind of your consumer has nothing to do with the logo itself, it is about their experience of you and your stuff. Number 20, ignore all negative feedback. Absolutely. Do not make this mistake the way that you deal with negative feedback can turn a disgruntled customer into a lifelong fan. So somebody just messes up and you deal with it the right way. They'll become very happy customers. I'll give you another example. I should have said this during the episode before the recap, but I'll give it to you here in Miami. There are two restaurants that I went to and ordered food from over the last week and one of them does a great job handling customer service issues.

Another one does a terrible job. So one of 'em is a company called Sweetgreen. Now I'm an investor in Sweetgreen. I own some stock in the company and Sweet Green is a national chain and they basically make, how do I even describe what they make? Do any of you know how sweet you can get? They make basically rice bowls, plates, they use fresh ingredients. I like the quality of the ingredients used in sweet greens. Usually Sweet Green is my go-to if I need to order food, my two go-tos, usually Chipotle and Sweet Green. Chipotle is higher quality. Chipotle is a little bit faster for me. So I sometimes get Chipotle, but I also do Sweet Green. So Sweet Green. Whenever they mess up my order, which they have a couple times like I've ordered delivery, which I don't usually do. Delivery, they take too long.

I'd rather just go get it myself. But sometimes the delivery job is taking too long and I'll mess with Sweet Green and they will make up for putting some credit into my account.

So your next order, you got $10 off or I'll give you a free drink or something like that. But they always respond positively and kindly and they always look to fix and make the situation right. Alright. Sweetgreen does a good job of that. It's one of the reasons why they're a national chain. You can't go natural without having that part down because you're going to have complaints from customers. It's guaranteed if you're doing that much volume. The other companies now they're Miami based and I believe they have two or three locations, maybe three, they're called the Mad Butcher and they have a location in the windwood section of town from which I ordered a burger two times.

I ordered the same thing. I ordered a bacon, cheese, burger and fries. The first time I ordered it for pickup, they had to order it when I got there and I just took the bag, went home, opened it, and realized that they forgot the bacon on my order. I was annoyed that they forgot the bacon didn't go back, but I just ate the sandwich as it was. I liked the sandwich. The overall quality of the sandwich was good. The fries were crispy. It was good. I sent them a DM on Instagram, on Instagram and showed them a picture of the receipt and a picture of the burger before I started eating it. Yo, y'all forgot the bacon and nobody responded to the dm. I even called the store, but nobody answered the phone. So I figured I'll get another shot. Maybe it was just an oversight.

Any company can overlook things one time. So I went back there a second time, and it happened to be this past weekend from when I'm recording this episode and I ordered the exact same thing, bacon, cheeseburger, fries, and I picked it up. Same way when you order something online, they have added a special note. So when I placed my order, I added a special note and said, Hey, last time I ordered here, y'all forgot the bacon. Please get it right this time. I was just saying it because it was never acknowledged the first time. And again, you can't go national making these. You can't just ignore your customer who complains because you'll go out of business because complain, they'll just beat you down. The customers will and they'll just stop buying from you. So you won't even have the revenue or the results to go national.

So anyway, I get to the Mad Butcher, I'm picking up my food, I tell her name and she and I say, Hey, last time I was here, y'all didn't put bacon on that burger. And the woman at the register said, oh yeah, I saw your note. I'm sorry about that. Said, don't worry, there's bacon on it this time. I said, all right, great. I stood right there at the counter and I opened the bag and I opened the sandwich right there in front of her because I wanted to make sure that the bacon was there the way she had just affirmed that it was. And guess what? Everybody, there was no bacon on the burger. They had forgotten the bacon again. And she saw me do it right in front of her. I showed her there was no bacon on the burger. And I said, miss, there's no bacon on this burger.

And she looked at it and she confirmed that I was correct, and she started talking to the cooks who were in the back. And this is not a big kitchen. So I can see her having this conversation with the cooks. The thing is they're speaking all in Spanish, and while I can understand Spanish, I'm not fluent, so I couldn't understand conversation. So she's talking to them and I start saying to them, I said, Hey, that's the second time. I said, that's the second time. It was two cooks in the back, a female and a male. I said, it's the second time. The same thing happened last week. Y'all did it again this week. And one of the cooks in the back, he's waving and apologizing. I'm sorry about that. And she takes the burger, she hands it to the girl who's back on the grill and they allegedly put bacon on the burger.

I'm standing there watching them do this. So she puts bacon on the burger, wraps it back up, hands it back to me, says, all right, I'm sorry about that. The woman at the front, she can speak English, she's bilingual, that's why she doesn't register. She says, sorry about that. She hands me the burger. I didn't see the woman put the bacon on it. So I opened the envelope again, right there in front of her. I did not leave. I opened a wrapper up right there in front of her to see this bacon that they put on the sandwich. And this bacon is completely uncooked bacon. Now, I don't know. Now this is a kind of a Latin based place because all the people there are Latin. The cooks are Latin, they don't even speak English. And the woman at the front, she speaks English and Spanish and everybody else working there looks like they only speak Spanish.

So I don't know if this is a Latin thing. Somebody who is Latin, let me know, is that a thing that y'all eat uncooked bacon? This bacon was like when you buy bacon from the grocery store and it is like pink and white. And that's how the bacon was. Now it wasn't cold, it was hot bacon. I don't know if this is a normal, I don't know if it's a Latin culture thing, but listen, in black culture, unless I'm completely out of touch of black culture, we don't eat uncooked fucking bacon. We cook the bacon, okay? I'd rather the bacon be crispy and burnt than be uncooked. Even when I order bacon anywhere I've ordered bacon on the sandwich, I usually tell the waiter or the person to make the bacon crispy. I want the bacon extra cooked, not okay, cooked, not undercooked, extra cooked. And I looked at the bacon and I showed it to the woman and I said, miss, this bacon is not cooked.

And she looked at it and I looked at it and I said, I can't eat this. This is uncooked bacon. You got to cook the bacon. So the woman starts speaking in Spanish again to the people in the back. Now this time the woman, the cook in the back seems a little bit confused. I guess maybe this is a normal thing. I don't know. Again, she couldn't speak English, so I don't understand what she was maybe saying to her colleague here. And they're having a conversation, and I guess the woman at the front is explaining to the woman in the back, Hey, you have to actually cook the bacon. These people don't want uncooked bacon. And while they're having this conversation, it immediately clicked in my head, and this happened automatically. Alright, if you make a mistake once, it's your fault. But if you make the same mistake twice and I accept it, then it's my fault.

And I said, you know what, miss? I interrupted the conversation, says to the woman at the front desk, just give me my money back. It was like $16 that I ordered. I said, just give me my money back. I'm good. And this is what the woman at the front says. She says, well sir, I understand, but you placed your order online and you paid online, which I had through a credit card. So in order to get your refund, you have to process the refund online. This is what she says to me. And I say to her, no, that's not the way that this goes. I placed an order. Y'all made a mistake. I showed you the mistake right here in front of your face. I want my money back. Just give me my money back. Can't you go in the system? I mean, it is y'all's system.

Can't you just give me the money? And she said, well, no, we can't do that because of the way the system is set up. You paid online. So maybe it's some third party system that takes the money. So I guess that's what she was saying. She said, you have to process the refund online. I said, well, I'm getting a refund from this company. I pay this company so you should be able to do it. And now that I'm talking it out, I understand what she was saying, but she wasn't able to explain it articulately enough, which is what she should have said . Look, there's a third party service that takes the money for our orders. So I don't have control over that third party service. So that's why I'm not able to directly give you a refund. And she should have said that. And then she should have said, however, because of this and because I saw this mistake happen right in front of me, let me tell you what I can do to make up for this.

Let me either, I could either do this or this or this. That's what she should have done. She didn't do that. Or she started telling me what she can't do. And when you already have a disgruntled customer in front of you, the last thing they want to hear is what you can't do. We already know what you can't do, which is make the order the right way. So don't tell me what else you can't do because that's only going to compound the problem.

And I'm not the type of person who's going to accept that. I said, no, that's not acceptable. That's all you have. Y'all messed up two times. The second one you saw right here in front of your face, you're not going to tell me what you can't do. I'm not accepting it. So this was starting to become a back and forth argument.

And a woman understood. I think she understood from my tone and from my energy that I was not going to accept her answer that she can't give me the refund. So what she did, this didn't take about 30 seconds. It's not like this was some long back and forth thing. About 30 seconds later, she just opened a register and gave me $16 in cash. I left the burger there, I left the fries there, and I just took the $16, walked out, and this area Miami called Wynwood. Luckily there's a bunch of places to get food around there. So I just walked two blocks and I got a burger at a different place. I'm telling you all that to tell you this, your brand is that experience. Fuck the logo. I couldn't point their logo out of a police lineup. But that experience, I'm always going to remember that.

And I will trash that restaurant forever because they made a mistake in my experience. Fuck the logo again, the brand. That's what people remember is that story right there. I'll always remember that story. Their names ever come up, and I'm just doing a recap here. I should have told you that during the content, but you listen to the whole episode, right? Anyway, anyway, right? Anyway, number 21, recapping point number 21, marketing and sales. I can be completely separated knowing they are not. Marketing is what you do to put yourself in position to sell, and your sales go easily when your marketing is done properly. If your sales are difficult, it's difficult for you to birth the baby of a sale. It's probably because your marketing is not good and you're basically attracting the wrong people. That's why your sales are not going too well. So your marketing, when that's better dialed in, you'll get people who already know they want to buy, like who walk into a gym when it's opening in the neighborhood and everybody's just signing up.

You barely got to do any selling. That's the way you want your sales to go. No matter what you're selling, the right people will buy immediately because they already know they want to buy because your marketing was done the right way. So that's why marketing is the lifeblood of your business. And that's why any one of these 21 mistakes I have told you, you are making about marketing, you cannot afford to make these. You literally cannot afford to make these mistakes because they cost you opportunities to make money.

#2828: What Does Seeing Other's Success Mean To You?

Let's get into the topic. What does seeing success, seeing others succeed, what does that mean to you? And let me give the context of what this question, what the question that we're going to address here actually means. This episode is really about a philosophical rhetorical question, but not really rhetorical because you're going to answer it in your own mind. It'll be rhetorical as I record it because you're not here to answer back. But we're going to dig into your mindset and the way that you look at life, the way you look at opportunity, and most importantly, the way you look at yourself. That's what this episode is about. We need to get clear on your answers to the main question and these other questions, how you look at life opportunity in yourself because it has a huge effect on what you actually do has a huge effect on what you try to do.

And both of those combined into what you actually, excuse me, what you actually achieve, your outcomes and your results in life. And if you listen here often enough, you know that I often use the phrase results based business that being life is a results based business. So the result does matter. Point number one, topic once again is what does seeing others' success mean to you? Number one, when you see success in another person, let's say you see another person achieve a success, maybe something that you are trying to achieve, they just did it maybe faster than you, maybe they did it bigger than you, maybe you weren't even thinking about achieving that success, but you see someone else achieve some success in some area that you're like, oh, that's cool that that person got that success. Maybe they reached their goal there, they were trying to get to a level eight goal and they got to it.

And you're right now at a level five, you're trying to get to a level eight goal that's different, but it's parallel and they did it. When you see someone else do that, you could see it as meaning that someone can do that thing. So if you see someone doing something that maybe you want to do, you haven't done it yet, but they did it, you look at that and say, okay, well that's proof that somebody can do it. Maybe not necessarily you but someone can do it because clearly there's the proof of that person right there. It is. Like you seeing somebody make a lot of money and you say something like, well, good for them, say or think good for them, but that doesn't really have anything to do with me because my situation is not directly their situation. So it's cool that they did it, but that has nothing to do with no necessarily me doing it.

While you are literally correct, it does not have anything to do with you. It could provide some clues for things that could have a lot to do with you depending on what it is. It depends on how you choose to look at it though, whether there are clues in there that you could use or if there's nothing in there that is relevant to you at all in any way, shape or form, nothing relevant whatsoever. This is all based on the way you choose to look at the situation. And this is the whole point. The whole point is how you look at a situation, even if it's someone who's in a completely different space from you doing a completely different thing in a different country, in a different industry, and you've never met this person and never met anyone who looks, sounds or smells like them, the fact that they achieved a certain level of success.

There could be some clues in there, but the way that you are mentally wired and you can alter your wiring in many different ways, the way that you're mentally wired will determine whether or not you even see the possibility there. Or if you don't, everyone following where I'm at here, what happens with many people is that they look at others who have created some level of success, even people who are in their exact same lane. So let's say you're a basketball player and someone else achieves a higher level of success than you in basketball, you're an entrepreneur who sells widgets and someone else sells that same widget and they're just selling a hundred times more than you. And they just had some great idea that popped off and they sold a bunch of widgets. Many people who look at someone doing the exact same thing as them achieve a high level of success.

And you know what these people do, and this is the tragedy, is that they don't even get curious about what did that person do? How did they do it? And look, how could I maybe borrow or steal from what that person did borrow or steal an idea from that person that I could use to boost my own success? What can I borrow from what I see this person doing? And again, this is a mindset, folks. This has nothing to do with your actual skills. It had nothing to do with your resume. It has nothing to do with the outcomes you have produced or failed to produce up to this point. This is all about just the way that you choose to look at the success that someone else has created. There is something in there that you could use, but you have to be looking for it.

You got to have your mind wired to look for, okay, what could I take from that that I could possibly use myself? And again, this is a way that you can train your mind to think like this. If you've been listening to this show for some time, you may have heard me talk about it. I often discuss my process for coming up with ideas for content because I get asked often enough when people see the depth of the content that I've created and the volume of content that I've created. People often ask me, Dre, how is it that you're able to create so much material? You put out material? I literally put out material every day. I've been putting out content every day since 2005. The subject matter has changed and the formats are not always the same, but I've always put out content. I put out content every day for them.

They're 20 years straight. And people often ask me, how are you able to come up with so many ideas? Well, one of the reasons is I have trained my mind to see, to seek possibilities for content in every single thing that I encounter, everything that I go through and deal with and engage with in life. I'm looking for an opportunity. What's the content that I could possibly get out of this? And it could be something short and quick like a tweet level or a status update or a text message level idea, or it could be something that goes a little bit longer like an episode of this show where I might talk for 45 minutes straight because I have something to say on a certain subject. Or it could be a YouTube video that's 10 minutes. Or it could be a reel that I put on Instagram or TikTok.

That's what, 90 seconds. So I have trained my brain though, to look for these things. The whole point is I've trained myself to look at this stuff. So in the series that I just did a seven part series on the 21 things you believe about marketing that are not true. Well, I told you all a story at, I believe it was the last episode, yesterday's episode where I told you how I went to go pick up a burger and fries and this place, they forgot the bacon on the burger two different times that I went to this place and then the person was trying to give me a hard time about giving me a refund, telling me I had to do it online because I had made the order online so they couldn't process the refund in the store and she was basically doing everything wrong that was really hurting the marketing that she was doing for that company that she worked for.

And she says she was the general manager and the difference between the general manager and an owner, she's a manager, not an owner, and the owner is not even going to realize that his or her company or if it was a group, they're losing money because they lost the customer in me. And anybody who I tell about it, anybody who ever mentions that place in Miami, they don't go there because they're terrible. Lemme tell you what they did and I'll tell you the bad story and my bad experience there. I'm costing them money because of the experience that I had with them and I made content out of that. That's the point. I wrote an article about it and I talked about it here on the show and I'll probably talk about it again sometime in the future. Alright, so I'm creating content out of every single thing that I go through, whether it be something positive or something negative or even things that are neutral.

It could be something random that happens. I went to Whole Foods a week or two ago and the price of the hot bar food is like 50% higher than it was five years ago, literally 50% higher. That's crazy. And I took that concept, put it into an article and I said, Hey, if you're an entrepreneur, you need to be level on your game up because if you're not giving more value to your audience, then they probably won't be willing to give you more money, which means you're not going to be able to keep paying for this food whose price is going up. Our Whole Foods price went up. I don't know if they made a big announcement about it, but that price did go up. It was $12 a pound to get food from the hot bar. I said, that's crazy. I'm not buying from here anymore.

Not that I necessarily can't afford it, but just on principle alone, I could probably get the same food for cheaper. I just may have to do a little bit more work. I'm willing to do it. I'm not paying $12 a pound for hot bar food. That's a little bit too much. And see, that's why I got a meal delivery service. I was just there on the weekend. But anyway, I went on a tangent there. The whole point is many times people just don't get curious about how they could borrow from what somebody else is doing. And again, this is about training your brain. I went on that tangent there to help you all explain when you train your brain, this is how you can start to pick up on these things without even, you don't even have to consciously be thinking about, but your brain is just trained to think, okay, my brain is trained to think, how can I get some content out of this When you see someone else being successful or what are they doing that I could borrow from?

Even if you're not, again, you may not even be in their lane. What are they doing that I could use? What's something in here that I could benefit from? Okay, when you see someone who's doing something similar to you, I would encourage you to look at that success this way. This is the way I would encourage you to do it. Don't necessarily drop everything that you're doing to try to copy everything another person is doing because you probably can't and probably not going to make sense for you anyway. But do consider what do you see in them that you could possibly again borrow or copy and use for your own purposes? And you should do this as much as possible if you're a person who's trying to become successful because you never know where you may get the right idea from, may get a great idea from something that again, has nothing to do with anything that you have going on.

Remember, I heard Kobe Bryant say this, he was talking about speed and agility and he was talking how he was watching National Geographic or one of those shows where the big cats like the cheetahs and the Jaguars and they go chasing after prey. And he said he was watching the show and he heard how the narrator was explaining that the big cats, I don't know which one it was, the cat, leopard, lion, cheetah. One of those when they're chasing after their prey, that their tail actually moves as a counterbalance whenever they're making sharp turns, that the tail actually balances them out when they're moving around so that they have maximum agility. And Kobe was drawing a parallel between that tail and something that he was talking about because human beings, we don't have tails. I think he was talking about his sneaker, I don't know exactly how it translated.

I don't remember the exact statement that he said, but I remember him saying that, that he noticed something about the big cat and that got him to thinking about how he trains for basketball, et cetera, et cetera. The whole point being Kobe's mind was conditioned to look for any slight edge he could get for himself so he could be the best player he could possibly be on the basketball court, and he got it from watching some cats chasing around Gazelles in Africa on National Geographic. That's the way that I want your mind to think when it comes to your success. Alright? The fact that someone else did it should be a clue to you and someone could be, again, it could be an iron or a teeter point. Number two, today's topic. Once again, what does seeing others' success mean to you? Number two, it could mean that anyone can do it.

Now, this is different from someone who can do it. Someone can do it means someone means somebody other than yourself, right? When you say the word to someone you're talking about, not me. But on the other hand, when you say anyone can do it, that means anyone including yourself, even that person over there who's doing nothing right now, me right here, who's somewhere in the middle, I could do it, they could do it. Anybody can do it. There's another way to look at success. See, this is the possibilities angle. See, the someone angle is the well someone but not me. This angle point number two here, this is the possibilities angle. Because someone did it, that means anyone can do it. You often hear people who have created success usually say this as kind of like a self-deprecating way of including the audience. When they say something, they'll say, well look, if I was able to do it, then you could do it.

You hear people say this on stages when it gives speeches, they'll say, well, I come from a background of poverty, or I didn't know both of my parents, or I flunked out of school, or I didn't even go to college or I dropped out or I went to jail or my first two businesses failed. They'll tell you all these self-deprecating truths about themselves as a way to help to basically minimize how you view them. So don't view them as some godlike character just because they're the successful person in front of you. But look where I started from. The person on the stage is saying this where I started from is lower than where you're at right now. So if I can do it, you can do it. Many of you have heard people say this, people say this kind of stuff all the time. It's a great sales tactic.

It is a great marketing tactic and it is a great motivating and inspiring tactic for an audience, especially when you're the exalted person standing on the stage because you want to humanize yourself and help the audience understand that the reason that you're on the stage is not because you're just so much better than them, but because you just did some things that they haven't done yet, but you're there to give it to them. So anytime you're selling from the stage, you probably want to do something like this. Depending on what you're selling and depending on your audience, there are nuances to it. But in general, any of you who have been in audiences and heard people selling anything from the stage, you have heard some form of this, someone just telling you how they're not that great. All they did was just plug into some simple things that you can plug into 'em too.

All you gotta do is sign up for my course and I'll show you exactly how to do it. People do this all the time. Again, not a bad thing. It's a good tactic that helps people understand, okay, this person is not just some God, that's not the reason they're successful. They're successful just because they have this formula that I don't have yet and I can just buy the formula by going to the back of the room and paying my money. So again, if I can do it, anyone can do it. This is the possible angle. So people will often add a presenter who uses this angle. They often add somewhere in their presentation about all the things that again, make them not great. I just told you this, I grew up in poverty. I had a low GPA. I barely made the team in high school.

My first product didn't sell anything. My first speed was horrible. Hear people do this all the time. I've even done it. I've used it a few times myself. I told you I barely made the team in high school when I was playing basketball, I walked on to play Division III college basketball, but I still had a pro basketball career. The fact that I shared those truths from my story with audiences in my basketball days helped me sell a whole lot of copies in my book called The Overseas Basketball Blueprint. And those are true stories. I'm not lying and I'm not even sensationalizing. I played one year of high school ball, walked on D three college balls. There's no sensationalism in that story. It's just the truth. And when I tell people that and then I tell them, Hey, I went on to have a damn near 10 year pro basketball career, here's how I did it.

Here's a book for you to learn how to do it. That's the reason why I was able to sell many copies of the book, not because of the logic of what's in the book. Now, the logic that was in the book is amazing, but the story is what allowed people to see themselves and myself and say, well, if he could do it, I played three years of high school basketball. This guy played one. So if I could play three, he could play one and he can make it pro, then why can't I make it pro? Let me get that book. I know I'm going to go pro. So that helps sell the book. Alright, this is, again, this is a good thing to do. Any of you who's a salesperson, so these are things again, you hear people do this all the time. As I said, humanize themselves.

They do this because they want to plant the seed. A possibility in your mind that you don't have to be amazing in order to be successful. You don't have to be as good as them to be successful. And as a matter of fact, you may already be better than them. And so which means you're guaranteed to be successful if you just do A, B, C, which usually involves you doing whatever they're asking you to do, you can replicate or even surpass their success. This is a possible mindset, which again, I would strongly suggest if you're going to be an entrepreneur, I would suggest you adopt this mindset. When my son gets old enough to talk, he's going to understand I'm going to help install this mindset into him. I'm going to let him know, look son, the things that I'm going to be teaching you from the time that you're five years old, I didn't understand these things.

So I was 25 years old. So you got a 20 year headstart and you got basically a mentor and a coach at home to teach you the stuff that I didn't learn until I was a fully grown adult. So you got to have a big headstart on me. Everything that it took me years to understand, you're going to understand by the time before you even become an adult. So it's no reason for you to not be 10 times more successful than I am. I'm going to teach him that and I'm not lying to him because I'm setting him up for a success that I was not set up for. So again, possibilities, mindset. This is a great tool, folks, not only for yourself to think in these terms, but also if you want to motivate and inspire other people, you need to implant these ideas in other people's minds because it excites and motivates them to believe that they can be successful.

Remember that most people are not successful. Most people are average and below average. Most people can't be successful. They don't even have any goals. So when you're trying to motivate and inspire people, especially when you're talking to the masses of people, just a random selection of humans, most of them are going to be average and below average. You have to give them some vision of the possibility of success in their mind because most people don't walk around with that as normal equipment. Most people don't go and intentionally go look for the kind of stuff that you're hearing right here today. They don't go look for it. And even if they came across it, they wouldn't even know what it was and they wouldn't engage with it. So if you want to move people to action, you must learn how to plant a vision in their minds.

You want to see someone who's very good at doing this. Listen to anybody who's running for president. They all do a very good job at this. Even the ones who lose, they do a good job at this because the only way you can even garner enough support to where you can even be mentioned in the people who are running for president is you have to get a lot of people to believe in you. And the only way you get a lot of people to believe in you, you're talking to the masses of people, is you got to plant a vision in their minds. They will not show up with the vision already in their heads. Most people don't have one. Everybody following me here, good. It doesn't mean that everyone else who does what you do is going to be successful, but again, you want to plant the vision in their mind that they can be because otherwise they won't even try.

Okay? So look at other people and always see possibilities for yourself. Again, this is a mindset. This has nothing to do with what you've actually done. Every successful entrepreneur looks at things like this, asks them, and you will see this point number three And another thing, one more thing on point number two is that many successful people look at things this way and they don't even realize that they're doing it. What I'm doing here today is I'm making it conscious for you so that you can start doing this on purpose. And you'll find a lot of successful people do this without even realizing that they're doing it. Point number three, today's topic once again is what does seeing other people be successful mean for you? We're going over the possibilities of what you could see. Number three, the main reason most people do not create success in life, and again, as I already told you by definition, most people are not successful.

They don't have goals, because most people's success, most people see other people's success as having nothing to do with them and having no bearing on their situation. Okay, this other person is successful, good for them. What the dang aint got nothing to do with me. That's how most people think. They may not say it in so many words, but that's how most people think about success. Alright, this person over here is successful. This person on the billboard in Times Square, they're successful. This person with all the followers on social media, they're successful. This person on tv, they're successful.

This person across the street, they're successful with. None of that has any bearing on what I'm doing, my situation or what I can do. This is the way most people think by default. This is why most people are average MBO, as I said.

And there is some nuance to this. When I see someone else create success, I do not drop everything that I'm doing, just watch the movie of the other person's success because then I'm abdicating my own responsibilities. But I do always look for little things that I can take from someone else's success and apply them to my own process. And again, you can get this from anywhere. You just have to pay attention. The key here folks, is paying attention and you can apply little things that you get from other people to your own process and you never know what it might be. This is why you gotta pay attention, you have to pay attention to things you never know where you may get a good idea from. I remember I was reading a book by Andre Agassi who was a former tennis professional, one of the top players in the world in his time.

Some of you may remember Andre Agassi. And in his book he talked about how he was struggling as a tennis player. He was already very talented. People knew he was good, but he was struggling. He was not performing the way that he wasn't performing up to his level of ability. And he went to see a tennis coach instructor, and the instructor said, okay, Andre, the mistake that you're making is that you keep trying to hit winners every time you hit the ball in tennis. And a winner is like when you hit the ball in a way that the other player can't return the shot, at least within the rules and you get a winning shot. So it's like a highlight shot that you get in tennis. So the instructor said, how about Andre? Instead of trying to do that, how about you just keep the ball in play?

Just keep the ball in play. When a ball gets hit to you, just hit it back to your opponent and just keep hitting the back and let your opponent make a mistake. Instead of you trying to force the highlight win, instead of trying to force the highlight play, just keep hitting the ball back and forth and wait for your opponent to give you an opening or to make a mistake and then you can win that way. And Andre Aze started following that and it did actually start working. And I'm sharing that with you to share this. First of all, why am I reading a book about somebody who played tennis? Because I was looking for that little nugget that I could get out of anywhere, and I found it through that point right there. And that was like four years ago, and I read that book, but I still remember that you get what I'm saying here.

So this is why you want to be eclectic and where you're getting your sources, your sources of information, insight and inspiration. And then you want to see what you can take from what you're taking in and see how you could use it yourself. So I always look for these little things that I can take from what other people are doing and apply 'em to my own stuff. And again, I never look at somebody else's stuff, even if they're doing a hundred times better than me and think that I can't possibly do that because there's something special or different about them as a human being, that's not true. Human beings, for the most part, are about 99% the same. All of us human beings, the main difference between us is the way that we think. Now, some people are short, tall, fat, small, different skin tones, color is genders, et cetera.

The main difference between us is the way that we think. And the good news about that difference is that you can change the way you think anytime you want. Alright? There's a book called Think and Grow Rich. There's a whole genre of books all about consciously altering your thought patterns in order to consciously alter your outcomes. There's a whole genre of books, and if you're watching this on video, I got a bunch of 'em sitting here, right here behind me. Alright? These are my books and there's a million people who've written books on these subjects. You should read them because you never know where you may get the good nuggets. So this is the way that you should look at things. Most people don't do this. And what did I tell you about opportunity folks? It's always the opposite. Most people are focused on their own small myopic worlds where they have created barriers in their own minds to their own success, to their own outcomes.

And these barriers are completely mental, they're not real barriers. And then these people, once they create these barriers, they live their whole life within these barriers. This is the tragedy right here. So when you see someone else doing a lot better than what you're doing, but don't bother to question how they did it or what they're doing, alright, those are the self-imposed limitations that are blocking you. So you can't become a successful person or even approach your full potential with self-imposed limitations blocking your mind from expansion. You can not become a successful person or even approach your full potential with self-imposed limitations blocking your mind from expansion. This is why the first piece of what we do in working on your game university is building your mindset, recapping today's class, which is what does seeing others' success mean to you? Again, it's a philosophical question.

I'm answering it for you and telling you what these things mean and how you should use them. Number one, when you see success, you could see it as meaning that someone can do it. This is kind of blocking yourself off from you being successful because you don't even consider what are the possibilities for you within what other people have done. Number two, you could see it as anyone can do it. In other words, if I can do it, then so can you. Or if she can do it, then everybody can do it. And again, you see a lot of salespeople and presenters, they do this often. They're letting you know that, Hey, I'm not

That's great, even though I'm the person up on the stage with all the lights on me. I just have these few things that I've done. And if you do the same things, you can be just as successful, if not more successful than me because you're probably better than me now than I was when I was at the stage that you're at right now. Again, you've heard this many times, and number three, the main reason most people do not create success in life is because most people look at other people's success and don't even realize that there are some possibilities for themselves within it because their brains are not trained to even consider it. That's why I'm strongly suggesting to you that you train your brain to consider this. There's a way of rewiring your subconscious and your conscious minds, but it has to be done intentionally.

It has to be done consciously. It doesn't just happen just because. And this is why the first thing you get when you come into work at your game university is the bulletproof mindset.

#2829: The Slow Bus To Success (And How To Get Off It)

Let's get into this topic, which is the scope bus to success and how to make sure, again, you ain't the one riding on it. This title that I mean literally is about getting to success slowly rather than getting there with speed and urgency. And in case you didn't know, you'd rather get to success with speed and urgency for a couple of reasons. Number one, when you're moving slower than without that urgency, sometimes you don't have the energy, you don't have the energy to move yourself to get things done and need to get done because you're okay moving slow.

So things that you could get done within one day is taking you a week. Things you could do in a week take you a month, things that could take a month or take a year simply because you don't have any urgency in, you're okay getting to things slow. The problem with getting things slow, the compounded issue is that every human being has a limited amount of time on earth before we reach death. So if you're moving slowly through life as if you have time, then you are basically openly defying biology, which says every human being dies. So when I say biology, you don't need to have a college degree to understand that, that any of you know a human being who's lived forever without dying, I don't think any of us does. So you shouldn't be moving slow, you should be moving fast just on that understanding alone.

You don't need any other understanding, but you understand at one point you're going to die and you don't know when, which means you should move fast to get all the success you can accumulate as quickly as possible because that success allows you to do things for yourself and for others that you can't do when you're dead. Is that a simple enough reason? Is that a good enough reason for anybody to move with speed and urgency? I believe it is. And again, all of us are running on a clock and when that clock hits zero, you know what that means. So we need to be urgent about creating our success as soon as possible. So today we're going to talk about the things you should avoid in order to engage the urgency. So if you're engaging in urgency, we're going to talk about the things that you should not do or the things that put you on the slow bus.

The slow bus is just the bus that moves too slow. You want to be on the bullet train, I think not in the United States, but in some country, maybe it's in Japan, I was reading about, might not have been in Japan, may have been in a different country. They have these trains that can basically go very far distances in a really, really short period of time. Trains are almost as fast as airplanes and they'll probably be here in America at some point when we get the technology. But you want to be on one of those. So you want to be on one of those bullet trains or the airplane to success, not know the bicycle to success. There's nothing wrong with riding a bike for your health, but we're talking about getting somewhere with speed. You probably want to get in something that can go a little bit faster.

So if you find yourself committing any of the errors I'm going to lay out here today, make the decision that you will stop making that error starting right now. As soon as you hear it and understand it and you know that it refers to you, you make the decision that no more. That's over point number one, today's topic, once again is a slow bust to success and how to get off it. Number one, thinking without doing, thinking without doing puts you on a slow bus to success. It's not that thinking is a bad thing. I said thinking without doing alright. I'm not saying it's just thinking by itself. Thinking is good. The most successful people in life, when they come up with an idea, which is usually a form of a fault, they do something to commit themselves to that idea or to maybe even try the idea right there on the spot.

They commit themselves to the idea to make sure that the idea doesn't just disappear and float off into the ether where someone else can steal the idea. They do it that day, not three weeks later, not a month later, not next year, not when the kids get out of school, not when it stops raining outside, not when the weather breaks. They do it today and they do it now. And when I say an idea, it doesn't necessarily mean you can go do the thing right now. Let's say you're driving in your car and you get an idea for an episode of your podcast that you should record. It's not that you should have a microphone with you and lighting and you set up in your car and record an episode of your podcast. What I mean is you have the urgency to do something about the idea.

You don't just think about it and not take action. So in the micro you could do something as simple as write down the idea of what you're going to record on your show so you're not trusting your long-term memory. Now you have it written down and then you just refer to that place where you write all your ideas down. You should have a place for that because that'll train your brain to come up with ideas. So you can do it when you need it, not just when you want to. And then you can just write it down in your formal place or you can just refer to 'em when it's time for you to pull your mic out and record. The whole point is you need to move immediately on the thoughts that you have, not just sit there and hold them in your head or think that you're going to remember them and that you'll get to them later.

People who end up being mediocre and worse in life have a bad habit of getting to things later. They have a bad habit of telling themselves and rationalizing that it's okay to not do it now because I can get to it later or I will get to it later or there is no need to do it right now. Or here's an example of somebody who they didn't get to until later and look at them, they became successful. All of this is bullshit and I've heard these types of things from anybody you can name. I've heard different forms of all of those things that I've just said is okay for me to get to it later because look at this person, they got to it later and they became successful. So that means I can get to it later. No, that doesn't mean you can get to it later.

And even though we're coming off the heels of what I just talked about in yesterday's episode, that seeing someone else be successful should be looked at as a possibility, that means you can also be successful. That doesn't mean you should take your time just because that person for whatever reason, took longer. Maybe they took longer because they had to, not because they chose to. There's a difference. And see, a lot of people tend to leave out those details when they call themselves modeling their behavior after another person. They only want to model the parts that are convenient for them. If you only model from convenience, you're not modeling. I remember in basketball, my basketball days, they used to have ball players who would come in and say, well Dre, they want to dribble like let's say someone like Kyrie Irving who's a very good, very good at dribbling the basketball, still playing to this day.

And players will say to me, well Dre, I heard that when Kyrie was young he would do this drill and this drill and they would point out these things that they heard Kyrie Irving did when he was a kid. I don't know where they heard this, I don't know if Kyrie said it himself, but they said they heard that Kyrie did this and they said, well Dre, do you think I should do the same thing that Kyrie Irving did? And I once made a video answering this question in a generality, not specifically about their Kyrie question, but just overall. And it was a message I was giving to everybody that if you heard that someone else did something and you also see that person as successful, that doesn't mean that you should just copy everything that that doesn't mean that you should just copy the thing that you heard they did, the one isolated thing that you handpicked from this person's behavior.

Because the problem with that is you're leaving out all the context that goes around the thing that they did. So you heard Kyrie Irving did a certain dribbling drill, okay, hey, maybe that might help your dribbling, but what about all the other things he did that might not be so easy or convenient for you? What if he was getting up at five in the morning so he could go outside and run three miles before school? What if he was lifting weights after school? What if he would spend a lot of time doing footwork drills that are not really exciting or highlight real worth, but they develop the ability to dribble the ball and move his feet at the same time, which he does. So you can't just leave out the parts that are inconvenient for you because you just want to highlight the real stuff.

So you got to get all of it. And this is one of the things that again, when you find yourself modeling another person, you gotta do it the right way. So the whole point here is successful people do things immediately. Okay? One big thing I see often when people who are on the slow bus to success is they get an idea, they think about things but they don't do anything. A lack of action is a commonality. We'll just say that. You find in people who are mediocre or worse, they have a bias to inaction. I have an episode action bias. Lemme tell you that episode, that was episode number 1199 Action Bias. Most people who are unsuccessful or mediocre or worse, they have an inaction bias or you want to be the opposite of that or you want to have the bias of doing stuff.

Now, I can't tell you how many times I've talked to an entrepreneur and they tell me what their challenge is at the moment and I ask them, have you considered this? Have you done anything about that, this, that, and the third? I'll throw a couple of things out there and often the entrepreneur will respond. You might think they may say, I never thought of that. But often the response is, yes, I have thought of that. I have considered that. I do know about that. I have been thinking about that. The problem is that all they did was think about it. That's all they did was know about it or hear about it. They didn't do anything. They haven't taken any action. And often when an entrepreneur responds and says that and they start telling me, yeah, I've heard of it, but I haven't done anything.

Or I'll ask them, well, have you done anything? And they say no. They'll usually laugh at themselves. They'll laugh in spite of themselves because they realize how silly it sounds that they've heard of this thing and I just suggested it to them and they already knew about it, but they still haven't done anything. And they laugh because they realize how silly it sounds when they get to say it out loud. Out. Okay? So I don't want that to be you. And again, at least a hundred times over the last five years, somebody has done this in a conversation with me. And if we go back even more years, I could probably get up closer to a thousand times. I've heard someone say something like this in some type of engagement. So don't be the next person on this list. Alright, this is the list you want to avoid.

When you get an idea, implement it doesn't work, throw it away. And if it works, do something simpler like that. But the big point here in point number one is you must implement your ideas when you get them. Do not wait till later because you'll call off. They will call off and you might even forget it if you didn't write it down. Point number two, today's topic once again is the slow bus to success and how to get yourself off of the bus, how to ring the bell on the bus so that it gets you off at the next stop. Number two, two months' time between idea and action. So this connects right to what I just talked about and I gave this one away, stepped on it a little bit in point number one. So going further on that, you must reduce the time between thinking about doing something and actually doing something for a couple of reasons.

Number one, humans, when we are thinking about an idea, that's probably the time that that idea has the best chance of actually happening. The moment you think of something is when it has the best chance of actually occurring. Now there are people who have created processes and systems in their lives and disciplined themselves to where they can still get stuff done. Even if they don't do it at the exact moment. I will put myself in that group. I can get an idea, for example, of something I may record for this show. I'll write it down. I may not get around to recording that specific idea until three weeks later, but because I have a process for capturing my ideas to make sure I don't lose them, I know I'm going to eventually get to it on top of the fact that I got a shoulder that comes out every day and therefore I have committed myself to recording enough that the material keeps coming out.

Most people don't have those kinds of processes for any idea that they have. Therefore the idea just comes through their head and they disappear and they go away. And then what happens is five years later, someone else does the thing that you had thought of five years ago. And you're right, that person stole my idea, your ideas if you owned the idea. See, the thing about ideas folks is that they're not proprietary. Nobody owns an idea. Ideas don't have owners, they only have implementers. Did everybody hear that? Ideas do not have owners. They only have implementers. And I think I did an episode on this, lemme say, yes I did episode 1203. Ideas have no owners, only executors. So execute, implement, using them interchangeably here you got to be the executor of an idea, not just the holder of an idea. A lot of people have thought of things but they never actually did it.

I'm sure there are people who thought that maybe I could do a solo show and put it out every single day, but they didn't actually implement it or they didn't implement it and stay consistent with it. Most of the things that I've done, I wasn't the first person in the world to come up with the idea. There may be a couple of things, may have been the first, but most of the things I've done, I wasn't the first person in the world to come up with the idea, but I may have been the first to consistently execute on it. And listen, maybe there are people who executed on it longer than me or before me or did it better than me. But the fact is, the execution is what creates the outcome folks. And we are in a results-based business. So you want to create outcomes, you have to execute, not just think about stuff and the way that you execute.

The easiest way to move yourself to a stronger habit of execution is by reducing the time between when you think about taking an action and when you actually take the action. So again, you can't wait until three months from now, six months from now when everything is calmed down, when everything is aligned, when I'm ready, I had somebody say this to me just the other day, I was looking in my message inbox on social media because sometimes we run ads on social media and people will send dms and my assistant will handle the messages that are coming through the dms. And I just go through and just see what kind of conversations are happening. And there was a person in there who there's a back and forth conversation happening between us and them and we got them to the point that we're like, alright, well here's something that we can offer you and we basically, we will give you the link to go and do it and you can sign up for it right now where they would make a financial investment to do something right now and this is something that they can invest in.

And they said, all right, that would sound great. And we told 'em what it was. We told 'em the price and everything and they said it would sound great. So we sent them the link and they didn't do anything. A day went by, we followed up with them and said, Hey, you had any issues with the link? You didn't do anything. We didn't say it in so many words, but we sent them a message to find out why they didn't do anything. They just said, everything sounds good. They didn't do it. And the person said, well, I'll do it when I'm ready. And not in a negative way, they said, I'll do it when I'm ready. I don't want to have one foot in and one foot out. I got to make sure I'm all the way ready to go do it. That kind of language.

Alright, this is the common rationalization that people give when it's time to take a step forward. Remember when we did the episode on courage versus Confidence? If you don't remember that episode, let me refer you to it. That was episode number 27-40. Confidence versus courage. When you're doing something that you've done before, you can just call on confidence because confidence is a belief in your ability and you have belief in an ability because you've done it before. Courage on the other hand, is your ability to do something even when you have no belief that you can do it because you haven't done it before, you have no past references to refer to. So courage is about how do I move myself to go do something that's brand new to me? And the challenge for this person, that little anecdote that I just gave you, this person needed to call on courage, but because they didn't, well, they were short on courage, they probably didn't realize that courage is what they needed.

What they were looking for probably was confidence. And they even said it in so many words, when I'm ready, well, you're never going to be ready to do something brand new. That's the problem everybody, you're never going to be ready to do something that's brand new. That's why you gotta be courageous and do it anyway. That's what courage is. It's action in the face of fear. The reason many people have ideas of things that they would do or could do and don't do 'em is because they're looking for confidence when they should be looking for courage. Did everybody understand that? And again, listen to episodes 27-40. If you want to learn more about that and everybody should listen to that episode, and if you heard it when it came out, I would suggest you go back and listen to it again because there's something in there that you need to remind yourself of that maybe you heard it that day but you forgot about it since then.

So you need to understand that this is a way of thinking, and has nothing to do with your tangible resources. Lot of times, a lot of things that I talk about here are about the way that you think. It has nothing to do with what you physically have or have access to or how much money you got or any of that, which means anyone can use these things. This is applicable by all of you. No matter where you are in life right now, whether you're at the highest level, you need this, you're at the lowest level just starting out, you need it. Most people stop themselves from doing this, like reducing that time between the idea and action. They stop themselves from doing it. And the reason that they stop themselves from doing it is because it takes courage to, again, adopt a new habit to do something that you're not used to doing.

If you're used to procrastinating getting an idea and thinking about it for three days, then do something. And then I say, alright then instead of thinking about it for three days, as long as you think about it for three minutes, then do something. Alright, that's new, that's a new behavior. And if you go looking for confidence to do that, you're not going to find it. And then you'll do nothing. And then you'll rationalize it with, well, I'm not ready yet. Of course you're not ready. I know you're not ready. That's the point. You're not supposed to be ready. You being ready is the reason why you're in a position where you need to do something different anyway, everybody gets what I'm saying? And the problem is a lot of people never get this concept to turn over in their minds. And unfortunately, I'll be honest, some of you listening to this right now, you are logically agreeing with everything that I'm saying, but you are having emotionally accepted this and you are going to go right back to doing the same thing you've been doing. Now some of you're going to listen to this and say, that makes sense and you're actually going to go do something, but not everybody's going to, because if I can get everybody just go do these things just by understanding me,

This alarm is going off in my building.

Okay? So let me restart what I was saying there. If I get everybody to just go do things that they're supposed to do just based on a logical, rational understanding of what I'm saying, then well I'd be, I would go run for president. I wouldn't be just doing this. I'd go do something where I could get a whole lot more ROI from what I'm doing and I probably have a million times more people in my audience because everybody would just listen to me say, that makes a logical sense. And they would just go do everything that I said. It doesn't work that way. If it did work that way, a lot of things in life would be a whole lot different. So anyway, the way most people stop themselves because they believe they're lacking resources, I don't have the resources, the time, or the readiness.

Readiness is a resource. The money, another resource. The way I would urge you to think instead is with resourcefulness rather than resources. Everyone has some living on a resource. Every human being on the planet has a limitation of resources. Your limitation could be money, time, attention, energy or focus. What the most successful people do is figure out how they can still take action even when plan A is not available. Plan A might be, well, if I had all the money, I could just buy this and we'd be done. But they find a way to do something even though they can't plan. Most people when thinking about doing something first they consider whether their first idea can be done. If they can't do their first idea, they don't do anything. So don't be like most people. This is where you need the resourcefulness, even when you act on resources.

Point number three, and by the way, let me give you a couple episodes where I've talked about resourcefulness because that is an important one. When you need to get something done that may not, it may not be so obvious how you can do it because the first thing that you think of, you don't have that option. So how can you do it? Anyway, we talked about this in episodes 24 and 97. The difference between levels is not resources. Episode 2089, how to be resourceful when you lack resources. Episode number 14, 67 and three resources that compensate for anything else. And when you are missing resources, here's what you can do. Listen to those episodes. Point number three, today's topic once again is a slow bus to success and how to get yourself off of it. Number three, doing one thing at a time.

There's another point that has some nuance and I'll explain it. When you're focused on a specific task at work, like you as a human being, like right now I'm recording the show, you should, and I should focus on just doing this. I shouldn't be thinking about anything else or trying to do another thing. At the same time I'm doing this, I shouldn't try to multitask this along with other things that I'm doing. And it's not really multitasking, it's task switching. You're giving a short amount of attention to something then going back and forth, back and forth. That's a bad strategy because your effectiveness will be diminished and you're not going to get either one of them done at a higher level when you're switching between activities. However, in the big picture of what you're doing in business, you should not only do one thing at a time, you should have multiple things going at once so that you can find what's working, identify what isn't, and put more kerosene on the things that do work and immediately delete the things that don't.

So if you got five things going on at once, and three of 'em are working by your measure and two of 'em are not, get rid of the two and do more of the three and then find maybe two more you can test. And so you got 30 things going at the same time. They're all working and that's the way that you should do things. Now, when it's time for you to actually do work individually as a human, you need to focus on the thing that you're doing and the task at hand that is in front of you. Alright, this is where, well, let me backup. Your business should always have multiple plates spinning, and your business can be you and your life. Your life has multiple plates spinning. You got a job, you got a family, you got kids, okay? That's three different plates right there just by itself.

That's three different plates. Alright, you got a bank account or you got a job, you got not a job, I got a human body. You go to the gym. Alright, that's four, that's five plates spinning right there. So again, when I say your business, it doesn't necessarily mean entrepreneurship, but it does mean entrepreneurship. But it's also those of you who are not entrepreneurs, your life is a business. You got more than one plate going in your life. So you always have multiple plates, meaning even when you don't want to. So with any person only focused on, again, any person involved in your life should only be focused on the task that's in front of them even though there are other tasks going on in the background. So this is where going back to business where you can use things like software, artificial intelligence, this can help all of us because we'll be able to do multiple things while using artificial intelligence to do stuff like watch or actually work on things while we are not personally doing them ourselves, paying attention to 'em in a moment.

So listen to my series on artificial intelligence and you can learn more about that. That is for the entrepreneurs out there, but also those of you who are not entrepreneurs. AI software is going to be part of all of our guys, whether you run a business or not. So you can use AI in your life the same way you could use it in your business. And again, that's episode 27 59 where I started talking about that. So with that out of the way, let's recap today's class, which is a slow bus to success and how to make sure you are not riding on it. And this is about how you can achieve success faster? And I'm telling you this in reverse order by telling you the things people do that make their success slow. Number one, thinking without doing, don't just think about things you're going to do.

Actually, do them. Take action on them immediately and put some standards in your life to where you are acting on your ideas instead of just thinking about them. Because a lot of ideas that get thought about never get executed because of this very problem. Number two, too much time between ideas and action. So this goes right along with point number one. You want to reduce the amount of time between when you think about doing something and when you actually do something successful people act with urgency. And anybody who is successful or thinks of the most successful people or people, notice that they act with urgency. Think about something, they do it, they think about it, they do it. When they get an idea, they immediately act on it. And if it ends up not being good, they delete it and they delete it just as immediately as they would implement it.

Number three, doing one thing at a time. Now again, one thing at a time. When you're focused on a specific task as an activity, do that one at a time. But in your bigger picture, life and business, you want to have multiple things going at once because you never know which one might actually work, which ones may not work, and you can delete the ones that don't work. You can put more gas on the things that do work, and then you can put systems and processes in place so that things can run even without your direct involvement. That's what I mean by not doing one thing at a time, having multiple things going, but you put the processes in place so that more than one thing can happen the way that it needs to. So this is, for example, one of the things that I talk about with entrepreneurs all the time.

I publish on every social media platform every day. So I'm looking at social media apps. We got X, you got Instagram, you got YouTube, you got LinkedIn, you got TikTok, you got Threads, you got Facebook, I got a Facebook group and a Facebook business page. So how many apps is that? It's like eight apps, something like that. I post on these apps every single day, but many of them I don't even log into the entire day. So how am I posting on 'em every day without logging into them? Well, my assistant handles about 70% of it. Then we can use automation and my assistant handles the automation. I know what parts I got to do, she knows what parts she got to do. We know what parts the AI has to do and she takes care of all of that. That's a way that I can have more than one thing going, even though I'm not literally doing it myself.

I can focus on the main thing I'm doing and we have a system that allows what I record here, for example, to flow into articles, the flow into social media posts, the flow into YouTube videos, the flow into reaching out to my email list. So there's a process that you can put in place for all of this stuff. Speaking of such, you want to put those processes, those systems in place in your business and in your life and start with your mindset.

#2830: Eclectic Input: Why To Get Info & Insight From Unique Sources

Let's get into today's topic, which is eclectic input, taking in information and insight from many unique sources. And this is something that I touched on just a little bit in the last couple episodes here on the show where I told you how I was reading a book about a tennis player Andre Agassi, and I got an idea from that that I got to apply and use in my own business even though I don't play tennis at all.

So this episode is about why you want to get input from as many sources as possible and why even though I'm a person who will encourage you to go deep in your area of expertise, you should also skim the surface of other areas of expertise that are not your specific areas because you could always find something useful in places that you would not normally think to look, and more importantly, your competition would not think to look there either. So you can get an edge on them by simply looking for things that they're not looking for and then looking in places where they are not looking. So this is where your advantage may lie because remember what I told you in episode 10 25, the opportunity is always in the opposites. So if everyone's looking this way to get to find their next idea and they're all your competition, you should look the other direction because you'll get an idea that none of them is even thinking about let alone using, and you don't even have to be better than them to outdo them simply because you have resources that they don't have.

Not because you have any necessarily talent or skill, it's specifically because you're looking in the direction that they're not looking. So let's get to it. Point number one, topic once again today is eclectic input. Why? To get information and insight from many different sources. Number one, you don't want too much of me two in your things in the things that you do. You don't want there to be too much. Me too, me too means what I mean by this is you don't want to be doing all the same things that all of your competitors are doing or the same things that others who could possibly be compared against you are doing by any eyes of the consumer. So the people who you consider to be your competitors may not be the same people who your consumer considers to be your competitor. You may think that if you have an app that you're only competing against other apps that are in the same space.

This is how many business people think that I got a fitness app, I'm competing against other fitness influencers. Well, yes, you are competing against the other fitness apps out there, but you're also competing against every other thing that the person who might download your app could be doing with their time or the money that they would need to pay to get access to the workouts in your app. So you're competing against much more than just other exercises you're competing against depending on who the person is who has your app, you're competing against doing nothing. They don't have to work out. Working out is not a legal requirement. Somebody's working out, they're doing it voluntarily. So are you competing against someone depending on who your app is for? Are you competing for people who don't work out at all and they're trying to get started?

Or is this someone who's going to work out? Definitely. Okay, then you are competing against every other way that person could work out because maybe they could do things other than an app. Maybe they're the type of person who will go outside and run five miles and they don't need an app to work out. So you're competing against that too. So keep this in mind folks. So the me too part is everything that your consumer, your prospect is comparing against you. You don't want to look or sound like them. You want to be completely unique to where the only way they can get what you're offering is they have to come to you. That's what you want. If you're in the basketball training space for example, and all your ideas for marketing and selling and doing your training comes from other people who also teach basketball trainers how to market, sell and train, then you're running into a problem.

Even if those people are really good, all your material is going to look and sound like everybody else in the space. And the same thing if you're an esthetician or a life coach or you tutor high scorers to do good on the SATs, everyone else who's in your space is looking at the same sources for ideas and information on how to be better and do better. They're all looking at the same things. So all of you are going to look and sound exactly the same because you're all getting your information from the same place. Everyone understand what I'm saying here? You don't want to look at the same things that they're looking at because again, you're all going to all come to the same conclusions and your outputs all going to kind of look and sound the same. And then you become a commodity in the eyes of the consumer and in that case the consumer says, okay, everybody here looks pretty much the same, so I'll just pick the cheapest one because they all seem pretty much the same.

And if in your heart of hearts that you are not exactly the same as everybody, you're different. You have to make it obvious that you're different so that the consumer can understand it. It can't be a secret, it can't be something that they only understand. If you get to talk to 'em for 20 minutes, they might not give you much time. They may only give you 20 seconds. So this is the marketing challenge. How do I make it clear and obvious that I'm different from everybody else out there? This is called again, the race to the bottom when you're a commodity because people say, oh, y'all are pretty much the same. It's like someone goes to the grocery store and they're going to get mustard. Is there a particular brand that you need for most people to answer is no. So they're all commodities.

You don't want to be that. Give you an example of this that I applied in my own life, and this is way before I could have explained this to anybody. When I was coming up in basketball, I wasn't that good of a player. I started playing when I was 14. So from ages 14 to 18 high school years, I knew that all the ball players went to the local playground and played pickup basketball, Findlay Recreation Center in Mount Airy in Philadelphia where I'm from. And I realized very early that if all the players around here are already better than me, then I can't only do the same things that they're doing because then I'm only going to get better at the same pace that they're getting better. Again, this is just my theory and therefore I can't catch up to 'em. They're already ahead of me.

Now we're all starting at the same time. Then maybe that could have made some sense but still wouldn't have made sense because I want to get better than them, more than they're getting better. And on top of the fact that I need to catch up. So I realized what I had to do, I need to do more than what they're doing because if I do the same as them again, they're already ahead. So we're all moving at the same pace, so I'm still losing. So I noticed by paying attention, I noticed that the local playground courts were always packed in the evenings when everyone would come outside, the sun was down. All the older guys, like the guys who had full-time jobs, would come home from work and they would come play basketball. So the playground was packed at night, so it was a good time to be there.

This is where you see all your friends, but at the same time I needed to get an edge on my friends and pass them. So what could I do? I noticed that around between 10 o'clock and two o'clock, 10:00 AM and two o'clock in the afternoon that the basketball courts would be completely empty, not because it was anything wrong with the courts, but because it was the middle of the summer and it was hot as hell outside and it was like 90 degrees and you're on asphalt. So I think that makes it even hotter. It absorbs heat and bounces it right back. I think it bounces it right back so it makes it even hotter. So nobody would be out there. It's too hot to be on the basketball court at this time of day. And I said, okay, that's my advantage. If it's too hot for everybody else, it won't be too hot for me.

And in those times, between 10:00 AM and 2:00 PM I would be on the basketball court practicing by myself not knowing what I was doing but just doing stuff and hoping that something worked. And that's where I started to slowly start to catch up to my peers and by the time I was 18, I was actually a solidly good basketball player. I wasn't doing the same thing that all my competitors were doing. That's the point. And I need you to have that same mindset with your stuff. You don't want to do the same thing that everybody else is doing and sometimes not doing the same thing as everybody else doesn't necessarily mean you need to go and do something that is so radical and different. I mean, what did I just tell you that is radical? What I did, all I did was just practice more than everybody else.

I just went to the court at a time, everyone else thought logically to them it's too hot. I said, well, it won't be too hot for me. And I just practiced it, there's nothing radical about that. I told you all about this when I talked about how to increase the depth of your knowledge. One thing you can do that can separate you from your peers is simply go read 20 books on your area of expertise. Just read 20 books about it and whatever it is, read 20 books. I guarantee you'll know more than 98% of people in the world on that subject. And it includes the people who do that thing for a living because most people who do stuff for a living, any of you who's ever had a job, look around at your peers, do they study the job? Okay, exactly. They don't, don't study the job, they just have a job.

They show up and they do the job, they do the training that the job requires. But besides that, what do your peers do to deepen their knowledge on what you all do for a living? Most of you who have a job, look around as your peers. Tell me what do they do besides just do the job and do what they're required to do? For the most part, the answer is nothing. They don't do anything, they do nothing. And it's even worse than the entrepreneurial space because in the entrepreneurial space there's not even a requirement of doing basic training. At least when you get a job, they train you on how to do the job. At least you got the fundamentals in place because they train you how to do it. When you're an entrepreneur, there's no training. You can just hang up your shingle and say, I'm an entrepreneur and start selling stuff and you need not have any expertise whatsoever and you can just start selling stuff.

Now, I don't know how you're going to sell anything, but you can try. And so this is the part that I want y'all to understand that doing something is different from everybody else. Folks doesn't necessarily mean doing something crazy, sometimes it just means doing the basics more than everybody else does the basics. In the sports world specifically, and this is also true actually in the business world and in your line of work, you probably noticed this is true as well. Actually as a matter of fact, the clients that I've worked with, I've heard them even say this. So I would say this applies in every level of professionalism that sometimes the easiest thing you can do to put yourself ahead of all the competition, you wonder what it is. Master the fundamentals, master the fundamentals, drill them, practice them, do them over and over again until they get boring and monotonous and then do 'em again.

That can put you ahead of everybody else. I remember, I'll give you one more note here when I was, we're still on point number one, topic once again today is eclectic input, wanting to get input and insight from many different places. When I was playing ball, I remember once I started to get good at basketball, I started doing this dribbling series. This is just a series of drills I would do. Every time I started my workout, it took about five, 10 minutes to just practice my dribbling skills. I wasn't that good of a ball handler when I first started playing, and probably by around 2009, once I started building an audience online, many years later, I made a video showing the dribbling series that I had been doing since I was probably 18 years of age. And by that point I was maybe 10 years later or close to it.

And I remember doing the drills and I showed the video on video, I showed the players who were watching what drills to do, do this drill. This drill was like 10, 15 drills and at the end of the video I said, do these drills every single day for five years and you will be a good ball handler. And I remember the most common comments I got on that video aside from thank you was Dre, do I really have to do it every day for five years? Man, that's a lot of work. LOL people didn't really want to do the work. And that's the point. I want y'all to get that. That's the point right there. If you could just know what the fundamentals are, be sure that those are the correct fundamentals and you just drill them, drill them, drill them until you master them, you'll be ahead of most of your competition. That's an eclectic idea simply because most people are lazy. They don't think and they don't read. Alright, I told you that already, right? So understand that eclectic input does not necessarily mean you need to go digging into the Amazon rainforest to find a new idea. Sometimes just the basic stuff that's right in front of your face. Point number two, today's topic once again is eclectic input. Why? To get insight from many different sources. Point number two, remember that a great idea can come from anywhere.

Speaking of basketball, the first product I ever created and sold on my own was called Hoop Handbook. It's a training program for up and coming basketball players that still exists today. And when I created Hoop Handbook, I started with two programs. One was a dribbling program for basketball players like that series I just told you about and included a bunch of other workouts and drills and then one for shooting, so one for dribbling and one for shooting. Now, where did I get this idea? And by the way, these programs, I was selling for $4 and 99 cents a piece and when I first put these programs out, I didn't even have what they call auto delivery. These days when you buy a digital product online or you buy anything that has a digital aspect to it, that as soon as you push the button to run your card and get charged and it takes the money, then immediately you get an email that says congratulations on your purchase and it has links and it has where you can go access the stuff and all that stuff.

You get it immediately, right? So when I first started selling my products, I didn't know that there was such a thing as automatically delivering the product to the customer. So when I made my first sales, the people who bought from me were following up from buying by sending me an email and saying, Hey Dre, I just bought your product. Can you send me the product? Because I didn't have auto delivery, so I had to manually go see what they purchased. Then I had to go send them an email with the program that they had bought attached to the email and I would manually email it to 'em. I did that for about a week before I realized, or I thought, I theorized there has to be a way to automatically send these to customers, and I googled something and I found it and then all of a sudden I had auto delivery.

I'm sharing all that to let you know how basic this was when I first started. Now the question here that I want to answer that you are not even thinking of, but I'm going to give it to you is where did I get the idea for even having a program in the first place? Because these days, all of you are thinking about it. You get an audience and a subject is to make a course or a program or a product and sell it. Well, yes, it's common sense these days, but 15 years ago this was not common sense and nor was it common to, there was no common process for doing it either. So I get the idea, I got this idea from a random commentator on YouTube because at this point I had a nice little YouTube audience of basketball players who were following me and I knew who these people were.

They were 13 to 24-year-old young men who were looking to advance in basketball, most of them in the 13 to 18 range, like high school age and one of the commentators on YouTube, no name, no face, no picture. They just suggested in a comment, Dre, why don't you just take the workouts that you already do, put them in a format where other players can learn from you and they can practice the same way that you practice. Now, he didn't say it so articulately, but that was the idea that he was getting across. And I read that comment because at that time, and still to this day, I read all my comments and given who my audience was at the time, again, I don't know who this person was, but I would guess he was probably some 15-year-old kid living in his parents' home who had no professional basketball experience and no entrepreneurial experience nor any sales experience.

But the suggestion was a great idea. Still it didn't matter that he didn't know. He probably hadn't played pro basketball. He probably wasn't an entrepreneur and he wasn't a salesperson, but his idea was still good. So I was open-minded to the idea regardless of the source of the idea. That's what I want you to understand. The fact that he didn't have expertise in the area in which he was offering a suggestion had nothing to do with the fact that the suggestion was still good. Everybody catch what I just said? And the reason I was able to turn it into a business opportunity is because I was open-minded enough to understand that. And I want you all to not get caught in the matrix of thinking that you can only listen to someone if they happen to have a certain level of expertise or credibility or accomplishment, et cetera.

Now, I'm not saying you need to deeply investigate every idea that comes from any random bum who's done nothing. However, I suggest you keep your mind open enough because the best idea often doesn't come from the place that you think the best idea is going to come from. The best idea for what you're doing often will come from someone who doesn't even do what you do. It might not even know anything about it. Doesn't mean they can't be smart, but they may not know much about that particular space. But because they understand certain things, they can see things that maybe you wouldn't see. This is the reason why I'm working on your game university. Most of the clients that we have in working on your game university folks are not former basketball players or even former athletes who just became entrepreneurs through the internet and putting content up before we were calling it content.

Like me, most of the people who are working at your game university do not have the same background that I have. So why are they clients of mine? Why do they come to me? Why do they believe that I can help them? Because I understand the fundamentals, I understand the principles, I understand the disciplines when it comes to mindset, strategy, systems and accountability. Notice that none of those four things has anything to do with a particular industry. You understand what I'm saying here? And this is why you gotta keep your eyes and ears open because you never know where the best idea may come from. And this is one of the reasons why even here for this show, I will listen to questions. I always read questions and comments and feedback that I get from people all over social media. Even if they're saying something banal and dumb, and sometimes you gotta deal with the banal and dumb stuff and trolls in order to get the good stuff.

I'm willing to do that because somebody may say something that might be a great idea for another episode that I can put out or another article that I can write or the next chapter of a book that I'm putting together. So this is why you gotta keep your eyes and ears open and don't close yourself off to people just because they don't have a certain standing in your mind. And this is something that I was talking about a few episodes back where I was talking about how to know someone's a true expert, how to prove that you're smart. That a lot of people in the academic space specifically, I don't know why I notice it a lot with those people, but they are extremely proprietary about listening to someone or even taking feedback from someone, especially when there's a disagreement. If that person doesn't have a certain level of accomplishment, well, you don't have the expertise or you're not an expert on this subject or you didn't study this subject or you didn't go to school for it, so that means you can't talk about it.

I see people saying this all the time and I'm like, do you understand that the best idea that you could get in that area probably comes from someone who doesn't work there? Because their mind is not just, their mind is not just set to this one way of thinking. They have a whole different way of thinking, but I can't change everybody. I'm not here to save the world. I'm here to save the people who want to be saved, but they have to be open-minded. This is why I'm suggesting that you keep your mind open, don't close your mind off to somebody or something just because it's not coming from a place that maybe you thought it would come from. Everybody understands what I'm saying here. So this person probably had very little expertise in the area in which they offered me a suggestion, but I was able to turn into a business opportunity anyway because a great idea can come from anywhere and again, it's often not the usual suspects.

This is why you want to diversify your sources when it comes to taking in information. You can get a great idea from somewhere that you never thought an idea would come from, let alone a good idea. This is the reason why I read books on subjects that are not directly related to my business. Alright? I told you that I read Andre Agassi's book, he's a tennis player. I have no, what's the word, ambitions for playing or even learning how to play tennis. But I read the book anyway because I figured there might be something in this book that I can use. As of this recording, I am just finishing up reading a memoir by the actress Mindy Kaling. Have any of you heard of Mindy Kaling? I think she had a TV show that was called Everybody Loves Mindy or something like that. I never watched this TV show.

I do remember her from a TV show, The Office, which I did watch 15 years ago. I did watch the TV show at the office, but I read her book, not because I'm necessarily a fan of Mindy Kaling, I just happened to see the book. I said, let me read this book. Who knows? Maybe there'll be something in there that is useful that I can use. Now I'm almost done with the book, I'm not finished yet. I'm not sure I grabbed anything necessarily out of it, but I'm okay with that. I'm okay with the trade off sometimes taking in something where I get nothing from it, but I know if I keep taking in eclectic things from different people with different experiences, I'm going to get something useful that I can use in my space that again, none of my competitors are using. So this is the reason why I will take in something like that and then I'll go right back to reading a book that's specifically about business and about entrepreneurship and marketing and sales.

That's the straight line way. Then I'll go to something that's completely off the beaten path and you should be doing the exact same thing. So you can mix this up. And it doesn't mean it's always going to happen. As I said, not like every comment that I read. Somebody gives me a business idea that goes and makes me money, but one of them will. And that's the reason why I keep myself open to it. Okay? So this should be a regular part of your information consumption routine. Point number three, today's topic once again is eclectic input. Why? To get information and insight from many different sources. Number three, breakthroughs and insights come from known things used in new ways.

Breakthroughs and insights come from known things used in new ways. What did I just tell you that a basketball fan watching me on YouTube said, why don't you just put your stuff down together in a program? It is not a new thing to create a program. It wasn't a new idea to create a program. He didn't even say create a program. He said, just write down all the workouts that you're doing and let other people see the workouts so that they know what to do. That's literally what he said. And I said, okay, I'll do that, but I'll put it into a pack. I'll package it up and I'll sell it again. Was any of that a new idea? Was that a new idea? No. Putting basketball on the internet was a new idea when it was combined, but the internet wasn't new and basketball wasn't new.

Again, new things combined in new ways, create new ideas. I remember reaching out to some people who worked. Give you another example. I reached out to some people who worked on the executive side of Nike basketball. This is probably about a little over

10 years ago now. I wanted them, the reason I reached out to them is I had a little bit of a relationship with Nike at this point because I had done some brand deals with them as an influencer. I had done some events with them. So I knew some people who worked in, not the basketball players at Nike, but the executives, the people who worked in the offices at Nike. They're the ones who called the shots. And I knew some of these folks. So I reached out to them and I said, listen, you all should have me as the person who runs your YouTube basketball channel, because at the time, I mean they probably still have one to this day, y'all have a YouTube basketball channel.

But the stuff that I'm doing on my channel, if we put it on the Nike basketball channel with the reach that you all have, it will help a whole lot more players. Of course it will help me. I would get served by it, but it would help Nike as well and shit. As a basketball player, why wouldn't you want to have a relationship with Nike? So this is a great idea, at least I thought it was. So I reached out to Nike, or at least the people I knew at Nike, and I proposed to them that we do this and I knew that I could improve on what Nike was doing. This is the reason why I reached out and I articulated all of this, and long story short, the executive who I knew at Nike, she took my message, she ran it up the chain of command.

She came back to me and said, Dre is not going to happen. And she said, no, from high on up. They said, we hear what you're saying, but we don't want to do it because we just want to focus on our social media. We're only going to use the athletes who are already endorsing our products. So are the Kobe Bryant and LeBron James of the world. And she said, and I said, well, is there any other, and I'm a salesperson, so I kind of pushed her and said, was there any other route we can go to kind of make this happen? Someone else, we can talk to some other route. Do you see any other opportunities to make this happen? And she said, no, it's probably not going to happen. She said, I'm pretty high up at Nike. I don't know their system, their, what's the word hierarchy at Nike?

But she said, I'm pretty high up. And from the response that I got, this is not going to happen. So sorry. Nice try, but no, it's not going to take place. So it ended up not happening. I ended up not doing anything with Nike, at least on that end. But what I did do is I was able to steal an idea from Nike. So here's what I did. I noticed that Nike would take their players who are in the Nike indoor season, and they would get those players to make little clips on YouTube and say, well, here's how I do this, move that move. And they would put those out on Nike. So what I did was say, alright, how about I just go take a move that Kobe or LeBron does, and I'll break down the move that Kobe or LeBron does, and I'll make a series of videos based on that.

Or here's 10 moves that LeBron does, and I'll make the LeBron series. I'll make a series about moves that LeBron does, or here's a series about how to play like Kobe. Here's a series about how to play whoever names a player. And I started making programs off of that, and I started selling those programs all because I was able to steal an idea from Nike after Nike wouldn't let me take what I currently do and use it for them. They wouldn't let me sell. Then I went and did it my own way. Those programs, when I started creating those pour lighter fluid on the sales that I was already making, and again, this is about maybe a little over 10 years ago. And the reason is the reason all this happened is not because I'm some genius. Again, Nike is the one who had the idea.

I just combined their ideas with my thoughts. I just combined two ideas. So I did about half the work, Nike did half the work as far as the ideas go. Then I did a hundred percent of work as far as the implementation. And again, a small amount of time between idea and implementation. Y'all catch that? I hope y'all caught that. Okay. So I got an idea from somewhere where a plan didn't work. I understand I went to Nike trying to do thing A and they said no. So I ended up doing thing B, which had nothing to do with my original idea. The only reason I went to idea B is because idea A didn't work. If idea A worked, I might not even come up with idea B. So I took an idea from something else, converted it into something else that I could use.

And this is how a person is doing for example, and I turned it into something I could use my own way. So this is how a person, if you run a dental practice, let's say you're a dentist and you got your own office, you can take an idea from the local plumber and you can use it in your dental office because the way that they market and sell to their clients, what do they do? They serve their clients. They want to get found, they want to serve clients, and they want to be the person that the client calls when they need something, right? Isn't that exactly what you want to be when you're a dentist? You want to get found, you want to serve your clients, and when they need something, you want 'em to come back. And as a matter of fact, at the dentist, you want 'em to come back every six months to get their teeth cleaned.

Unlike a plumber who you probably hope you never had to call the plumber, right? So you can take an idea. The plumber can take an idea from the dentist. The dentist can take an idea from the plumber. And this is why you gotta be looking at different places. Don't just look at the thing that you do and hope you get all your ideas from there. An author, for example, you could take an idea from an electronics company and use it to sell more books. Why? Because electronic companies want to sell their product the same way an author wants to sell your product. The only difference is the product, but the process is not different. You want to have customers, you want to sell to them, you want to make money and you want to sell to 'em again, right? Okay, well how many different industries do that?

So you shouldn't limit yourself to the book world. Everybody understand what I'm saying here? This is why you want to diversify your sources. All that said, let's recap today's class, which is eclectic input. Why? To get info and insight from many different sources. Point number one, you don't want to have too much. Me too. And this only happens when you're doing the same things and getting information from the same sources as your competitors. All you have to do is do what they're not doing. So just look around. The opportunity is in the opposite sometimes in doing the basics more than they're doing it. Number two, great ideas can come from anywhere. Again, the first product I ever created came from a nameless, faceless person who probably had no basketball experience, no business experience, and no sales experience. But they gave me an idea to take basketball, make it business, and sell stuff.

Alright? So again, great ideas do not have to come from someone who is unquote credible in that space. It can come from someone who has no credibility, but a good idea is a good idea regardless of the source. And number three, breakthroughs and insights come from known things used in new ways. This is why you want to look around and see what's working and ask yourself, how could I use that? How could I use that? How can I use that? And if you just ask yourself that question, it opens your mind, it challenges your mind to think, and you will come up with ideas. So again, I've gotten plenty of ideas for business based on things that other people were doing. I get plenty of ideas from this very show, from things that I hear other people say, things that other people say to me.

Questions, people ask me, comments, people leave. And again, they're not trying to give me an idea like Dre, he's just doing an episode on this. I get people who say that, but most of the time people say that to me. They're offering me something that I've already done. But when people give me comments, when people say stuff, when people just speak from their heart and their mind of what they have going on in their lives, it often gives me an idea of something that I can create that I think will help them and help others. So again, this is why you gotta keep your mind open. You can train your mind to do this unconsciously.

#2831: The Inequality "Gaps" That No One Talks About [Part 1 of 3]

Let's get into the topic. Now you have probably heard about something like you hear people talking about the wealth gap.

Everybody's heard people talk about the wealth gap, how certain groups have more wealth than other groups in aggregate. We know that there are outliers in every group, but people want to remind you that certain groups are behind in the race or certain groups are behind because they started off further behind in other groups for whatever reason. And many of these reasons people will happily and loudly tell you about over and over again. You probably heard about those and it's not that they don't exist, it's just that you've heard about 'em so much that I don't need to give time to those because you already heard about it. But there are also other gaps such as literacy gaps, general success gaps and other things that I'm not thinking of at the moment that I'm sure there are people who will tell you a lot about those that well, in addition to the wealth gap and even write entire books about these gaps, and actually there are probably people who've done all of these things today.

Here's what I'm going to do that's different from all of that. I'm going to talk about the gaps that are clear. They are obvious, but when you think about them, you don't hear anybody talking about them, at least not in the form of them being gaps. You hear people talk about them, period, but you don't hear people talk about them as gaps. As a matter of fact, you've heard me talk about some of the things I'm going to talk about in today and tomorrow's episode. You've heard me talk about them in general as general concepts, but you haven't heard me talk about them for a minute. One of the reasons why one person and another person, there's a gap between their outcomes is because there's a gap in this thing, this thing, this thing, this thing, those things. That's what I'm going to talk about in today's episode and tomorrow's episode.

So what I'm going to do is fill in the gap in the marketplace of these gaps not being discussed. You see what I did there? Point number one, today's topic once again is the gaps that nobody talks about. Number one, the discipline gap. Let me ask you a question. Is there a discipline gap in society? Any of you who's a successful professional in what you do? Let me ask you a question. Are there some people who started out at the same time as you and basically at the same level as you who are right now not at the same level as you and you have gone significantly further than they have? If the answer is yes, let me ask you a question. Is there a gap in your discipline and their discipline? Is there a gap between your ability, not ability, but your execution of showing up consistently to do your job versus their execution of showing up consistently to do their job?

Is there a gap between you and them? All of you are probably even laughing to yourself right now because you know that there is a gap, there has been a gap, there continues to be a gap and in the future there probably will continue to be a gap. And that discipline gap probably plays a role in the fact that you are where you are and some of your former peers are where they are. I mean they may still be your peers, but it doesn't even look like it anymore based on where you're at versus where they're at. Can we agree to this? You hear me mention every day when I open up this show showing up every single day to do the work, right? That's the first thing I mentioned when we talk about the work on your game philosophy, why? Because discipline is the most important aspect of everything.

Work on your game is about, I don't care if you're an athlete, entrepreneur, anywhere in between. How many people do you know? I'm talking to everyone now who wants to be successful, yet they don't have the ability to show up every day and just do the damn work. That is a foundational requirement of success. How many people do you know who just don't show up for whatever reason? This is not showing up, but they say they want to be successful. Being that you know so many people who fit this description and to be honest, listen, some of you listening to this might be one of these people. How many people do you think across the entire population of the world who also fit this description? How many people, maybe just in your industry who fit this description, probably millions of people, can we agree that showing up every day to do the work plays a huge role in somebody's outcomes and ultimately in their success or lack thereof?

Do we agree to that? Does anyone disagree with that? That showing up consistently to do the work plays a huge role in somebody's outcomes? Does anybody disagree with that? So since you agree, here's a follow-up question. Why does nobody ever talk about the discipline gap? Why don't you hear anybody talk about it? Why hasn't anybody written a book about the discipline gap? Oh, as a matter of fact, somebody did, I called it the third day, I wrote a whole book about it. You can get it for free by going to third day book.com, but that's, I'm kind of cheating there because I didn't write the book as, hey, here's the difference between one person and another. It kind of is because the subtitle literally says the decision that separates the pros from the amateur. So I kind of did talk about it that way, but the entire book is not framed around you versus other people.

The entire book is framed around you versus you. It's about you helping yourself. It's a self-help book because one of the principles over here working on your game, we got a lot of principles. One of 'em is that leaders look in the mirror, not out the window. So the book ain't really about you comparing yourself to other people. It's about you comparing yourself to yourself doing what you need to do. And if you do that consistently enough, eventually you'll be so far ahead of all those other people that it won't even matter what they're doing. That's what we do over here at work in your game world, not to say we can't look around and compete because competition is part of the game as well. Remember I come from the sports world, so competition will never go away and that will never be devalued here.

But the most important competition is you being better than yourself. You keep doing that consistently. Eventually the other people won't be competition because they ain't got the discipline to do what you're doing. Everybody follow? So why aren't there any Netflix specials about the discipline gap? Why is nobody pushing bills and laws through Congress about closing the discipline gap? But you got a bunch of people protesting about closing the wealth gap because they say, well this group should be given some reparations or they should write a check to every person of this group or this color in this place in order to make up for lost time or lost wealth or lost whatever. But nobody's saying, Hey, what do we do to close the gap about discipline? Just something for you to marinate as we move on. There's a simple answer to this because in order to close the discipline gap, people would actually have to take some accountability and do things personally.

So you close the wealth gap, theoretically you actually wouldn't. But theoretically you can close the wealth gap by just writing everybody a check. Alright, hand everybody a bunch of money. Now the wealth gap is closed now nobody can bring it up anymore. That technically is not going to close the wealth gap because wealth is not just giving people some cash, but this is the way that keeping it very simple, this is the way that people are thinking. See, to close the discipline gap, you can't just hand somebody something, they actually have to do something. And because humans will always be human, the discipline gap will never get closed. And what did I tell you? All the opportunities are opposite. So knowing that the discipline gap will never be closed because humans are always humans. Let me read between the lines for you. There will always be lazy people who will not show up and do the work regardless of how much resources they have available, regardless of how many opportunities are placed in front of them, regardless of their talent.

Therefore your opportunity will always be in being one who is willing to show up and do the work because there will always be so many people who won't. Everybody got it? Good. I will tell you a quick story I remember. I don't know if I had this in my notes for a later part of this series, but lemme see if I have it in here. It might be in a later part of the series'. If it is, then I'll hold it until later. But if it's not then maybe I'll just share it here. Let me see. I'm just looking to see if I've got it

And it's not there and it's not there.

And looking for one more. Okay, I don't think it's in here. So I know I have it in here somewhere. Maybe it's in a different episode that I'll be talking about it. But years ago I used to go to this basketball gym every single day not far from where I am, even to this very day. And it was where I recorded most of my YouTube basketball videos and the gym would often be empty. And the whole concept of the third day, speaking of such, came from the fact that a lot of ball players would often ask me, Dre, why are you always in an empty gym? How do you have that gym to yourself? Because it's not normal for a nice pristine, beautiful gym. Like the one I used to train in would be empty because usually there'd be a bunch of players in there practicing the same way that I was.

But the gym was often empty. And the whole concept of the third day was me explaining to people that the gym's empty, not because people don't know about it and not because I rented it out or that I own the gym and blocked people from coming in, but because people simply don't have the discipline to show up every day the way I do, which was true. And you had proof of it because you could see me in that gym every day empty. And one day there was every once in a while there'd be some striker who would come in. So there was this kid who came in there one time and he was about my size, but he was younger than me and he wanted to practice basketball. I asked him to play me in a game I was practicing by myself so often I welcomed the idea of playing somebody one-on-one just to make sure the stuff I was practicing actually worked, played by him.

And I said to him and he said to me, actually, how often do you come in here? And I usually would get that question after I worked out with somebody because they wanted to work out with me because they could see working out with me would help them get better. So he started asking, I could tell by the questions he was asking that he wanted to continue working out with me. And I found out a little bit about him. He's a young guy, he was from the neighborhood and he didn't have anything going on at that time. He wasn't playing basketball anywhere. He wasn't in school. He was going to go to school, but he wasn't in school at the time. He was a young guy, maybe 19, 20 and he didn't even have a job. So basically he had nothing going on in his life, which I'm not saying that as a knock against him.

I'm saying that as that was actually good for me because that meant he had no excuse to not come to the gym if he wanted to work out. So I said to him, look, I come to the gym every day at this time from this time to this time I'm at this gym. If you want to work out with me, alright, we can work out. But here's the thing, here's the time that I start. The time is over. You just told me you ain't got nothing else going on so you have no excuses. Make sure you're here one time every day and you can work out with me, but if you don't show up you can't work out with me anymore. And I told him that straight up from the beginning. This is the first day we just played one-on-one, I just met this kid. I said, if you don't show up then I don't know you anymore. Make sure you show up. So he showed up for about, let me ask y'all actually, before I even tell you the punchline here, how many days do you think this kid showed up to the gym?

Those of you who are not familiar with my basketball work from back in the day on YouTube, I put videos out on YouTube every single day for about 10 years straight. This was just basketball on, I still put videos on YouTube to this day, but back then it was 10 years straight, just basketball workouts and often there were times I was putting out 2, 3, 4 videos a day. I had so much content. I went to the gym Monday through Friday every single day. It was like a nine to five. Now I wasn't there from nine five, but I went to the gym every single day Monday through Friday, as long as the gym was open, as long as it wasn't a holiday, I was at the gym every single day and I told him, keep coming to the gym, you can work out with me.

How many days consecutively do you think he showed up before he broke the agreement that we had and he didn't show up? How many days do you think he lasted? That's the question. The answer is three days. This kid showed up for three days. We worked out three days in a row after that and we would do our drills and then we placed him and I got all the stuff on video and you can find the videos on YouTube. I didn't put his name in it or anything, I don't even remember his name. But when you see me playing somebody, one-on-one, he was a Latin Latin kid, bought my height and he didn't have a shirt on so he would work out with no shirt on. So if you can find those videos on

YouTube, that's him for three days and he stopped showing up and I didn't see him or hear from him for about two weeks.

I didn't hear from him, nothing happened. And then about two weeks later he came into the gym one day and I completely ignored him and he was on the court and he kind of dribbled past the court I was on I guess trying to get into my non vision to get my attention. I completely ignored him, acting like I didn't even see him there. I was like, I acted like he was a ghost and I just kept working out. I didn't talk to him and that day I completely ignored him, left the gym, said nothing to him, and the next day he didn't come back and I haven't seen him since and that's the discipline yet. Now this kid could have become, I mean I don't know if he was no serious, I don't know mentally what his makeup was as far as what he was going through with basketball, but if had he kept working out with me every day, he would've become a significantly better basketball player in about 90 days.

But he blew the opportunity. I told him, just keep showing up. You're good If you don't show up, we have a problem unless you reach out to me. I gave him my number too. Said, look, if you ain't going to make it, let me know if you got a problem or something like that. But I'm expecting you here every day. You ain't gotta call me. We ain't got to text. We ain't got to verify every day just what time the gym opens. I'm going to be here, just be here. He ain't showing up. And that was it. That's an example, just an example of the discipline gap. Point number two. Today we're talking about the gaps that no one talks about. And again, I'm going over several of 'em. It seems like a lot of people don't talk about these. Number two, the effort gap.

Effort gap and discipline gap are cousins. But let's talk specifically about this effort. One showing up is one thing. See it's one thing to just show up. It's another thing to actually give an effort to be successful. That's the next step. See, showing up means you're physically in the facility. Now what do you do once you get there? How many people do have ability, talent or desire to be successful? Maybe all three at least from what they say and probably damn near. Everybody has some level of ability. They have some type of talent and most people, at least if you listen to 'em talk, they want to be successful. Can we agree? Okay, probably. Damn everybody fits that description. So conversely, how many people do you know of all those people? How many of them actually give an effort that is commensurate with their alleged desires?

In other words, their effort aligns with their desires, they say they want to be successful. Do you see their actions reflecting someone who wants to be successful? Now that number may be a lot smaller versus the number who actually say it, the number who actually do it, notice it not the same, right? Everybody sees where this is going. I kind of just told you there are plenty of people out there who have ability, opportunity and allegedly a desire to succeed, yet they don't do the damn work. Would you agree? And it was here that I was going to, I would've told you that basketball store had already told you, I told this kid, just be there every day and we're good. And when people would ask me again, how do you have this gym all to yourself all the time in Miami that you're working out, excuse me.

Because of this effort gap, because of the discipline gap and the effort gap. Again, this gym is not some mysterious hidden location. This is a big gym, but with big windows, it is in a prominent location. It's very easy to find. You could Google a basketball gym and this gym will come up on Google. It was a publicly owned facility, so we're not talking about some Equinox. It costs $200 a month. This is a publicly owned facility. You know how much the membership was to this gym that I was going to. It was $10 a month. Yeah, so literally one zero $10 a month, meaning anyone could get into this place and even if you didn't have a membership, you just wanted to use the gym that day. The buy-in fee to use the gym one time was like $3 1, 2, 3, $3. Anybody can get into this gym and everybody knew about it and I was the most known basketball person on YouTube for a good probably eight years before most other people started to jump in.

So everybody in Miami who had access to the internet, who played basketball, knew who I was. They knew where I was working out and they knew exactly where that facility was at. I was a very easy person to find. Anybody could have come into that gym. Yet 98% of the time I was in that gym working out. It was an empty effort gap. Nothing I'm telling you is an exaggeration. Everybody in Miami knows where that gym is to this day. Effort gap. That's the difference. And again, I told this kid I didn't even practice with other people. One of the reasons why that gym was empty and I never went and took the initiative to get somebody else to come to the gym with me. I could have and went and found somebody to come work out with me. I knew a lot of ballplayers in Miami.

I could have easily told somebody, Hey, come to the gym. This is where I work out every day. I could have easily told someone or invited someone or asked someone to come work out with me. I never did because I didn't really like working out with other people. Honestly, I was never a big fan of bringing other people into my workouts. I liked working out by myself, but when he came around and he showed interest, I said, okay, I'll use this guy as a practice dummy. That's what I was going to do. I was using him as a practice dummy to basically use him to work on the stuff that I would do by myself.

Now I could just use a human. He was like a crash test dummy that I would use to work on my game and I figured that my audience also, because a lot of ballplayers who were watching me on YouTube, they would often say, well Dre, I see you doing this stuff by yourself, but it'd be interesting to see you execute these same drills against a live human being because I want to see what it looks like when there's some actual resistance going up against you.

And I said, okay, that's a great idea. All of these things went through my mind when this kid came around to the gym, so I figured I would use him. I said, just show up every day. He couldn't show up every day. Sometimes it's just the simplest parameter that will eliminate people. All you gotta do is show up every day and that's it. Again, he didn't last a week. These days basketball's over. I don't play basketball anymore. I go to a boxing gym a few times a week. I'm just at the gym today and I'm recording this in early January. Anybody knows anything about the fitness world, especially if you're in the gym space, you go to gyms or you ever owned a gym or worked at a gym. January is the most popping off time of the year for a gym because everybody has allegedly made some New Year's resolutions to get in shape.

So everybody's at the gym working out for some reason. I don't know what's going on. There's something in the water down here or maybe in the world period. But the gym's been pretty quiet. I'm recording this in January. The gym was pretty quiet. It doesn't look that much different from December. The gym that I go to now, I don't know if other gyms are different now. Sometimes in my building there's a building, there's a gym in my building and sometimes when I walk past that gym in the evenings when I'm taking my son on the walk, I see a good number of people in there, but I don't know if it's that much different than the number of people who were in there in December. I don't go to the gym during peak hours when there's a bunch of people in there. I like going during off peak hours, but again, even during off peak hours in December, it looks the same as it looks now.

I would expect there to be more people in some new faces, but I actually see fewer faces. And again, the same thing happens in the gym. Any of you who go to a gym, you go to the gym consistently on the same days, at the same times you start to notice the same faces. Even people, you don't even know them. You don't even know their names, but you know their faces because you see 'em at the gym same days, same times all the time, right? Same thing in this boxing gym. I notice the same faces and their consistent faces who I see again all the time, but these people are not as consistent as I am and I'm not even trying to become a professional boxer. I mean, I was and was aiming to remain a professional basketball player in my basketball days. So it made sense. My consistency.

I'm not trying to become a pro boxer, but I'm more consistent coming to the gym than some of these people who claim that they want to box. These are people who want to be pro boxers, amateur boxers and amateur boxing is not the same as amateur basketball as a whole. There's a whole different realm of the way things work in boxing as opposed to basketball. I have no intentions of getting into a ring for an official fight with anybody yet I still come to the gym more consistently. Some of the people who claim that that's what they want to do, and I've talked to these people. They told me that they want to be boxers or they want to get into amateur boxing or they want to get into inboxing. They have this thing for different age groups and my trainer was telling me about it. He's been trying to encourage me to maybe get involved in it.

I don't think that's going to happen. Never say never, but I don't think it's going to happen. But he's like, there's a group where over 40 men can fight and there's championships and all this stuff and you can do local and then there's regional and then there's national. There's a whole national competition for this. Let's say a man who's over the age of 50 and he's 160 pounds, there's a championship belt for that in boxing. I have no desire to achieve any, no glory, sports glory at this point. I did what I needed to do in sports. I just like to stay in shape. I like to be in professional athlete shape and boxing just happens to be my vehicle for doing that right now. I have no aspirations for doing anything in boxing. Again, I don't have anything to prove as an athlete at this point.

The whole point being, I'm sharing all that to say this. There are people who do have something they want to prove as an athlete, and these mofos don't show up to the gym as consistently as I do. That's the point that I'm making here. This is the effort and the discipline gap that I'm talking about. So the ability to show up and actually give a damn effort is so lacking in society these days that this gap needs to be explored a lot more than it gets explored. Nobody talks about this. Everybody wants to talk about these gaps and outcomes. Nobody wants to talk about the gaps in inputs. Why doesn't nobody talk about this? Well, we know there are reasons people don't talk about this because it means holding people accountable for their own actions and lack of actions, which again, your favorite politician or influencer is not going to gain a lot of fans by doing that. But again, my job ain't to gain a lot of fans just amongst average people because I don't want no average people in my audience. Average people probably couldn't afford me anyway. I'm looking for people who want to do the work and they're serious about going to their highest level. So if that's you, keep listening. Point number three, today's topic. Once again, we are talking about the gaps that nobody talks about. Number three, the implementation gap.

Implementation gap. Now I talked about this recently in the episode where I talked about why you should take in less material, not more material just a few days ago. And the definition of implementation is a process of putting a decision or plan into effect, also known as executions. So you can also call this the execution gap. Just because you are consuming material, whether it's free material or paid material or you're going to events, you're talking to other people or anything else you do to get access to information, ideas for things that you could do does not mean you will actually implement any of it or put any of it to good use. Just because you have access to something doesn't mean you're going to use it. That's the implementation gap. How many people do you know who buy books, attend events, sign up for webinars, sign up for free challenges, even join coaching programs, but don't implement any of the stuff that they get access to?

How many people who fit that description, they got access but they don't do shit with it? Alright? There's a gym in the building that I live in. If you live here, the gym comes as it comes with the fact that you pay whatever you pay to live here. There's still people out of shape living here. They don't use the gym. They don't implement the thing that they have direct access to. You know how many ball players I talked to over the years when I was playing ball basketball? Who would tell me, Dre man, I just don't have access to a gym or a court. The closest court is two miles away and my parents won't drive or they won't let me, et cetera, et cetera. So many people I would hear tell that story and who knows if they were telling me the truth or not.

I was just taking 'em at their word. But there were many people I know who live here in Miami where there are parks everywhere in Miami. Miami has more parks per square footage than any city I've ever lived in or the Florida period. Just all of south Florida. So I don't care if you're talking about Boca Raton, Naples, Miami, Fort Lauderdale, Tampa Bay, Tampa, the city, Clearwater, they're all part of Tampa Bay. I've lived and spent time in these places. There are parks everywhere in Florida. You can't walk a mile in Florida and not come across a park where there's grass, there's a basketball court, there's parks everywhere out here. I don't know about where any of you live, but now here in Florida, there are parks everywhere and there's still out of shape people in Miami and just Florida period, not just Miami, Florida, period.

There's places to work out everywhere, alright? That's not the problem. The problem is implementation folks do not have access. A lot of people complain of lack of access and some of you may be actually are dealing with a real lack of access, but down here ain't no lack of access and most of you who are listening to this right now, you have access to a, you have a data connection, you got wifi for the most part, 99% of you, I don't want to hear that shit. I don't want to hear that shit. You don't have an access issue, you have an implementation issue, you have an effort issue, you have a discipline issue. That's your real problem. Most people don't implement the material that they have access to and I know for a fact that many people do not implement most of the stuff they get access to whether they got it for free or even if they paid for it.

I told you, I go to conferences, I ask people who I meet at conferences, I go to conferences, I talk to damn near everybody. Anybody that approaches me at a conference, I'll talk to 'em. I'll stand in a lobby at conferences and just wait for somebody to approach me and just converse with people. I stood in the lobby all day. I was still in the lobby for hours talking to people when I go to conferences because I go there to meet people. That's the reason why I go and I'll ask fellow attendees, alright, you came to this conference, what are you going to do now that you came to the conference? What are you going to do differently based on what you learned or heard or got inspired by At this conference? 99% of the time when people answer that question, they tell me they're going to do something that they already knew they needed to do before they came to the conference that they still would've needed to do.

Whether they had come to the conference or not. So a person. Last conference I was, I was speaking to this woman, I said, what are you going to do now if you came to this conference? She said, well, I got to finish writing my book. Said, how long have you been writing the book? How long have you been working on the book? She said, I've been working on it for like two years now. Alright, so she didn't need to come to the conference and know she needed to finish writing that book. Now maybe what she learned at the conference or what she heard got her energized and inspired to finish the book. Maybe that's what it did and hopefully it did and hopefully she finished the damn book. The whole point being what stopped her from implementing before she came to the conference. Nothing. That's the whole point.

People simply don't get things done. You come to work with me, we are not taking two years to write a book. I don't care what you're writing about. Let's try for two months. We implement here, we get things done. If that sounds like you, then you need to be scrolling down to underneath, wherever you're listening to this and clicking on that link for work on your game university.com or just simply typing it into your browser. Work on your game university.com and let's get it going. Alright, so somebody will tell me something like, well I need to finish this book I started three years ago. This is at conferences. When I'm talking to fellow attendees once on a website that they've been working on, it is rarely that they're going to go do something that they just heard 30 minutes ago. That's not usually the thing people say they're going to do. You know that most books they get bought don't get read past the first chapter. Most courses that get purchased do not get consumed past module two and a lot of courses are like 6, 7, 8, 9, 12 modules. This gap plays a big role in the outcome differences between people. Point number four, I'm deciding if I'm going to put this into a separate episode. Lemme see what I got here.

Yeah, what we're going to do is we're going to make this into a, actually instead of a two part series, we'll make this into a three part series. So tomorrow we'll pick up on point number four. So let me recap what we got here today. So we're talking to gaps that nobody ever talks about and again, you hear people talk about things like the wealth gap and the income gap and the outcomes. People are talking about the outcomes. So let's talk about the inputs. That's what I'm talking about here. Number one, the discipline gap, showing up every single day to do the work. How many people do you know who want to be successful yet they don't show up? Exactly. Point number two, the effort gap. How many people show up but they don't do shit? They don't actually put the effort in, they don't actually do the work.

Alright, I'm going to a boxing gym. I'm not trying to be a boxer at all on any level. I meet people at the boxing gym who say they want to be boxers and I'm in the gym more consistently than they are. Alright? This is the effort gap. And number three, the implementation gap. How many people get access to information, access to stuff, buy books, sign up for webinars, sign up for free challenges, courses, et cetera, and then they don't even implement the stuff that they got the access to. How many people got a bookshelf of books and they ain't even read the damn books? Alright, this is the implementation gap and all of these are within your human control. It has nothing to do with your ancestors, the past, what anybody else is doing, the government, anything like that. All of you have access to all three of these.

You can do them whenever you want. This is a matter of you deciding that you're going to move yourself to these actions. If you have challenges with these, that's completely fine. It just makes you human, but it is not completely fine to not do anything about it.

#2832: The Inequality "Gaps" That No One Talks About [Part 2 of 3]

Let's get into the topic. Now you have probably heard about something like you hear people talking about the wealth gap.

Everybody's heard people talk about the wealth gap, how certain groups have more wealth than other groups in aggregate. We know that there are outliers in every group, but people want to remind you that certain groups are behind in the race or certain groups are behind because they started off further behind in other groups for whatever reason. And many of these reasons people will happily and loudly tell you about over and over again. You probably heard about those and it's not that they don't exist, it's just that you've heard about 'em so much that I don't need to give time to those because you already heard about it. But there are also other gaps such as literacy gaps, general success gaps and other things that I'm not thinking of at the moment that I'm sure there are people who will tell you a lot about those that well, in addition to the wealth gap and even write entire books about these gaps, and actually there are probably people who've done all of these things today.

Here's what I'm going to do that's different from all of that. I'm going to talk about the gaps that are clear. They are obvious, but when you think about them, you don't hear anybody talking about them, at least not in the form of them being gaps. You hear people talk about them, period, but you don't hear people talk about them as gaps. As a matter of fact, you've heard me talk about some of the things I'm going to talk about in today and tomorrow's episode. You've heard me talk about them in general as general concepts, but you haven't heard me talk about them for a minute. One of the reasons why one person and another person, there's a gap between their outcomes is because there's a gap in this thing, this thing, this thing, this thing, those things. That's what I'm going to talk about in today's episode and tomorrow's episode.

So what I'm going to do is fill in the gap in the marketplace of these gaps not being discussed. You see what I did there? Point number one, today's topic once again is the gaps that nobody talks about. Number one, the discipline gap. Let me ask you a question. Is there a discipline gap in society? Any of you who's a successful professional in what you do? Let me ask you a question. Are there some people who started out at the same time as you and basically at the same level as you who are right now not at the same level as you and you have gone significantly further than they have? If the answer is yes, let me ask you a question. Is there a gap in your discipline and their discipline? Is there a gap between your ability, not ability, but your execution of showing up consistently to do your job versus their execution of showing up consistently to do their job?

Is there a gap between you and them? All of you are probably even laughing to yourself right now because you know that there is a gap, there has been a gap, there continues to be a gap and in the future there probably will continue to be a gap. And that discipline gap probably plays a role in the fact that you are where you are and some of your former peers are where they are. I mean they may still be your peers, but it doesn't even look like it anymore based on where you're at versus where they're at. Can we agree to this? You hear me mention every day when I open up this show showing up every single day to do the work, right? That's the first thing I mentioned when we talk about the work on your game philosophy, why? Because discipline is the most important aspect of everything.

Work on your game is about, I don't care if you're an athlete, entrepreneur, anywhere in between. How many people do you know? I'm talking to everyone now who wants to be successful, yet they don't have the ability to show up every day and just do the damn work. That is a foundational requirement of success. How many people do you know who just don't show up for whatever reason? This is not showing up, but they say they want to be successful. Being that you know so many people who fit this description and to be honest, listen, some of you listening to this might be one of these people. How many people do you think across the entire population of the world who also fit this description? How many people, maybe just in your industry who fit this description, probably millions of people, can we agree that showing up every day to do the work plays a huge role in somebody's outcomes and ultimately in their success or lack thereof?

Do we agree to that? Does anyone disagree with that? That showing up consistently to do the work plays a huge role in somebody's outcomes? Does anybody disagree with that? So since you agree, here's a follow-up question. Why does nobody ever talk about the discipline gap? Why don't you hear anybody talk about it? Why hasn't anybody written a book about the discipline gap? Oh, as a matter of fact, somebody did, I called it the third day, I wrote a whole book about it. You can get it for free by going to third day book.com, but that's, I'm kind of cheating there because I didn't write the book as, hey, here's the difference between one person and another. It kind of is because the subtitle literally says the decision that separates the pros from the amateur. So I kind of did talk about it that way, but the entire book is not framed around you versus other people.

The entire book is framed around you versus you. It's about you helping yourself. It's a self-help book because one of the principles over here working on your game, we got a lot of principles. One of 'em is that leaders look in the mirror, not out the window. So the book ain't really about you comparing yourself to other people. It's about you comparing yourself to yourself doing what you need to do. And if you do that consistently enough, eventually you'll be so far ahead of all those other people that it won't even matter what they're doing. That's what we do over here at work in your game world, not to say we can't look around and compete because competition is part of the game as well. Remember I come from the sports world, so competition will never go away and that will never be devalued here.

But the most important competition is you being better than yourself. You keep doing that consistently. Eventually the other people won't be competition because they ain't got the discipline to do what you're doing. Everybody follow? So why aren't there any Netflix specials about the discipline gap? Why is nobody pushing bills and laws through Congress about closing the discipline gap? But you got a bunch of people protesting about closing the wealth gap because they say, well this group should be given some reparations or they should write a check to every person of this group or this color in this place in order to make up for lost time or lost wealth or lost whatever. But nobody's saying, Hey, what do we do to close the gap about discipline? Just something for you to marinate as we move on. There's a simple answer to this because in order to close the discipline gap, people would actually have to take some accountability and do things personally.

So you close the wealth gap, theoretically you actually wouldn't. But theoretically you can close the wealth gap by just writing everybody a check. Alright, hand everybody a bunch of money. Now the wealth gap is closed now nobody can bring it up anymore. That technically is not going to close the wealth gap because wealth is not just giving people some cash, but this is the way that keeping it very simple, this is the way that people are thinking. See, to close the discipline gap, you can't just hand somebody something, they actually have to do something. And because humans will always be human, the discipline gap will never get closed. And what did I tell you? All the opportunities are opposite. So knowing that the discipline gap will never be closed because humans are always humans. Let me read between the lines for you. There will always be lazy people who will not show up and do the work regardless of how much resources they have available, regardless of how many opportunities are placed in front of them, regardless of their talent.

Therefore your opportunity will always be in being one who is willing to show up and do the work because there will always be so many people who won't. Everybody got it? Good. I will tell you a quick story I remember. I don't know if I had this in my notes for a later part of this series, but lemme see if I have it in here. It might be in a later part of the series'. If it is, then I'll hold it until later. But if it's not then maybe I'll just share it here. Let me see. I'm just looking to see if I've got it

And it's not there and it's not there.

And looking for one more. Okay, I don't think it's in here. So I know I have it in here somewhere. Maybe it's in a different episode that I'll be talking about it. But years ago I used to go to this basketball gym every single day not far from where I am, even to this very day. And it was where I recorded most of my YouTube basketball videos and the gym would often be empty. And the whole concept of the third day, speaking of such, came from the fact that a lot of ball players would often ask me, Dre, why are you always in an empty gym? How do you have that gym to yourself? Because it's not normal for a nice pristine, beautiful gym. Like the one I used to train in would be empty because usually there'd be a bunch of players in there practicing the same way that I was.

But the gym was often empty. And the whole concept of the third day was me explaining to people that the gym's empty, not because people don't know about it and not because I rented it out or that I own the gym and blocked people from coming in, but because people simply don't have the discipline to show up every day the way I do, which was true. And you had proof of it because you could see me in that gym every day empty. And one day there was every once in a while there'd be some striker who would come in. So there was this kid who came in there one time and he was about my size, but he was younger than me and he wanted to practice basketball. I asked him to play me in a game I was practicing by myself so often I welcomed the idea of playing somebody one-on-one just to make sure the stuff I was practicing actually worked, played by him.

And I said to him and he said to me, actually, how often do you come in here? And I usually would get that question after I worked out with somebody because they wanted to work out with me because they could see working out with me would help them get better. So he started asking, I could tell by the questions he was asking that he wanted to continue working out with me. And I found out a little bit about him. He's a young guy, he was from the neighborhood and he didn't have anything going on at that time. He wasn't playing basketball anywhere. He wasn't in school. He was going to go to school, but he wasn't in school at the time. He was a young guy, maybe 19, 20 and he didn't even have a job. So basically he had nothing going on in his life, which I'm not saying that as a knock against him.

I'm saying that as that was actually good for me because that meant he had no excuse to not come to the gym if he wanted to work out. So I said to him, look, I come to the gym every day at this time from this time to this time I'm at this gym. If you want to work out with me, alright, we can work out. But here's the thing, here's the time that I start. The time is over. You just told me you ain't got nothing else going on so you have no excuses. Make sure you're here one time every day and you can work out with me, but if you don't show up you can't work out with me anymore. And I told him that straight up from the beginning. This is the first day we just played one-on-one, I just met this kid. I said, if you don't show up then I don't know you anymore. Make sure you show up. So he showed up for about, let me ask y'all actually, before I even tell you the punchline here, how many days do you think this kid showed up to the gym?

Those of you who are not familiar with my basketball work from back in the day on YouTube, I put videos out on YouTube every single day for about 10 years straight. This was just basketball on, I still put videos on YouTube to this day, but back then it was 10 years straight, just basketball workouts and often there were times I was putting out 2, 3, 4 videos a day. I had so much content. I went to the gym Monday through Friday every single day. It was like a nine to five. Now I wasn't there from nine five, but I went to the gym every single day Monday through Friday, as long as the gym was open, as long as it wasn't a holiday, I was at the gym every single day and I told him, keep coming to the gym, you can work out with me.

How many days consecutively do you think he showed up before he broke the agreement that we had and he didn't show up? How many days do you think he lasted? That's the question. The answer is three days. This kid showed up for three days. We worked out three days in a row after that and we would do our drills and then we placed him and I got all the stuff on video and you can find the videos on YouTube. I didn't put his name in it or anything, I don't even remember his name. But when you see me playing somebody, one-on-one, he was a Latin Latin kid, bought my height and he didn't have a shirt on so he would work out with no shirt on. So if you can find those videos on

YouTube, that's him for three days and he stopped showing up and I didn't see him or hear from him for about two weeks.

I didn't hear from him, nothing happened. And then about two weeks later he came into the gym one day and I completely ignored him and he was on the court and he kind of dribbled past the court I was on I guess trying to get into my non vision to get my attention. I completely ignored him, acting like I didn't even see him there. I was like, I acted like he was a ghost and I just kept working out. I didn't talk to him and that day I completely ignored him, left the gym, said nothing to him, and the next day he didn't come back and I haven't seen him since and that's the discipline yet. Now this kid could have become, I mean I don't know if he was no serious, I don't know mentally what his makeup was as far as what he was going through with basketball, but if had he kept working out with me every day, he would've become a significantly better basketball player in about 90 days.

But he blew the opportunity. I told him, just keep showing up. You're good If you don't show up, we have a problem unless you reach out to me. I gave him my number too. Said, look, if you ain't going to make it, let me know if you got a problem or something like that. But I'm expecting you here every day. You ain't gotta call me. We ain't got to text. We ain't got to verify every day just what time the gym opens. I'm going to be here, just be here. He ain't showing up. And that was it. That's an example, just an example of the discipline gap. Point number two. Today we're talking about the gaps that no one talks about. And again, I'm going over several of 'em. It seems like a lot of people don't talk about these. Number two, the effort gap.

Effort gap and discipline gap are cousins. But let's talk specifically about this effort. One showing up is one thing. See it's one thing to just show up. It's another thing to actually give an effort to be successful. That's the next step. See, showing up means you're physically in the facility. Now what do you do once you get there? How many people do have ability, talent or desire to be successful? Maybe all three at least from what they say and probably damn near. Everybody has some level of ability. They have some type of talent and most people, at least if you listen to 'em talk, they want to be successful. Can we agree? Okay, probably. Damn everybody fits that description. So conversely, how many people do you know of all those people? How many of them actually give an effort that is commensurate with their alleged desires?

In other words, their effort aligns with their desires, they say they want to be successful. Do you see their actions reflecting someone who wants to be successful? Now that

155

number may be a lot smaller versus the number who actually say it, the number who actually do it, notice it not the same, right? Everybody sees where this is going. I kind of just told you there are plenty of people out there who have ability, opportunity and allegedly a desire to succeed, yet they don't do the damn work. Would you agree? And it was here that I was going to, I would've told you that basketball store had already told you, I told this kid, just be there every day and we're good. And when people would ask me again, how do you have this gym all to yourself all the time in Miami that you're working out, excuse me.

Because of this effort gap, because of the discipline gap and the effort gap. Again, this gym is not some mysterious hidden location. This is a big gym, but with big windows, it is in a prominent location. It's very easy to find. You could Google a basketball gym and this gym will come up on Google. It was a publicly owned facility, so we're not talking about some Equinox. It costs $200 a month. This is a publicly owned facility. You know how much the membership was to this gym that I was going to. It was $10 a month. Yeah, so literally one zero $10 a month, meaning anyone could get into this place and even if you didn't have a membership, you just wanted to use the gym that day. The buy-in fee to use the gym one time was like $3 1, 2, 3, $3. Anybody can get into this gym and everybody knew about it and I was the most known basketball person on YouTube for a good probably eight years before most other people started to jump in.

So everybody in Miami who had access to the internet, who played basketball, knew who I was. They knew where I was working out and they knew exactly where that facility was at. I was a very easy person to find. Anybody could have come into that gym. Yet 98% of the time I was in that gym working out. It was an empty effort gap. Nothing I'm telling you is an exaggeration. Everybody in Miami knows where that gym is to this day. Effort gap. That's the difference. And again, I told this kid I didn't even practice with other people. One of the reasons why that gym was empty and I never went and took the initiative to get somebody else to come to the gym with me. I could have and went and found somebody to come work out with me. I knew a lot of ballplayers in Miami.

I could have easily told somebody, Hey, come to the gym. This is where I work out every day. I could have easily told someone or invited someone or asked someone to come work out with me. I never did because I didn't really like working out with other people. Honestly, I was never a big fan of bringing other people into my workouts. I liked working out by myself, but when he came around and he showed interest, I said, okay, I'll use this guy as a practice dummy. That's what I was going to do. I was using him as a practice dummy to basically use him to work on the stuff that I would do by myself.

Now I could just use a human. He was like a crash test dummy that I would use to work on my game and I figured that my audience also, because a lot of ballplayers who were watching me on YouTube, they would often say, well Dre, I see you doing this stuff by yourself, but it'd be interesting to see you execute these same drills against a live human being because I want to see what it looks like when there's some actual resistance going up against you.

And I said, okay, that's a great idea. All of these things went through my mind when this kid came around to the gym, so I figured I would use him. I said, just show up every day. He couldn't show up every day. Sometimes it's just the simplest parameter that will eliminate people. All you gotta do is show up every day and that's it. Again, he didn't last a week. These days basketball's over. I don't play basketball anymore. I go to a boxing gym a few times a week. I'm just at the gym today and I'm recording this in early January. Anybody knows anything about the fitness world, especially if you're in the gym space, you go to gyms or you ever owned a gym or worked at a gym. January is the most popping off time of the year for a gym because everybody has allegedly made some New Year's resolutions to get in shape.

So everybody's at the gym working out for some reason. I don't know what's going on. There's something in the water down here or maybe in the world period. But the gym's been pretty quiet. I'm recording this in January. The gym was pretty quiet. It doesn't look that much different from December. The gym that I go to now, I don't know if other gyms are different now. Sometimes in my building there's a building, there's a gym in my building and sometimes when I walk past that gym in the evenings when I'm taking my son on the walk, I see a good number of people in there, but I don't know if it's that much different than the number of people who were in there in December. I don't go to the gym during peak hours when there's a bunch of people in there. I like going during off peak hours, but again, even during off peak hours in December, it looks the same as it looks now.

I would expect there to be more people in some new faces, but I actually see fewer faces. And again, the same thing happens in the gym. Any of you who go to a gym, you go to the gym consistently on the same days, at the same times you start to notice the same faces. Even people, you don't even know them. You don't even know their names, but you know their faces because you see 'em at the gym same days, same times all the time, right? Same thing in this boxing gym. I notice the same faces and their consistent faces who I see again all the time, but these people are not as consistent as I am and I'm not even trying to become a professional boxer. I mean, I was and was aiming to remain a professional basketball player in my basketball days. So it made sense. My consistency.

I'm not trying to become a pro boxer, but I'm more consistent coming to the gym than some of these people who claim that they want to box. These are people who want to be pro boxers, amateur boxers and amateur boxing is not the same as amateur basketball as a whole. There's a whole different realm of the way things work in boxing as opposed to basketball. I have no intentions of getting into a ring for an official fight with anybody yet I still come to the gym more consistently. Some of the people who claim that that's what they want to do, and I've talked to these people. They told me that they want to be boxers or they want to get into amateur boxing or they want to get into inboxing. They have this thing for different age groups and my trainer was telling me about it. He's been trying to encourage me to maybe get involved in it.

I don't think that's going to happen. Never say never, but I don't think it's going to happen. But he's like, there's a group where over 40 men can fight and there's championships and all this stuff and you can do local and then there's regional and then there's national. There's a whole national competition for this. Let's say a man who's over the age of 50 and he's 160 pounds, there's a championship belt for that in boxing. I have no desire to achieve any, no glory, sports glory at this point. I did what I needed to do in sports. I just like to stay in shape. I like to be in professional athlete shape and boxing just happens to be my vehicle for doing that right now. I have no aspirations for doing anything in boxing. Again, I don't have anything to prove as an athlete at this point.

The whole point being, I'm sharing all that to say this. There are people who do have something they want to prove as an athlete, and these mofos don't show up to the gym as consistently as I do. That's the point that I'm making here. This is the effort and the discipline gap that I'm talking about. So the ability to show up and actually give a damn effort is so lacking in society these days that this gap needs to be explored a lot more than it gets explored. Nobody talks about this. Everybody wants to talk about these gaps and outcomes. Nobody wants to talk about the gaps in inputs. Why doesn't anybody talk about this? Well, we know there are reasons people don't talk about this because it means holding people accountable for their own actions and lack of actions, which again, your favorite politician or influencer is not going to gain a lot of fans by doing that. But again, my job ain't to gain a lot of fans just amongst average people because I don't want no average people in my audience. Average people probably couldn't afford me anyway. I'm looking for people who want to do the work and they're serious about going to their highest level. So if that's you, keep listening. Point number three, today's topic. Once again, we are talking about the gaps that nobody talks about. Number three, the implementation gap.

Implementation gap. Now I talked about this recently in the episode where I talked about why you should take in less material, not more material just a few days ago. And the definition of implementation is a process of putting a decision or plan into effect, also known as executions. So you can also call this the execution gap. Just because you are consuming material, whether it's free material or paid material or you're going to events, you're talking to other people or anything else you do to get access to information, ideas for things that you could do does not mean you will actually implement any of it or put any of it to good use. Just because you have access to something doesn't mean you're going to use it. That's the implementation gap. How many people do you know who buy books, attend events, sign up for webinars, sign up for free challenges, even join coaching programs, but don't implement any of the stuff that they get access to?

How many people who fit that description, they got access but they don't do shit with it? Alright? There's a gym in the building that I live in. If you live here, the gym comes as it comes with the fact that you pay whatever you pay to live here. There's still people out of shape living here. They don't use the gym. They don't implement the thing that they have direct access to. You know how many ball players I talked to over the years when I was playing ball basketball? Who would tell me, Dre man, I just don't have access to a gym or a court. The closest court is two miles away and my parents won't drive or they won't let me, et cetera, et cetera. So many people I would hear tell that story and who knows if they were telling me the truth or not.

I was just taking 'em at their word. But there were many people I know who live here in Miami where there are parks everywhere in Miami. Miami has more parks per square footage than any city I've ever lived in or the Florida period. Just all of south Florida. So I don't care if you're talking about Boca Raton, Naples, Miami, Fort Lauderdale, Tampa Bay, Tampa, the city, Clearwater, they're all part of Tampa Bay. I've lived and spent time in these places. There are parks everywhere in Florida. You can't walk a mile in Florida and not come across a park where there's grass, there's a basketball court, there's parks everywhere out here. I don't know about where any of you live, but now here in Florida, there are parks everywhere and there's still out of shape people in Miami and just Florida period, not just Miami, Florida, period.

There's places to work out everywhere, alright? That's not the problem. The problem is implementation folks do not have access. A lot of people complain of lack of access and some of you may be actually are dealing with a real lack of access, but down here ain't no lack of access and most of you who are listening to this right now, you have access to a, you have a data connection, you got wifi for the most part, 99% of you, I don't want to hear that shit. I don't want to hear that shit. You don't have an access issue, you have an implementation issue, you have an effort issue, you have a discipline issue. That's your real problem. Most people don't implement the material that they have access to and I know for a fact that many people do not implement most of the stuff they get access to whether they got it for free or even if they paid for it.

I told you, I go to conferences, I ask people who I meet at conferences, I go to conferences, I talk to damn near everybody. Anybody that approaches me at a conference, I'll talk to 'em. I'll stand in a lobby at conferences and just wait for somebody to approach me and just converse with people. I stood in the lobby all day. I was still in the lobby for hours talking to people when I go to conferences because I go there to meet people. That's the reason why I go and I'll ask fellow attendees, alright, you came to this conference, what are you going to do now that you came to the conference? What are you going to do differently based on what you learned or heard or got inspired by At this conference? 99% of the time when people answer that question, they tell me they're going to do something that they already knew they needed to do before they came to the conference that they still would've needed to do.

Whether they had come to the conference or not. So a person. Last conference I was, I was speaking to this woman, I said, what are you going to do now if you came to this conference? She said, well, I got to finish writing my book. Said, how long have you been writing the book? How long have you been working on the book? She said, I've been working on it for like two years now. Alright, so she didn't need to come to the conference and know she needed to finish writing that book. Now maybe what she learned at the conference or what she heard got her energized and inspired to finish the book. Maybe that's what it did and hopefully it did and hopefully she finished the damn book. The whole point being what stopped her from implementing before she came to the conference. Nothing. That's the whole point.

People simply don't get things done. You come to work with me, we are not taking two years to write a book. I don't care what you're writing about. Let's try for two months. We implement here, we get things done. If that sounds like you, then you need to be scrolling down to underneath, wherever you're listening to this and clicking on that link for work on your game university.com or just simply typing it into your browser. Work on your game university.com and let's get it going. Alright, so somebody will tell me something like, well I need to finish this book I started three years ago. This is at conferences. When I'm talking to fellow attendees once on a website that they've been working on, it is rarely that they're going to go do something that they just heard 30 minutes ago. That's not usually the thing people say they're going to do. You know that most books they get bought don't get read past the first chapter. Most courses that get purchased do not get consumed past module two and a lot of courses are like 6, 7, 8, 9, 12 modules. This gap plays a big role in the outcome differences between people. Point number four, I'm deciding if I'm going to put this into a separate episode. Lemme see what I got here.

Yeah, what we're going to do is we're going to make this into a, actually instead of a two part series, we'll make this into a three part series. So tomorrow we'll pick up on point number four. So let me recap what we got here today. So we're talking to gaps that nobody ever talks about and again, you hear people talk about things like the wealth gap and the income gap and the outcomes. People are talking about the outcomes. So let's talk about the inputs. That's what I'm talking about here. Number one, the discipline gap, showing up every single day to do the work. How many people do you know who want to be successful yet they don't show up? Exactly. Point number two, the effort gap. How many people show up but they don't do shit? They don't actually put the effort in, they don't actually do the work.

Alright, I'm going to a boxing gym. I'm not trying to be a boxer at all on any level. I meet people at the boxing gym who say they want to be boxers and I'm in the gym more consistently than they are. Alright? This is the effort gap. And number three, the implementation gap. How many people get access to information, access to stuff, buy books, sign up for webinars, sign up for free challenges, courses, et cetera, and then they don't even implement the stuff that they got the access to. How many people got a bookshelf of books and they ain't even read the damn books? Alright, this is the implementation gap and all of these are within your human control. It has nothing to do with your ancestors, the past, what anybody else is doing, the government, anything like that. All of you have access to all three of these.

You can do them whenever you want. This is a matter of you deciding that you're going to move yourself to these actions. If you have challenges with these, that's completely fine. It just makes you human, but it is not completely fine to not do anything about it.

#2833: The Inequality "Gaps" That No One Talks About [Part 3 of 3]

Let's get into the show, which is how to create your blue ocean. So first of all, let's get clear on what a blue ocean is. For those of you not familiar with what it is, then I'll explain how to create it. There is a book out there called the Blue Ocean Strategy, which if you have not read it, you already know what to do. If you hear me mention a book on the show, you need to go buy it and you need to read it and you should probably read it more than once. And if you are an entrepreneur or a marketer, the concept of a blue ocean first starts with the understanding of a red ocean. A red ocean is, and I'm going to give you an analogy here so you can understand it.

It's like an ocean that has a lot of fish and fish need to eat, fish get hungry, but the ocean becomes red because there's not enough food for all the fish to eat. So hence what happens is the fish start attacking each other so they can basically win. They're competing for the little bit of food that's available because there's more mouths to feed than there is food. So they start attacking each other and they start bleeding when they start attacking each other. Therefore, you got a lot of blood in the water. That's the red ocean. There's the ocean with a bunch of blood in it because there are too many mouths to feed and not enough food. A blue ocean conversely is an ocean where there is plenty of food to feed all the fish who are there and hungry and looking for food. So the blue ocean strategy means you can still be within the crowded ocean and there's a reason you want to be within it.

I'll explain that in my points. And then you carve out a space that is distinctively for and about you so that within that red ocean you have an oasis that's only for you and there's plenty of food for just you to eat, hence the ocean remains blue. In other words, there's in that ocean that none of the other fish is trying to eat and only you're eating it so you're not competing with anybody because nobody else is trying to eat the food that you're eating. It's food that's specifically for you. So again, do not take this simplified explanation of the blue ocean strategy to be a substitute for you reading the actual book and don't even take this entire episode to be a substitute for you reading a book. If I mention a book here, go get it and read it. If you're serious about your craft, I shouldn't even have to tell you that.

Now, getting into these points today, once again is how to create your blue ocean. Point number one, find a space where activity is already happening. Yes, you heard me correctly. This is the part of the blue ocean strategy that people don't quite understand. I'm going to explain it here today. When you are creating a blue ocean folks, a blue ocean does not mean you go to a place where there is no competition and there are no other fish trying to eat. Don't do that. You don't want to do that. You want to go to a place where there are other fish where they are actively eating. You want to go where there is competition. See, some people think they want to go somewhere where there's no competition whatsoever so they can completely dominate that space and not have anyone to compete against. Lemme tell you why this is a bad idea.

That will generally put you out of business relatively quickly if there is no competition in your market, meaning there are no other businesses trying to sell the same thing that you're selling. You know what that also means? That means that there are also no customers. See, when you step into a space and there are no other companies selling anything similar to what you're selling, that also means there are no buyers buying what you're selling because if there were buyers, there will be sellers and there are sellers. That means there are buyers. So if you go somewhere, there are no sellers. That means by definition there will also be no buyers. Everybody understands this. Now, some of you may be thinking, you may be thinking a step ahead of me. You're clever, you said, oh well Dre, I'll go to a place where there are no sellers and I will create my space and I will attract the buyers.

To me that sounds like a great idea. Lemme tell you why. That's also not the best idea. It is not an impossible idea, but it's not the best idea because if you go to a place and you try to create a market that does not currently exist, you know what's going to happen. You are probably not smarter than the last 200 years of humanity, which means you're coming up with an idea that is not brand new. It has been tried, it has proven that it doesn't produce money, which is why nobody else is doing it. It's not that you're the first one to come up with it. I'm going to make the guess that you're not smarter in the last 200 years of humanity than in the last 200 years of selling and marketing. Now if I'm wrong, then you are free to go and prove me wrong and then you should start your own show and explain why I was wrong.

What I mean by this is when there is a market, that means there are people who are already spending money for the thing that you're doing and that means someone already thought of it and someone is already doing it. And again, they may not be doing the exact way that you're going to do it and hopefully not as well as you can do it, but they have already cracked the code of showing the world that there is something that you would want to spend money on and it's this thing over here. You want to step into that space and then you're going to do what I'm going to tell you in points number two and three in order to carve out the space that is specifically for you. But the point here in point number one is to make sure you understand this, never step into a market that does not already exist.

Because what you would need to do if you did that is create a market from scratch, which can be extremely time consuming and very financially consuming. It can cost you a lot of money and time to create a market from scratch because what you would need to do is educate the world as to why they need to do the thing that you are asking them to do, not just that they can do it with you. Let's say if someone wanted to hire someone wanted to sign up for a gym, alright? Most people already understand the concept of having a gym membership. They understand what happens in a gym and they understand generally what they would do if they were to go to a gym. Almost everyone listening to this understands the concept, even if you are not currently a customer or a client of a gym, but everybody understands how it works.

Now, if you were to create a brand new market for something that does not currently exist, the first thing you would have to do is get the world to understand and accept the thing that you are about to sell before they buy it. You got to get them to understand it. Then you got to get them to appreciate its value and then you got to get them to accept that they probably need it. Then you can make money. Now, how much of your resources would it take for you to get all those three things in understanding, appreciation and exception? Those cost a lot of time and they cost a lot of money. When we think of an industry that is relatively new that did something like this in order to get people to understand, appreciate and accept the market. So let's think about the bottled water industry.

Those of you who remember, maybe we go back to maybe the nineties, 1990s, around that time before that, up to that point, if someone wanted to drink water, generally what you did was you just turned on the faucet in your kitchen and you poured the water into the glass and you drank it. That was pretty much it. Now, there were some people, it wasn't widespread, but there were a good amount of people who would get water filters and they would filter their water. So you would pour the water into a pitcher and the pitcher would have a filter on it or you could put a filter onto the spout in your sink, your kitchen sink, and they would filter the water so that you were drinking filtered water instead of just regular, excuse me, tap water. Now, that was the start of the bottled water industries.

The bottled water industry's grand plan was to get people to understand they had to break your false belief. Your false belief was it's okay to drink water out of the tap. There's nothing wrong with it. They had to break that false belief and install a new belief that drinking water out of tap was very harmful to you. It could kill you, it would destroy your brain cells, it would make you sick, it'll kill your kids, et cetera, et cetera. They had to take time and they had to spend a lot of money to get people to understand, appreciate and accept that. Once people accepted that, then they were able to take them to the next step, which is okay, now you got to do something about that. Tap water. Here's a filter. Or here you can buy bottled water. Water's already in a bottle. It comes from a Poland spring.

It comes from some place where it had deers and mountains and that's all bullshit. It's really just municipal tap water. That's what it is. It's tap water. They just put it in a bottle and give it a fancy name. It makes, it sounds like it comes from some far away place and you spend money on it. That's really what the bottled water industry is. It is a great mental psyche of what the bottled water industry is, and you're drinking water out of plastic, which is probably just as if not more harmful than drinking water out of a kitchen faucet. But anyway, different conversation for a different day. But what they did was they basically hoodwinked people mentally into thinking that you're doing something healthy by drinking water out of a damn plastic bottle that's disintegrating every minute that the water is disintegrating the plastic, but again, different conversation for a different day.

What the bottled water industry did successfully was teach people that drinking water out of a tap was a bad idea and thus, you needed an alternative and then they happen to be the ones providing the alternative, which is buying water out of bottles. What I suggest you do today, if you don't want to drink tap water, that's fine. You need to get yourself an AquaTru water filter, which costs less than bottled water because you don't have to keep buying cases. It produces a lot less waste. So you're not throwing plastic bottles away all the time or putting 'em into recycling bins and they don't even get recycled most of the time. You have one filter, one water filter machine. You pour tap water into it, it produces a clean filter, purified water, and there's no waste. How about that? So you can get your AquaTru water filter.

There's a link down below in the description. They're one of the sponsors of Work on Your game, so just go to work on your game.com/at what stands for true work on your game.com/at stands for AquaTru. That is not a, I didn't even plan on it, it just happens to be something I'm talking about at this point. So that's one way you can create a brand new market, but you need to understand the bottled water industry spent millions of dollars and many years teaching people like you and me to believe that there was something wrong with tap water. Now, personally, I don't actually believe there's anything wrong with tap water even though I'm an AquaTru water filter user. If I had to drink tap water all day, I would be completely fine and I would do it and I wouldn't think twice about it. Many people don't think that way because the bottled water industry successfully taught people that there is something wrong with the water coming out of the tap and depending on where you live, it can be, there can be something wrong with the water coming out of the tap.

So let me make sure I add that in. Give you another example of a company that had to create a new market. Think of the smartphone. So Apple pioneered the smartphone and what they did was a little bit different than the bottled water industry because they weren't really creating a brand new thing out of nothing. They weren't just taking an idea and saying, don't do that, do this. They were taking something that we had already accepted and they just expanded upon it. So we already had the idea of mobile phones at the time that the iPhone came out. We were all very familiar with the mobile phone because you had a bunch of phones that had been out that were becoming more high tech. So the first regular cell phones people had you look at, let's say the mid to late nineties and going into the early two thousands, we had cell phones that did text messages and phone calls For the most part, all of us had access to a phone that could do that and the iPhone did have that, but what the iPhone also did was combine the iPod, which was a pocket sized MP three player that could hold thousands of songs on it.

It took the iPod, which we had accepted was a great idea, great breakthrough, and Apple had to spend a lot of money on marketing and teaching the world that they should want one of these things because it wasn't a common thing at the time. It was an MP three player that wasn't the first ever, but they pioneered it and they dominated that market. Then they took the computer, the web browser that we all were familiar with, but we were used to using computers on a desktop. You had to be sitting down in a seat or maybe if you had a laptop, but it was a big bulky, no book size or bigger device that you could get on the internet with. All Steve Jobs did was, and I say all as if it was very simple, but all he did was take these three concepts, a cell phone, an mp, three player, and a web browser.

He combined them all into one device and any of you who is not familiar with your marketing history, any of you who's in a marketing world, you should know your marketing history. You should go online, go to YouTube and look up the presentation. When Steve Jobs introduced the iPhone, it was a legendary marketing presentation, one of the most legendary presentations in the history of marketing. You should know about it if you're in the marketing space because you need to know the history of where things come from, especially those of you who have iPhones. How do you not even know the presentation when he introduced the iPhone? You need to know about it because the way he presented it, Steve Jobs did what I tell you all great experts in their field do. He simplified and clarified what that device was and made it easy for even a fifth grader to understand what it was.

By again, he repeated over and over again a web browser, an MP, three players and a phone, and it's again, a legendary presentation. So go look that thing up on YouTube. If you have not seen it yet or before, even if you've seen it before, go look it up again and watch it again. The whole point is you don't want to be stepping into a market where the market does not already exist unless you happen to have the genius of Steve Jobs and the resources of a company like Apple. If you don't have that, you don't want to do this. See, in that case, again, you're creating a market from scratch and you may not have the resources or the time, time being one of your resources to do that, to educate the world on why they should want that thing. Now, every once in a while this can work and you hit the lottery, you introduce something brand new to the world, they realize that they want it, and you can dominate that market as if you were the first one to market.

But often, the first one to market is the person with all the arrows in their back and they die because they take all the bullets trying to teach something new to the world and the world does not want to hear it, and then everybody else comes on the back end. They make all the money, so you don't want to be the first one. There's an entire graveyard of entrepreneurs who thought they were going to create a brand new market that did not already exist and they all were wrong. So when you walk past the cemetery, the entrepreneurship cemetery, you are stepping over their bones, their scouts, their fossils because they're dead, because they died trying to prove it. Alright, so get rich or die trying. Most of 'em died, alright? They didn't get rich, they died trying, alright? You don't want to be that person who steps into a market that already exists.

Point number two, today's topic once again is how to create your blue ocean for your business. Number two, identify what is happening in that ocean that you can from. In other words, what makes you different and unique and new compared to what already exists in the current red ocean. So when you step in a red ocean before the other fish start killing you because they want to stop you from getting to the food, ask yourself, what can you do in this market that is different from what everybody else is doing so that you are not participating in the bloodbath of fish killing each other in the red ocean? This is where you had to differentiate yourself, and there are two ways to go about this and you can do this from opposite ends. One way is to look at yourself and simply decide what you are going to do differently than what already exists.

All right, here's what everybody else is already doing. Why? Why don't I just do it this way? The other way is to look at what already exists and figure out what they don't have or what they are not doing that you do have or that you can do or what they are doing that you will not do either. One, how are you going to differ by looking at them as opposed to looking at you This way is sometimes easier because then you're not creating your idea from scratch. See, if you're stepping into the red ocean and trying to create an idea from scratch, you're just going to decide, okay, I'm just going to come up with something and it's going to be different from what everybody else is doing. This is harder than doing it the other way. The other way is when you say, all right, here's what everybody else is doing.

Let me find the cracks in their process. Let me find the holes in there, their walls. Let me find the fly in the ointment and figure out how I can improve on what they are missing. What are they not doing that I can do? What do the customers want from them that they're not getting that I can actually provide? So I'll be an improvement on them knowing that people already want this because the customers have already made it clear that they want it. See, this is just simple market research. Look at what already exists and you are simply finding and filling the available empty spaces. Again, you can look at what people are already doing and just find what they're missing, find the holes in their processes. This is your opportunity. Either way, you have to identify what will make you different from what already exists.

And again, this must be a true differentiator. It can't be something so simple and basic that your competition is just looking at what you're offering and adding it to their own mix tomorrow morning. So if they can just look at it and see what you're doing and say, all right, we'll go do that, then it's over. You don't really have a differentiator. And these two literally are different. So if any of you watch Shark Tank and if you're an entrepreneur, you should watch Shark Tank. It's a very informative show when it comes to entrepreneurship and business in general from the people knowing their numbers to the questions that investors want to ask of you if they're interested in investing in your business to how people present their businesses to people just explaining their business models. So a lot of things you can learn from it and be entertained at the same time.

So on the Shark Tank TV show, often what happens is someone will come in there with a product, especially when they have some type of food product. This happens often with food products. There's one of the sharks named Kevin O'Leary, also known as Mr Wonderful. He's created and sold several businesses how he made his money, and I believe he created and sold a company called The Learning Company, and that was one of the ways that he got his start as far as being a millionaire entrepreneur, and whenever someone comes with a food product, he's often the one who says something like, and actually he does this with smaller products than anything retail based is really his thing. Anything that's a retail product, whether it's food, a widget, a toy, something like that. He says, some people over in China or some of the big supermarkets if you have food, he says some supermarket companies because the margins there are razor thin.

The margins are like one or 2% in the supermarket. Those of you don't know what that means. Margin simply means how much money is left over after you sell and then you pay for the fulfillment of the sale and the margin being 1%. Meaning if you sell a product for $100, the money that you actually take home in your pocket is $1, which is 1% of $100. That's the kind of margins you have in the supermarket space, and he's not exaggerating. That's the real number. The margins in the supermarket space are like 1%. So you sell a hundred dollars worth of product, you actually take home literally $1, and he explains that and he'll say that about retail space and stuff like that as well. He says, some company that's watching this on TV right now is going to just knock off your product. In other words, they're going to make a cheap copy of your same product and they're going to put you out of business.

They'll completely crush the cockroach that you are. That's the phrase that he used. He uses that phrase all the time. So if you watch Shark Tank, you'll hear him say that oftentimes the whole point being your true differentiator needs to be a true differentiator, not just you saying that you're different just because you believe it. Nobody cares what you believe. Can you prove that you're different? Can you be different in such a way that someone can look at your product and they can't copy it even though they see exactly what it is and they know you're succeeding with it? Can you do that? If not, then you're not truly differentiated. So it needs to literally be different. So for example, what I do, let me backup. I've lost my place here in my notes. For example, What I do here as a coach, even here on this show, is based on the fact that I am a professional athlete, I'm willing to talk about subjects that many people are unwilling to talk about, and I like to look at the things as objectively and straight up and down as possibly objectively and logically as possible.

Now, while none of the things that I just said is necessarily a breakthrough idea, the combination of all of them makes me unique because there are so few people who are either A, capable or B, willing to do that, not all of them all together. There are some people who have some of those, but not many people have all of 'em. So even though I'm openly telling you what differentiates me, I have little competition because how many people do you know can and will do it? Not many. How many do you know will talk about the things that I talk about in the way that I talk about them? Not many, at least not publicly. They won't do it, very few.

So when I say a true differentiator need not be some secret formula, like the formula for Coca-Cola, but it does need to be something that cannot be easily duplicated or copied. It needs to actually be unique, truly unique, so that again, even if people can see it, they can't do anything to copy it. Point number three, today's topic once again is how to create your own blue ocean for your marketing and business. Three, make your marketing focus on emphasizing the difference and making sure everyone understands that difference must remember what marketing is, is the relationship you have with your public, whether it be people who already know you, people who just got to know you, and people who don't know you at all. One of the reasons that I put this show out as often as I do every single day, it's part of my marketing mix that I put on every day.

Any subject you could possibly ask me about, I have probably done an episode on that subject. So every day I'm giving myself another opportunity to do what, to get myself seen, heard, and known by someone who otherwise may not have known about me, and to reinforce the idea of who I am and what I'm about with people who have heard of me before. So I'm just continuing to market this. Part of my marketing mix is to give you this show on a daily basis. That doesn't mean you have to have a show that comes out every day. You want to do once a week, do once a week, whatever it is you want to do, but it needs to fit what you're trying to do marketing wise and business wise. So every day, because my unique ability is my approach, not necessarily the subject matter, I'm giving my unique ability more exposure to more people because my approach is the unique ability.

It's not the topic because you notice that I'll jump around on this show from a marketing topic to a mindset topic to some social issue, to who knows what else. I'll talk about anything in between, but it's not always the same topic as far as industry and line of work. One day I might talk about publishing books and the next day I might talk about courses. Next day I'm talking about coaching. They are all under the umbrella of business, but there are different aspects to business. My approach that makes me unique is not the subject matter itself, even though I am pretty damn good at the subject matter. So even if you skip around on this show, let's say you just turn to the feed, you just skip around in different episodes and you pick and choose which ones to listen to. My unique ability is the same regardless of the subject.

That's the key. This is why I use other social media applications. When I get on an app like X, formerly known as Twitter, I do the same thing there that I do here on the show just in a different format and it gets a different kind of response because it's a different format. I respond to other people's posts there. I ask questions all for pushback. I objectively challenge things that I see other people posting. Same stuff that I do here. I just do it in a different way and with people who I don't even know and who don't know me, but I'm exposing my unique ability in the exact same way and the people who want it come further, deeper into my world. And the people who don't want it, they go the opposite direction. This is how it works. There's just different formats for doing it, but I know what makes me unique.

I know what the unique ability is and the more I emphasize it, the better I do. Simple how it works. All that said, let's recap today's class, which is how to create your blue ocean in business. First, getting clear on what the blue ocean is, is a space that you occupy within a red ocean where the food is only for you and you are not in a blood bath against all the other fish for limited resources. Number one, find a space where activity is already happening. Yes, you want to go where there is already business taking place because that means there are buyers. If there are no buyers, that's the reason why there are no sellers. And if there are no sellers, that means there are no buyers. You don't want to get into that space unless you have the

Time and the money to invest in educating the public as to why they want your thing. And most entrepreneurs who I know, you're probably not in that space. Number two, identify what is happening that you can diverge from. What can you do that makes you different from everybody else out there? Either figure out what you already bring is different or look at what everybody else is doing and see what they are missing that you can bring to the table. Number three, make your marketing focus on emphasizing this difference and making sure everyone understands this difference. So believing that you are different is one thing. Getting other people to understand and believe that you're different is a whole other thing. So one of the reasons I put the show out consistently is so people can get exposed to it and they can experience my unique ability and my unique ability.

Again, there is no fluff, straight to the point. Brass tacks, no bs, no dancing around topics and being willing to talk about things that a lot of people are not willing to talk about. Again, people can see that and they know it, but they can't duplicate it and they can't beat me at it because I'm doing things that they won't do, and this is a way that you create your blue ocean out of the way. Folks, make sure you're text me to get my text community, my numbers down below the description and work on your game university. That is the place where I do all my coaching. If you had to be coached on me directly, you want to help me find your blue ocean and your space so that you don't feel like you're competing against everybody. You don't feel like you're just putting stuff out there and nobody's paying attention. It is not bringing you the revenue or the attention or the eyeballs that you want.

#2834: How To Create Your "Blue Ocean" In Business

Let's get into the show, which is how to create your blue ocean. So first of all, let's get clear on what a blue ocean is. For those of you not familiar with what it is, then I'll explain how to create it. There is a book out there called the Blue Ocean Strategy, which if you have not read it, you already know what to do. If you hear me mention a book on the show, you need to go buy it and you need to read it and you should probably read it more than once. And if you are an entrepreneur or a marketer, the concept of a blue ocean first starts with the understanding of a red ocean. A red ocean is, and I'm going to give you an analogy here so you can understand it.

It's like an ocean that has a lot of fish and fish need to eat, fish get hungry, but the ocean becomes red because there's not enough food for all the fish to eat. So hence what happens is the fish start attacking each other so they can basically win. They're competing for the little bit of food that's available because there's more mouths to feed than there is food. So they start attacking each other and they start bleeding when they start attacking each other. Therefore, you got a lot of blood in the water. That's the red ocean. There's the ocean with a bunch of blood in it because there are too many mouths to feed and not enough food. A blue ocean conversely is an ocean where there is plenty of food to feed all the fish who are there and hungry and looking for food. So the blue ocean strategy means you can still be within the crowded ocean and there's a reason you want to be within it.

I'll explain that in my points. And then you carve out a space that is distinctively for and about you so that within that red ocean you have an oasis that's only for you and there's plenty of food for just you to eat, hence the ocean remains blue. In other words, there's in that ocean that none of the other fish is trying to eat and only you're eating it so you're not competing with anybody because nobody else is trying to eat the food that you're eating. It's food that's specifically for you. So again, do not take this simplified explanation of the blue ocean strategy to be a substitute for you reading the actual book and don't even take this entire episode to be a substitute for you reading a book. If I mention a book here, go get it and read it. If you're serious about your craft, I shouldn't even have to tell you that.

Now, getting into these points today, once again is how to create your blue ocean. Point number one, find a space where activity is already happening. Yes, you heard me correctly. This is the part of the blue ocean strategy that people don't quite understand.

I'm going to explain it here today. When you are creating a blue ocean folks, a blue ocean does not mean you go to a place where there is no competition and there are no other fish trying to eat. Don't do that. You don't want to do that. You want to go to a place where there are other fish where they are actively eating. You want to go where there is competition. See, some people think they want to go somewhere where there's no competition whatsoever so they can completely dominate that space and not have anyone to compete against. Lemme tell you why this is a bad idea.

That will generally put you out of business relatively quickly if there is no competition in your market, meaning there are no other businesses trying to sell the same thing that you're selling. You know what that also means? That means that there are also no customers. See, when you step into a space and there are no other companies selling anything similar to what you're selling, that also means there are no buyers buying what you're selling because if there were buyers, there will be sellers and there are sellers. That means there are buyers. So if you go somewhere, there are no sellers. That means by definition there will also be no buyers. Everybody understands this. Now, some of you may be thinking, you may be thinking a step ahead of me. You're clever, you said, oh well Dre, I'll go to a place where there are no sellers and I will create my space and I will attract the buyers.

To me that sounds like a great idea. Lemme tell you why. That's also not the best idea. It is not an impossible idea, but it's not the best idea because if you go to a place and you try to create a market that does not currently exist, you know what's going to happen. You are probably not smarter than the last 200 years of humanity, which means you're coming up with an idea that is not brand new. It has been tried, it has proven that it doesn't produce money, which is why nobody else is doing it. It's not that you're the first one to come up with it. I'm going to make the guess that you're not smarter in the last 200 years of humanity than in the last 200 years of selling and marketing. Now if I'm wrong, then you are free to go and prove me wrong and then you should start your own show and explain why I was wrong.

What I mean by this is when there is a market, that means there are people who are already spending money for the thing that you're doing and that means someone already thought of it and someone is already doing it. And again, they may not be doing the exact way that you're going to do it and hopefully not as well as you can do it, but they have already cracked the code of showing the world that there is something that you would want to spend money on and it's this thing over here. You want to step into that space and then you're going to do what I'm going to tell you in points number two and three in order to carve out the space that is specifically for you. But the point here in point number one is to make sure you understand this, never step into a market that does not already exist.

Because what you would need to do if you did that is create a market from scratch, which can be extremely time consuming and very financially consuming. It can cost you a lot of money and time to create a market from scratch because what you would need to do is educate the world as to why they need to do the thing that you are asking them to do, not just that they can do it with you. Let's say if someone wanted to hire someone wanted to sign up for a gym, alright? Most people already understand the concept of having a gym membership. They understand what happens in a gym and they understand generally what they would do if they were to go to a gym. Almost everyone listening to this understands the concept, even if you are not currently a customer or a client of a gym, but everybody understands how it works.

Now, if you were to create a brand new market for something that does not currently exist, the first thing you would have to do is get the world to understand and accept the thing that you are about to sell before they buy it. You got to get them to understand it. Then you got to get them to appreciate its value and then you got to get them to accept that they probably need it. Then you can make money. Now, how much of your resources would it take for you to get all those three things in understanding, appreciation and exception? Those cost a lot of time and they cost a lot of money. When we think of an industry that is relatively new that did something like this in order to get people to understand, appreciate and accept the market. So let's think about the bottled water industry.

Those of you who remember, maybe we go back to maybe the nineties, 1990s, around that time before that, up to that point, if someone wanted to drink water, generally what you did was you just turned on the faucet in your kitchen and you poured the water into the glass and you drank it. That was pretty much it. Now, there were some people, it wasn't widespread, but there were a good amount of people who would get water filters and they would filter their water. So you would pour the water into a pitcher and the pitcher would have a filter on it or you could put a filter onto the spout in your sink, your kitchen sink, and they would filter the water so that you were drinking filtered water instead of just regular, excuse me, tap water. Now, that was the start of the bottled water industries.

The bottled water industry's grand plan was to get people to understand they had to break your false belief. Your false belief was it's okay to drink water out of the tap. There's nothing wrong with it. They had to break that false belief and install a new belief that drinking water out of tap was very harmful to you. It could kill you, it would destroy your brain cells, it would make you sick, it'll kill your kids, et cetera, et cetera. They had to take time and they had to spend a lot of money to get people to understand, appreciate and accept that. Once people accepted that, then they were able to take them to the next step, which is okay, now you got to do something about that. Tap water. Here's a filter. Or here you can buy bottled water. Water's already in a bottle. It comes from a Poland spring.

It comes from some place where it had deers and mountains and that's all bullshit. It's really just municipal tap water. That's what it is. It's tap water. They just put it in a bottle and give it a fancy name. It makes, it sounds like it comes from some far away place and you spend money on it. That's really what the bottled water industry is. It is a great mental psyche of what the bottled water industry is, and you're drinking water out of plastic, which is probably just as if not more harmful than drinking water out of a kitchen faucet. But anyway, different conversation for a different day. But what they did was they basically hoodwinked people mentally into thinking that you're doing something healthy by drinking water out of a damn plastic bottle that's disintegrating every minute that the water is disintegrating the plastic, but again, different conversation for a different day.

What the bottled water industry did successfully was teach people that drinking water out of a tap was a bad idea and thus, you needed an alternative and then they happen to be the ones providing the alternative, which is buying water out of bottles. What I suggest you do today, if you don't want to drink tap water, that's fine. You need to get yourself an AquaTru water filter, which costs less than bottled water because you don't have to keep buying cases. It produces a lot less waste. So you're not throwing plastic bottles away all the time or putting 'em into recycling bins and they don't even get recycled most of the time. You have one filter, one water filter machine. You pour tap water into it, it produces a clean filter, purified water, and there's no waste. How about that? So you can get your AquaTru water filter.

There's a link down below in the description. They're one of the sponsors of Work on Your game, so just go to work on your game.com/at what stands for true work on your game.com/at stands for AquaTru. That is not a, I didn't even plan on it, it just happens to be something I'm talking about at this point. So that's one way you can create a brand new market, but you need to understand the bottled water industry spent millions of dollars and many years teaching people like you and me to believe that there was something wrong with tap water. Now, personally, I don't actually believe there's anything wrong with tap water even though I'm an AquaTru water filter user. If I had to drink tap water all day, I would be completely fine and I would do it and I wouldn't think twice about it. Many people don't think that way because the bottled water industry successfully taught people that there is something wrong with the water coming out of the tap and depending on where you live, it can be, there can be something wrong with the water coming out of the tap.

So let me make sure I add that in. Give you another example of a company that had to create a new market. Think of the smartphone. So Apple pioneered the smartphone and what they did was a little bit different than the bottled water industry because they weren't really creating a brand new thing out of nothing. They weren't just taking an idea and saying, don't do that, do this. They were taking something that we had already accepted and they just expanded upon it. So we already had the idea of mobile phones at the time that the iPhone came out. We were all very familiar with the mobile phone because you had a bunch of phones that had been out that were becoming more high tech. So the first regular cell phones people had you look at, let's say the mid to late nineties and going into the early two thousands, we had cell phones that did text messages and phone calls For the most part, all of us had access to a phone that could do that and the iPhone did have that, but what the iPhone also did was combine the iPod, which was a pocket sized MP three player that could hold thousands of songs on it.

It took the iPod, which we had accepted was a great idea, great breakthrough, and Apple had to spend a lot of money on marketing and teaching the world that they should want one of these things because it wasn't a common thing at the time. It was an MP three player that wasn't the first ever, but they pioneered it and they dominated that market. Then they took the computer, the web browser that we all were familiar with, but we were used to using computers on a desktop. You had to be sitting down in a seat or maybe if you had a laptop, but it was a big bulky, no book size or bigger device that you could get on the internet with. All Steve Jobs did was, and I say all as if it was very simple, but all he did was take these three concepts, a cell phone, an mp, three player, and a web browser.

He combined them all into one device and any of you who is not familiar with your marketing history, any of you who's in a marketing world, you should know your marketing history. You should go online, go to YouTube and look up the presentation.

When Steve Jobs introduced the iPhone, it was a legendary marketing presentation, one of the most legendary presentations in the history of marketing. You should know about it if you're in the marketing space because you need to know the history of where things come from, especially those of you who have iPhones. How do you not even know the presentation when he introduced the iPhone? You need to know about it because the way he presented it, Steve Jobs did what I tell you all great experts in their field do. He simplified and clarified what that device was and made it easy for even a fifth grader to understand what it was.

By again, he repeated over and over again a web browser, an MP, three players and a phone, and it's again, a legendary presentation. So go look that thing up on YouTube. If you have not seen it yet or before, even if you've seen it before, go look it up again and watch it again. The whole point is you don't want to be stepping into a market where the market does not already exist unless you happen to have the genius of Steve Jobs and the resources of a company like Apple. If you don't have that, you don't want to do this. See, in that case, again, you're creating a market from scratch and you may not have the resources or the time, time being one of your resources to do that, to educate the world on why they should want that thing. Now, every once in a while this can work and you hit the lottery, you introduce something brand new to the world, they realize that they want it, and you can dominate that market as if you were the first one to market.

But often, the first one to market is the person with all the arrows in their back and they die because they take all the bullets trying to teach something new to the world and the world does not want to hear it, and then everybody else comes on the back end. They make all the money, so you don't want to be the first one. There's an entire graveyard of entrepreneurs who thought they were going to create a brand new market that did not already exist and they all were wrong. So when you walk past the cemetery, the entrepreneurship cemetery, you are stepping over their bones, their scouts, their fossils because they're dead, because they died trying to prove it. Alright, so get rich or die trying. Most of 'em died, alright? They didn't get rich, they died trying, alright? You don't want to be that person who steps into a market that already exists.

Point number two, today's topic once again is how to create your blue ocean for your business. Number two, identify what is happening in that ocean that you can from. In other words, what makes you different and unique and new compared to what already exists in the current red ocean. So when you step in a red ocean before the other fish start killing you because they want to stop you from getting to the food, ask yourself, what can you do in this market that is different from what everybody else is doing so that you are not participating in the bloodbath of fish killing each other in the red ocean? This is where you had to differentiate yourself, and there are two ways to go about this and you can do this from opposite ends. One way is to look at yourself and simply decide what you are going to do differently than what already exists.

All right, here's what everybody else is already doing. Why? Why don't I just do it this way? The other way is to look at what already exists and figure out what they don't have or what they are not doing that you do have or that you can do or what they are doing that you will not do either. One, how are you going to differ by looking at them as opposed to looking at you This way is sometimes easier because then you're not creating your idea from scratch. See, if you're stepping into the red ocean and trying to create an idea from scratch, you're just going to decide, okay, I'm just going to come up with something and it's going to be different from what everybody else is doing. This is harder than doing it the other way. The other way is when you say, all right, here's what everybody else is doing.

Let me find the cracks in their process. Let me find the holes in there, their walls. Let me find the fly in the ointment and figure out how I can improve on what they are missing. What are they not doing that I can do? What do the customers want from them that they're not getting that I can actually provide? So I'll be an improvement on them knowing that people already want this because the customers have already made it clear that they want it. See, this is just simple market research. Look at what already exists and you are simply finding and filling the available empty spaces. Again, you can look at what people are already doing and just find what they're missing, find the holes in their processes. This is your opportunity. Either way, you have to identify what will make you different from what already exists.

And again, this must be a true differentiator. It can't be something so simple and basic that your competition is just looking at what you're offering and adding it to their own mix tomorrow morning. So if they can just look at it and see what you're doing and say, all right, we'll go do that, then it's over. You don't really have a differentiator. And these two literally are different. So if any of you watch Shark Tank and if you're an entrepreneur, you should watch Shark Tank. It's a very informative show when it comes to entrepreneurship and business in general from the people knowing their numbers to the questions that investors want to ask of you if they're interested in investing in your business to how people present their businesses to people just explaining their business models. So a lot of things you can learn from it and be entertained at the same time.

So on the Shark Tank TV show, often what happens is someone will come in there with a product, especially when they have some type of food product. This happens often with food products. There's one of the sharks named Kevin O'Leary, also known as Mr Wonderful. He's created and sold several businesses how he made his money, and I believe he created and sold a company called The Learning Company, and that was one of the ways that he got his start as far as being a millionaire entrepreneur, and whenever someone comes with a food product, he's often the one who says something like, and actually he does this with smaller products than anything retail based is really his thing. Anything that's a retail product, whether it's food, a widget, a toy, something like that. He says, some people over in China or some of the big supermarkets if you have food, he says some supermarket companies because the margins there are razor thin.

The margins are like one or 2% in the supermarket. Those of you don't know what that means. Margin simply means how much money is left over after you sell and then you pay for the fulfillment of the sale and the margin being 1%. Meaning if you sell a product for $100, the money that you actually take home in your pocket is $1, which is 1% of $100. That's the kind of margins you have in the supermarket space, and he's not exaggerating. That's the real number. The margins in the supermarket space are like 1%. So you sell a hundred dollars worth of product, you actually take home literally $1, and he explains that and he'll say that about retail space and stuff like that as well. He says, some company that's watching this on TV right now is going to just knock off your product. In other words, they're going to make a cheap copy of your same product and they're going to put you out of business.

They'll completely crush the cockroach that you are. That's the phrase that he used. He uses that phrase all the time. So if you watch Shark Tank, you'll hear him say that oftentimes the whole point being your true differentiator needs to be a true differentiator, not just you saying that you're different just because you believe it. Nobody cares what you believe. Can you prove that you're different? Can you be different in such a way that someone can look at your product and they can't copy it even though they see exactly what it is and they know you're succeeding with it? Can you do that? If not, then you're not truly differentiated. So it needs to literally be different. So for example, what I do, let me backup. I've lost my place here in my notes. For example, What I do here as a coach, even here on this show, is based on the fact that I am a professional athlete, I'm willing to talk about subjects that many people are unwilling to talk about, and I like to look at the things as objectively and straight up and down as possibly objectively and logically as possible.

Now, while none of the things that I just said is necessarily a breakthrough idea, the combination of all of them makes me unique because there are so few people who are either A, capable or B, willing to do that, not all of them all together. There are some people who have some of those, but not many people have all of 'em. So even though I'm openly telling you what differentiates me, I have little competition because how many people do you know can and will do it? Not many. How many do you know will talk about the things that I talk about in the way that I talk about them? Not many, at least not publicly. They won't do it, very few.

So when I say a true differentiator need not be some secret formula, like the formula for Coca-Cola, but it does need to be something that cannot be easily duplicated or copied. It needs to actually be unique, truly unique, so that again, even if people can see it, they can't do anything to copy it. Point number three, today's topic once again is how to create your own blue ocean for your marketing and business. Three, make your marketing focus on emphasizing the difference and making sure everyone understands that difference must remember what marketing is, is the relationship you have with your public, whether it be people who already know you, people who just got to know you, and people who don't know you at all. One of the reasons that I put this show out as often as I do every single day, it's part of my marketing mix that I put on every day.

Any subject you could possibly ask me about, I have probably done an episode on that subject. So every day I'm giving myself another opportunity to do what, to get myself seen, heard, and known by someone who otherwise may not have known about me, and to reinforce the idea of who I am and what I'm about with people who have heard of me before. So I'm just continuing to market this. Part of my marketing mix is to give you this show on a daily basis. That doesn't mean you have to have a show that comes out every day. You want to do once a week, do once a week, whatever it is you want to do, but it needs to fit what you're trying to do marketing wise and business wise. So every day, because my unique ability is my approach, not necessarily the subject matter, I'm giving my unique ability more exposure to more people because my approach is the unique ability.

It's not the topic because you notice that I'll jump around on this show from a marketing topic to a mindset topic to some social issue, to who knows what else. I'll talk about anything in between, but it's not always the same topic as far as industry and line of work. One day I might talk about publishing books and the next day I might talk about courses. Next day I'm talking about coaching. They are all under the umbrella of business, but there are different aspects to business. My approach that makes me unique is not the subject matter itself, even though I am pretty damn good at the subject matter. So even if you skip around on this show, let's say you just turn to the feed, you just skip around in different episodes and you pick and choose which ones to listen to. My unique ability is the same regardless of the subject.

That's the key. This is why I use other social media applications. When I get on an app like X, formerly known as Twitter, I do the same thing there that I do here on the show just in a different format and it gets a different kind of response because it's a different format. I respond to other people's posts there. I ask questions all for pushback. I objectively challenge things that I see other people posting. Same stuff that I do here. I just do it in a different way and with people who I don't even know and who don't know me, but I'm exposing my unique ability in the exact same way and the people who want it come further, deeper into my world. And the people who don't want it, they go the opposite direction. This is how it works. There's just different formats for doing it, but I know what makes me unique.

I know what the unique ability is and the more I emphasize it, the better I do. Simple how it works. All that said, let's recap today's class, which is how to create your blue ocean in business. First, getting clear on what the blue ocean is, is a space that you occupy within a red ocean where the food is only for you and you are not in a blood bath against all the other fish for limited resources. Number one, find a space where activity is already happening. Yes, you want to go where there is already business taking place because that means there are buyers. If there are no buyers, that's the reason why there are no sellers. And if there are no sellers, that means there are no buyers. You don't want to get into that space unless you have the

Time and the money to invest in educating the public as to why they want your thing. And most entrepreneurs who I know, you're probably not in that space. Number two, identify what is happening that you can diverge from. What can you do that makes you different from everybody else out there? Either figure out what you already bring is different or look at what everybody else is doing and see what they are missing that you can bring to the table. Number three, make your marketing focus on emphasizing this difference and making sure everyone understands this difference. So believing that you are different is one thing. Getting other people to understand and believe that you're different is a whole other thing. So one of the reasons I put the show out consistently is so people can get exposed to it and they can experience my unique ability and my unique ability.

Again, there is no fluff, straight to the point. Brass tacks, no bs, no dancing around topics and being willing to talk about things that a lot of people are not willing to talk about. Again, people can see that and they know it, but they can't duplicate it and they can't beat me at it because I'm doing things that they won't do, and this is a way that you create your blue ocean out of the way. Folks, make sure you're text me to get my text community, my numbers down below the description and work on your game university. That is the place where I do all my coaching. If you had to be coached on me directly, you want to help me find your blue ocean and your space so that you don't feel like you're competing against everybody. You don't feel like you're just putting stuff out there and nobody's paying attention. It is not bringing you the revenue or the attention or the eyeballs that you want.

#2835: How To Never Get Punked Or Bullied In Life

Getting into this topic I was thinking of one day randomly when I came up with this topic, I was thinking of my basketball experiences growing up, playing on the city playgrounds of the city of Philadelphia, where I come from, and playing against guys who really had nothing to lose and guys who had no ambitions of elevating or ascending in the game of basketball, meaning they were playing street pickup ball.

They were not trying to make it to any leagues. They weren't trying to go back and play in college. These are grown men. They're not trying to go play in colleges. These are guys who would go to work from nine to five when they got off work, they would come to the playground and play pickup, but they were still relatively young enough to be pretty good, at least compared to me as a teenager. And these are the kind of guys I grew up playing against. And what happens is, and some of them even younger, what happens is when you play ball in the playground, especially in cities like the moment where I come from, at least back in the day when I was growing up, I don't know how it is these days, things are a little bit different now because a lot of people don't even play outside on the playgrounds. People go and play in the gyms and y'all are playing in equinoxes and Lifetime fitnesses and all that shit. But when I was growing up, you played on the playground, that was the only court you had access to was the playground

There. All these indoor leagues, I mean they existed but it wasn't as normal, let's just say, or ubiquitous as it is now. And what would happen is, and by the way, even when we did play in leagues, a lot of times the leagues you play outside, the leagues weren't inside leagues were outside anyway. Sometimes you're going to go up against players who can't compete with you on skill or talent. So if you happen to be a highly skilled or a very talented player, sometimes you're going to play against players who simply cannot compete with your talent or your skill. You know it and they know it. So what they do is default to turning the game into a nastiness game of nastiness. They turn it into football, basically basketball players playing football or football players playing basketball is a better way of saying it.

They would turn the game nasty because that was the only way that they could possibly compete. In other words, they want to junk up the game, muck up the game, make the game much more nasty, much more physical and turn it towards something that they could have a better chance at competing in. And when you play ball, if you were a highly skilled or talented player, you know exactly what I'm talking about here because you would inevitably run into these players the more you play it because if you're good, most of the players you play against ain't as good as you and they know it. So they have to figure out a way to compete with you. They're not going to just sit there and let you kick their ass all day, especially guys playing in the street. They have pride and they will try to turn the game into something that they can win if they can't win a game of skill, which is what basketball actually is.

So if you found yourself in one of these games and you shied away from these individuals, these people who would try to basically bogle you off the court, if you shied away from their nasty tactics, you could be the better player by far and lose. And this what happened, I've seen it happen. As a matter of fact, I've had it happen to me when I didn't understand. What I'm going to explain to you here today is that you can lose to a player who is not as good as you simply because you allow them to punk you. And that's what we call it. Allow 'em punk you or bully you out of your game and beat you even though they had no business even competing with you in the first place. So all this means folks, especially those of you who are highly skilled, you need to know how to deal with this type of person in awe of life.

It is not just a sports subject. I'm using sports as an analogy here, as a frame, but you need to know how to deal with these people in all of life because they exist. They are numerous in number, and the more skilled you are, the more numerous they will be because you're going to be, the more skilled you are, the more skilled you're going to be than most of the people you meet. And you're going to eventually run up against some people who are not just happy letting you kick their ass. They're going to compete back and they're going to compete in a way that they have a chance which ain't on skill. Now everybody is following me? So this is not just related to sports. These people exist. There's a lot of them. And when they realize they can't beat you on ability, they will try to beat you.

They're just going to try to beat you in a different way. So you better be ready to deal with these people instead of trying to avoid them or allowing them to beat you because they ain't got no business beating you because they ain't got the game to beat you, but they got other things. And so you need to match them with what they got and then beat them on skill. Let's get into it. Point number one, the topic once again today is how to never get punked in life. Number one, accept that these football players exist. And when I say football players, I'm using that as a, I'm using that term metaphorically. So when I say football players throughout the rest of this episode, what I mean is a person who is not as skilled as you. So this is a relative term because each of you has a different skill level.

A person who's not as skilled as you yet they are just as competitive as you and they're going to try to turn the situation nasty because they can't beat you just using, they can't beat you by following the regular rules of the game. So you're going to try to beat you in some other way. Has any of you who's listening to this ever dealt with a person like this? Many of you have, alright, this happens in the office, office politics, and I have some clients of mine who tell me about this office politics that they got to deal with in their jobs, jobs that maybe they're either trying to leave or they're trying to figure out a way to move to a different department. They have to deal with some football players, some nasty people who don't like the fact that you are who you are and they are who they are.

Maybe they don't like your position relative to theirs and they're going to try to turn the game nasty because that's the only way they can compete with you. They can't just beat you on disability, they can't beat you on performance, so they're going to beat you in another way. You need to accept that these people exist in life and there are a lot of them. And basketball, again, we would call these people football players like, oh, we are about to play against these football dudes. And they weren't really football players. Sometimes they were literally football players who just liked to play basketball for fun and they would take their football mindsets, let's just say, and football physicality. And they would bring it over to the basketball court and basically again, try to bully you off the court or just beat you up. If they couldn't beat you on skill, they would try to beat you with their muscles.

This is what they do. And again, football is a much more physical game than basketball for those of you who don't know. And football is much more about hitting and physically beating up your opponent than it is about dribbling and shooting and doing moves because again, these football players understand that they can't win if they just play by the normal rules. They can size you up and they know who they are and they're like, okay, well I ain't going to win that way. How can I win? As I told you in the introduction, you must accept that these people exist and you must accept it. You must be prepared for these people because the only other option you have is to avoid them or try to appease them. I would suggest you not do that because you're going to lose confidence in yourself and before you know it, your skill is rendered completely useless because you're not willing to use it.

Robert Green tosses about this in a book he co-authored with 50 cent. He has a book called The 50th Law. If you haven't read it, go get it. And in that book, one of the chapters talks about when you need to know when to be aggressive, when to be a lion in a situation, when do you fall back and let people kind of hang themselves and when do you become a lion and you go and actually kill them directly? Machiavelli talks about this in his book called The Prince, another book you should read. He says, A leader must know when to be bad and aggressive and when not to be. There is time for everyone. You have to be willing to be aggressive and nasty and maybe even violent in your life and in your endeavors. And if you are not, you'll be taken advantage of by people who are willing to be nasty, aggressive and violent because they will use your unwillingness to be that.

They will use that against you. And again, you have enough experience in life, in business and in any type of office setting. And when I say office, I don't mean it has to be. Some type of corporate business could be you could be working in a school and deal with politics between employees and coworkers and people who are just nasty for whatever reason. And people who don't like you because you're prettier than them or you're younger than them or you make more money than them or you're just more talented than them, you're going to deal with these kinds of people everywhere that you go. You're going to deal with these people in school, you deal with these people in your local church group. There ain't going to be no money involved. Some people will just get nasty because you have something that they don't have and they don't like that and they're going to try to undermine you in any way that they can.

This is a reality of life. You can ignore this at your own peril. Point number two, today's topic once again is how to never get punked or bullied in life. Number two, understand these people's strengths and weaknesses because they have both. Every human on the planet has strengths and weaknesses. And understand that this type of person who I'm describing these football players, you cannot avoid them. Don't try to back away from these individuals because that's exactly what they want. Again, they're bullies. A bully likes when someone is afraid of them because the bully will just keep picking on you because they know that you're afraid of 'em. They know that you're not going to fight back. And a bully is after easy victories. A bully could look at somebody and know that they could beat them in a fight, but if they know they're going to have to fight, they'll probably leave you alone because it's much easier to just beat up on somebody who's not going to fight back.

So this is the mindset that you have to have knowing that maybe you're not at an advantage if you go to war with these people, but knowing that you're willing to go to war, the bully will probably leave you alone just because they don't want to deal with the war in the first place. War is costly. Isn't it much easier to win without having to shed any blood? Of course. So the bullies are looking for easy targets. They're looking for the people who are afraid. And when you're afraid you get taken advantage of, this is how life works. This is a life point that I'm giving you here. You can take this out of work. You can take this just to your everyday life. Bullies are looking for easy victories. And when you present yourself as someone who is an easy victory, and in the environments that I come from, sometimes people refer to people like that as food.

When you present yourself looking like food, you're going to get eaten. This is just how it works. You have to let people know that there is going to be a cost to messing with you even if they still win, if they know they're going to incur a cost. Again, as I said, there's a whole bunch of people who are scared in life, they're punks and they would love, they would allow themselves to be taken advantage of. Those are the ones who the bullies will go after. They're going to go after the ones they got to fight and beat up again even if they know they're going to win. So either when you're dealing with these football players, you either have them join you on a level of mutual respect or you gotta beat them. And usually those go hand in hand and there is no in between.

When you deal with these types of people and they make it clear that they don't like you and they're not trying to compromise with you, then you gotta be ready to put your hands up and fight. Sometimes literally and sometimes metaphorically. I remember back in 2008, I made a video on YouTube and I was explaining to my basketball player audience how, because a lot of players were asking me questions about how do you play against a player who's taller than you or stronger than you or bigger than you? Because it seemed like a lot of players were having this problem. I am playing against this other guy, Dre. He's taller than me and stronger than me. So he just goes to the basket and he just scores on me very easily. And then when I try to score on him, he just blasts my shot and I can't do anything. What am I supposed to do against a player like this? So I made a video explaining what to do against a person like this on a basketball court. And I explained to him that the first thing you gotta understand is just a natural truth about human beings is that any breathing organism, anything that breathes or bleeds can be defeated.

Lemme repeat that. Anything that breathes air or it bleeds blood can be defeated. It doesn't matter what it is. Think about it. Think about anything that is a breathing thing.

They can all be beaten because they all can be killed. They're all mortals. Any breathing or bleeding thing is a mortal, which means it can die, which means it can be beaten. And I remember a lot of athletes would make a lot of players on that YouTube video make sarcastic comments, oh, I get it, Dre, just bring a knife to the court and just chop my opponent up and then it'll solve all the problems. LOL, right? I remember when Mike Tyson was, and lemme back up. This is the first thing you get to understand about any opponent. First of all, that's the number one thing you must understand about any opponent is that you can't look at them as if they are unbeatable.

Because if you think they're unbeatable, then they will appear to be unbeatable and everything they do will just confirm what you already believe, your fear. I remember when Mike Tyson was at the peak of his boxing powers and he was defeating every fighter he went up against through those of you who remember Mike and his days, or you want to go on YouTube and look up his early fights. The opponents that he was beating, it was about 50% intimidation and other 50% boxing skills. Mike Tyson's a very skilled boxer. A lot of people don't know that, but Mike Tyson was an extremely skilled boxer. He was also a very intimidating boxer. He was such a hard hitter, a power puncher. He was an aggressive boxer. He was the type of boxer who always comes forward and coming forward means he's always stalking you and coming at you and bringing the fight to you.

Whereas there are other fighters who kind of let you come to them and then they just pick you apart when you come after them. Think of somebody like Floyd Mayweather. He's more of a counter puncher. He waits for you to try something and then he attacks you. Whereas Mike Tyson is the kind of guy who just comes straight at you and forces the action upon you. Mike Tyson is that type of fighter. He would intimidate his opponents and he would just beat him up. And many people, including myself, at least back in the nineties, thought Mike Tyson was unbeatable. I thought nobody could beat Mike Tyson. He was just too tough, too strong. And I didn't understand. Back then I was just like, nobody can beat him. Nobody was beating him. But time told us that this was not the case and it was just that nobody had identified or exploited his weaknesses yet.

Maybe people had identified it, but identifying someone's weakness and doing something about it or two different things. If you're playing against Shaquille O'Neal and I tell you he's going to back you down, turn around and dunk the ball, you might identify that that's what he's going to do. But being able to stop it is a whole different ball game. So any opponent you face, especially those who have only one tool in their arsenal and these football players that you face in life often they only have one tool, which is to be aggressive and nasty. That's their only tool and they only got one tool. You can beat them. You just have to figure out what you do to neutralize the one tool that they have and how to counter it. So the first thing you have to do before you do any of that, and this is what I was told by the basketball players in that video back in 2008, same thing I'm telling you now.

I told them that the first thing you gotta do is unwrap yourself from your emotional reactions. You got to stop feeling like a pussy and feeling like you can't beat these people because as long as you have that in your mind, it doesn't matter what I say, you're not going to do anything. First thing you have to accept is that this person can be beaten until you accept that nothing else I say is going to matter. Once you accept that, now we can move on to point number two. Understand that. So the first thing is wrapping yourself in the emotions. The second thing is understanding they can be beat. And the third thing is you have to identify how they can be beat. 1, 2, 3. It's not feeling like a pussy. Stop. Basically punking yourself makes you more scared. That's number one. Number two, accepting that this person can be beat the same way that you can be beat.

And number three, let's figure out how to beat 'em. But you don't get to the strategy part until part three. Step three, everybody follows that be, do, have. Okay? And that strategy is just part two. Alright? So the first two parts are all part of the being. That's part of the mindset, getting out of your emotions and accepting a reality. That's all part of the being. The thing is, let's figure out a strategy and then you have to actually execute on it. And having is the outcome. So with Mike Tyson for example, the reason he intimidated and defeated most of his opponents is because most of them, again, Mike Tyson, was the type of fighter who would come forward. You watch Mike Tyson videos of him boxing in his day, even to this day, even now, well not now, he doesn't fight anymore.

But even in his later years as a fighter, Mike Tyson's style was always the same. He was a forward, he would come forward, he would come at you and force the action upon you. And anytime he did that to other fighters, well guess what the other fighters would do. They would play into his hands, they would back away. He would come at them and they would back away from him. They would back away and they would get on their heels. And once Mike Tyson got you on your heels, it was over. He would just destroy you. He would just devour you and take you apart. So finally, Mike, and there were some fighters who tried over the years to kind of not let him do that. And they had some success, but all of them ended up losing anyway. And so eventually he went up against two fighters, specifically who I'm remembering.

And he lost more than two fights, but he lost to more than two fighters. But these are two that I'm thinking of. Cause they were the first two to kind of do it in a textbook way that everybody else was able to learn from. One of them was named Evander Holyfield, the one was named Lennox Lewis. Both of those fighters did the same thing to Mike Tyson. What they do is that instead of letting Mike bring the fight to them and attack them, they went on the offensive and they attacked Mike. They didn't let Mike attack them. They went on. They went at him. So specifically you think about when Mike Tyson fought Evander Holyfield. Evander Holyfield came, he was a come forward fighter as well. So it was forward versus forward. And Evander Holyfield did a better job of coming at Mike and basically putting Mike on his heels than Mike was able to do to put Evander on his heels.

And Evander just picked Mike Tyson apart and basically beat him up. And Le Lewis did the exact same thing. So all of a sudden Mike Tyson looked very beatable. When people stop playing into his hands, it's the same thing when you deal with aggressive people in life. When you stop playing this in their hands and giving them what they want, they are not as tough or unstoppable as they once appeared to be. Moving on to point number three, today's topic once again is how to never get punked in life. Number three, prepare and equip yourself to handle them. In other words, you have to be able to beat them at their own game if you must. So the examples I just gave you at the end of point number two is those work, but only if you're prepared to actually do anything. So Evander Holyfield and Le Lewis, it's one thing to say, Hey, don't let Mike Tyson walk you down and just stalk you and intimidate you, but you actually have to have the ability to actually execute on that plan.

It's one thing to have a plan, another thing to do it. And Mike Tyson is often credited with being the one to say this. I don't think he's the first one that said it, but he's credited with it. Everybody has a plan until they get punched in the face. So do you have the ability to actually execute on this plan that I'm giving you here? And again, you can apply this to anything. Just because you identified a weakness in an opponent again, does not mean you can exploit that weakness. You must have the resources to actually do it. Speaking of boxing, again, think of a fighter like Floyd Mayweather. Floyd famously didn't ever watch film of the opponent that he was about to face. So he was going to fight somebody. They would do these TV shows that would show you why both fighters were getting ready for the fight.

It was actually a pretty entertaining series. And anytime Floyd was fighting probably the last maybe 10 years of his career, they would do this. And the other fighter, whoever Floyd was about to fight, you would always see them. There'd always be a scene of that fighter and their trainers and all that stuff sitting around watching video of Floyd's previous matches of which he had won all of them. But they would find little pieces where the opponents had had some success. They say, alright, we're going to learn how to do that. Oh, see how that hurt him? See how that made him uncomfortable? We're going to do that. And you would see the other fighters game planning for how to beat Floyd. But Floyd would never watch a film of the guy he was about to fight. He would just not watch it. Floyd would say, I don't need to watch films.

I'll just wait until we get in the ring. I'm going to see what you're trying to do then I'm going to just take it away from you. I'm going to pick you apart and I'm going to beat you. It was a famous boast that Floyd would always do what he would say, every opponent that I fought, and somebody would say to him, well this opponent you're about to fight. Well, he has a game plan. He had a plan, he's going to do this and that and that. Floyd would always respond the same way. He would say, well, I fought X number of people, whatever his record was at the time, I fought 40 people and 40 people had a plan and 40 people lost. So this guy, and I'm about to fight, he's going to be number 41 on the list. He had a plan too, and he's going to lose just like everybody else who had a plan.

And we can't challenge it because he ended up beating everybody. So just because you can point out or identify an opponent's weakness does not mean you can do anything about your opponent's weakness. That's a whole different thing. You must identify and develop the ability to exploit a weakness that you notice, not simply be able to talk about it. Just talking about it doesn't get the job done. I remember when I was playing basketball in college, we would play pickup basketball every day and it'd be a lot of us, the same guys playing pickup every day. And I remember I used to, there was a time where I favored doing this reverse layup, so I would drive the baseline and when someone would challenge me on one side of the rim, I would just reverse it and make the way up on the other side of the rim.

So I would just do this reverse layup move often. And it was often successful in our on-campus pickup games. I remember one of my teammates, or at least it was a former teammate at that time, an unathletic white guy, he couldn't really jump. So he couldn't really challenge me at the rim, but he would be in the right position, but he couldn't do anything and I would do the reverse and score on him all the time. So I remember one time I was driving to the hole and before I even jumped, he yelled out, he's going to do a reverse. He yelled it out and I just did it anyway and I made it. And I remember saying to him, well hey, pointing it out is one thing, but doing something about it is another thing. It's the same thing for you. So again, I told you what Evander Holyfield did to Mike Tyson, but only Evan Holyfield was able to pull it off.

So putting Mike on the defensive can defeat him, but you have to have the ability to actually do it. Again, those are two different things. The knowledge that you can do it and then the skill to actually do it. So make sure you don't miss out on that part here. With that said, let's recap today's class, which is how to never get punked or buoyed in life. And again, I thought of this just thinking of my experience as a basketball player, how when you are a skilled person in anything you do, you're going to stir up envy and resentment in people who are not as skilled as you. And they're going to find ways to muck up the game, so to speak, to shift the terrain more to an area that is better suited for them. And you better be ready to deal with these people because they will come at you.

Point number one, accept that football players exist in life. And again, football players are people who will turn a situation nasty and physical and rough because that gives 'em a better chance to beat you than if they just play with you off of normal skill because they can't beat you off skill and they know that. And out of respect for you, out of respect for the fact they can't beat you on skill, they're going to try to beat you in another way. You need to accept that these people exist and there are a lot of them. And the more skilled you are, the more of them you will meet. Number two, understand their strengths and weaknesses. And alright, anything that breathes or bleeds has weaknesses as well as it has strengths, you just have to first of all, get yourself out of your emotions about what this person is doing or can do.

Secondly, understand that anyone can be beat, which I just told you. And third, start probing for the weaknesses so you can figure out what to actually do about this person rather than just shying away from them. And point number three, now you have to prepare, equip yourself to handle these people. So now you know that they can be beat, you've accepted they can be beat. Now you have to develop the tools to actually do the beating. Alright? You're going to actually beat them. You have to develop the ability to do it. So beating them at their own game, if you must, again, think of you Vander Holyfield versus Mike Tyson. Nobody thought anybody could beat Mike Tyson. And

Holyfield realized and proved that there is a way to beat him. You just can't do what every other fighter had tried to do was try to run away from him.

No, you got to go at him and make him run away. And when Holyfield did that to Mike Tyson, Mike Tyson had no recourse. But again, you have to have the skills of holyfield to actually execute. There's one thing to know, it is another thing to do it. As Floyd Mayweather said, 40 people had a plan, 40 people lost. So just because you have a plan doesn't mean you can execute on it. You got to work on your game and develop the skill to actually do this stuff.

#2836: The 6 Pieces Of A Successful Book [Part 1 of 2]

The topic today is the six pieces of a successful book. Now I'm an author of 35 books officially as of the recording of this episode. Now, if you were to look me up on any writing or book platform, you'll see that I probably have more. I probably have close to a hundred titles listed, but I officially call myself an author of 35. Officially I got a hundred titles, but again, 35 full-fledged books that I would say, and I talk to 'em here from a lot of people who are writing books and want to write books naturally.

So today and tomorrow I'm going to do a short miniseries on the six things that must be in place if you want to release a book successfully. And let's define this word successful because people throw that word out but don't really give flesh to it. So when I say successful, what I mean is you put the book out, you get it in front of your target readers and they actually go get the book however they need to get it, whether they download it, they buy it, whatever, they read it and they get value from it. And value can mean a lot of different things. Value can mean they just read it and they laughed or they read it and they cried or they read it and they got information or they read it and they actually went and applied the stuff that you told 'em to do.

It depends on what's in your book, which one they're going to do. Maybe they do all four or something else that I didn't mention. So when I say successful, that's what I mean in the context of books in this series. Okay, so successful, I'm giving flesh to that. So anytime you throw around that word successful, make sure you give flesh to what success actually means. Because what success means for you may not be what your listener thinks success means. So you need to be clear what you're talking about when you use that word because it's one of those relative words, one of those slippery words that can mean a hundred different things to a hundred different people. Now that you know that, let's get into it. Point number one, topic once again is the six pieces of a successful book. Number one is editorial. What does editorial mean?

Editorial simply means some people may be intimidated by that word, but it actually means a very simple thing. What is the book and what is it about? Alright, what the book is. Alright, I wrote this book called The Third Day and it's about how you show up and give your best effort when you least feel like it. That's editorial. What is the book and what is it about? That's it. Alright. In simple terms, the writing of your book, that's the editorial because whatever you call the book, whatever the title, the subtitle, and then just the basic premise of what someone would get if they read it, that's the editorial. So you should be able to explain it in a sentence so that someone gets it again, doesn't mean they need to go buy it. Just as I told you that doesn't mean you're going to jump out of your chair and go to third day book.com and get your free copy of that book.

What you should do doesn't mean you're going to do it, but you understand what it is. That's it. People just need to know what it is and understand what it's about. That's all editorial means. Now you have to actually write the book so that it actually fits what you say it is about. That's your job. But this should be clear. Your editorial needs to be clear, okay? So when someone reads your book, what's actually in it? What are they going to get from it? You should be writing your book with your reader in mind. The book is not for you, it's for the reader. If you want to write a book for you, then you can go get a diary or a journal and don't ever show it with anybody. But if you're writing a book to put out to the public, the book needs to be for the person whom you want to go and acquire your book, the person you want to go and read your book, okay?

Whatever that happens to be. So if you should be, again, write your book with the reader in mind, give them what you believe they need or what they want. So if your book is based on entertainment, then it should be entertaining for your ideal reader. Again, not for everybody, just your ideal reader. You want them to feel some type of emotion, anger, sadness, anything like that. Your writing should reflect that. Alright? You should be asking yourself if you are getting that done as you write. Alright, is this book doing what I said the book is going to do or what I told myself the book was going to do? You can also ask your editors or your proofreads if you are doing that job, if you have editors or proofreaders, and I would suggest if you're not sure with your editorial, have somebody else read the book say, Hey, is this book actually doing what it's supposed to be doing?

So if your book is based on getting someone a certain type of results or changing their mindset, something like that, my books are usually in that category, then you need to make sure your book is doing the job that it was assigned to do. Okay? So the editorial is simply about making sure your words are a reflection of what you say the book is going to be about your words being, the words in the book need to be a reflection of what the words out of your mouth say that the book is going to be Everybody following me? So as you're writing, you need to keep your reader in mind so that you are serving the reader, not just serving yourself by just doing something that feels good to you, but it doesn't actually do what you are selling the book as everybody following me here, this is the editorial and this is why having editors is a good idea.

That's why if I was to say someone's asking me, Dre, what's your best written book? I would say in my book, work On Your Game because it went through a very, very arduous editorial process where we made sure the book did exactly what it said it was going to do and that's why the words in that book came out perfect because the editing was so, it was very thorough. It was extremely thorough editing. Now again, that doesn't mean the rest of my books are trash. The rest of my books are actually very good too, but the whole point being it was a lot of editing and the editorial made sure the book did exactly what it was supposed to do. So that's why if somebody asked me Which book would you recommend anybody read, they never heard of you. They just want to start with one book.

I would give 'em work on your game for two reasons. One is the one I just told you the other reasons because it encompasses the entire work on your game framework in one book. Whereas every other book I have is kind of a sub framework within the work on your game framework. So the third day is under the framework of discipline, the mirror motivation is a little more mindset super you is about confidence work on your game. The book is about all of these things and everything put together business, mindset, basketball, all of it into one book and the framework that created this whole thing is all in that book. So that's the reason why I give people that book. Moving on to point number two, today's topic once again is the six pieces of a successful book. Number two, the design of the book design means the layout of the book.

That means what does it look like? What are the pages going to look like? What are the chapter headings going to be? What kind of fonts you're going to use, the spacing, the paragraphs, all of that stuff. The little boxes, if you're going to have little boxes in between your paragraphs, the layout, the cover of the book, the images in the book, if are any the formatting, if it's going to be any, again, the size of the fonts are you going to have page numbers are going to be in the bottom little corner. They're going to be on the left, they're going to be at the top. You're going to have the name of the book on every page. You're going to have your name on the other pages. What is it going to be? All that's part of the design of the book and this does matter.

Now is the most important thing. No, but is it important? Period? Yes, this is one that every author understands, but unfortunately many authors try to do this on their own when they're much better at writing than they are at designing. Alright? Most of you authors are authors, you're not designers, most authors are not authors and designers and most designers are not authors. So you got to stay in your lane. Which lane are you in? Are you an author or a designer? If you're not a designer, here's the good news these days you can get good design work done for relatively cheap. And when I say relatively cheap, sometimes that means free because there are a lot of templates when it comes to formatting that you can just plug your book into so that you don't, number one, don't have to worry about trying to pay to get it done. Maybe you don't have the budget for it or everybody has the budget for it if you're writing a book, but maybe you don't want to come up with any extra money to get your book out there. And number two, you don't don't have to make the investment, the mental investment of trying to figure out graphic design. And I agree with you, you don't want to and you shouldn't, even if you could because you ain't no graphic designer, this is all important.

What I'm saying here, if you have listened to this show for some time, you've heard me rant and rave about how people who are not graphic designers need to stop graphic designing, whether that's an author, an entrepreneur, a salesperson, if you business title is not graphic designers don't do graphic design. Alright, everybody got it? The layout cover, images, and formatting of your book are graphic design jobs that you are unqualified to do and I hereby ban you from doing them. Okay? So don't do this, don't do any graphic design. The good news again today is there are plenty of templates that you can just plug your book into so you don't have to do any designs, just plug into a template that's already designed and they're mostly free and there are thousands of 'em to choose from, so you don't even have to make this decision, okay?

So get help with all of this stuff so that your graphics look as well as the words read. So don't let your graphics kill the quality of the writing, alright? The quality of the writing is good, I know because you're an author, so don't kill that with poor graphics because you simply didn't do your job as far as outsourcing work that you personally just should not have been doing in the first place. Everybody follow me here? So get help with this stuff. So again, the graphics can do justice to your writing. Okay, everybody with me? Great. You are an expert at writing words, so hiring someone who's an expert at graphic design. Alright, have I stressed that point enough? Do I need to say it another 10 times? Good. You have heard the saying that you should never judge a book by its cover. And the reason people say that is because people judge books by their cover.

Alright? All human beings judge books by their cover. We judge people by their appearance and we judge books by their appearance. Alright? You could be the best in the world, but if your appearance looks and people are going to assume that you're sloppy and many of them are not open-minded nor objective enough to give you the time of day to find out if their snap assessment was actually true, they're just going to assume that it is true and they won't listen to you because they assume you're sloppy and they don't want to hear someone who's sloppy. You can look sloppy, but be a great performer. You can look sloppy, but be the smartest person in the room. But if people think you look sloppy, they won't even listen to find out how smart you are because they've already decided, because they judged your book by your cover.

Do you follow me? This applies to your book, it applies to you personally. It applies to everything that you do. There's a very small percentage of people who are open-minded enough who can look at you and think you look sloppy, but still be willing to listen to you and find out if it's true. Most people decide something and they just decide everything that they judged you about based on one little thing. They just decide that's the whole case and they don't want to listen to anything else. I was on X the other day, the app formerly known as Twitter, and somebody had posted this picture and it was two couples sitting at what looked like a baseball game in the bleachers and the picture was taken from behind them. Somebody was sitting a few rows up from them and there's two couples and there's one couple where both a man and a woman and one couple, the man is sitting there and a woman is sitting behind him and she has her elbow up on the seat behind them and her head is on the back, her hand is on the back of his head leaning in towards him like this or leaning in towards him period.

If you're not watching on video, she's leaning towards him and her hand is on the back of her man's apparently hit the other couple is sitting right next to them and the man is sitting there, he's sitting in his seat the same way that the other guy is, but the girl is sitting in her seat and she's leaning forward a little bit. You can't see their faces. She's leaning forward a little bit, almost as if maybe she might be looking at her phone. You can't tell, but you can see that she's leaning forward and at the moment that the picture is taken, this couple is sitting on the left. There's no physical contact between them, but the other couple of the woman has her hand on the back of her man's head and the caption of the person who posted this photo said, which couple do you think has a more loving and happy relationship?

Couple A or couple B. And I left a comment that was the objective answer, the objective right answer. I'm kind of being tongue in cheek but I'm not, which was, how the hell are we supposed to judge that based on a picture? You have no idea what's going on with these couples. You don't know anything. All you got is a snapshot. You can't judge anything from this. And I was like, that's ridiculous. It's ridiculous for you to even ask that question, but this picture had thousands of comments on it of people basically psychoanalyzing who's a happier couple just based on this little photo. And I know some people were doing it kind of as a tongue in cheek joke, but there are people who do this.

They seriously were responding so well, look, she's touching him and she's not even, there's no contact.

They're probably not happy. They're probably arguing. I'm like, yo, how the hell can you draw that conclusion based off of that? I'm saying all that to say this, most people do this all of life. They get one little tiny piece of information about a person and they make all these judgments about the entirety of that person's life, their business, everything that they're about with no information whatsoever. And understand they do this when it comes to your book. So do not kill your own book's success with a trashy presentation because there are a bunch of non-thinking people who otherwise would buy your book, who won't just based on it looking trashy from the outside. So don't let your poor graphic design skills strangle your great writing skills. So make sure your books are as professional as your writing is point number three. Today's topic once again is the six pieces of a successful book. Number three, market planning. Now let's get to the business side of this. Well, this is all the business side, but this is the meat and potatoes of the business side is market planning.

So who is it for which we talked about a little bit already and how are they going to know that it's for them? So this is about you actually getting the word out to the world that you have a book that they should read. And when I say the world, I mean the people who you actually wrote the book for doesn't have to be every human on the planet. An important thing to know about writing books is that you need to be selling and marketing your book before the book comes out. Let me say that sentence again. I want to make sure everybody in the back heard me. An important thing to know about writing books is that you need to be selling and marketing your book before the book comes out, not when it comes out. You don't start talking about the book the day that it releases.

You need to start talking about the book before it comes out. Did everybody hear me? Authors? Did you hear me? Okay. When I say selling the book before it comes out, what I mean is you can be collecting money if you want for your book, meaning you can actually have a presale available. So if you have a mockup of your book that is simply just an image of the book on a screen, you don't actually have the physical book yet because you didn't finish writing it. But if you have a mockup that can show people the book so they can see visually this is what I'm going to get and allow them to give you money, you can do that. That's one way of doing it. But you don't necessarily have to do that before your book comes out if you don't want to.

Many authors these days do a presale of their books, but you don't have to do a presale. One thing that you can also do when I say selling is you're selling people on the idea of the book so that they are anticipating the release of the book before it comes out. So you don't have to have a presale, you can just put the book out the day it comes out, and this is the regular price and it's regularly available today, but you've been talking about it for months before it came out. That's what I mean when I say sell the book before it comes out. So you can literally sell it, but you can also sell the concept of the book just letting people know that something's on the way. Anyone who does any type of launch in business, this is what they do.

Any of you who follow any influencer on the internet, you notice that a lot of 'em do launches and they'll just tell you something's coming. They won't only tell you what it is, something's coming, then they just kind of lead up, beat up, beat up, beat up. Then they finally tell you, oh, this is the thing. This is my course and it's going to be this and it's going to be that, and it's going to have these and it and you're going to get this, this, and this, and you're going to learn how to do that and I'm going to solve all these problems. And then they may pre-sell it or they may just keep telling you, well, on this date it's dropping. They keep telling you about that date. It's coming, it's coming, it's coming, it's coming. And then the date that drops, they want to build up so much momentum that everybody's ready to go buy it.

The date comes out, what are they doing? They're selling you on the product before the product is available to be bought. You need to be doing the same thing with your book. Just let people know it's coming. And notice that people do this damn near everything. People do this with events. Have any of you ever been to someone's event? What do they do? Alright, this event is coming up June 5th, it could be January. Alright, the event's coming up on June 5th and they just keep talking about it, talking about it, talking about it, talking about it, and they're getting you all excited for this event. And then when the event finally comes, they want everybody to be excited to be at the event they've been talking about for months. You don't just wait till it comes out on the day of the event. Hey everybody, I'm having an event, you want to come that's too late.

You got to get people excited early. And remember human beings are hard headed. Now we get to hear the same thing over and over and over again before we actually do something because we are lazy. We don't think and we don't read. So you got to, and even though I'm talking about books, ironically, you have to tell people things over and over and over and over again and you gotta tell 'em ahead of time and tell 'em again and again and again. Otherwise they will forget and they will, life will get in their way.

Okay, so I remember when I was talking about my book the third day and I was talking about it months before it actually came out. If I was to put a new book out now and in the way that I did the third day, I'd probably talk about it like eight months before the book came out.

Whereas with the third day, I didn't start talking about it until maybe June. The book came out in August. So I did maybe about two or three months ahead of time. But if I was to do something like that now, I'd probably talk about it like six to eight months ahead of time, maybe even a year ahead of time, depending on the kind of book that I was putting out. Now I do my books a little bit differently than a traditional normal book, but I would get the whole point of getting your audience ready before you even have a way for them to purchase. So you want to start selling it. And so I was doing it two months before it came out, and again, I was talking about it like eight months before it came out, but I would've been selling it even harder.

I would've pre-sold it even earlier than that if I was doing it again today. So you need to be doing this because you want to build your audience before you actually sell them a thing again, build your audience before you sell them a thing. And this applies to any product. This is not limited to just books. Your market planning is meaning thinking about your ideal audience, where can you find them and how you'll be getting in touch with them. So let them know you have something on the way and after it comes out, let them know that your book came out. Alright? So you're going to be doing this. This is an ongoing thing. Marketing. You heard my series about marketing, right? Marketing is an ongoing thing. It's not a start and stop thing. It's not Oh, I did my marketing, no marketing. You don't do marketing.

Marketing is ongoing, you live marketing, you're in a business, you're an entrepreneur, you live marketing. Marketing is the number one thing you do in business. You're not doing marketing, you're not doing business. So your business is not your book. Your business is your ability to sell your book. Your business is not the book swap out book business is not your course, it's not your event, it's not your coaching program, it's not your consultations, it's not your speaking events, it's not your speech, it's not the product or service. Your business is your ability to sell the thing. If you don't sell it, there's no business, okay? Just because you have it doesn't put you in business. The fact that you can sell it puts you in business. Business is the exchange of money folks. So the only time there is business happening is when you're doing something that is putting you in position to exchange money.

So just creating something is not business that's creating, that's art, that's artistry. Selling is the business. Everybody follow me? Alright. If you remember anything from what you hear from Dre Baldwin, at least when it comes to business, that's the part you need to remember. Marketing is ongoing and the business is when something gets exchanged. So I just told you, I told you it was one, I just gave you two for the price and one. So let's recap tomorrow we're going to get into the second part of this, the six pieces of a successful book. Again, I've written 35 books officially, and a lot of people ask me about books and talk to me about books. And I'm going to give you the six things you need in place if you're going to put a book out, number one, editorial, what the book is going to be and what it is about in your writing as you're writing the book, you need to keep this idea in mind and make sure that you are delivering on the promise that you have in your mind about your book.

Number two, the design. This is the layout, the cover, the image, the formatting. Remember that people do judge books by their cover. That includes people, it includes books, it includes courses, it includes houses, clothes, cars, everything. Life. We judge by their covers, even though we say not to do that, everybody does it anyway. So make sure your cover, cover, including literally your cover, are representative of the quality of your writing. And number three, market planning. Who is it for? And how will they know that it's for them? You need to be selling your book, the idea of the book, or literally selling the book before it comes out. You want to be building up your audience before you ask them for anything. And you do this by giving them quality, content, quality, value, useful stuff that are around the concept of the book. So when you do drop the book, they're already ready to buy from you.

They already know you're an expert. They already know you can help them and you've already given them value.

#2837: The 6 Pieces Of A Successful Book [Part 2 of 2]

Let's get right into this. Picking up from where we left off yesterday, we're on point number four. We were talking again to six pieces of a successful book and again, this is holistically the entire book, not just the putting out of the book order writing, but all of it. Number four, financial, financial peace here. What I mean is with the pricing of your book, that's part of it. And the pricing also includes how much money you want to make holistically from the fact that you even have this book coming out. So that can be more than just the

Actual cost of the book itself. So let's say you want to charge 20 bucks for your book, that's part of the finances also, but let's say you have more than one book. Do you want to bundle this together with other books? Do you want to use your book to sell other things such as coaching or courses or your professional speaker as well? Those are all things you can bundle into the pricing of your book. So understand that your pricing, whatever you're going to price your book, let's just say with the book itself, we keep it simple. It needs to factor in who your audience is, where this book is going to be placed, meaning who it is going to be in front of. When I say placement positioning, that positioning is how you talk about the book. What are you saying about it and what impression do people have of your book based on how you talk about it that's positioning the value of the book.

What are people going to get out of it? What kind of change is going to happen? What problems get solved? That's the value. And also your hard costs. Hard costs are simply how much does it actually cost you to get one copy of your book printed? How much does it cost to get the book shipped based on where you're shipping it? How much does that cost? If you have inventory that you need to hold somewhere, are you paying for the inventory costs? All of that does the hard costs. That's the stuff that you can actually count on a calculator. So if you are writing a book, I would assume that you have probably read some books before you started writing a book. I don't know too many people who've written a book but they've never read a book before. And that would mean since you've read books before, you have a pretty good idea of how books get priced.

You have a general idea of how much a book costs, right? And work on your game university. I work with people on the pricing of their books and other products and talk about how they can subsequently make more money off the book besides just the price of the book. Again, it doesn't have to be from book sales directly because we know that they book costs. What anywhere up to maybe 30 bucks is how much somebody's going to charge for a book. Well, if you want to make a lot of money, let's say you want to make something like $10,000 a month, and this is the number I hear often from entrepreneurs. First of all, you have to sell a lot of $30 books in order to make $10,000 a month. That's a lot of sales and that's assuming you sell the book for 30 bucks.

What could you sell for $15? I mean, we can just do the math on this. You can know how much money you stand to make based on the cost of your book. So if you want to make $10,000 a month and you were selling your book for $15 was about a common price that I see, it means you got to sell 667 books every month. It's technically two thirds of a book, but we'll just say 667 books every single month and that makes you $10,000. That would get you right at $10,000 if you sold 667 books at $15 a month. I did an article on this sometime ago where I talked about entrepreneur math and I called it $250,000 math. And if you want to make a certain amount of money, you just need to do the math on what you are going to be selling it, how much you're selling it for, and how many of them you would need to sell in order to make the money that you want to make.

And also this is not counting your out of your outbound costs in order for every book that you sell, first of all, you have to print it, you have to ship it, you have to pay for the label, you have to pay for the envelope. That book goes in, you have to pay for whoever is housing the book. So if you're selling 667 books a month, those books have to sit somewhere or they have to get shipped to you. So there's a cost for that. There's probably going to be some type of software system that is tracking every order and making sure that the orders go where they're supposed to go and no tracking numbers get sent out and emails get sent, notifications, all of that, and that's going to cost you something. So it's not actually $10,000. I mean revenue wise it is 10,000, but then after all your costs are going to be significantly less than $10,000.

The whole point being we want to work on, and this is what we do and work on your game university, we work on what other ways can you monetize the fact that you have someone's attention from your book and make yourself more money in ways that are even higher margin. So for example, a course you can make more money selling a course than you can make selling a book and the course usually doesn't have as much, it doesn't have as much fulfillment cost as a book because most courses are online. So I sell you a course, it doesn't cost me any money to make the sale to you and for you to get access to the full course. It doesn't cost me any money because I already have the website, I already got the backend set up, I already got the course materials on there.

None of that's costing me any money to just get it to you. But if you buy a book from me, a physical book, I have to, again, I have to print a label, I have to put it in an envelope, I have to actually get the book printed and I have to pay for the shipping. So all of that stuff costs me money. So this is why you want to look for higher margin things that you can couple with the fact that you have a book that can allow you to make more money than just the sale of the book because again, that's how a lot of book sales you got to make in order to make the kind of money that I hear a lot of entrepreneurs talk about wanting to make. So it does not have to be just from the sale of a book.

So when you're writing books, you probably, most people I know who write books and almost everyone, not almost, but everyone I work with who writes a book, you have other things to sell besides just your book, things such as courses. You can sell more than one book. You can sell bundles of books for example, over here we have the bulletproof bundle, you have coaching, you get speaking consulting, you can sell webinars, you can do some type of training and many other things that I'm not even listening to here. So the financial part of your book is about the price of the book, factoring in your costs to actually get the book into the hands of the buyer, but also what are the ways that your book can produce money for you and your business that go further than just whatever the book costs. This is all part of your marketing and business strategy. So you need to be thinking about all of this stuff as your marketing, your book. Point number five, today's topic, once again, we are talking about the six pieces. You need to have a book to have a successful book. Again, this is all with the book. This is the whole life cycle of a book, not just putting it out. Number five is the production. Production means getting the actual book in your hands so that you can get it into the hands of

You mean you actually have a physical book or what needs to happen in order for you to get that book in your hands. So all of these things, all of this is part of it too that I didn't even get into. So this is an important part of putting books out that people have become more knowledgeable of these days simply because of the ubiquity of self-publishing and the ubiquity of self-Publishing makes it easy for anyone, even yourself to write a book, put it out and actually have a physical copy of the book and you can wave it around and show everybody, Hey, here's my book. It's pretty easy for anybody to do that these days. Relatively easy because so many authors these days are self-published. It used to be a thing back in the day, it actually is still a thing today. It's still a badge of honor for an author to write a book with a traditional publisher where you sign a contract with a traditional publishing company and they technically own the publishing rights to the book, you sign those publishing rights away.

That's what a publishing deal is. You sign away the publishing rights to actually own the publication of the book, but it still has your name on it and you get all the credit for it. But the publishing company actually owns the rights of the book. So anytime an author writes a book, the traditional publisher, the publishing rights are owned by the company, not by the individual who wrote the book. Now, later on, there are other details of that where you can buy back the ownership of the book, but usually it takes a certain amount of time because the publishing company wants to make their money, right? That's the reason why they did the deal. They want to make some money off the book. They're not just going to give it to you just because you signed the contract. So I mean, you really have no recourse to say, Hey, give me the publishing rights back.

And if your book is extremely successful, probably in your lifetime, you're probably not going to get a chance to buy those publishing rights back because the company wants to keep it and keep making money off the book. So you think of any extremely successful book that sells a lot of copies, the publishing company who did that deal is not selling the rights of that book back to the author, even if the author wanted to, because why would they? And they're making money off it. Anyway, this is why, again, you want to look at other ways to make money from your book. So since so many authors these days are self-published IE, they put their books out themselves and that allows you to retain complete 100% ownership over the book that you have published. And because so many authors may not even have the option of publishing through a traditional publisher, and many authors think they do, but they actually don't.

Once you have written your book, you need to get your book actually available so somebody can buy it, okay? So that's what the production pieces need to be available. So someone could buy it if they wanted to and not just buy it, but also read it. Hopefully they read it, whether it be a digital book or a physical or an audio. So getting a physical book printed is becoming super easy these days. Platforms that offer physical printing such as Amazon's Kindle Direct Publishing also was, which is abbreviated as KDP, they give you templates that all you have to do is just download the template and you can take all your book content, slap it into the template, and it is already perfectly formatted to fit Amazon's requirements. And then you get a cover designed and you can have your book in your hand within the next 10 days.

You have a physical book in your hands, and again, it'll be printed properly, it'll fit on the pages the way it's supposed to and all of that. And they show you exactly how to do this on Amazon's KDP, they show you how to do this. And again, you don't have to do all this stuff yourself, folks, you can just hire somebody who knows how to do this stuff. You can get with somebody who understands it, who can walk you through the process. You don't have to bang your head against the wall trying to figure it out. But in a general sense, once you've done it a time or two, it is relatively easy, relatively easy. But just because something is easy doesn't mean everybody's going to do it. And that's why I'm bringing this up. So you need to consider the production, how you're going to get your books printed, how are you going to get them ready for the public?

And then there's the next step, which we'll get to in a moment. So how are you going to actually do this? If you want to sell that 667 books per month, you need to think about, alright, how often am I going to order a new shipment of books? If you're selling that many books, 667 books a month, what does that mean? You're selling about 10, 20 books a day. Yeah, 20, 22, 23 books every single day you're selling those. So how are you going to ship those? Are you going to do the shipments yourself? Are you going to take the books to the post office every single day? Are you going to buy all those labels? Are you going to do all the shipping, printing? How are you going to do all that? Somebody has to take care of that. So again, think about these things and when you're going into any business, how am I going to do the fulfillment?

Fulfillment is what you do after somebody buys something from you, and that's the process of you getting the thing that they bought to them. How are you going to fulfill the order once it is paid for? Amazon has a great fulfillment process and part of it, the front facing part is called Amazon Prime, which states that if you have Amazon Prime, many products that are sold on Amazon, you can get it shipped to your house within the next two days. Often it'll be one day depending on the product, if it's a very ubiquitous product, you get the product one day. If you order early in the morning, some of you have probably seen this, especially if you live in big cities, you get the product the same day. I can go on Amazon at seven in the morning and order something. They say, well, we could get it to you by 12 o'clock this afternoon, depending on what the product is.

That's fulfillment. Now they have a whole system that allows 'em to fulfill that fast. There's a company speaking of shipping called Uline. A lot of you who ship physical goods, a lot of us use them. And if you do ship physical goods, you should use Uline because they have pretty much anything you could need to ship physical goods and everything else, anything that goes in a warehouse or an office building, they got it. All types of stuff. Mop, ringers, those yellow caution signs that you put on the floor when you mop the floor, you don't want anybody to slip and fall, bubble mailers, all kinds of things. Anything you could think of. Their catalog, their product catalog is super thick with all these products that they sell. And Yuon has warehouses all over the United States, at least in the United States, and they have a very

Tight fulfillment process. Whenever I order from U Line, they say, as long as you place your order before 6:00 PM Eastern, then your product is guaranteed to be shipped to you and arrive to you within 24 hours. They do the next day's shipping. You don't have an option of anything cheaper. So the cheapest shipment I can get from U on is like $22 for shipping. So what I do is I wait until I need a couple products and I just order 'em all at the same time. I know I got to pay $22 in shipping, and that's just the process. The whole point is they have a solid fulfillment process. So if you're going to ship a lot of books and take it from me as a person who has, I remember in the last year I really focused on selling books, just selling books, and I wasn't really, not that I wasn't selling other things, but I was selling books and I was running a lot of my front end ads just to sell books.

I just wanted to sell book after book after book, just ship as many books I possibly could. When last year I did, that was 2020, it was 2021 and going into 2022, so it was 2021 mostly. And then summer 2022, I did this. And the fulfillment process is it can be an arduous process if you're making a lot of sales and I was making a lot of sales, and you have a book, imagine if you're selling 20 books a day. Imagine if you're selling 20 books and then you got a bunch of upsells and people buy the bundles, and now you need a bigger envelope and you got to fit all the books in there, and now you got 10 orders you got to fulfill. Now you have to make sure people's addresses are correct and somebody didn't give you their apartment number or somebody's emailing you a, Hey, I ordered the book three weeks ago and I never got it.

And now you have to figure that out. You gotta go dig through and you got to take the books to the post office or whatever the process is to get 'em shipped out. It can become a job in itself just fulfilling the orders if you're making a lot of sales. So you want to think about all of these things. Don't just think about the end game of how much money you're going to make. You're thinking about what you have to do because you're making that money. Okay? So to make money, there's something you have to do and you want to think about your margins, you want to think about your fulfillment, you want to think about the costs. And the costs are not just in dollars, folks. The costs are also in time and energy that you have to give up in order to fulfill what you just sold.

Alright? That's all part of the game. Point number six, we're talking here today is what we're talking about today is six pieces of a successful book. Number six is distribution. Distribution means literally getting the book in front of people who need to know about it. In other words, getting yourself seen, heard, and known. And distribution applies to products the same way it applies to people. Any of you who's good at what you do, but you feel like not enough people know about you, then you have a distribution problem, also known as marketing. We call it marketing when we're talking about people, when we're talking about products, we call it distribution. You can also call it marketing as well. Distribution just means getting the word out about what you have so that the people who might be interested can at least be eligible to find out about it. Now, of course, we have readers. Those are the people who will buy your books, but also you want to think about the people who have access to your readers, people who have access to your readers is where you would use

The Dream 100 strategy. I talked about the Dream 100 in episode number 24, 84, 85, and 86. I did a three part series on the Dream 100. So if you haven't listened to that, again, it's episodes 24, 84, 85 and 86. And the Dream 100 strategy is simply finding people who have an audience of people who might be your readers and figuring out how you can collaborate with the person who has that audience and get your message in front of that audience such that their fans can also become your fans. So that's a form of collaboration, and this is something that I do all the time over here at Work On Your Game. We do a lot of collaborating. I have appeared on since 2015 when I went full-time into entrepreneurship. I've probably appeared on three to 400 different platforms of other people's shows, and the bulk of those have been over the last three years, or we'll say 2020.

So between 20, 20, 21, 22, 23, maybe the last four years, the bulk of that number that I just gave you has happened over the last four years, and that's upwards of 5,200 appearances every year on other people's platforms. So basically every three days I'm appearing on somebody else's platform because we have a process for leveraging the Dream 100. Why do we do that? Because it allows me to get my message in front of other people who already have an audience, people who already know I can trust them. I get some of that to rub off on me. I get in front of that audience and I can get new fans into my world, and at the same time, I can create an opening where now I have a new connection in business and this person is already out there and they already have traction. How can we figure out ways that we can work together even further than maybe even just appearing on their shelf?

So there are other things that we can do. So these are forms of collaboration, and this is all called the Dream 100, and this is something that you want to do on an ongoing basis because the Dream 100 is a marketing strategy. Dream 100 is not to say a tactic, it's a strategy and strategies you want to operate on a consistent basis. This is the process piece. So when I talk about work at your game university and I talk about mindset, strategy, systems and accountability, this is the system Dream a hundred. There's a system for how we do the Dream a hundred, and any of you can create a system for how you use the Dream a hundred based on who your audience is. So that's part of the distribution process, and again, you can run advertising as well. That's another thing you can do to distribute your products.

You can make content to get your book sold. And there are many other subcategories under each of these three that I just mentioned. So it's different ways to do the Dream a hundred. There are a million different ways to run ads, and there's a lot of different content that you can put up. So in other words, once your book is out or is about to be out, you need to think about what are you going to strategically do to make sure that people know that it's out, that people know the value of the book and what is going to do for them if they were to buy it and read it. So you need a plan for this. This is not something you should just be randomly doing. Now, you might think of a new idea today, but you need an overall plan for what am I going to tell people about this book, what I'm going to tell 'em it's going to do for them, and why?

When I get their attention, what am I going to tell them why they should? What am I going to tell them to help them understand why they should go get it? You need answers to those questions. So you don't want to be doing what we call random acts of marketing. You want to be consistently marketing with, you should come up with ideas consistently, but also you want to have a process into which those ideas can fit. That's the best way of saying it. Same way that I have a process for recording the show. I came up with an idea. I might come up with an idea five minutes from now, but I have a process for what I'm going to do with that idea. So the process is already in place. New ideas get thrown into the filter, and they get put in the place that they're supposed to go because we have a process, we have a system.

This is one of the pieces again that we have in work at your game university and how I help entrepreneurs like yourself. With that out the way, let's recap. Today's class was part two of series miniseries here, six pieces of a successful book. Number four is financial. This is the pricing of your book. This again, factors in audience, placing, positioning, value, your costs. Also, the other ways that you can make money from the book besides just the sales of the book, because there are a lot of other higher margin things that you can sell, like coaching, speaking and consulting, and courses on the back end of selling a book. So the book may just be the front end introductory offer rather than selling more stuff on the back. Number five, production. That means getting a book in your hands so that it can go into the hands of your readers.

This is an important part of putting books out that people are more knowledgeable about because we have self-published these days. So people are used to going through the whole process of coming up with the idea of the book, then getting it done and getting it out. Then actually physically having a book in their hand that you need to think about. This is if you want to sell a lot of books, you have to do a lot of production, and you need to think about who's going to be handling all that process, including the fulfillment, because that can become a job in itself. If you're selling a lot of books, trust me, I've been there. And number six, distribution, getting a book in front of people who need to know about it. Readers of course, but also people who have access to your readers. This can be the Dream 100.

This can be your advertising. This can be your content. So you want to have a plan, a full-fledged plan and strategy for how you are going to, and a system for how you're going to get the word out about what you're doing so that the people who need to know about it can know about it, and they can do something with what they know, which is of course go by your book.

#2838: Traits Of The Top 2%

Let's get into today's topic, which is traits of the 2%. Now what got me thinking of this topic because this is something that I have, I've actually talked about this before, I might not have talked about it. And yes, I did talk about this episode number 24 24, what the top 2% do that you don't do. So there we were talking really about the actions of the top 2%. Here we're going to talk more about the mindsets, the mental habits of the people in the top 2%. So this is a sister episode to that one, but this one is going again more to the mental side of it than just the activities.

So what got me thinking about this was I heard this story, I read this story that Pizza Hut in California was laying off about, I think they said 1200 employees. They were laying off because it was a response. According to the article, they were laying these employees off as a response to the minimum wage increases in the state of California. And I remember having some conversations with some people on social media about this, some people who agreed and some people who disagreed. And I remember some people were saying that was my solution, because I was having this back and forth conversation with several people and my solution was saying that well, people who really have a problem with the way that employees or staff or now laid off staff get treated, should cease being employees and just become CEOs. They could just become the person who owns and runs their business.

They don't have to worry about the way that employees get maybe treated poorly or they're underpaid or all these things that people were saying about employees and basically bad mouthing companies saying, well these companies are just greedy and they're just using employees and they're not treating 'em right because they're laying them off and they should just eat the costs and pay more money to their staff and all this stuff. And I said, well no, they shouldn't do that. The staff should just stop being staff and become a boss. So now you don't have to worry about how staff gets treated because you ain't staff. And some dummies in those comments, in the comments to the things that I was saying, they replied to me and they said, well Dre, if everybody became a CEO, there wouldn't be anybody left to work. Now theoretically they are correct that if everyone decides to be a CEO, there wouldn't be any workers because everybody would be a business owner and there wouldn't be any employees.

Doesn't mean that we couldn't still have businesses because everybody could just be a solopreneur running their own company. But that's besides the point I got. The directionally what they were trying to say, which is everybody can't be a CEO and they're a hundred percent correct. They cannot literally say that will not happen. Everybody becomes a CEO and I'm going to address the idiocy of that talking point and I don't think they meant it literally. I think some of them maybe did, but directionally I got what they were saying. I'm going to address why either, whether literally or directionally this will never happen. And I'm going to explain to you why today and what I'm going to try to help you understand, especially those of you who are listening to this show, is that it is not your job to worry about what the 98% are going to do.

You need to make sure that you are part of the top 2%. Alright, everybody else is their business. You are your business. So let's get into it. Point number one, topic once again today is traits of the top 2%. Number one, people who are in the top 2% have a heavy amount of drive, D-R-I-V-E drive. And I don't mean operating a vehicle. I mean top 2% performance have a level of drive that, and when I'm talking tom 2%, I'm talking about the type of people who are willing to do what everybody else doesn't do, such as make themselves the boss of their situation so that they don't have to worry about what the boss does. You won't have one anymore, you are the boss. So if you're going to join the top 2% and CEOs are in this group, and this is where this all came from mentally and physically, your drive to succeed must be stronger than that of almost everyone.

If you join the top 2%. And again, when I was telling these people who were I guess defending people who are staff who are getting laid off from their jobs at Pizza Hut, I said, why don't those people just become those people or whoever you're talking about, why don't they just become a CEO O and then you don't have to worry about again, complaining about CEOs and saying CEOs are overpaid or they're greedy or they're not worth the money that they make, but if they're overpaid, why don't you just become a CEO? I mean if your issue is money and you see that this job is overpaid, why don't you just take that job unless you think it's something morally or ethically wrong with it, which a lot of them kind of did allude to and I think that's kind of just a cop out. It's just a mental cope that people come up with so they can basically justify staying in the same space that they're in while complaining about it.

That's a little bit of a different conversation than what we're having here today. If you're going to be in the top 2%, your drive to succeed must be stronger than that of almost everyone you know shouldn't know anybody who's more driven than you. The reason why there will never be a problem of everybody on the planet becoming a CEO at the same time and leaving nobody to work is that most people don't have the drive to become a top 2% performer. They don't even have the drive, let alone the skill or the knowledge or the thought or the idea. They don't have the drive.

The reason I know this to be true is because I can subjectively look at the actions of people and you can as well now that you're thinking about it, look at the actions of the people you see around you. If you want to know what someone is truly about and what they truly believe, don't listen to anything they say. Simply watch their actions, watch their behavior. You don't have to watch them every day like some private investigator to see what a person is about and you can look at who they are and where they are today. Then check on them in five years or 10 years from now or someone who you've known for a while. Look at them today and ask yourself, who were they five or 10 years ago? Have they changed much? Have their circumstances changed much? Are they that much of a different person besides of the fact that they got older, fatter and uglier?

Besides that, has anything changed? When people only change by getting older, fatter, and uglier, this is a representation of them lacking drive. They don't have any drive, which is fine. I'm not saying it's to badmouth them, I'm saying I'm just pointing out the truth. Most people don't have drive, they just get older, they gain weight and they don't look as good as they did when they were younger. This is pretty much what happens with most people because they don't have any drive to do anything different, so they just live by default. And when you just live by default, the only things that happen is you get older, fatter and uglier. That is what happens. Again, I am kind of being tongue in cheek with this and being facetious, but I'm also telling you the truth. If I got this wrong, somebody let me know. What else happens to people when they live by default, they don't get better.

They don't just make more money naturally, that doesn't happen. You have to have a drive in order for things to get better on purpose in your life, and the only way things get better is on purpose. Things do not get better when you're just left alone. The only time in life when things get better by being left alone is during puberty. That is when your body naturally grows and it gets to a certain point where puberty ends and you stop growing and any growth you get after that has to be on purpose. Most people are not on purpose at all in any aspect of life. This is why most people's growth ends at puberty. Everybody follows point number two, today's topic once again is traits of the 2%. Number two, determination. The word determination, the root word of determination is determined.

What does it mean to determine something? It means to make a decision, right? If you say TBD, which stands for to be determined, what does that mean? That means that somebody somewhere needs to make a decision about what's going to happen in this situation. You might see that if you're going to go to a sports game that you see three weeks from now, the Lakers are going to play against the Knicks in New York. What time is the game? It says TBD to be determined. We don't know what time the game's going to be yet somebody's going to make a decision though about what time that game's going to be right? That's what determined means. That's what it means to determine something. So determination is the trait of a person who has made clear decisions about who and what and where they will be in life.

Determination is the trait of a person who has made clear decisions about who and what and where they will be in life. And let me let you in on a secret. 98% of people never make any decisions about who they are, what they will be or where they will be. So in other words, 98% of people have no determination because they don't determine anything. They just allow life to happen as it happens. That is not determination. That's the opposite of determination. That's the status quo. That's inertia or what many of you will call stagnation, one form of inertia. Most people don't determine anything and this is how most people end up wherever life decides to send them, not where they have consciously chosen to be. And there's a big difference between the two. You can end up where life wants you to be or just where it tosses you.

Life doesn't really consciously think about where it sends you, it just sends you wherever it sends you and if you allow it, you'll just end up wherever doing whatever with whoever. But you have a 2% of people who actually get determined about where they want to be in life and regardless of the circumstances put in front of them, they find a way to alter the situation and use circumstance to their advances regardless of what the circumstance is because they have already determined, predetermined where they're going, who they're going to be and how it's going to work. That is what determination sounds and looks like. Now, again, let me ask you, how many people do you know who fit that description? Hopefully you can say the person in the mirror fits that description and maybe you might know a handful of people, meaning you can count them on the fingers on one hand who fit that description. Almost nobody else fits that description. Most people don't fit that description. By the way, if you think 50 people who are like that, I highly doubt it unless you happen to be part of some type of high level mastermind. But other than that, just random people that you know just by living life, no, no way at all.

Again, this is how most people end up wherever life sends them, not where they have consciously chosen to be. Most people have zero determination. The top 2% of people have high levels of determination, which means regardless of the circumstances that are placed in front of them or the situation in which they are placed, they always find ways to turn circumstances to their favor. Now, while I tell you that 99% of life is out of your control, you don't actually control circumstances. The more control you take over the 1% that you do control, the more you can influence circumstance and you can start to turn circumstance almost as if you are controlling it in your favor. Your determination level is so high that you seem to be able to manipulate circumstances and because of your strong influence over the things that happen around you. And the only reason any person has a strong influence over the things that happen around them is because they have a high level of determination. In other words, they have already determined what's going to happen here and all they're doing is shaping the situation to fit what they have already determined it was going to be. That is determination, that's taking ownership, that's self ownership. That's the first principle when I talk about the 12 work on your game commandments is ownership. Taking ownership of your situation is determination. They are. You could use them interchangeably in this context.

So understand some folks when it comes to circumstances and when it comes to determination, 2%, people always find ways to turn circumstances to their favor regardless of the circumstance. They always turn that circumstance to their favor regardless of what it is. And again, this is not some magic trick. It's not some skill that's only available to a certain person. This is a skill that's only utilized by certain people, but it's available to everybody. This skill does not require any specific amount of resources. It doesn't require any resources at all. As a matter of fact, people have decided that they are going to be a certain thing and they set about making it real. That's it. Determined people have decided I'm going to be this, and then they go out and they become that thing. And it doesn't mean it happens overnight, it doesn't mean it happens just because they snap their fingers and it damn sure does not mean it's easy.

But because they have determined that they're going to do it, they're willing to go through the challenges the third day, if you will, to make it happen. And they have the mental toughness to keep pushing. This is what determined people do top 2% performance. This is what they do. 98% of people don't do this. They don't decide what they want to be. And since they haven't decided they can't go out and influence anything because they don't know what they're trying to influence, they don't know what outcome they're trying to get to. See. If you haven't made a decision, you have no determination, you haven't determined anything, then you can't really have any influence because the only way you can influence something is if you are clear on what you're trying to influence, who you're trying to influence, why you're influencing, and what outcome you want to get to see. If you haven't determined anything, then none of those things matter. They don't even come into the equation. So this is why determination matters so much. 98% of people don't do any of this stuff. So if you want to be in the top 2%, I'm telling you the formula right here for what you need to do that will separate you from 98 out of every 100 people. Point number three, today's topic once again is traits of the top 2%. Number three, discipline. Now this is one you should know pretty well.

Why should you know it? Well, I opened the show with this every single day, showing up every day to do the work. You heard me say that a thousand times. How many people do you know who do this? How many people do you know who show up every single day to do the work? I would bet for most of you, I would bet very few people who fit this description, even though it is a pretty simple concept, show up every day, do the work. How many people do you know who do it? And the reason so few people who do this is not because those people who don't do it, it's not because they lack the resources to show up. Everybody has the resources to simply show up. Anybody can just get out of bed and know where you're supposed to be and just be there on time.

Anybody can do that. Why do so few people actually do it though on a consistent basis? That's the question. Resources have nothing to do with this reason. People don't do this. They have no discipline. People just have no discipline. And so you may be thinking this may sound a little bit circular. Why do people not discipline? They have no discipline. Well, where the discipline comes from, let's back up. Discipline comes from structure. The reason many people can't show up consistently to do the work IEB discipline is because they have no structure. When there is no structure, discipline will eventually evaporate. When you don't have structure, your discipline will evaporate. I am more disciplined in my schedule throughout the day, throughout my workday when I have back to back items on my calendar and know exactly what needs to happen next and next and next.

Therefore, there are no gaps of time in my schedule. I'm more disciplined on those days and on days when I have gaps in the schedule because when the structure goes away, so does my discipline. So I'm just as prone to this as any other human being is. And this is why you want to have the structure in place. And this is why we have worked on your game university, where we bring the structure to you, we implement the structure into your business and into your life so that the discipline will happen as a natural byproduct.

So discipline comes from structure and many people lack discipline again simply because they don't have the structure because a lot of people don't even understand that discipline comes from structure. So therefore, because of this, they don't show up every day. They can't show up every day. And without that consistent work of showing up, they can't produce results.

And when you're not producing results consistently, guess what? You also don't have consistently. You don't have confidence. Now, would you be confident if you were consistently not producing results? Of course not. And when you are not consistently producing results, thus you add confidence, you are ineligible to be a self-determining individual because you don't have the confidence to even believe you can do anything because you ain't doing it. Remember where confidence comes from? It comes from a belief in your ability to do something. Where does that belief come from? It comes from past experiences. So if you haven't experienced any success, you have no reason to feel why you can experience success in the future. This is why your determination is weak because you don't have the confidence. You don't have confidence because you have no discipline. You have no discipline because you have no structure. So you see how all this works together.

So you see how this stuff connects and this is why having one piece naturally leads to the next piece and naturally leads to the next. So this is why I can confidently state there will never be a problem of everyone being a CE at the same time. That would mean everyone in the world has decided to be self-determining, structured, disciplined and thus confident. What are the chances of that happening? Chances are somewhere very close to zero. Know how silly that sounds? Everybody can become a CEO. Everybody's going to become a business owner. Nobody's going to want to be a worker because everybody's just going to be super self-determined and disciplined and believe in themselves. Really, you really think that's going to happen? I would love to take that bet, how much you want to bet on that and let's put some parameters in place so I know when I can collect my money because that's an easy win.

Point number four, today's topic. Once again, we are talking about the traits, mental traits of the top 2%. Number four, the will and ambition to be wildly successful. Now, you may notice that some of these words may sound pretty similar to you. So we talked about determination, we talked about discipline, we talked about drive, and I'm talking about the will and ambition to be wildly successful. But if you listen to the way I'm describing each word, you'll notice that there are slight distinctions between them. And also I will give you that. Usually when you have one of these, it often is accompanied by others. Usually you usually won't find someone who has a strong drive, but no ambition, no determination and no discipline. Usually it doesn't happen. Someone who's super disciplined usually has strong drive, they're determined and they have some will and ambition, usually these travel impacts, but they are different, and I'm telling you what each one of them does and why each one of 'em has their own position on the team. So ambition folks means a strong desire to achieve something. Often that requires a lot of hard work and effort. Most people, if you ask them, will tell you that they have ambition.

You ask most people, Hey, are you ambitious? Most people will say yes, no. You may get a few people who will honestly say, yeah, I ain't really that ambitious. I'm alright where I'm at. Again, it may not use the exact word ambition, but they will tell you that they want to achieve big things. So if someone wants to achieve big things that are not easy to achieve, that is a reflection of ambition. Whether they're lying or telling you the truth is a different question. But if someone says that they communicate that that is a reflection of being an ambitious individual. Again, whether it's true or not, it's a different story and that takes it to the next point. It's the next sentence rather. At this point, very few people actually take actions to get towards their set outcomes, let alone do they actually achieve them.

Even though many people will tell you that they have big goals and big dreams, if you watch them, their mouths say they have big goals and big dreams, right? But if you watch their feet, you watch their behavior, you'll notice that they never do anything to move themselves any closer to those big goals and big dreams. So which one should we believe? Folks pop quiz class. Which one do you believe? Somebody tells you one thing, but they do something that is different than what they said. Which one do you believe in, the actions or the words? Of course we all know the answer is you judge people on their actions, not on their words because words are a dime. A dozen words are slippery by nature. You can interpret someone's words to mean one way when it actually means something different. Actions are much harder to misinterpret because they're clear. Actions can be felt, words can be felt sometimes, but not all the time. And again, words can deceive. Actions are not as apt to be used for deceit as words are. Actions are harder to fake. It doesn't mean they can't be faked, let's be clear. But words are, you're easy to lie with words. It's hard to lie with actions.

So ambition is a strong desire to achieve something. Again, that requires hard work and effort. Most people say they're ambitious, but look at their actions. They're not ambitious.

No one wants to sound like an idiot or a dummy who has no goals. So if you ask somebody if they're ambitious, they'll say yes because they don't want to sound stupid or sound like a loser who doesn't have any goals. But most people, if you actually look at them, you will notice that they don't have any goals. They don't want to sound like they don't have goals, but if you look at them, it is obvious that they don't have goals because they're not doing anything to reach anything other than where they're at. They're not doing anything other than maintaining the status quo. This is how most people live their entire lives. I'm being facetious when I say that. A lot of people don't want to sound like idiots or dummies by saying they're not ambitious, but most people are idiots and dummies who are not ambitious. Is this what it is? I'm being facetious. I'm also telling you the truth.

Most people have no ambition. Most people are not going to do what it takes to achieve things that are not easy to achieve. So if you want to do something that's not easy, I mean that's hard in itself. Just the fact that you even told yourself you're going to do something that you know is not easy, that's hard. And if you can't be a boss in your own life, if you can't boss yourself to start doing these things that we talked about, you're not qualified to be the boss of anybody else. You have to have these things in abundance. This will and ambition to be great in addition to the other things that we talked about here. Moving on to point number five for Ask Point here today we are talking about the traits of the top 2% of performers out there. Number five, I have a rhetorical question for you. Who do you know who has all four of these traits? Discipline, determination, discipline, determination, drive, drive, discipline, determination, and will who has all four

Driven to be successful? They have the discipline to show up consistently. They have determined that they're going to be successful and they have the will, the strength of will and ambition to push themselves through challenging situations and challenging times to keep going on their path. Who do you know has all four of these? And you can unequivocally say, this person has all four. I would bet most of you the answer is very few people. In other words, you can count on one hand how many people you know who fit the description. Most of you, I would be surprised if most of you can say more than one person. Again, some of you may work with these types of people all day every day and you do it as a specialty. So maybe you know a thousand, but people know maybe one person who fits the subscription. Some of you don't know any, some of you are zero and that's okay. It doesn't mean you're doing anything wrong, but we're just trying to point out what's true. Okay, that's it.

Very few people have all four traits. So because very few people have all four traits, I'm going to let you all in on an open secret. There will never be a shortage of workers. While there's nothing wrong with being a worker, these workers who I run into, again when I'm on social media, they are complaining about the situation as if someone else is forcing it upon them as if they can't change the circumstance by simply getting these four traits that I just talked about. They can't just get these traits and they can live a completely different life if they wanted to. There will never be a shortage of people who just simply want to be told what to do. And there's nothing wrong with wanting to be told what to do. I mean that's the life that you want to live. You are entitled to live it

With no judgment from someone like myself. But the people who I find myself talking to on social media who call themselves defending the workers, they complain about the situation as if they have no choice, as if they have no options. And then when I say, well, you know, actually have options, right? You don't have to keep staying in this situation. You can become an entrepreneur. And then they'll say something like that that reflects their lack of knowledge of what entrepreneurship actually is. They'll say, well, these entrepreneurs, they all got millions of dollars that they inherited or that the government handed them or they got all these resources. That's the reason that they're entrepreneurs. No, it's not. You can become an entrepreneur with no money and you could do it right online or using all free stuff. See, a lot of people just had these false beliefs in their minds that they have never actually examined or allowed to be examined. So they go through their entire lives thinking that they're smart when they're actually stupid going through their entire lives thinking that they're doing things that are helping them when they're doing things that are actually hurting them.

But

With all that said, if you acquire and implement these assets that do require effort and hard work to acquire them and to implement them, and that's effort and hard work that most people are not willing to do. If you are willing to do so and you do, you can move further ahead than everyone else by leaps and bounds. Pretty simply acquiring and implementing these assets requires effort and work that most people will not do. Not your fault, not my fault. That's their decision and it's their right to live. And most people are destined to be the average masses. Most people are destined to be part of the masses. That's not a knock on people and it's not a knock on anyone who maybe you find yourself part of the masses right now. It's just the truth. And if you want to be one of the top 2% performers, you just gotta make sure you are not doing what the masses of people are doing. What are you doing right now that the masses do? Are you doing something that most average people do? Are you sitting around watching tv?

Are you mindlessly scrolling through social media? Those things are all average person behaviors. You have to catch yourself and you want to make sure that you are not amongst average people when it comes to your behavior, unless of course you want to be average. Now, if you want to be average, then I don't even know how you made it through this whole episode, but assuming that you have some clear purpose and some clear direction in your life, you know what your options are and you know what the trade off is of each one of these options. Let's recap today's class, which is traits of the top 2%. Again, I was thinking about Pizza Hut laying off employees while I was talking about it on social media. And some people were saying, well, the company's treating employees badly. And at one point in the conversation I said, well, why don't these employees just start their own businesses?

And people said, well, that's not so easy. And someone also said, well, if everyone became a CEO, there wouldn't be anybody who has to work. I've had more than one person say that to me. And today I'm explaining to you why the people who become that are in the top 2% and it still gives 98% of people to do everything else. So that will never happen, that there'll be no one working because everybody owns a business. Number one drive. Top 2% of people have a level of drive that no one around them has. Your drive to succeed must be stronger than that of almost everyone. Full stop. Number two, determination comes from the root word Determine. What does determine mean? It means to make a decision to know what you're going to do. Many people fall short in life because they never determine what they want to achieve, so actually, they don't even fall short because they don't even know where they're going.

You can only fall short when you get a goal. They don't go anywhere in life because they never determine where they want to go, why they want to go there when they'll get there, who's going to go with them? Never consider any of this stuff. So it's impossible for them to be successful. They don't set themselves up with a goal. You can't score without a goal. If you can't score, you can't win. Determine. People have decided that they're going to be a certain thing and they're going to live a certain way and they set about making it real through point number three, discipline. This one you should know well, because again, I open a show with this every single day. How many people do you know who have talent but don't have discipline? Alright, many of you probably work with some of these folks. Maybe you have hired them.

Maybe you've been hired by them. Talented people, skilled people, but they have very little discipline. Many people lack discipline simply because they have no structure, alright? Structure creates discipline. So if you're going to show up every day and do the work, then you can't produce results. You'll have no confidence. Then you're eligible to be a self-determining individual. So all this stuff connects. So you want to be self-determining. You got to be disciplined, you got to get the structure in place. It doesn't have to be your structure. Plug into our structure, come to work on your game university and plug into what we got. We will help you. Number four, we want ambition to be wildly successful. Ambition is a strong desire to achieve something that requires effort and hard work. Most people will tell you that they're ambitious, but if you look at their actions, you'll notice that most people are not ambitious.

They're okay being okay. And if you want to achieve things that are not easy, you have to go after them. Alright? You can't be a boss in your own life. You can't be a boss in other people's eyes. You haven't become a boss in your own life. So you got to start setting yourself straight on all of this stuff. And number five, who has all 40 traits? For most of you, the answer is very few people. And most of you may know one person, maybe you know one person who fits the subscription. And listen, this is why there will never be a shortage of workers in life. There will never be too many CEOs and not enough workers. Again, there's nothing wrong being a worker, but the workers who I run into who complain about the situation as if someone has forced it upon them, I don't agree with these people fundamentally.

So acquiring and implementing these assets requires effort, hard work that most people are not willing to engage with. And again, it's not your fault, it's not my fault, it's their decision and it's their life to live. Most people are destined to just be part of the average masses. This is not a knock on those people, it's just the truth. Just make sure you are not one of them unless of course you want to be. So by the end of this episode, you'll now know what your options are and the trade off of each, which I just did.

#2839: Why You WANT To Be Emotional

Let's get into this topic here today, which is again why you want to be emotional. How many people, especially males, I hear this often with males, they talk about getting emotional or accuse a person of getting emotional as if it's a negative thing, as if you have done something wrong or you have taken a loss in a situation because your emotions have gotten engaged somehow some way.

Now to them, I'm going to tell you how getting emotional is actually a good thing. Now, getting emotional, there's a wide range of how emotional a person can be, but what I want to talk about here today is why engaging emotions is actually a good idea and it's something I strongly recommend you do if you have big ambitions and large goals that you wish to reach. Now again, the disclaimer to what I'm saying here today is that getting emotional can mean a very wide range of things. So let's say there's a percentage of how much emotion is, how much of your emotions are engaged. It could be anywhere from one to 100%. So getting emotional could be 2%, it could be 99%. So take what I'm saying here to mean of course to be in a controlled way. So I didn't put that in the title. Why do you want to be emotional in a controlled way, but you want to be emotional?

You want to be emotional in a way that the emotions are not completely controlling you, but you are engaging them and using them. And once I get into these points, you'll understand what I mean when I say engaging and using your emotions at the same time, not allowing your emotions to completely run your life. Because we already talked about how you're in the emotional management business in an earlier episode of this show and how emotions are great gas pedals but terrible steering wheels, those points are still true. They still apply, but at the same time, that doesn't mean you want to turn your emotions completely off because if you turn your emotions off, you're going to be missing out on some opportunities that I'm going to detail here today that are only available when your emotions are engaged. Point number one, the topic once again is why you want to be emotional. Number one, emotions are lighter fluid, jet fuel and the gas pedal to your desired outcomes,

Your desired outcomes, you can light them on fire, I mean in a positive way where they just get heated up and there's more energy going on. So light it on fire in a positive way, jet fuel to push you forward. And the gas pedal, everybody knows what happens when you push the gas pedal in the car, right? The car moves forward as long as it's not in an emergency brake. They are the gas pedal to your desired outcomes. If you have big goals and big ambitions, you must know your emotional reasons for wanting to reach those ambitions and goals. If you have big goals and ambitions, you need to know your emotional reasons for wanting to reach those goals and ambitions. Now the question is why does someone need emotional reasons to reach their goals and ambitions? Why can't they just have logical reasons to reach their goals?

Dre, why do you need emotional reasons as well as logical reasons to reach their goals? I'm just supplying the question that you should be asking and I'm going to answer right now. The reason is because there will be times where urological and rational plans are not working as smoothly or as simply as you expected them to work. Sometimes things just don't work as easily or as smoothly as you thought they would work, and you're going to have to do a little bit more to make them work than what you thought you would need to do. And your logical brain and your rationality will not be enough to eat enough, be enough to push you over some humps that you're going to have to get over to push you through some slow times that you're going to have to work through to get you solving some problems that you have been previously unable to solve.

Sometimes you're going to need to engage your emotions to move yourself forward because your logical thinking can't take you any further. You're going to need emotion for this logic and logic is it. Logic and rationality are not always enough because if logic and rationality was all we needed, then again, all you would need is a library card. You could sit in the library all day and you would have all the ammunition you needed to reach all your goals, but instead you got people at the movies, you got people watching tv, you got people watching comedy, you got people listening to music. Why? Because of all of those things, people working out know what all these things do. They get our emotions engaged in some way, shape or form, different ways for different people, different triggers for different individuals. But we need our emotions engaged because that's what makes us human.

See, if all it took was just logic and rational thinking, then robots and artificial intelligence could outdo every single one of us because they don't make mistakes, they don't mess up, they don't take off days, they don't slip up, they don't forget things the way human beings do. But it is our ability to relate emotionally and our ability to touch others' emotions and our own emotions that is, excuse me, the last frontier between us and robots. Because if all it was was logic and rationality, then humans would be phased out in a relatively short period of time. Okay? So you need emotion and it doesn't mean that your logic and rationality can't work. I'm extremely logical and I hope I am a rational person, but you need a little bit of extra oomph every now and then behind your plans in order to move them through the resistance.

Alright? Sometimes you're going to face resistance in which you need an emotional reason more than you just need a logical reason. And this is where again, the emotions come in. This is why emotions are a great gas pedal, terrible steering wheel. All you do is turn the steering wheel in a car you never press on. The gas car may move, but it ain't going to go too far and it's going to take a very long time to get there, right? You might even get pulled over from going too slow. Jim Rowan famously stated that many people come up short on their goals, not because they don't have the knowledge or resources or abilities, but because they simply don't have strong enough reasons to be successful. If you listen to some of your favorite motivational speakers out there, even some of the speeches that I give when I give professional speeches, they are on the motivational side.

And when I say motivational, what I mean is they touch people at their emotional cores, not just their logical course. Because if all I gave them was logic, then it wouldn't move people to action. Logic is not often enough to move people to action. There's a small percentage of people who can be moved to action just by logic alone, and most of us don't fit that description. Even those of us who are very logical people, someone like myself, we still want some emotion to kind of trigger. It triggers our energy, it lights us up, it again pours gas in the tank. We need that. So your reasons to be successful are the gas pedal to your internal drive. And people who are strongly driven usually have very strong emotional reasons for that drive. Whether you know about the reasons or you don't, you might not know about them, but they have them.

So you think of some of your most known speakers who are known for motivating, think about Les Brown, think about Tony Robbins. Think David Goggins. Think Eric Thomas. Think Jim Roh. You think about these people and you listen to the stuff that they say in their speeches. Notice that most of the stuff that you remember from them has nothing to do with logic or rationality. Now, you may remember some of the things that they said, but the things that they said, you remember because it triggered you and touched you in some way emotionally, not just logically. And often the thing you remember about those people are their stories and stories are not talking to the logical part of the human brain. Stories talk to the emotional part of the human brain because when someone tells you a story, you if this story is told, well, you can imagine yourself in their situation and you can understand maybe how you would've felt or maybe they supply you by telling you how they felt and how that feeling you felt it somehow some way in your life.

So then you relate to them even though it's a different story than what you went through. But you relate to the emotion and that's how it touches you and that's how you stay connected to that person because they told you a story, they felt this way and you remember when you felt that way through something different and now you connected to that person because they have felt in a way that you felt and that's how you connect with them. And it is one way that a good salesperson can get across to an audience by touching them emotionally. And remember that emotions move people to action more easily than logic. I told you all when I was looking to play pro basketball, yes logically I was a good player and I could dribble, I could shoot, I could jump high, I could do all the basketball stuff.

That's all some of the strong drivers that I had. I wrote about this in my book, Work On Your Game. When I came home from college, my parents asked me a series of questions about my goals to be a pro basketball player and I didn't really have any real plan on how I was going to make it happen. And they basically held a mirror up to me and in my circumstance, and they were right, they were right in holding the mirror up because he just showed me that I didn't really have a real strategy for making it happen, which I did. And that moment gave me an emotional peak. It put me to an emotional peak to where I told myself I was not going to let the situation defeat me. And that energy, that emotional energy got combined with my logical ability and my thinking and my reasoning.

And that drove me over the next year plus before I got my first chance to play professional basketball. And it continued to drive me after that. And I would say it could still drive me today if I wanted to get myself in that state or think about it deeply. I could get myself in that state right now if I wanted to. And also when I was in college. So last coach that I played for, I ended up not in the program anymore. I butt heads with that coach and my emotional drive to want to make sure that that coach's decision did not end my career. That didn't become the last statement of my basketball career, meant I had to get to the next level. So I was able to combine these situations as emotional fuel to go with my logical and rational ideas to go and make it happen.

So even for again, a person like me who is an extremely logical individual, when I say extremely logical, I don't mean logical like I'm smarter than other people. I mean if you have a hundred percent of a pie and some percent is logic and some percent is emotion, I'm like 90% logic. Even someone like me, that 10%, I still need that 10% of emotion to go with the logic. And you need it as well no matter what your breakdown is. Point number two, today's topic once again is why you want to be emotional. Number two, learn to identify, accept and channel your emotions in the direction in which you want them to go. So this is what I just touched on at the end of point number one. So once you identify your emotions, remember we're in the emotional management business, so you can't let your emotions just run amuck and dominate you because again, they'll run you into a wall.

That's for anybody. You want to identify your emotions when you have an emotion, accept the fact that there is an emotion there, recognize it, and then you want to channel that emotion in the direction in which you want it to go. Alright? This is your next step. Once you understand its value, now you have to learn how to use it. So once you are clear what your emotional reasons are for anything and your triggers for knocking into that emotion and wanting to be successful, then you got to learn how to control and direct your emotions based on how you want to use them and also how you don't want to use them or you don't want them to use you. So you have to learn how to control your emotions. So it's not just about having it and just letting it go crazy. I just told you great gas pedals, terrible steering wheels.

Any of you have ever been in a car and your foot was stuck on the gas pedal and you couldn't get it off. I doubt any of you have been in that situation. If you did, you'd probably be dead right now because the car would've just kept accelerating and you couldn't stop it. You would've crashed into something and it'd be over. So none of us wants to get in that situation. This is why you gotta learn how to take your foot off the gas. You have to learn how to use the brakes and not always press on the gas. Alright, so you understand how this analogy makes sense. Emotions, again, great gas pedals, but there are terrible steering wheels and when you're driving in a car, you need to press on the gas to make the car move. But you don't just slam on the gas the entire time that you're driving because again, you'll end up dead and you'll probably kill some other people in the process.

So you have to control the gas pedal, alright? You don't just slam on it just because it's there, you control it. And it's the same thing when it comes to your emotions. So in any type of high stakes situation such as in business or playing a sport, you need an emotional drive to give you the energy. However you can allow the emotions to just take over and control you because the emotions will disturb you, they'll disrupt your steadiness, they'll disturb your thinking and it can cause you to spiral out of control behaviorally. So you think of something like basketball is a sport that I played. It's yes, you can use emotion to get yourself locked in and focused and ready to go for the game. Whether you're going to be angry, whether you want to be cool and steady, whether you want to tap into your killer mindset, whatever you want to call it.

Different people have different ways of languaging it and different things that work for them. But if you get too emotional in a game of basketball, it's hard to dribble. It is hard to shoot because shooting is a fine motor skill and if you're too emotional, those fine motor skills go out the window. Dribbling is a fine motor skill passing. These are fine motor skills. So you can't just be out there all emotional because you can't just go running around crazy in basketball because you need a combination of power and fine muscle movements and you can't just be all angry shooting a three pointer ball, probably not going to go in the basket. So you have to learn how to channel the energy. Whereas in another sport, let's say something like football, emotion can help. If you're a defensive player in football, you don't really need to think too hard.

You can just be all emotional and just try to hit people as hard as you can because that works for football. If you're on offense, on football, however you probably can't do it that way. Maybe you're running back. But other positions probably not even an offensive lineman, definitely not a quarterback. You think of a sport like boxing, you might think of any kind of combat sport, it may look from the outside in. That is just emotion. Just get angry and just go out there and just swing. But if you go up against someone who actually knows how to fight and you're all emotional, they're going to bait you and they're going to use your emotion against you and probably knock you out. So it's not even that, that is not the deal either because if that's all it took, then they would just take some random guy off the street and need to just be beaten up by professional fighters.

And not to say that they couldn't, but most of the time it doesn't work that way because you need some thought, you need some logic that goes into it as well. So again, remember that emotions are a tool folks, remember they're a gas pedal. The gas pedal is a tool. You can't go through the whole world, just whole life rather just slammed on the gas, you're going to die. They are terrible. Steering wheels use emotions the way they should be used, which is not everywhere and not all the time. Again, they are a tool, they're not the mechanic. If you can follow that metaphor, everybody gets what I'm saying here. A mechanic controls the tools. The tools don't control the mechanic. You are the mechanic. The emotion is the tool. You use it when you need it and when you don't need it, you put it back on the shelf.

Point number three, topic once again today is why you want to be emotional. Number three, if you want to engage and influence other people to action, you must learn how to touch their emotions, not just their logic. As I said, there's a small percentage of people who you can move them with just logic alone. But everyone else, you need to touch their emotions on some level to get them to do anything because most people, everyone listening to this right now, including myself, we have some things that logically we know that we need to do, but we're not doing them. Why? Because we haven't found an emotional trigger that will move us to actually do something as opposed to allowing the status quo to remain the status quo. This is the law of inertia. It's easier to stay in one position the way that it is, whether it's moving or not moving than it is to change the situation.

This is inertia. To break your inertia, you need energy and emotion is energy. Energy is 85% of the job in life. Energy is one of our five forms of investment along with time, money, attention and focus. You need energy. If all it took was to move people to action was logic, there would be a long line again outside of the library instead of outside the movie theater. Notice that logic is not one of the five forms of investment. Energy is logic is not, doesn't mean don't have logic, but it's not one of the five forms of investment. People like me. If all it took was logic to move people to action, then people, podcasts would be more popular than musical artists. But the reason that music is more popular than a podcast is because music touches your emotions in a way that a podcast does.

Not to say the podcast can't touch your emotions, but the rhythm and the beat of and the melody of music touches humans emotionally in ways that just the spoken word cannot. Now again, there are some spoken word artists who are great at touching your emotions, but you get what I'm saying here and this is not the way the world works, that just the speaking, just the words, just the logic is enough to move someone to do something. You got to get them emotionally. People are engaged in influence when their emotions are touched, not when their logic is touched. Again, most of the time there are some exceptions. As a matter of fact, I will say that most people do very little logical thinking. Most of their most thinking that most people do is not super logical. And even when people do think of things logically, they usually don't do anything about what they just thought about when all their thoughts are just logical.

So I know when I'm being logical, I'm only reaching a small percentage of the population or I'm only reaching a small percentage of you and who you are. And even when I'm trying to reach other people, I have to limit how much logic I give them. Thus I may go less. I go over the 24 hour limit of logic. Some people just can only take but so much logic before is like, alright is enough, I need something else. In the sales world, you often hear that facts tell and emotion sells. If you've ever been in sales, you probably have heard someone say that before and you should remember it because it's true. It's a cliche because it's based in reality, it's based in truth. Best way to get anyone to do anything is to trigger them emotionally. Don't worry about logic, you gonna' have to use logic at all for some people to move them to action.

And there are a small percentage of people, again, logic will work, but everyone is triggered through emotion. Now there are some people who you can trigger through logic, you can trigger any human being through emotion, but it depends on what emotion and you got to touch them in the right place at the right time. And some people have to work harder than others to trigger their emotions. So don't think that the emotion that worked on person A is going to work on everybody else. Your job is to figure out what that level is for others. You have to figure out how to do it consistently. And if you want to influence and persuade people, you must figure out how to reach these people emotionally. You're going to be in the sales world and understand everybody in the world is in sales. You better learn how to trigger people emotionally.

Alright? This is an absolute when it comes to selling and when it comes to trigger people emotionally in sales, there are certain sales triggers. Things such as to gain praise, to be praised by other people is an emotional feeling. If people praise you or you stand in front of them and always get a standing ovation that triggers an emotion. If you want to avoid pain or if you have some pain going on in your life and yet pain was completely alleviated, would you feel emotionally better? Of course you will. Let's say your pain is you don't have any money, but now you start making some money. Now you have money to take care of all your needs. Would that emotionally make you feel a whole lot better? Of course it would. Those are forms of triggering people's emotions. So you want to think of these three dimensions as not just anger, sadness, happiness, yes, but what leads to that?

What can lead to happiness? If you made an extra $10,000 in the next 24 hours, would that make you happy? Yes, that's an emotion. Alright, so understand this is how logic and emotion work together. They're not independent, they're not mutually exclusive. They work together. Views need to figure out how my logical points trigger someone emotionally? And then you gotta tell them, you got to explain it to 'em. Don't leave it for them to read in between the lines of that. So with all that said, let's recap today's class, which is why you want to be emotional. And again, you hear many males these days, especially talking about someone getting emotional if they're doing something wrong, as if it's a bad idea to get emotional. Getting emotional is actually a good thing. And here I'm telling you why number one, emotions are the lighter fluid, jet fuel and gas pedal to your desired outcomes.

If you have big goals and ambitions, you have to have emotional reasons for doing it because that will push you through the times when your logic and reason aren't enough. Number two, learn to identify, accept and channel your emotions in a direction in which you want them to go. So you have to control your emotions. I told you, you're in the emotional management business. You have to manage emotions. That is not, you're not suppressing your emotions, you're managing your emotions and understand that your emotions are a tool. You are the mechanic. You use tools. You don't just let the tool use, you use the tool. So you have to control the tool, put it on the shelf when you need it, take it off when you don't or grab it off the shelf when you need it. Put it on the shelf when you don't.

And number three, if you want to influence people to action, you must learn how to test their emotions, not just their logic. And every human on the planet can be moved to action through emotion. There are a small percentage of people you can move with logic, but everybody can be moved with emotion. And if all it took was logic to move people to action, then again there'd be a long line at the library instead of a long line at the movies. People are at the movies because the movies are emotional, the library is logical. Not to say that the library is not valuable. Remember the opportunities and the opposites, but you need a mix of both. They work together. You think of the logical things that will make sense for another person If you want to influence another person and ask yourself how can this logical thing make sense for them emotionally?

And if you can translate it into that language, you're much more likely to have it work and produce a result for you than if you just give 'em the logical point. Because most people will agree with your logic if your logic is sound, but it doesn't mean you're going to do anything. And if you want people to do stuff, that's what influence and persuasion means. Then you got to give them a reason to do something. And usually emotion will give people a reason much more than logic with a reason.

#2840: How To Get The "Second Dollar" In Business

Let's get into this topic. How to get the second dollar in your business. It doesn't matter what kind of business you have today. As a matter of fact, as I was meeting with a gentleman, a friend of mine, he runs a brick and mortar business and his brick and mortar business, what they do is they help restore and repair dress shoes. So being that I wear so often and I'm wearing dress shoes with my suits and I walk a lot now in these dress shoes, the shoes, the soles of the shoes get worn down from all the walking that I'm doing and I needed to get the soles replaced.

Now these are shoes that I've invested a lot of money into buying. So I was willing to pay to get the bottom of the shoes, the bottoms of the shoes restored because it is worth it to maintain this investment that I made into these shoes. And I went to the place and this guy was fixing my shoes and he started to start asking me questions about what I do. I told him I'm a business coach, and he said, well hey, I happen to be looking for something like that. And he and I sat down and had an ongoing conversation about how I can help him in his business. Does he give you all an example? Now do I know anything about restoring shoes? No, but I don't need to. I know nothing about, I know a good amount about his business, he told me about it.

But the whole point being folks, I want you all to understand those of you who are considering my offer when I tell you to go to work on your game university and you're thinking, well, Dre does this online stuff and the podcasting and the books and stuff like that, but my business is nothing like that. I like his messages, but I'm not sure he could possibly help me. I'm giving you an example so that you understand that I can and I'm bringing him up because when you're trying to get the second dollar in your business, he needs to get the second dollar from his customers. The same way that you who sells books online, you need to get the second dollar from your customer the same way that someone else who is a, what's another business? Somebody can run, you have a house cleaning business, you need to get the second dollar from your customers.

If you run a financial services company, you need to get the second dollar from your customers. Every single one of us who sells anything, we want to get the second dollar from our customers and our clients. So what does the second dollar mean? This is referring to when a person has already paid you for something, they have become your customer or client in some way. They have given you money, the exchange has happened. Now you want them to make the decision to make another exchange, a second exchange either for more of the same thing or something different. It doesn't matter. The point being they made a second exchange with you. So when I say the second dollar, I don't mean that the first exchange had to be $1 and the second one was for the dollar. Number two, I mean that metaphorically meaning they had made a second business transaction with you.

That's what I mean when I say the second dollar. Again, it can be the second, third, fifth, eighth, all future transactions I'm referring to here when I say the second dollar. So today I'm going to explain how to get to this and also why it's so important for every business owner to understand the value of that second dollar as opposed to the first point. Number one, today's topic once again is how to get the second dollar in business. Understand that you must continually market to your customers. If you listen to my series on 21 Mistakes people Make in 21 Entrepreneurial Mistakes, people making businesses not understanding the value of continuous marketing and that's marketing not only to the people who have never heard of you because you want to bring new people into your business, which all business owners want and many business owners unfortunately however, focus exclusively on bringing new people into the business to

The detriment of servicing the people who are already there. Alright? In other words, you are missing out on the second dollar. You forgot to service the accounts of the people who have already given you their first dollar. So marketing does not just apply to people who've never heard of you before. It also applies just as much if not more to people who have heard of you and they've even done business with you. Just because someone bought from you yesterday does not mean they'll buy from you tomorrow. Even if they need more of the same thing, there's no guarantee they're going to come to you to get it. Now, how many of you have done this? You bought something from one place and the experience was fine, you have no complaints, but then the next time you need to buy that same thing, you went somewhere else, you just tried somebody else.

Maybe it was just more convenient. Maybe you were price shopping. Maybe you just wanted a change and maybe it was just more convenient to go to the other place than it was to go to the first place. Or maybe you were just looking for an experience that was a little bit different for whatever reason and you just didn't go back. Or maybe you just forgot about the place you bought from the previous time. And then when you bought from the new place for your second transaction, you then remembered, oh yeah, I bought from the other place the other time. Maybe I should have gone there, but you forgot about 'em and they forgot about you obviously. So hey, they lost out on the money. How many of you have had this happen? I bet all of us have had it happen.

Many of you probably don't even remember that this happens because many businesses do not market to their internal customers.

IE the people who have already given the money, they only market the people who never gave the money before. This is a mistake. Business owners, this is a mistake. We all do this. We buy from one place, then we go buy the same thing from a different place just because we forgot about or did not remember or we're not reminded to come back and do business with that same place again. And it's not our fault as consumers, it's their fault or your fault if you're the salesperson. The reason this happens is because the first dollar, the business that acquired the first dollar, that's you. If you're listening to this, you as the business owner, you got lazy or you just were lazy. Maybe you didn't even get lazy. Maybe you were lazy all alone, you just lazy period. You were lazy about making sure you got the second dollar.

In other words, you did not do anything to ensure or entice or ask your current customer to be a customer. Again, again, do not assume that someone will remain a customer for life just because they were or are a customer. Once you stop marketing to your customers, they stop being customers. So understand that marketing is not just about bringing new people into your world. I've said this three times already here today. You need to keep marketing to people who have already come into your world to make sure they don't leave. You want to keep relationships warm because again, just because you know somebody doesn't mean you're going to keep knowing them. If you stop talking to 'em, then the relationship falls apart. This is how it works. So it doesn't mean people are going to keep knowing you if you're not consistently communicating with them. Any of you have friends that you haven't talked to in a while, if you just don't reach out to them and they don't reach out to you, then a relationship kind of goes away and there is no relationship anymore and neither of you did anything wrong necessarily, but since you are the one listening, I'm going to put the onus on you. You have to maintain that relationship by staying in touch with that person. So here's the thing about marketing and all

Marketing is folks, is the relationship that you have with your audience. Marketing never ends. There is no end to marketing When you run a business, you are in the marketing business forever. It doesn't matter what your business is. When you have a business, you are in the marketing business. Everyone understand what I'm saying here? You're in the marketing business until you get out of business, period. As long as you own a business, you are in the marketing business. Doesn't mean you have to do 100% of the marketing yourself, but you are in the marketing business. If there's no marketing happening, you won't have a business. Most important thing that any business does is marketing because if you're not marketing, there's no way anybody can buy anything from you. So if you're not in marketing, you can't sell. They work together. Point number two, today's topic once again is how to get the second dollar in business. Number two. Now let's talk strategically about how you get people to want to give you a second dollar? So now you understand the concept of the second dollar. How do you actually put this into action? Well, the simplest thing you need to do is you need to have a next thing for people who are already buyers.

In other words, if someone's already giving you money, you need to give them a reason to give you money. Again, you need to give them a logical reason. Okay, you bought this. Now here's the reason why you should buy this, whatever the next thing is going to be. Now let's get more tactical and logical here. So if you're going to get a second dollar from a client or a customer, you need a reason for them to do it. In other words, you need another thing to sell them. Now, some businesses have this already built in because of the nature of their products. They have it built in, but it doesn't mean they should get lazy. So this is where a lot of companies get lazy. So you think about something like lotions, potions, makeup, cosmetics, any type of food, perishables like food, things that people consume and it's gone and they need more of it.

These things always run out. So what does the consumer have to do? They have to go and buy more of that same thing, but just because it's already built into your product, that is going to run out and people will need more. Do not assume that they're going to come get the most from you just because you're there, they might not start going somewhere else. So it's built into somebody's going to need more bread, more lipstick, more toothpaste. So let's talk about this and companies get lazy with this. So I eat a lot of bananas, which is my favorite fruit. Bananas and apples I eat the most of and I eat. Lemme see, I eat two bananas in the morning to work out. I put a banana inside my protein shake and I might eat another one over the course of the day. So I'm going through at least four bananas a day.

So over the course of a week I'm going through about 30 bananas because a couple times during the day I may just eat a banana as a snack. I'm going through somewhere around 30 to 40, 30 to 35 bananas every week. So I have to keep mine. It's not like you can just buy a thousand bananas and they'll just stay ready until you're ready. They're not like foods with preservatives in 'em. They're actual fruits, which means you have to eat them in a certain timeframe. Then you gotta go get more when they're fresh and they don't last that long, right? Bananas you can keep in your house for what? In five days and then that's pretty much it. I used to get all my bananas from Whole Foods and Whole Foods is fine, but Whole Foods would be a little bit shaky with the bananas.

They have some bananas that are a little bit too ripe, but I know they aren't going to last long. I like my bananas to have a little bit of yellow with a good amount of green because the green means they're not quite ripe yet, which means I can get them and let them sit and by the time I'm ready to eat them, they're ready. And I like the Bananas Firm and ripe and I don't like any bruises on the skin and none of that stuff, but Whole Foods getting kind of lazy with the bananas and once in a while I'll go to Trader, there's a Trader Joe's that is about equal distance in the other direction from where I live to get there at Trader I was getting some products from there that only Trader Joe's has. They have some bananas there and I get organic bananas.

The organic bananas at Trader Joe's are consistently higher quality than the organic bananas at Whole Foods. It's just the truth of the situation. So Whole Foods lost a banana customer and me. I stopped buying my bananas from Whole Foods. Stop buying 'em from Trader Joe's because Trader Joe's has been more consistent. So this is an example. Just because I'm always going to buy bananas doesn't mean I'm always going to buy 'em from you. Alright? That's an example. And you can also think of other companies that have products that are replenishable. Sometimes you can build your whole business just around that one product. You don't have to have a thousand different products. Think of a company like Ag One who is a sponsor of the work on your game show. If you go to ag one.com/work on your game, that's where you can get your first shipment of one.

You'll get a year supply free of vitamin D two, K three, and also a five travel packs to go with the age one. And that link is down below in the description by the way, and I think it's drink a one.com, not a one drink ag one.com/work on your game. That link is down below in a description. So don't take what I say, just scroll down and see it and click on it. It'll take you right there. Ag one's entire business and I'm going to pull it up here on the podcasting app that I'm looking at myself just to make sure I gave you the right link. Ag One's entire business is just that product. So it's drink ag one.com/work on your game. So I'm clicking on the link myself just to make sure it works and yes it does work. So get your starter kit when you start.

Now you're going to get a one, you're going to get a shaker bottle, you're going to get the D three K two, you're going to get the five travel packs. I'm looking to see what this is. Five travel packs. You'll get the monster supply ag one, a little container to put all your ag one inside. And again, this is all coming in your first pack. Ag one's whole business is one, don't have any other products. One sells one product, but it's a perishable product, which means when you run out, when your first month of packaging runs out, then they're going to get you another one. Then another one and another one they put it on what they call in that world, they call it an auto ship. Auto ship is you just put your card on file and every month they charge your card and they just ship you another package.

And many of you probably are signed up for a month of these. I've signed up for a lot of auto-ship products in addition to that. So electrolyte pills, my protein that I use in my protein shakes. What else do I get consistently from Amazon? I'm signed up for a bunch of what they call subscribe and save, which is an example of autoship is getting people to pay every month and you just continuously and they give you a little discount because paying every month because they know they have recurring revenue and many businesses want to have recurring revenue, there's a certain amount of money coming in every month. Now let's flip it on the other side. So I gave you the perishable replenishable side when you're selling something that people naturally will need more of, again like food, lotions, potions, makeup, et cetera. But what if you're selling something that is not in this realm, something that's not naturally I ran out of anymore.

Let's say you're selling something like coaching work on your game. University is a coaching program. It's not naturally something that you just need to go get more of just because you already have it. Well, if you're selling something like a book, I sell you a copy of my book the third day just after you finish reading the third day, it's not like you need to go buy another copy of the third day. Alright? The book gets sold one time and there's no reason for you to go buy the same book again. So what about that? What if you only have one book? I got 35 books. What if you have one book? What about that? What can you do in that situation? What if you sell a course, you get a course like Bulletproof Mindset 2.0, which you can't buy individually, but you do get access to it when you're a member working in your game university Or what about something in this space?

Now you sell something that's in this space you need instead of showing people that they need to buy the same thing again, which doesn't make any sense, you need a next thing for your customers and clients to want after they got the first thing. So what is the next thing that someone would want naturally after they get the first thing that you have, it is your job to figure out what that next thing could or should be or you need to be around someone like me who can help you figure out what that next thing is going to be.

And this is why you should be a member of work at Your Game university because this is one of the things that I'm an expert at helping you figure out what is the next thing in your business after they buy the previous thing again.

Because again, it doesn't make sense for 'em to buy two other previous things. They already got your book, they already got your course, they're not going to buy it twice. So what's the next thing they can buy? You need to know what this is and you need to have it ready so that when you sell them the first thing, you already are ready to sell them. The second thing, because some people will buy the second thing right there on the spot, but if you don't offer it, they can't buy it. Everybody follow? Okay? So you gotta have it ready so you can present them, you can present with them the next thing and why it's good for them in the process. So any of you who has bought a book for me, you've been through my sales funnel, I'm not talking about you bought it on Amazon, but if you bought it through our websites like third day book.com or mirror of motivation.com, if you ever bought a book for me through those, you went through our sales funnel.

Now it does not necessarily mean just because you went through the funnel, you're going to buy everything that we offer because we offer a lot of things in that funnel, alright? You could spend two to $300 within our sales funnel even though you came in on the premise of getting one book. The one book does not cost you $300, but if you buy everything in the funnel, you will spend $300 because we're giving you value, we're giving you like a thousand dollars worth of value for 300 bucks. So it's actually a steal. The point being we offer you the next thing. So when you get one book, let's say if you go to mirror of motivation.com, and I know how this funnel works as I put it together

Myself, when you mind a mirror motivation, we're going to make you an offer right there on the spot. Hey, how about you get the whole bundle? We call this the Bulletproof Bundle, which includes the super you, the Mental handbook and 100 mental Game best practices because I mean who reads this one book anyway, if you read books, you're going to read more than one book. So I'll sell you all four books at the same time instead of just one book. That is a way of me getting the second dollar, I'm offering you the next thing right on the spot. So next thing ladies and gentlemen does not need to be the next day or a month later or a year later, you can sell people the next thing right on the spot when you're selling 'em. The first thing, same way that when you're selling a car for example or an interview , have you ever bought a car.

When you're buying a car, what do they do? They try to sell you all the extras. They say, oh, how about a sunroof? How about a Bose sound system? How about the formats? How about whatever other extras they can add to a car? It's all kinds of stuff. What about tenant windows? How about some 20 inch rims instead of the eighteens, they always try to sell you some extra stuff, right? They sell you the next thing, they sell you on a they may be some kind of warranty they sell you on or they sell you on, who knows, whatever it is they sell at car dealerships and you just bought a car lately. Look at your receipt, you can see all the next things that they sold you that you didn't need to buy but you bought because they did a good job selling it to you, right?

So what is that next thing going to be? You can get the Bulletproof Bundle When you get the mirror motivation after that we're going to offer you the super duper mental game super duper bundle, which includes work on your game, the mental handbook, Bulletproof Mindset and 30 days of Discipline. And after that we're going to offer you something else. I may offer you to sign up for a coaching call at an extremely discounted price and on that coaching call I may try to sell you a coaching period. So look at all these next things that we're going to try to offer you all in one sales funnel and this all can happen in the scan of 10 minutes. Now the coaching call doesn't actually happen in 10 minutes, but when you get on that call then I'm probably going to try to sell you something else because this is what we do.

This is what marketing is, alright? We got to put ourselves in positions to make sales and it's okay folks, I want you to understand as you're listening to me, I'm telling you all these things we can sell. This is not a bad thing, this is a good thing because customers like to buy and people especially in the world that we live in in western society, we like buying things, alright? We are consumers, that's what we do. We consume, we buy, we spend money. And that's a good thing because when we spend money, that money goes to the entrepreneur. The entrepreneur or the business takes that money and they go buy stuff and the people they buy from take the money and they go buy stuff and the money circulates through the economy and the money comes right back around to you. This is all called circulation.

And when that circulation is happening at a high rate, at a high rate of velocity, this is called a healthy economy because there's so much money moving around and everybody's getting a piece of it and everyone's doing good. When the flow of money slows down and people aren't spending money as much, they call that a recession or a depression because the money's not moving around as much. So moving money around is a good thing. So you as a salesperson, it is your job to help the economy by selling things and getting people to move the money because when they move the money to you, you move the money to somewhere else to pay your staff or to pay for services that you use and they move the money somewhere else and they move it and they move it and it gets right back to that customer. The customer comes right back to you and spends money again. And now we have an economy.

Everybody understand? So that's a little finance lesson for all of you out there. Economics lesson I guess. So here's the secret folks, actually before I tell you the secret, lemme tell you this. You have to figure out what the next thing is. Have it ready so you can present it to them and tell them why it's good for them. The secret is this, ask people who have already given you $1 what they would want. That could become dollar number two. So if any of you is unsure what your second thing can be, ask your customers.

Any of you has a first thing and you sold some of them, ask the people who bought from you, okay, now that you got that from me, if I was to sell you something else, what's the next thing you would want or need based on what you got from the first thing? That's the question. Based on what you got from thing number one, what should thing number two be? Now not all your customers are going to have a good answer to this, but if you ask enough of them, you probably will get a couple good answers. And if you come into work at your game university, I'll give you 50 good answers as to what your next thing can be in your business. But you got to meet me halfway and come into the university, ask yourself after you ask your customers, what problems does a person now have that your first dollar product solved?

Now that your first dollar product solved a previous problem, what's their next problem? So I'll give you an example. So the first product that I ever created was Hoop Handbook. It was a basketball training program website that I still have to this day and I was selling a shooting program and dribbling program. That's what I was selling to basketball players. And then I made a whole bunch of programs about basically every skill you could do in basketball. So I'm helping these players work on their games and become better at playing basketball. So the question is what is the natural next problem? Because every time you solve someone's problem with one product, it is going to create a new problem with the next product that they meet. So the next product that is going to create a new problem that your next product can solve, whatever that next product or service is going to be, is going to create a new problem for them.

So let's back up here and I'll come back to the basketball thing in a second. If you sell cars, for example, let's say you sell a car, somebody buys a car, they have a car. Now what's the next problem that they have? Well, it's a couple problems. First of all, they need auto insurance. They're going to need gas, they're going to need to do something to protect their car. They may want a warranty or an extended warranty. There is going to be ongoing upkeep on the car. So certain vehicles, they have services like hey, every thousand miles you get a service. Whatever it happens to be. I don't mean it's an oil change, but I mean a full scale service. So automobiles like Lamborghini's, BMWs, Mercedes, they do this. They tell you, hey, you need to get a service on your car or whatever that is going to be and they do all this stuff to it that's specifically done for that car by that company. So these are all the next things that someone's going to need now that they have a car. Everyone understand this? So when I was selling basketball training programs, the ball players, I asked myself what's the natural next problem that a basketball player has. As he gets better at the game, he's better at playing. What's the next problem he's going to have? Well, he's probably going to have a problem getting on the team. So I wrote a book about 30 days of tryouts. How do you get ready for Basketball

Tryouts? I wrote a book called How to Play as Well As You Practice. So I'm giving you all these skills to help you practice good, but then the players will say, well Dre, I practice really well but then I get in the games and I mess up again where I get this idea from folks not because I'm some evil genius sitting in the basement, I got the idea my customers were telling me, re I'm practicing, I'm getting better, thank you for that. But when I get in the game, I'm still messing up. What can I do about that? So I wrote a book explaining to you how you can take your skills from the practice court to the actual game. It's literally called How to Play as Well As You Practice. I'm showing you the book right here. So any of you who's watching this on video, you can see it right here.

It's called Basketball How to Play as Well As You Practice, you can get this book for free. It covers the shipping. You heard that somewhere before, right? Go to who handbook.com/free FREE who handbook.com/f free. You can get a copy of that book, how to Play as Well as You Practice. And guess what's going to happen when you go get your copy of that book, we're going to offer you more books. Alright? Everybody understand this? Alright, this is not random, alright? There's a science and a structure to what we do here. And again, when you're a member of your game university, I will teach you how to do this. I'm telling you what we do, I'll teach you how to do it, why to do it and help you put this all together in your own business. So all of you, whatever you sell there is a natural next problem because there's no human being on the planet who has no problems and there's a lot of people who have a lot of stuff that they bought, they still have problems.

So what is the natural next problem that comes with the product that you sell? So let's say, let's come up with another one. Let's say, let's say I was helping women lose weight and get in shape and get makeovers. So let's say I was doing all of that. I did a whole full service. So a woman comes in and she feels like she's 25 pounds too heavy and she doesn't feel pretty or sexy and her wardrobe is like 10 years behind the times. So I help her get in shape. So now she has this great body, I help her fix up her wardrobe so her clothes look the way it this supposedly look and I help her just with her overall femininity and the way that she presents herself in the world so that more men will be interested in her because she's single and she's single divorced and she's just trying to get back out on in the game, but she doesn't feel like the game is really feeling her right now.

So I help her with all that to where she's at the point that the game will be feeling her and everywhere she goes, men will be stopping and looking and she'll be turning heads and now she's getting all this attention from men. What's the next problem that this woman has naturally? Next problem is she doesn't know how to deal with these men because now she's got all these different men coming at her and she's not sure how many of them are serious. How many just want her for sex? How many of 'em want to build a family? How many of them are the type that she should deal with? So now she's going to need some type of coaching, maybe relationship coaching, maybe relationship coaching is getting herself back into the right stance so that she is aligned with the type of man that she's trying to meet.

So there's the natural next service that I can offer to her. Maybe I don't offer it, maybe I can go find someone who does that and they do that full time and I will make a partnership with them. So I say, Hey Mrs. Dating coach, I got this woman makeover business. Every time someone goes through a makeover, the next thing they need is dating coaching. How about every time I send one of my clients to you, you just give me a 20% kickback on whatever they do with your program. The dating coach will say yes, boom, we got a business deal. That's a collaboration folks, everybody catches that Now they're getting customers that they didn't have to go out and work for. The dating coach is getting money that I don't have to do any work for on the backend, so I get the money, but I don't have to do any of the work. I don't have to provide the service she does. And now we got a great business deal going and we're servicing our clients at an even higher level because we're giving them everything they need without them having to go look for it themselves. We are saving them time, money, energy, attention and effort and we're making money in the process. This is what business looks like.

Now I'm going to pause there and make sure you all caught everything that I've said here the last 20 minutes because there's a lot that I just gave you there and if you're paying attention, the light bulb should be going off in your head right now. Any of you who runs a business, okay, no human being, no matter how successful, how rich, how happy, how healthy or anything else is ever completely devoid of problems. Not one. Nobody. I know people with million dollar homes, I know people who make millions of dollars a month. I know people who have whatever it is that you think would be the nirvana type of life. I know people who have those types of lifestyles and guess what, they all still have problems. As a matter of fact, many of 'em have more problems when they have stuff than when they don't have anything.

Everybody has problems, which means entrepreneur, there's always a customer for you because that's all entrepreneurs do. All we do is solve problems and people pay us for it. So as long as you can identify and solve problems, you can always make money. Notice I said you can make money. I didn't say you will. You need the right structure and systems and accountability to make sure you do make the money, but the opportunity to make money never goes away. Point number three, today's topic once again is how to get the second dollar in business. Number three, recovering past customers is easier than acquiring new customers.

This is a mindset piece. Recovering past customers is easier than acquiring new customers and working at your game university. You got a four part framework, mindset, strategy, systems and accountability. Notice the first one, mindset. It is the first piece of what we do and work on your game university and there's a reason why it's first is not random because the way that you think needs to be laid is the foundation upon which we can build the activities you're going to do. We know the process, be do have. You got to be first before you do. If someone has given you money in the past but hasn't given you money recently, you have a better chance of selling to that person and just bringing them back into the fold than you do selling to a new person who's never heard of you before and never given you money.

Why? Why is this true? Because with the previous customer, you already have some known like and trust factors already built in with the previous person rather. But with the new person you don't have any of that. You got to build all that up from the beginning. Again, not impossible, but it's easier to work with someone who already knows who you are. You just have to revive the relationship and you didn't do anything wrong. They didn't do anything wrong, but they just kind of drifted away from you because you didn't do your job and stayed on top of them and made sure that they didn't drift away. So now you have to go bring him back and it's easier to bring up someone back than it is to go find somebody brand new. Now I don't say that applies to everything in life, but in business that applies, this is all assuming that the reason they stopped giving you money doesn't mean they didn't have a bad experience with you or they don't hate you or anything like that.

In which case everything I just said is null and void. But just assuming that they just drifted away, you were just not paying attention, you can bring them back. Point of this being do not assume just because someone stopped buying from you, they are not still in the market to buy. Alright? Just because they stopped buying from you does not mean they stopped being a buyer. They're still buyers. You just haven't paid attention. That's why they stopped buying from you. They just forgot about you or you forgot about them and you can control the one about you forgetting about them. So it doesn't matter if they forgot or not, not your business. It Doesn't even matter if they forgot. They could be thinking about you every day just not buying from you. You need to reach out to them, remind them you're thinking about them too and that might be enough to bring them back into your space.

Okay? So look through your list of past customers, come up with a strategy and a system for getting back in touch with some of those past customers because some of them may be ready to buy if you remind them that you exist. You just gotta let them know that you're here, that you're a guy, that you are available and you got something that could possibly help them. Sometimes that's all it takes. Sometimes that's all it takes is you just got to reach out to someone and remind them that you exist and they say, oh yeah, you do exist. Matter of fact, I got a problem that I think you can solve and boom, you got yourself a second dollar from a past customer, but you got to do this work.

You have to do the work of actually reaching out to this person. They're probably not going to reach out to you. You got to reach out to them. Most people are not proactive, but they will do something if you can be proactive. Remember personal initiative folks, what's personal initiative? Being a go-getter who makes things happen instead of waiting for things to happen. Alright, the things that we preach here we're actually doing and you come into our world. I will coach you on how to do these things and how to do them efficiently, how to do them systematically, how to do them predictably, how to do them in a way that produces revenue, okay, profitably. That said, let's recap today's class. It was how to get the second dollar in your business. So when I say second dollar, again, I just mean someone giving you money after the first time.

So second, third, eighth, ninth time is the second dollar. Number one, understand that you must continually market to your current customers. Just because someone has already given you money. Do not assume that they are there forever and they will never go away. This is a false assumption because they always go away if you stop doing the marketing work. Number two, have the next thing. For people who are already buyers, you need to give them a reason to give you more money while they already have it while it's open. And you need to think of what is the natural next thing that they need to buy after they buy this thing. Some products and services, it is natural that they just keep paying over and over again. IEA gym membership or someone going to a gas station. But if you have something that doesn't make sense for them to buy it twice like a book or a course, you gotta ask yourself what's the next thing they would buy after they bought my book or after they bought my course?

What is the natural new problem that solving the old problem has created? So if you solve the problem with someone having a car, now the problem isn't needing insurance, now they need gas, now they have to replace the tires. Now they have to keep the car clean. So you have to think about what is the natural next thing a person needs after they buy your product. There's always the next thing because in America we are consumers. All we do is buy stuff. So all you gotta do is sell it because all people do is buy. Number three, recovering past customers is easier than acquiring new ones. Reviving a customer is pretty easy if you just reach out to a customer and communicate. Most of the time relationships fade simply because of a lack of communication, not because anybody's mad at anybody, not because anyone actually did anything wrong.

Sometimes that does happen, but often it is simply people just stop talking because nobody's reaching out, nobody's communicating and you are an entrepreneur, you are a salesperson. What is the fourth principle that we talk about here? The initiative to go make things happen instead of waiting for things to happen, not expect your customers to come looking for you. You go looking for them and I guarantee you go looking for a bunch of your past customers who haven't been around in a while. I guarantee you some of them are going to say, damn, I'm glad you reached out to me because guess what? I happen to have a problem that I think you can solve and boom, you just got to sell some customers or you just revived some customers. I guarantee you this will happen when it happens for you.

#2841: How To Communicate Concisely

Today's topic once again is how to communicate concisely. Number one, brevity. What does brevity mean? I did a whole episode on brevity. Lemme tell you about that episode that I did on brevity. So for those of you who are not familiar with it, it's one of my favorite episodes, episode number 1738, the skill of making your point without talking too much, that's what brevity means.

That's in my language. But the definition of brevity is concise and exact use of words in writing or speech. So brevity and being concise are cousins who will say brevity means don't use tenured words when you can use four. As I just said, there are three levels to brevity. Let me give you three levels of brevity. One is your ability to simplify your ideas and make them as easy to understand as possible, which usually means using fewer words and leaving yourself less room for someone drowning in your verbiage. People should not drown in your words because you've said too many of them. And often what people do is they make a good point and then they drown the good point with too many extra words around it to where the good point gets lost. It gets diluted. Don't do this brevity. Use four words instead of 10.

And this takes work. It takes work to be concise. It takes more work to be concise than it does to be verbose because it means you have to think about how to cut extemporaneous language out of my communication that takes work in writing. We call this editing today. I was actually working with a member of a game university and we were working on this. We were working on editing a manuscript for a book, a couple of books that she is putting together right now. And I said to her, more than once while we were working on this, Hey, we got to be concise here. Let's take this 15 word sentence and let's say the same thing in seven words. Make it half short and twice strong. Shout out to the genius. That's a rapper, by the way, by the name of the gza from Wu-Tang clan.

Most of you don't know what I'm talking about, but anyway, that's what I thought of when I said that line because he's the first person I heard say it. So one level of brevity is simplifying your ideas to make them easy to understand. Again, fewer words, let's run for someone to drown. You ever been in a conversation with someone who had a point to make, but again, they said so many extra things that you forgot to point. You ever been in a conversation with someone and they said something and you wanted to respond to that thing, but they weren't done talking. So then they kept talking and by the time they finished speaking you forgot the thing that you wanted to respond to. And of you've been in that conversation, men who are listening to this, you ever been in a conversation with a woman?

I'm sure this has happened. I'm kind of joking, but I'm not. And ladies, you know that you're guilty of this. So this is when people drown in your words too many words, people will drown, okay? And it is not about people having short attention spans, it's just that if you want people to remember things, understand something. Just simple logic. The more you give them, the less chance they're going to remember it. If you want someone to remember something, make it as simple and short as possible so that there's less chance that they forget what you said. Simple as that. Everybody got it? Okay. Think about Johnny Cochran's famous on OJ Simpson trial. Alright, everybody knows what it is, right? Let's all say it together. If it doesn't fit, you must have quit seven words, probably the most famous statement ever made in the courtroom and everyone remembers it.

Why? Because it was concise. There was brevity in his statement. That's why it's so memorable. If he had said 72 words, you wouldn't remember it. You might say it was great, but you couldn't remember what he said. We know exactly what he said. It was so concise. It was the brevity of the statement. Notice that, but also notice that he made his exact point. He summed up the entire OJ Simpson trial with that one sentence. Can we agree? Okay, so the second level there was, so the first level, I said there's three levels to this, but I think I only told you once. So let me make sure I'm going in my notes here to make sure I didn't miss something. So the first level of brevity, I'm going back to where I was. So one is your ability to simplify your ideas. And I think I might've skipped a second one.

Maybe I said three levels and I only meant two. But anyway, lemme give you the other level here of brevity like with Mr. Cochrane in the OJ Simpson trial. The third level, or this would be the second level, I don't think I gave you a second level, is when you understand something at an expert level, the service that you do for the public is simplifying the concept. That's what I'm doing here with this show. I understand things at an expert level. That's what I talk about each day on the show. Whatever it is I decide to talk about and I condense the topic down because every topic I talk about, there are books written on these subjects and you should read the books. But what I do here is I simplify the subject to where I can explain it to you in 20 to 30 minutes.

If you need an hour to explain something, maybe you need to make it more simple for you so that you can do the same for others. This is actually an exercise that I follow when I'm on X the app, formerly known as Twitter. I try to fit all of my responses to people or even the things that I say into one post, except when I'm making a thread on purpose where I'll use multiple posts. But if I'm going to say somebody says something, I'm responding to what they say and maybe I have a lot of thoughts to give. I try to fit all of my response to them within 280 characters, which is a skill because oftentimes I got to cut down on the things that I wanted to say just to make it as concise as possible and I got to take out the extra whatever the extra words may be.

So make it simple so you can make it simple for everybody else. Again, on a tactical level, this is called pruning your communication. So pruning just means you're cutting off the extras. So any of you who's ever done the yard work, when you're pruning your bushes and your trees, what you do is you're trimming the hedges. What you're doing is you're trimming hedges, you're cutting the extras off of it so that it's nice and neat and you're getting the extra leaves out of there. So the tree or the bush doesn't start growing all wildly and out of control In writing. Your editing process usually means what? Cutting down on words, not adding to them. Usually when you're editing, you're cutting things away and if you do any video editing, what are you doing? You're getting rid of extra stuff so that you only got what's left. You might record for two hours to make a 20 minute video, right? That's the whole purpose of cutting, of editing. You're cutting down.

This is deleting stuff even on the cutting room floor. Again, usually not addition when you're editing, if you want to be a concise communicator, get good at editing your communication. In other words, saying more with less. Number two, today's topic once again is how to be concise in your communication. Number two, clarity of points. Your points need to be clear. Remember what concise means. It means brief, but comprehensive need to be clear on the point you're attempting to make so you can be brief while at the same time making your point. So being brief doesn't mean that your point gets missed. Being brief means your point is made clearly and you don't need too many words. This is a skill, and again, as I said, when I'm on an xap, you get 280 characters. So when I'm responding to somebody else's comment or their assertion, especially when I'm disagreeing with somebody, I always challenge myself to fit my response within that two 80, even though I technically could go over, I have the blue check where you can write, I could write as long as I want if I wanted to, but I try to make it fit in the two 80 because I know a lot of people are not going to read if I go over.

So I could write an entire article telling them why I think they're wrong, but instead I try to tell them why they're wrong in 280 characters or less. And again, that's why that forces me to make my point as clearly as possible with as few words as possible, literally as few words as possible as I'm on a limit. So it's a practice ground for conciseness. When I make my point clearly, I usually get a very strong response from people. Whether that response is people disagreeing with my disagreement or agreeing with my disagreement either way is fine because the point is I just want to know that my point was so clear that everybody got it. That's the point. You see, my point is not clear and people can't quite understand what I'm saying. Then usually I don't get much of a response because people don't understand me.

But when they understand me, I get very strong responses. Again, positive or negative, doesn't matter to me. I can deal with the backlash because otherwise if they don't understand me, there's no reason for 'em to respond because they don't know what they're responding to. Okay? So you got to be clear as possible. You should get clear responses from people because they get what you're saying now. They don't get what you're saying. Again, there's nothing for them to push back on. Point number three, today's topic once again is how to communicate concisely. So that second point again was making sure your point is clear. When things are clear, you don't have to say too much. And number three, leave your emotion at the door. Now this is an important part because there is a place for emotion when you're trying to influence and persuade people. There is a place for emotion, but not all the time because emotions can cloud

Judgment. They often cloud judgment. So use it when that's what you want to do. If you want to cloud people's judgment or make them not think so logically or rationally, then go ahead and use emotion because it will bypass their logic. If you want people thinking clearly, then leave emotion out of it. And it depends on your style of communication. I happen to be a very logical communicator. I tend to not try to use emotional persuasion when I'm, especially if I'm disagreeing with someone, I try not to use emotional things. I notice when people do that that they're often using these fallacies. There is literally a logical fallacy called the appeal to emotion. So it appeal to emotion. Fallacy is when you try to use emotion to overcome somebody's logic, and again this works in sales, but in conversation, someone who understands fallacies and they understand logical thinking will easily point these out and basically dance circles around you.

So let me give you an example of an appeal to emotion. Fallacy is actually there's a couple fallacies wrapped in one here. So let's say I said something like, I like eating hamburgers and somebody pushed back against me because they're a strict vegan and they say, so you're saying that you want to kill every animal on the planet and you want us to have no destroyed ozone layer? Is that what you're saying? See, that's an appeal to emotion fallacy because I just said I like to eat hamburgers and if you have a problem with hamburgers, then say what your problem is. But they first of all posed a different question, a straw man of something that I didn't say and they're asking me to respond to something that I didn't say was a fallacy in itself. And secondly, they're appealing to the emotion. Oh, you're just trying to kill all animals.

That's an appeal to emotion because killing animals is an appeal to emotion. I didn't say that. I just said I like to eat hamburgers. That's an example. And people do this actually, there are people who are very skilled at doing this. You see 'em on social media all the time, and I enjoy pointing out the fallacies in their arguments. I do this all the time. So I don't know if any of you's ready for the Twitter battlefield. It's not a place for the faint of heart. But anyway, that's an example. You want to leave emotion at the door if you're trying to make a logical point. There is a place for emotion, but it's not everywhere. If you want people thinking clearly, leave emotion out. And again, this is of special importance when you are disagreeing with a person or pushing back against something someone said, or you're trying to help someone understand something that they may not understand, you want to make it logically make sense for them.

That's the way that I look at it. Now, some people do this the exact opposite way, but you're listening to my show, so I'm going to tell you the way that I like to do it. I like to make people understand things logically, and if you want to add emotion to it, that's fine, but your points need to be logically sound. It's just the way that I think human beings make decisions based on emotions, but we justify those decisions with logic. In other words, our short-term decision making can be based on emotions, but our long-term thinking is based on logic. How many of you have ever made a bad short-term decision based on logic? Every hand should be up. We've all done it, but we need to use our logic to decide what makes sense in the long term of life. We usually, our lives in the long term are a reflection of our logical thinking.

So someone ends up not doing too well in the long term. They're failure at logical thinking. And anybody could do good in the short term based on the right emotion with the right person at the right time and in the right place. But we can't judge someone's life off a short term thing. We got to judge it off the long game. And the long game is based on logical, rational decision making, not emotion. Everybody understand that emotions run, they run out, they're like roller coasters. So eventually you get tired of riding on that ride. You just want something steady and calm and normal. That's your logic. And if your logic is flawed, then your long-term results will be just as flawed as your logic. Everybody understand me? Good. So if you want to help a person's way of thinking, be altered, you want to alter how someone thinks and thus you want to alter their actions.

First thing you need to do is help them logically understand what you're giving them. They have to logically get it and understand why it makes sense for them. If you only need to use someone in the short term, then you can depend on emotions and you can probably get them to do something just based on emotion because you only need them in the short term. But in the long term, again, emotions eventually wear out, emotions burn out. So if you need to work with someone over a long period of time, do not depend on emotions only because eventually that person will come to their senses and they'll start thinking more logically. That's what when someone says come to your senses, that's what it means. It means their emotions are no longer controlling them and now their logical brain is thinking. And now you have to make a decision of what makes sense here.

And if what you showed them didn't make sense in that their emotions are no longer triggered, what are you going to do now? You are stuck in a hard place. So when I coach people, for example, I like to explain things to them logically and sometimes concisely. Sometimes I'll explain it even deeper. So because I want to make sure they get it and I want the person who I'm working with to be permanently changed based on what I'm showing and teaching them and helping them with. In other words, I want to transform my knowledge to them, which is why I explained not only what but why. And I was just talking to someone today as a matter of fact about this exact thing that when you're working with me, I'm not only going to tell you what we're going to do, I'm going to explain to you why we're doing it so that this knowledge is no longer just my knowledge, it becomes your knowledge.

So now you are that much stronger and better after working with me or because you worked with me, I'm going to even say after because we can continue working. It's more things that we can build on what I already taught you. So I'm not expecting this to end, but you will be stronger from working with me than it is not like you're going to be strong while I'm around. Then when I'm gone, you go back to being who you were before. The skill level continues to elevate because I'm continually making you better. Okay? So that's what I aim to do when I work with people. So any of you who've been thinking about working with me, that's another benefit. They just keep coming. Alright? The benefits just keep coming. So if I only use emotion, I might be able to alter someone's behavior in the short term. And most of us can have our behavior altered in the short term by emotional triggering, but it doesn't really help to change a person and it doesn't really help that person in the long term if that's all you're doing. So with that said, let's recap today's class, which is how to communicate concisely, defined in a way that is brief, but comprehensive. And again, this is a skill, which means it is a learned and

Practiced ability. Anyone can get better at this. Number one, brevity. Do not use 10 words when you can use four. Again, there are a couple levels to this. One is your ability to simplify your ideas, make them as easy to understand as possible. And another level is sort worth three that I gave you. Another level is keep your communication as short and necessary such that it is easy to be retained. In other words, you want someone to remember something, don't give 'em too much information. That information piece number three, drowns out information piece number two. And the third level of brevity is when you understand something at an expert level, the service you do for the public is in simplifying the concept. This is what journalists were supposed to do originally. They were supposed to go find out what actually happened. A reporter tells you what happened, journalists dig deeper into why it happened, and then they explain to us objectively why it happened.

But journalism doesn't do that anymore. Now there's a lean to everything instead of just telling you things straight up and down. So now we are responsible for getting our own information and we have to go and figure things out on our own. And many people don't want to do that. And this is how we've gotten the concept of fake news because nobody's telling us the objective truth anymore except people like me. Number two, clarity of point. Remember what concise means. It means brief, but comprehensive. If your point is clear enough, you don't need to use too many words. You can explain it very briefly with brevity and people will get it immediately and they'll be able to retain it again. Remember Johnny Cochran at the OJ trial. Number three, leave emotion at the door. There is a place for emotion when you're trying to influence and persuade people.

But if you want to influence and persuade people for the long term, you can't just go off emotion. You may use emotion to get them moving, but you need to give them logic because that's the only thing that lasts. Long term logic is a slow burn, long fuel way of long fuel resource, let's put it that way. Whereas emotion is a high burn. It's fast burning, but it's a very short-term thing. So if you only need someone for the short-term, trigger their emotions, use 'em and get out of there. But if you need someone for the long-term, you have to give 'em the logic, otherwise it won't last.

#2842: Why Some People Always Win – And Others Always Lose

Let's get into the topic, which is why some people always win, others always move. This episode is really about habits of thought and which lead to habits of action and consistency of outcomes that almost everyone experiences in life. We all experience some outcomes consistently in life and we do this because there are certain things that we are doing or not doing and that's because there are certain things that we are thinking or not thinking that lead to it.

There is a chain here and they're all connected. So today I'm going to articulate what these are. I'm going to explain how they lead to certain outcomes in life so that you can be more conscious and intentional about how you are using these chains of behavior in life, these causes set in motion and how you can use them more and intentionally in your own life and then it will be more obvious to you why others create the outcomes that they create in their lives or why they don't. So when you're more conscious about this, then you can be more intentional about choosing the past that actually works for you and produces the results that you actually do want in your life so you can get more of the outcomes that you want in life. Point number one, the topic once again today is why some people always win and others always lose.

Number one is choice. Choice. This is one of the main reasons that some people win and some people lose both successes and failures. Success and failure rather are conscious choices. Both of them are conscious choices. If you make no choice then you end up usually failing. So the only way that you can succeed in life is by consciously choosing to succeed. If you do nothing, then you usually fail. And if you choose to fail, of course you fail. Now why is this true? Because of the law of entropy, which we talked about not too long ago. Let me give you that episode where I explained that was episode number 28 0 6. So from here about two months ago all of it was explained where if you do nothing in life, you just do nothing. You just stay exactly where you are and try to maintain the status quo.

What happens is you usually end up going backwards. Most people think that they are being neutral, but there is no such thing as being neutral in life that doesn't exist. It is either forward or backward. You are either building or destroying. Alright? People who become successful in life are successful because they have chosen to be successful and they have made the decision to be successful. People become successful because they have chosen to be successful and they have made the decision to be successful. It must be chosen. It does not just happen. So this point could be called a decision as well as it could be called a choice. So anyone you know who succeeds consistently, ask them what is the key to their consistent success. Most of 'em will probably start telling you about their habits and the actions that they take, and at least in their eyes, the actions that are leading to their success that are most responsible for their outcomes.

But understand something, those habits are consciously chosen habits, success habits must be consciously chosen. You do not just randomly do stuff that produces success on a consistent basis. Now you might randomly do something that works once in a while and not even realize how you did it, but if you do something that works consistently, that's because you're choosing to do so. And again, these things don't just randomly happen to them. Alright? And I really want you to understand this point, successful people are doing it on purpose. They do it consistently on purpose because they're consciously choosing to do certain things that lead to certain outcomes.

Point number two, today's topic once again is why some people always win and other people always lose. Point number two, conditioning, conditioning, any habits performed consistently becomes conditioned in you, meaning you get used to doing it. I was talking to someone today, I can't even remember who I was talking to. I think I was talking to someone on a zoom call and they were telling me how they get up early in the morning, they get up at like five o'clock in the morning and I was telling 'me I get up a little bit before four o'clock in the morning every day. And they were like, man, I don't even know how I would even do that. Get up at the time that you get up Dre. And I said, well, if you just do it consistently, you go to bed early enough and you just start getting up at that time consistently, even if you don't go to bed early enough, you just get up at that time consistently.

You get used to it to where it becomes abnormal to not get up at that time. And this applies to any habit or behavior in life. And this could be something that you feel is productive and helping you and also something that is reductive and something that is sending you backwards. So smoking cigarettes was a bad habit. Even people who smoke cigarettes probably would agree it is a bad habit, but if you do it often enough, you get so used to it that it becomes normal to not smoke cigarettes or drink alcohol or anything else. You could become addicted to gambling, whatever, anything that you do consistently, your body and mind will condition itself to doing it and it will get used to it and it will expect to do it even when you try, you try to not do it. So any habit does this, any way of acting, any way of thinking can become habitual.

It can get conditioned into you and hopefully you can get a combination of both of the things that you want. So if you're doing something consistently and you're constantly thinking about it and it's helping you get to where you want to go in life, you want that to be conditioned to you so that it becomes normal for you to do it and it becomes abnormal to not do it. So if you know waking up early and going to the gym is helping you get in shape and stay in shape and you like being in shape, then you want that to get conditioned in you so it becomes abnormal to not work out. Not working out is like you feel crazy if you don't work out. And so it's like anywhere you go, anywhere you're at, you got to find a way to work out all you want that to be conditioned in you when it comes to the success that you have in your business or how you feel positively about yourself or anything that you do that you want to happen, you want it to get conditioned in you.

So my book, work On Your Game, the very first chapter of that book, which you can get at work on your game book.com, very first chapter of the book is mental conditioning. When you get your mind in the right space that controls what your body does and it controls the actions that you take, of course what your body does is literally your actions. When you get your mind in the right space, it leads to you taking certain actions. When you get your actions aligned with your goals and your actions are based on accurate information and accurate formulas, then you get the outcomes that you want. This is how life works, everybody follows that, get your mind in the right space, choose your actions and then make sure your actions are based on accurate formulas and you have no accurate measurements of what it's going to take.

You will get the outcomes that you want, assuming that you have some outcomes that you're looking to achieve, IE you have goals and you have all that, then there's no way you can't get the outcomes that you want. When people lose in life, they lose because they are conditioned to lose. They are expecting to lose and therefore because you expect something as an outcome, notice the outcome, your actions will be reflective of that expectation and your thoughts are reflective of your actions because you expect to lose. You expect to lose, you're going to do things that lead to losing and your outcomes will be losing. This is how it works. It works the same way forwards as it does backwards. I remember having teammates in my sports years, I remember I had teammates in basketball who as soon as our opponent started to have some success in a game against us, so we're playing the game against another team.

As soon as the other team scores three times in a row, I would have teammates who would start getting their heads down and they would just start moping around and I could tell that they expected to lose. They had an expectation of losing. So as soon as something happened in the game, this could be the first quarter of the game and the other team is starting to look like they have some momentum. I had teammates who were already ready to quit because they were predisposed to quit. They were just looking for a reason to do so. They were just looking for an excuse to quit. And other teams scoring three times in a row became an excuse to quit. And again, I played with a lot of players who had this mindset because again, they'd rather lose and get angry about the fact that they lost because this is their comfort zone than win and be happy about the fact that they won or get angry about the prospect of losing and thus transmute that energy, that anger about losing into the success actions that lead to winning Napoleon Hill in his book Think And Grow Rich.

Also in the book, the Law of Success, he talks about transmutation taking energy from one situation and carrying it over to a different situation to produce the outcome that you want. So you can take the energy of anger over a disappointment in your life, transmute that energy because energy is neither created nor destroyed. May we transfer from one object to another. You can take the object of energy, you can take the object of that energy from the anger and you can translate it over to doing something positive that leads to you having the outcome that you want. Take the energy of you didn't make the sports team, you're disappointed. You can translate that energy over to, okay, let me practice a lot now so that next year I do make the sports team or the energy of I lost the last game to make sure I don't lose the next game.

So this is how you can transmute energy, but if you don't transmute that energy and this energy that's leading to an outcome that you don't want, you're going to keep getting it over and over and over again and understand this concept of transmutation, taking energy from one space and moving it to another. This has to be conscious and intentional. It does not just happen just because it doesn't happen just because you thought about it or I mean, excuse me, doesn't happen if you don't think about it. It's a better way of saying it. You have to think about it and order for it to happen and then you have to have intentions, then you have to have a process for moving it over. So it takes, even though I use these terms conscious and intentional all the time, just because you're conscious and intentional about something doesn't mean it's going to happen just because you're thinking about it, you have to do something in order to make it happen.

So again, I've seen people in life who they expect to lose. So as soon as something comes up that even looks just a little bit like things going in the direction that they don't want it to go, they just push it even further because they have the expectation of losing. So it conforms to their expectations. And these people, again, they were conditioned and expecting to be losers and for the most part they lost. And if I was teammates with them, depending on their energy and my energy, their strength and my strength, their energy of losing might have overcome anything anybody else wanted to do. So when you get too many people with that mindset and one group expecting to lose, well guess what? Y'all just keep losing. Your team will never succeed. So when you get a player who is very influential with any mindset inside any group, and when I say a player that could just be a member of any group, get a member of any group who is an influential individual with a strong inclination towards any type of mentality, they will infect the entire group in a positive way or a negative way.

If they have negative energy, it will cause the team to fail. If their energy is positive, it will uplift the team of people who might not be that good and the negative energy can pull down the team. That could be otherwise very good. Moving on to point number three, today's topic once again is why some people always win and other people always lose. Number three, expectations, which you've already talked about a lot here.

Both your choices and your conditioning are reflections of your expectations. So what do you expect of yourself? Do you expect to win or do you expect to lose? When you look in the mirror, who do you expect to see? When you go into a situation without knowing the outcome, what do you expect is going to happen? What's your expectation? You go into a situation where the outcome is not clear, it can go either way. What's your expectation? What is your mental plan? I'm asking you what you know is going to happen because oftentimes you don't know. I'm just asking you, what do you expect? If you're a salesperson, you go into a sales call, do you expect to close the sale?

Is that your expectation? If you're a salesperson and you have a product that you sell for a thousand dollars and you have three sales calls in your calendar today, how much money do you expect to make today? It should be $3,000 because that's a thousand times three. Assuming you don't have any upsells, you're just going to sell the product yourself. Alright, three sales calls, a thousand dollars product, a thousand times three equals 3000 bucks, your expectations are going to be a thousand. Or if I close one, I'm good. No, you got three sales calls you expect to close. All three, not closing, should be the exception. The expectation is every single sales call closes and close just means a person says yes, they agree, they give you money, you give them the service and everybody's happy. When I say close, that's what it means. So what is your expectation?

If you're an athlete, do you go into a game expecting to win the game? It sounds like a simple question, but you'd be surprised. Again, I just gave you an example. You'd be surprised. Some people go into situations expecting to lose. I mean, they do all the right things, say all the right things, but their expectation is they want to lose. And often you can tell by their behavior, you can tell by their energy and you can tell by the way they respond to stimuli happening around them. As I said, I'll have teammates who as soon as the other team got a couple positive plays in a row, that teammate would just pretty much mentally give up. They didn't physically give up, but they mentally gave up. Their energy went down. So if you're an athlete, do you go into the game expecting to win?

It is a simple question, but again, this is a yes or no, though it's a yes or no thing, do you have the expectation of success? If your expectations are weak folks, then it makes sense that your actions are also subsequently weak, and that's probably because your mindset is weak. When your actions are weak, your mind is weak. When your mindset is strong, you can take a weak body, a weak tangible resource and produce strong results because the mind controls the body. And again, understand, all this stuff works in a chain, it all works together. So when you have negative expectations, you have to be in the greatest shape, have the greatest resources, tangible, physical resources of anybody, and still fail. And have you ever seen that before? You ever see the person who's seen to have all the tangible resources available to them, yet they still fail.

Why? It was their mindset, something in their mind was causing them to fail over and over again. It's not because your eyes deceived you and they didn't have the resources, they had the resources, they just didn't have the mind to use those resources in a way that would produce the outcome that they wanted. It doesn't mean they can't develop it because all this is developable, developable, developable, if that's even a word. I don't know if it is, if it is not. Just made it up. So recapping today's class, which is why some people always win and others always lose. This is about habits of thought and again, which leads to consistency of actions and consistency of outcomes. Number one, choice, success and failure are conscious choices. So if you make no choice, you usually end up failing. Why? Because the law of entropy says you leave something to its own devices, it usually gets worse actually, not usually.

It always gets worse. You're either moving forward or backward in life. There is no neutral, there is no in-between you're either building or destroying you or winning, you're losing, you're getting better or you are getting worse. There is no neutral. Number two, conditioning. Any habit which is performed consistently, becomes conditioned in you. This can be a way of thinking, a way of acting, and hopefully it's a combination of both. And again, this applies in a positive, the same way it applies in a negative point. Number three, expectations by both your choices and your conditioning are reflections of your expectations. So what do you expect of yourself? Do you expect to win? Do you expect to lose? What do you see when you look in the mirror? When you go into a situation and the outcome is not clear? If you go either way, what is your expectation or do you expect to win?

If you have two sales calls and you've got a $1,500 product, your sales day should be expected to be $3,000 at least, because that's two calls, two closes, $1,500 a piece equals $3,000. If your expectations are weak, you're expecting, let me get one. Or I don't know if either one of these is going to, I don't know if they have the money, or they may say, no, they might not like me. If you go in there with that expectation, usually you get less than what you expect. Usually that's what happens in life. Your expectations are weak and it makes sense that your actions are also subsequently weak, and that's probably because your mindset's weak. Again, this all works in a chain.

#2843: Why You Fear Success [Part 1 of 10]

Let's get into this topic. Again, this is part of a 10 part series. Why do you fear success? Now almost anyone you ask if you ask them directly, if you ask people a direct question, do you want to be a successful person?

Almost everybody you would ask would say yes. I think any of you should listen to this right now. If I asked you, you would say yes. And I believe that you're telling the truth. And this is what most people do. Their actions are a reflection of it, right? Because you go to work every day and supposedly the reason you work every day is because you're aiming to be more successful than you were the day before. However, some people are driving with the emergency brake on. So it's not that you're not driving, it's not that you're trying to go somewhere, you're just going there with the emergency brake on. Any of you who's ever driven with your emergency brake on probably can't do it in a newer car. It's been in older cars where it was just a break grinding up against your gears. You can't go as fast as you could.

You can't go as fast as the car is capable of knowing because you got the brake on. So while you're doing all the things that outwardly look like and aim towards success, you may secretly or even consciously fear being successful, which is why you're driving so slow, you're driving with the brake engaged and you are basically impeding your own forward progress. And what I'm going to talk about over the next 10 episodes in this series are what are the things that we may be either consciously or unconsciously concerned with that are causing us to sabotage our own success and keep us from getting to the success that we say we want to get to. So you need to listen to the next 10 episodes of the series and ask yourself, do any of these things that I'm going to lay out apply to you? Because if you're not getting to your success at the speed at which you want to get to it, I guarantee you that there is something either in your consciousness or your subconsciousness that is holding you back whether you are consciously thinking about it and doing it on purpose or you're doing it in a way that you're not even aware.

But this 10 part series can be maybe a bit therapeutic for you in the process. So that's out of the way, let's get into it. Point number one, we are talking today again, why you fear success number one is change. Number one reason people consciously or subconsciously fear doing anything is because of the change that is on the other side of the action. There is always change on the other side of any significant action in life.

Lemme say that again. There is always change on the other side of any significant action in life. If you take significant action and make more money, then you're going to have more money. Now you have a whole different set of things to deal with because you have that more money, you take significant action working out, your body is going to be in a different space. You take significant action in doing X.

Anything you're working on right now, you take significant action is going to be a serious change that happens there. And that change comes with a set of its own challenges. Because in life there are no perfect scenarios, there are only trade-offs. You learn this in episode 2174 with success comes change. And when I say success, let me be clear here as we start this series. When I say the word success over the course of this series, what I mean is you are achieving significantly more than what you've achieved up to this point. So when I say success, that's what I'm referring to. So everyone can define their own success and success is defined as pursuit of a worthy ideal. You get to choose what the worthy part is and the ideal part. So when I say success in this 10 part series, what I mean is you significantly outperforming your current self.

Alright? So whatever that is. So if your current self is making $250,000 a year, success might mean $500,000 a year. If you're making 50 grand a year right now success might mean $125,000 a year. I'm just using money as an example here. If a success for you is you can do 10 pullups success might mean you can do 50 pullups. So success is just significant. You choose what significantly means for you because that's another relative and subjective term. You choose what means significantly higher than where you are now. So when I say success, that's what I mean you getting significantly above your current self. Okay? Now that we got that out the way with success comes change because whatever you define as success means you are changing your current situation, right? Everybody agrees with that. Alright? For you to be successful or more successful than you are now you have to change the current situation. So you are saying goodbye to the status quo. That's the current, you introducing yourself to a new normal in your life, which means by definition there's change. Many human beings are extremely

Resistant to change because of the law of inertia. And we've talked about the law of inertia. Let me give you the episode where we talked about this. I talked about everything here on the show, but the law of inertia we discussed in episode number 24 76, I mean 24 66, excuse me, 24 66 is the law of inertia. And the law of inertia in simple terms says it takes more effort to change your situation than it does to leave it as it is. That's one simple thing that the law of inertia states. It's easier to just stay where you are than it is to change. This is one reason why many people don't change and it doesn't matter whether you're changing it for better or worse. Most people would rather keep things exactly as they are, than do anything that's going to disrupt the situation. Because change means saying goodbye to what you are used to and saying hello to something that you are not used to.

Even the thing that you are not used to, even if the thing that you're not used to is having 10 times more money than you have right now or 10 times the status and accomplishments than you have right now. It is still a change. Most people would rather stay where they are than undergo that change, even though the change is leading them closer to the thing that they say that they want. And this is where people end up self-sabotaging or where you may look at yourself in the mirror and say, I know I want to achieve this success. Why do I keep doing these things that are sending me in the opposite direction? This is one of the reasons it may be an unconscious thing that is holding you back. Point number two, today's topic once again is why you are in fear of success.

Number two is responsibility. Responsibility, which is if you break responsibility up into two words, it is your ability to respond, your response ability. Now why would your ability to respond hold you back from wanting to be successful? Why would that make you fear success? Because having responsibility also means that now you have some expectations, you have some ownership and there's an impetus on you. There will be eyeballs on you, yours and including others because you have responsibility. Most people don't have responsibility in life. Most people want as little responsibility as possible. And because of this, the trade off of having no responsibilities, that you have no power, you have no influence. Remember that power and influence are a package deal. They come with responsibility, ownership, and expectations. So with success and accomplishment, it usually comes, as I said, power, which is just your ability to have influence over a situation and over yourself.

With success you'll have more influence and control over the circumstances of your life and often over the circumstances and outcomes of other people's lives. So any of you who's a head of household who's listening to this right now, you have more than one person in your household besides you. Okay? As you achieve more success now you have more influence and control and more power over what happens with the people in that home that you're responsible for. Just by the fact that you've achieved more success. Not because you announced it, not because everyone sat down and agreed to this, but because you've achieved success. Guess what? Everything's in your lap now.

It just happens naturally. A lot of times in life there is no discussion. It just happens. Alright, you have all this success, okay, well we're going to put everything on you. Everybody's just going to sit back and watch you and let's just let you be.

Everyone's going to get behind you. They may not just sit back and do nothing, but they're going to get behind you and watch you lead the way because they ain't leading the way. So you're going to lead the way just because you have the success. Again, this is not even something you have to aim for, it just happens. It is a natural occurrence in life that most people do not want to lead. Most people do not want the responsibility and the expectations that come with leadership. So when you do things that give you more power and influence, other people will naturally just start following you simply because you've done things that they haven't done. So it's just natural for them to follow. And because most people don't want to compete with you for the leadership role anyway, you ever find yourself in competition with another person for a leadership role, you and that person, y'all are in rare, y'all in rare air because it's very rare that two people are battling for the leadership position, knowing what comes with it, the responsibility and the ownership.

Most people don't sign up for that. And most people will gladly take the second place, the backseat to someone who's willing to take all that. And if you and another person both want it, that's a rare thing. It's like two people getting struck by lightning on the same day in two different streets anyway, on the same street. Rather, there's a better way of saying that. So when you do this and you have more influence over people's eyes, people are just going to follow you naturally just by the fact that you are achieving more success. People who don't have as much success as you, that is they will now be looking to you to be the person who can help influence their outcomes in situations. Just because you've already done it again, not because you announced it, not because they asked you to, not because you had some kind of contract that says whoever achieved success first has to help everybody else.

It's not any of that. It's just because you did it. People are just going to follow you. People are going to get behind you. And this means you now have more responsibility on your shoulders again that you didn't even ask for, which comes along as a package deal. When you are powerful and successful, you just get more responsibility. Again, one day you're just going to wake up like how I get all this responsibility. I didn't ask for this, I didn't sign up for this, I just did this to help myself. Now all these people are looking at me. This is just how it happens folks. This is just life. This is human nature. Human beings, most human beings want to follow someone. They want someone to lead them so that they can follow. They don't want to take the lead, they want to be led. Most human beings want to be led.

And when you step up and show that you have leadership capabilities by creating success, that is an unconscious demonstration of leadership capabilities because most people don't do that. People are going to get behind you and you just got these people following you just because again, you didn't even have to try. Okay? So this is going to happen. So this is where the resistance to responsibility can cause you to not want to be successful because this is going to occur and you may even start to notice it occurring as you achieve more and more success. Because the more success you achieve, the more people you are surpassing and they're going to look at you. So you achieve that success and decide that they're not going to go after it the way that you did. And this just gets behind you. So now you have these people following you and you didn't even ask them to follow you. Everybody following what I'm saying here? This is what happens. So this comes as a package deal. So even though many people say that they want more power, almost everybody says they want to have more power and influence over their own lives. By definition, influence is power.

So what happens though in action, people do things that are a lot different than what they say. Have any of you ever noticed it? People say they want A, B, and C, but then you look at their actions and it looks like they actually want D, E, and IF. This is what happens with human beings. Look at people's actions. You want to know they really want not to listen to their words. So when people try to avoid one thing, they actually avoid the other thing. When you avoid responsibility, you also avoid power. And this is another reason why people are afraid of success even though they don't know that it's success that they are ducking and dodging away from, they think they're dodging one thing where they're actually dodging Two things. When you dodge responsibility and expectation, you also dodge influence and power and control. See, these are the things that come with success.

And again, it's a package deal. Keeping in mind folks, there are no perfect scenarios in life. There are only trade-offs. Everything you do in life, there is a trade-off. So anything you're looking at, many of you have heard the saying the grass is not always greener on the other side. Well the reason that that saying is cliche based in truth and the truth that is based around is that anything that looks perfect from the outside looking in, meaning you have not experienced it yet or lived it yet and it looks way better than the situation you have now, maybe it is better than the situation you have, but it's not perfect. There is a trade off to that scenario that you just don't know about. And what you should do is find out what the trade-off is before you jump over there, before you jump to the other side of that fence because you might not be able to jump back over and when you realize that you jumped into something that you probably shouldn't have jumped into.

Point number three, today's topic once again is why you fear success. Number three, imposter syndrome. Now many of you have heard of the concept of imposter syndrome. I talked about in episode number 2 0 9 5 how to handle imposter syndrome. This is the feeling that maybe you are just not as good as the success that you are creating when you have basically out kicked your coverage, as we say metaphorically. And what that means is you have performed at a level that is above where you see yourself. So you see yourself as a hundred thousand dollars person, but here you are having generated $300,000. You see yourself as a million dollar person, but here you are with $10 million, you get the imposter syndrome. I am doing a lot better than I thought I could do. I'm doing a lot more than I even think. I don't even see myself as a person at a level 80, but here I am at a level 102.

Alright, how does that happen? And this is the mindset. This mindset, imposter syndrome is one of the things that stops people from doing things that might take them to a higher level. They simply don't see themselves as that person yet because they look at themselves in the mirror and the picture that they have of themselves, also known as your self image. And you don't see yourself as worthy of being at a level that is 10 or 20 times higher than where you currently reside. And this is again, that's the imposter syndrome. When you even consider, hey, maybe I could do this or maybe I could do that. If you don't see yourself at that level, then you're never going to get there. Alright? And this is why the do have principle applies and why I talk about it so often and why mindset's the first piece of what we do in working on your game university.

Because if you come to me and say, Dre, I want to make three or four or five times more money than I'm making right now, I say that's fine, but the first thing we have to fix is not me giving you a formula for how to sell your stuff or how to write your book or how to launch your course or how to price your stuff or how to find new customers or how to run ads on Instagram, even though that's what a lot of people come to me for. The first thing we have to do is get your mind right because your mind is not fertile soil for you making five times more money than you're making right now. Because if it was, then you would already be making it. We got to get your mind in the right place first. Then we put the actions in.

We cannot install it. You can't install a Ferrari engine inside of a Toyota framework, alright? It's not going to work, alright? It's going to destroy the car. The car is not built for it. You got to build, you gotta put the right mindset in first, the right frame around first, then you put the engine in. The engine is the activities, the frame is the mindset. So until we get the right mindset, the actions are never going to work. This is why there's so much information available online these days. Relatively cheap, cheap or free. Yet you still have the same percentages when it comes to people being successful. 1%, why are we successful? 4% doing pretty good, 15% still working towards success and the other 80% doing nothing or out of the game completely. Those percentages have been the same for 60 years. Folks, that's not an exaggeration. Actually, in 70 years, those percentages have not changed. Even though it's much easier to start a business, we have much more access to information. It's much more of an even playing field than it was 70 years ago. Yet the percentages have not changed at all. Why? Because you know what hasn't changed? Human beings, humanity has not changed. You can change all the technology you want until people change being people. The numbers are still going to be the numbers. Everybody follows this.

So when you don't see yourself as being that person who can be 10 or 20 times higher than you are right now, you would rather do things to keep you in the same place. And this is what people do. And this is why you look at someone and say, wait, why aren't you doing this or this or this? Why are you doing that stuff to still keep you down there? Because it's consistent with their self image. And until you change your self image, you're never going to change your actions. No human being can behave for a consistent period of time in a way that is out of line with their self-image. I talked about this in, lemme see if I did an episode on this. I think I did. It was, yes, it was episode number 1,198. 1198. Why do we stay on B Courts for so long?

And that is a metaphor from back in my basketball playing days when I was about 15 years old in my neighborhood in Philadelphia, the playground that I played at was called Findlay Findlay Recreation Center. And there were two full courts. There was one that we call a court, that's where all the best players, the grown men and the best players played. And then there was B Court, that's where the younger kids and also grown men, but grown men who weren't hardcore basketball players, they kind of just played for fun. They would play on B Corp. And when I first started playing, I didn't start playing until I was 14, I would play on B Corp and just kind of sharpening

My game is getting better. And one of my peers and my youth, he goes into my neighborhood, this kid named James, he was the same age as me. We were in the same grade. And around this time, around age 15, I would be at Findlay playing a full court game on B Court. And James would walk by and he would be with these older guys. He used to hang with these guys who were older than him and he would go over to a court and play on a court. And James would sometimes say to me while I was playing on B Court, he's like, Dre, why are you still playing on B Court? He didn't encourage me to play on a court. He would just say it kind of derisively Dre, why are you still playing on B Court? And James wasn't even that talented of a player.

He didn't, I don't even think he played high school basketball, he didn't play college basketball. By the time I was playing pro basketball, James was doing other things in the neighborhood besides basketball, let's put it that way. And the thing is, even though I was more talented than James and I had more skill than James and I was more serious about basketball than James, he had a mindset that he belonged playing with the older guys. And I still had a mindset that I should still be playing with the younger guys. And that's what I talked about in episode 1198. And this is an example of what I mean when I say the self-image will hinder us. Even though you have the tools, you can have the tools to be anywhere you want to be, but if you don't have the self-image to match those tools, and you'll still hold yourself back and then you'll be looking at yourself like, why am I only doing this when I got the tools to be doing that?

Or someone else may say it to you again, we do things that are consistent with our self image, not consistent with our abilities. Those are two different things. We do things that are consistent with our self image, not things that are consistent with our talent, potential and abilities. The fix for this is that you have to change your self image first, the way you think and the way you're being before you can change your behavior. Again, this is the be, do, have process in action. Recapping today's first of a 10 part series, why you fear success Again, everybody says they want to be successful. And when I say success in this series, what I'm referring to is you doing significantly better than you're doing right now. Point number one, change with success comes change. Most people are very resistant to change. This is the law of inertia that it is easier to stay in the same place and not change anything than there is to go to a different place and change something.

And this is why many people don't change in life. They simply don't want to deal with the change that comes with changing. Point number two, responsibility. When you achieve more success, other people who don't have your success naturally fall in line and they will just start following you and they will be following your lead. Even though you did not ask them to lead, you did not want to lead them and you didn't even tell 'em to do it.

They just naturally do it because human beings are naturally followers. We want someone to lead us. We want someone to show us the way we want someone to tell us to do. Tell us what to do. Being a leader is not a natural thing for most human beings, 99% of us. So when you step up and achieve more success than other people, other people will naturally follow you because they've been waiting their whole lives to follow somebody and use this to make themselves available. That will happen. And that responsibility comes with power and influence, but it also comes with responsibility, expectations. And now you got to deal with the things that

Go along with being a leader because now other people are looking to you and depending on you, even though you didn't ask 'em to, this happens. And point number three, imposter syndrome. You may start to see yourself getting to a higher level, and if your self-image, your mindset has not caught up to that higher level of accomplishment, then you will self-sabotage your success and you won't be able to sustain it. No human being can perform at a level that is inconsistent with their self-image for an extended period of time. So you have to get your mindset right first before we start taking the actions. Or if you have already achieved a higher level, but your mindset is not there yet, it is an emergency, an emergency, an emergency that you must do something about that mindset quickly before your mindset pulls your success back down to the level at which you see yourself. And that will happen unless you do something about it asap.

#2844: Why You Fear Success [Part 2 of 10]

Let's get right into it and pick up where we left off in our series of why you fear success. This is part four of what we are projecting to be a 10 part series. So part point number 10, loss of identity. No human being can perform for an extended period of time in a manner that is inconsistent with his or her self-image.

One challenge with becoming successful, especially if you have been less than successful for a long time, is that now you must step into a new identity and a new way of seeing yourself in the mirror if you want that success to sustain. So if you have been less than successful for a while now by your own estimation, by your own measure of what success means and then you become successful, the first thing that needs to change is your self-image. The way that you see yourself, the way you personally see the individual in the mirror. If that does not change but your success has changed, what's going to happen is your self image is going to pull your tangible success right back to the level of your self image. You will always perform at a level that is commensurate with how you see yourself. So if you see yourself as an average level performer but your outcomes right now are way above average, eventually those above average outcomes will pull themselves back.

You will regress to the mean as we say, and you will come back to the average level person that you see yourself as. Your results will be reflective of how you see yourself. If on the other hand you see yourself as a wildly successful individual and you are not that right now, as long as you can maintain that self image, you will then be moved to take actions that will get you to have your success measured up to the way that you see yourself. You always end up getting what you expect of yourself and you always end up living out how you personally see yourself. So one challenge with becoming successful, especially again if you haven't been successful, is that you must step into this new identity to match up to the outcomes that you have. And this is very uncomfortable for people, not because they don't want to be successful but because you are stepping outside of your comfort zone of who you have always known yourself to be.

If you've been the same type of person for the last 10 or 20 or 30 years and now you want to get a whole new level of success, understanding your self image must change as well as your outcomes. They both have to change. Now all of a sudden after 20 years of being the same type of person, now you're going to become this whole new individual all of a sudden just overnight just like that. Usually it doesn't happen that way. I'm not saying it's impossible, but it's highly improbable and that's difficult for people because they would rather not most people, and it may seem ironic, but it is true, it's a paradox most people would rather not become successful just so they can stay in the comfort zone of being the person that they've always been rather than becoming successful and get out of their comfort zone and step into a new self-image.

Most people would rather stay the same, even if that means staying average because it's comfortable than change, even if the change means being 10 times better than they were before because the change is so uncomfortable that they'd rather not deal with it. And this is the reason why you've heard me say over and over and over again on this show, people do not change and the reason people don't change is not because they don't consciously want to is because it's very uncomfortable to change and it takes a significant amount of resources to make real change in life. It takes no resources to just stay the same even though you're not technically staying the same, you're actually slowly regressing, but it feels to most people like they're staying the same. It's much easier to do that. Most people rather stay in their comfort zones and this is a real thing and it's a serious identity challenge for people when the circumstances of your life changes.

The good news about this is that this often happens when someone gets to having or doing before they change the being. So if you get to having an outcome or you suddenly have a change in behaviors forced upon you before your self image has changed, then it is thrust upon you that you have to adjust your self image or you're not going to be able to maintain what you have or what you've been doing. For example, when a person wins the lottery, let's say a person's been making $40,000 a year all their life and they're 50 years old and then they win a lottery, now they have $10 million in cash that they never had before. The most important thing this person needs to do is not hire an accountant or not get somebody to help 'em with their taxes or a money manager they don't need.

That's not the first thing you need to do. First thing this person needs to do is invest in their mindset and in some personal development because if they don't adjust who they see themselves as, they have to adjust from being that $40,000 a year person to being a $10 million person. If they don't make that adjustment, eventually their mindset will pull their actions and their outcomes back down to that $40,000 a year person. This is why any of you have heard these stories. You hear that a lot of people who win the lottery, they eventually end up going broke or going right back to the state financially that they were in before they won the lottery simply because their self image never changed, their outcomes change. We know we have the B do in half, and I'll tell you that you achieve in that order. You have the B first, then you do, then you have.

But if someone jumps the line and they just go from being do, to have one way, then all of a sudden they're just changing and they haven't done much and they haven't changed who they are. Winning the lottery, you don't have to do anything. All you had to do was buy a lottery ticket for $2 and now all of a sudden you got all this outcome that you didn't really do any work for and you didn't do anything to work on yourself or you got a problem. There's a conflict there. One of those has to change. Either your being has to change to match what you now have or you're having to change to match who you still are. And usually it happens in the second way. You're having changes, IE you lose all the money so you can go back to being the person that you've always seen yourself as.

This is the reason why. So when you hear people talk about people winning the lottery and they end up going broke or a pro athlete makes a lot of money as an athlete, then a few years later they don't have any money left. It's not because of what they did, it's because of who they are. It's because of their mindset. Your mindset never changed. You never do any work on your mindset. You're going to go right back to the same place. This is how an athlete, let's say an athlete comes from a poor or middle class or a lower middle class background, they go become a professional athlete and make a whole lot of money is publicly noted how much money they make. It's usually these stories that happen with athletes where you know exactly how much money they make, you can look it up and you Google people's salaries and all that.

So they made all this money, say an athlete makes $50 million in their entire sporting career, which is a lot of money by any measure, and then their career ends and five years later they barely have any money left. And people are like, how the hell did this person lose all this money? And what you'll hear a lot of people saying, especially people who work in the finance space, they'll say, well, this person didn't invest or they were over leveraged or they bought all these houses, they bought all these depreciating assets and they were taking care of too many family members and they lived this lavish lifestyle that was too big for their after athlete life. And all of those things are true, but notice what all those things are. Those are all actions. Those are all doing things that caused that outcome according to what many people will tell you.

They just did all these things or they didn't do certain things that led to those outcomes. But where do actions come from folks? Where do actions come from? They come from the way that we think. You can't take an action without somehow having some thought in your mind that leads to it. There has to be some notion in your head that leads to any action that you've ever taken. Think about that almost every action you've ever taken in life, there was some thought that crossed your mind before you did it, whether it was conscious or subconscious, there was some kind of thought that crossed your mind before you did every action. So it's really the mindset that needs to change. You get an athlete, let's say an athlete goes from being in the hood and his family makes $50,000 a year per household and a whole household and now he's making $10 million a year for the next 10 years.

The first thing he needs to do is go invest in some personal development. And even if the first thing he actually does is go get himself a money manager or a financial advisor or whatever that hopefully that money manager or financial advisor says, Hey, listen to what Dre Baldwin said and go get yourself some books. Go to the library, I'll give you a $500 allowance and buy yourself some books or invest in your mind because that will last a lot longer than your ability to dunk a basketball or catch a football or hit a baseball. That's the main thing that needs to change for any of you when you're having all of a sudden changes in ways that maybe your being has not caught up to. Everybody follows what I'm saying here. So if you're going to become successful, usually you have to do it in the normal order, which is B, then do then half.

But if somehow things get out of whack, you need to as an emergency measure, make sure that your mindset catches up to the changes in having even though you haven't actually done all the other work yet. Point number 11, today's topic once again is why you may fear success. Number 11, lost connections. Now this is one that we've touched on a few times already in this series, and as you become a more successful person, and again, success is relative. So however you measure success, as your success grows and increases, you will lose touch with some people for multiple reasons. One reason is it's the natural progression of life where some people choose to consciously and intentionally make themselves better while others choose to stay in the same place and simply not improve. This just happens in life sometimes. Some people like you who listen to a show like this one, you are consciously and intentionally doing things to make yourself better, whereas most people are not going to do that.

They're not interested in that. They'd rather do something that's entertaining or something that's more of a stress relieving activity like watching TV or hanging out or going to the movies. Whereas you're doing things that are growth inducing such as listening to a masterclass or reading a book or taking a course or joining a coaching program. Those things are growth inducing, but they're not easy to do. You can't put your brain on autopilot and do those things you got to actually think. Whereas most people would rather turn their brain completely off and do something that is mindless, IE watching tv, scrolling, social media, playing video games, et cetera. So if you're going in one direction, growth inducing and other people are going in the other direction, stress relieving, well, what do you think is going to happen over time? You and that person are going to grow apart.

Y'all are doing two different things. You're on two different paths that are going in divergent directions. So this is one of the reasons why you lose connections as you create more success. Not everybody else is willing to do the things necessary to create success like you're doing again, consciously and intentionally. Two phrases you'll hear me use a lot here on the show, and so naturally you and those people have less in common. Another reason why you may lose connections is because as you become more successful, some people may not be able to see life through the same lens through which you see life because again, they don't have the experiences that you have. They're not living the life that you have. They're not doing the stuff that you're doing, so they just can't understand what you understand. This is how any of you out there who has children and you have friends who you had kids before them and maybe your kids are growing up and getting older, your kids are now five years old, 10 years old, they're going, they're in high school, they maybe going to college.

And the friends that you had when you first had children, they didn't have kids then and they still don't have kids now. They can't relate to your situation because anytime that you talk to them, you're probably telling them about something's going on with the kids. Because when you have kids, for the most part, that's one of the biggest things. A lot of your attention and focus is on what's going on with the kids for the next 18 years at least until they get out of the house and they're on their own. And that other person can't relate to that because they don't have the same experience. So not like that person stops being your friend completely, but they may not be able to relate to you as well and the connection may get weaker just because y'all can't talk about the same things, you can't do the same things or they're going and doing stuff that a single person can do or a person with no kids can do.

Let's say you as a person with kids can't do those same things. You got kids now. You can't make the same decisions, you can't go to the same places, you can't stay out as late and you have to think about the kids before you think about anything else, even yourself. So this is one example that I'm giving you here of how two people can have divergent experiences, life experiences, and it causes the connection to weaken simply because they're just not doing the same things. So also some people may be only able to live vicariously through you because maybe they just want to watch what you're doing. I remember when I first went over a seizure to play basketball, I would write a lot of the first iteration of my writing. I would write blog posts on my Facebook profile and I would just write little basic articles, my Facebook profiles just about my experiences playing overseas and stuff like that.

And a lot of my friends from back home would read those posts because it was interesting. What was interesting about it was I was doing something that most of them would never do and they were able to live that life vicariously through me. So in some ways that can create more connection depending on your style and depending on who those people are. But in other ways somebody might see that and they may shun the idea of you simply because what you're doing is a reflection of what they're not doing. Again, you've heard me say that three or four times already in the series, so that allows them to stay comfortable in their identity to just completely block out anything that you have going on because it's so different from what they have going on. Point number 12, today's topic once again is we are talking about why you fear success.

Point number 12 is vulnerability. This is another thing that may be causing you to fear success and want to stay away from it. As we have established already in this series, success makes you more visible than you previously were. You are more seen, you are more known. Even people who already knew who you were are now more aware of your presence simply because of your success, your presence has enlarged. You have an enlarged presence simply because you're doing more than you were doing before. So because of this and also on top of the fact that the more successful you become, there are fewer people on your same level, the higher up the success ladder you go. It's not like you all of a sudden are by yourself. There will always be other people on the ladder, but there are fewer people on the ladder. There's more elbow room.

The higher up the success ladder you go. And because of that, you are more visible simply because there's less of a crowd around you. So there may be a crowd of a million people at level one of success. Level two, there's only 800,000. Level three is only 500,000. Level 10, there might only be 20,000 people up there. So you're more easily seen, more easily known, and more easily identified simply because, so you have relatively fewer peers than who you had before. So because of this, the attention that you're drawing could possibly cause you to feel vulnerable simply because you are so visible. Now you don't have to feel vulnerable, but this is a possibility, which is why I'm including it in this list, in this series. I've heard many people who have not yet created, let's say, financial success. This is a good example and I've heard this from multiple people.

They haven't yet created a certain level of financial success, but they will say something like, well, maybe I don't want to be so financially successful because they are projecting in their minds all the attention that comes with financial success and how they believe that when they have financial success, especially the success that is publicly noted, meaning people know that you have a certain amount of money, it will draw too much stress on them, such as somebody trying to sue you, somebody trying to steal money from you or somebody trying to get money out of you, dishonestly stealing from you, people asking you for money, and you got to deal with the requests and other maladies that come with having financial success. And again, this is similar to my friend who was worried about having too many muscles before they started lifting weights. So let's first of all get you some money, some money period is to make sure all your bills are paid first for you worried about having too much money and everybody wanting to take some from you, alright?

Again, you're making down payments on problems that you don't even have and then using those down payments as an excuse for not doing anything to get to success. And this is how again, many people think themselves out of success based on things that have never even occurred just based on their imagination. Literally, this is imagination. I would suggest that any of you who's thinking about a future problem that will come with increased success, accomplishment or achievement, I would suggest you get the problem and deal with it as it is. Go get the success, get the problems that come with it because remember, everything in life has a trade-off episode 2174, I told you that there are no perfect scenarios. Only trade-offs. Get the scenario of success. See the trade-offs and learn to deal with them. That's it. Just learn to deal with them because understand, since I just told you, everything in life has a trade off.

Being average has a trade off too. If you do nothing and stay in the same space as you are in life right now for the next 10, 20, 30 years, there's a trade off to that too. In other words, there's a penalty for that. The same way there's a penalty, if you get 10 times more successful, there is no perfect scenario you could be in where nothing's going to happen. Only scenario you could be in where nothing's going to happen and you don't have to deal with anything. It's called death, alright? Other than that, you are always going to have to deal with something, alright? That's what we call life. That said, let's recap today's class, which is again, we are on part four of what's going to be a 10 part series on why you fear success. Number 10, point number 10, loss of identity.

Your identity must change when your success levels go up. Actually, your identity must change before your success levels go up. 99% of the time, you must change who you see yourself as and how you see you in the mirror before you can change your actions or change the effect of your actions before you can change your outcomes. If you happen to do this out of order, IE, you win the lottery before you have changed your mindset, you better change your mindset quickly or your financial level is going to go right back down to where it was and meet your mindset where you were before. Number 11, lost connections. Sometimes you lose connections because you are going in a growth direction where other people are basically receding because they're not trying to grow. If you're not growing, you're dying. It's one of the others, you may lose connections that way.

And also as you create more success, people just can't relate to your life the same way simply because you're living a way that they're not living and these connections can be lost and some people fear losing those connections. These are people like and trust and love. You don't want to get disconnected from them, so you'd rather stay average so you can stay connected to those people. And number 12, vulnerability. Alright? As you become more successful, you become more seen, you are more known, you may feel like you are becoming more of a target and you may even hear people who are successful talk about these things and it calls you to psych yourself out and think, well, maybe I shouldn't become successful because then I'll be vulnerable and somebody might want to sue me or attack me, or I might need security or somebody's going to be stalking me or I'm going to get all these haters on the internet.

How about you just get to the success first and worry about the problems later? How about that? Instead of putting a down payment on problems that you do not yet have because you don't even have the success that would bring those problems, how about you go get the success and let's see what those problems actually look like and deal with them as they come. I bet you'll be able to deal with them if for you to become successful, you got to build yourself up so much that I guarantee you'll be able to deal with things like whatever problems come with being successful and you'll be much better off dealing with the problems as a success than dealing with the problems of being average.

#2844: Why You Fear Success [Part 2 of 10]

Let's get right into point number four here, picking up from yesterday's masterclass. And we're talking again about the reasons why you fear success. Number four, attention and criticism. So what you'll notice when I'm talking about these reasons why you fear success, these are all things that either, sometimes it's someone has already achieved some level of success and you start to notice these things happening and you fear them.

So you push away or you are anticipating what will happen when you're successful, maybe because of what you saw from other people or with your imagination and you're like, well, I don't want that. So you do everything you can to stay away from it. So sometimes you have actually experienced these viscerally and sometimes you're just thinking about them, but they all do happen. They are all real. So as you create more success, you naturally will draw more attention to yourself. And we've already talked about why this is because most people are not successful. So when you create success, most people don't even try to be successful, let alone do they become it. And the more attention you draw to yourself for whatever reason, you will naturally draw some people who have something to say about you, whether it's positive, negative or neutral. Simply because you are visible and in front of them.

The more attention you draw, the more people are going to have an opinion about you. It doesn't matter what the opinion is, they'll just have an opinion. Why? Because you're there and they're going to talk about it. This is what human beings do. But if you happen to be in front of a lot of people and you are successful and people note your success, meaning your success is visible or it's publicly noted for whatever reason, and again, public can mean within your community, doesn't have to be to the whole world. You'll get even more criticism and more negativity from other people because of the success when you're noted for having achieved at a high level. Now, why is this? Well, because some of you may be thinking about when somebody's wildly successful or wildly noted for being a success, don't they get more praise?

Don't they have fans? Don't they get followers? Don't they become influencers? They have all these people who like them and people who buy from them and people who give them money. Yes they do. At the same time they get more negativity. Just think about it. If you just think about that, that makes sense, right? If you just think about this a little bit, anybody you know who is known and they have fans and they have customers that they got money or whatever it is that you think comes with being successful to good stuff, guess what? They get a lot of negativity for it too. You might not see it or hear it all the time, but it's there. And if you look hard enough, you only have to look that hard. You'll find it. Now, why does this happen? Because most people by definition are average or below average, alright?

That you already know. You've heard me say that a hundred times on the show. So when they see you, these average and below average people, again, you are a mere mortal just as they are and you created this level of success that they have failed to create or not even tried to create. What are you to them? You got to understand how they're thinking. I'm going to tell you how they're thinking. You are a reflection of their shortcomings. See, when you see another person being successful, there's a couple different ways you can look at it. You can look at it and say, alright, that person is successful. Good, that motivates and inspires me. I can be successful too. What can I extract from what they're doing that I can use for myself? That's one way of looking at it. That's the healthy way of looking at it.

That's the way that would say about 2% of people look at success. Then there's a person who looks at it and says, well, that has nothing to do with me. I don't even care. I would say a good about 40% of people look at it that way. Then the rest, that means it's about 58% of people. They look at it the other way that your success is a reflection of their lack of success. And they have two choices from that point. They can either A figure out why you got the success and they didn't. They can do the work to close the gap, or B, they can come up with a story in their own minds that makes you lesser than you are. Doesn't literally make you lesser just in their mind. It makes you lesser so that they can feel okay and they can sleep at night knowing that even though you had a success, you only have it because of this or because you're this color or because you're this gender or because you're a cheater or because you're a bad person or you're immoral or because the world just gave you all this luck or you were born with a silver spoon in your mouth and they weren't.

And they can just craft all these rationalizations to make them feel okay about the fact that you have more success in them. This is the choice people have and a good percentage of people choose this option I just gave you. Again, people do have the option of looking at you as an inspiration to figuring out how they can create some of the success for themselves that you created for yourself. They could do that. Most people don't choose that. They just find a way to pull you down mentally again in their own minds so they can reconcile their failure to be as successful as you are. This is why the more successful you are, the more you'll be criticized and attacked by average people because the average person is average because they don't want to do the work to get to success the way that you have done the work to get to success.

This is just how it works. And they will craft stories in their minds to rationalize this exact activity. And a lot of times, again, this happens unconsciously, subconsciously. People don't even realize that they're doing it, but they do it. And the more you listen to people talk, the more you'll start to understand what's going on in their minds. The words are a reflection of people's thoughts. Point number five, today's topic. Once again, we are on part two of what's going to be a 10 part series, why do you fear success? Number five, judgment. Now, this is one that we kind of just touched on a little bit, but I want to talk about it a little bit more. Now. This judgment that I'm referring to is not just from other people, it's also judgment that you have of yourself looking at yourself in the mirror.

So first, let's start with the judgment you get from others. As I just told you, most people are average and worse and many people have very healthy, unhealthy, excuse me, many people have very unhealthy ideas when it comes to success in any form such as health, finance or career success. Many people are very unhealthy in the way that they think about how success happens. In other words, you ask someone about how you can make a good amount of money in life? Many people have some really negative ideas of how people who have money get money or how to be successful in a career. They think, well let's talk about this. Let's go into this a little bit. So you ask some people who are not very physically healthy, what does it take to be healthy? Oh, well, I don't want to be in the gym all day.

I don't want to be drinking damn protein shakes. I don't want to have to eat a rabbit and eat grass all day and be eating all that stuff and be in the gym all the time and lifting weights and I ain't got time for all that. They come up with all these negative stories that they make up in their minds about being healthy so that they can justify being unhealthy. You understand when it comes to finance, and this one is I think the most pernicious, the worst one because when I'm on social media on X, which is the only app where I actually engage in commentary between people, this one is extremely unhealthy. There are some people who I would see as far as their career goes, careers go. These are some people who are doing fine in their careers, they're making fine money, but they are incentivized to preach to their audiences that in order to be successful financially, you have to be some type of negative or bad person.

And there's a whole game around this. I've talked about this on some levels, but there are many people out there, many people. And this one is again, I think this is the most pernicious person who believes that to be successful financially, you must be some type of negative person. You have to be greedy, you have to use other people, you have to not care about other people. You have to just be a miser who's just trying to get everything for yourself and you will get all the equity out of other people with no apology and no remorse. And there are many people who think like this. There are many people especially who think like this about entrepreneurs. You'd be, I don't know if you'll be surprised, but I was surprised even and I have talked to a lot of people and heard a lot of stuff, I have been surprised with the kind of things I hear people say about entrepreneurs, just general ideas they have about entrepreneurs that are not based in any type of reality, but they believe them.

It's their reality, they believe it. What is such a thing as your reality? There's such a thing as your truth. There is such a thing as your reality. But a lot of people believe that to be an entrepreneur you have to be this negative person who is just using your staff and you are giving them as little as possible and you are just some greedy billionaire who got financed by some corporation or by the government or somehow you got access to these billions of dollars that are locked up in your safe that you swim around in every day by screws, McDuck, and you're just using your financial leverage against everybody else to make the world worse and just to make your pockets fatter. And there are people who really, really, really believe this. And again, these are the kind of ideas that people have in their heads and you're not going to change their minds, by the way. Alright? Don't even try. And when it comes to career success, same thing. Oh, the only reason you moved up in your career is because well you kissed up to the bosses or you let people talk to you any kind of way or you just gave up all your self-respect or these negative things that people come up with again is they're just rationalizations to make them feel okay about the fact that you are further ahead than they are.

Instead of figuring out how they can get to the same level as a successful person against success being relative. Most people just put a negative label on the people who have that success so that they feel okay not having it. So they will judge you and they will judge you harshly. And some of these people will be willing to voice their judgment of you. And when there are more of them, and the more of them there are, the more confident they are to voice their negative judgments of you. We call this the vocal majority. The vocal majority. These are the people who feel they have some negative idea they have of you. And when they feel supported, there are other people who have the same idea. All of them will get louder and stronger in their voicing against you. Let's just put it that way, and this is something that I know to be true, I'll probably do an episode on this soon after this series is done, is that people tend to agree with you privately and quietly and in private when people agree with you, they tend to do it quietly and in private, especially when you're talking about something that maybe people don't want to jump into that hot water because there may be some pushback and opinions are divided.

People tend to disagree with you loudly and in public. So you need to learn to take this with a grain of salt if people disagree with you. When I'm on, again an app like X, which used to be known as Twitter, I tend to jump into conversations where I know there are divided opinions and I like jumping into those conversations. I get to add something to the conversation that's not already being said. If I agree with somebody on something, I usually don't say anything because I don't have anything to add to the conversation. They already said it. I tend to jump in conversations when people disagree and when people disagree my pushback of the disagreement is very loud and it's very public and a bunch of people will jump in, I'll get 60 comments to people who disagree with something that I said. Especially on topics like politics, race, money, those are probably the top three where there's a lot of pushback and negativity.

Pushback is loud and it's heavy. But the people who agree with me, they don't really say anything. They just quietly agree with me. They might like my posts, they might follow me, but they don't, don't get into the conversation and defend me verbally because they don't want to deal with the backlash that comes with it. And I get it and I ain't mad at those people. But you need to understand this and you have to have your mind in the right place to be able to deal with this if you're going to get yourself into the public space. And that doesn't mean you need to be on social media talking to people in comments, I don't recommend it. It's not for everybody. You have to have a certain type of mental makeup for doing this. I have it and not everybody has it and not everybody needs it.

But as I'm saying here, instead of figuring out how to get to the same level as successful people, most people just put negative labels on you so that they can feel better about themselves. And again, on social media, I hear people talk about entrepreneurs, they're evil, greedy, they're exploiting people. This can be further from the troop, but a lot of people do truly believe this and other forms of judgment you have. The flip side of this is you judging yourself. This is a judgment you have to be aware of as well. And this is the worst judgment because you have to deal with yourself all day. You can put your phone away and not hear people saying stuff about you on the internet. You can't put yourself away. Well you can, but I would suggest you not alright? Because most people are average. It is inevitable that you've been around a lot of average people your whole life, alright?

Most of you can't avoid being around average people. You have no choice. You go to school, you go to work and you go outside, you go to the grocery store, alright? There are average people everywhere, alright? You can't avoid them, it's too many of them. So a lot of those average loser thinking ideas that you would get from average people are embedded in your brain the same way they are embedded in their brains. You got these if you went to school, I guarantee you got a bunch of losers thinking about average ideas because school is designed, designed to create and manufacture a bunch of average people to live average lives. It's designed that way. So unless you were homeschooled, there's no way you could avoid this. So when you start to create success, these loser ideas that have been planted in your brain, they might start to creep up in your mind.

So you must have the tools to deal with these. And guess what? We happen to have that tool. It's called the Bulletproof Mindset System. And that's the first thing you're going to access when you join work on your game university at work on your game university.com. Point number six, we're talking today, we're on part two of our what's going to be a 10 part series? Why you fear success number six, future failure. Yes. This is another reason people fear success is because they don't want to fail in the future that they haven't even gotten to yet. Alright? So they call when you are too focused on what's happened in the past, they call that anxiety. And when they say you're too worried about what's going to happen in the future or too concerned about what is going to happen in the future, they call that worry.

So future failure is a form of worrying. Many people hesitate to do things that would lead to success tomorrow because you may feel you're setting yourself up for a fall from grace the day after tomorrow. So if I am at level 10 today and I do the work that'll give me a level 12 tomorrow, then the problem is what if I fall back to a level eight the day after tomorrow? Well, I might as well not get to level 12. Why not just stay where I'm at and keep it neutral the whole time? This is how people think, excuse me, this is how people think. This is the rationalization that they go through and therefore they sabotage their success and do nothing and they rationalize and they come to the conclusion it's better to do nothing at all than to move up and then have to move back down because you have created success in the present. Now you create an expectation. I will tell you that that's true. When you create success, you create an expectation with yourself and through others to do it again.

And you need to maintain that success. You want to maintain success. Any of you who's created success, you want to maintain it, right? You want to stay up there. And if you doubt your ability to maintain or expand on your success, which means you may fail in the future compared to your present achievements, it doesn't make you a failure, it just means you have failed to maintain the success. So if you're used to a level 10, you move up to a level 12 and you can't maintain a level 12 and you fall back down to a level 10 again while you fail to achieve the level 12. Alright? That's what I mean when I say fail and some people get sensitive about me saying the word fail. If that's you, I would suggest you get over it. You're going to be working on your game world.

We don't play that shit, alright? I'm just going to give you the language as it needs to be said. So if you fail to maintain that level 12 or you fear that you'll fail to maintain that level 12, you will not even try to get to the level 12 in the first place and you'll just stay at level 10 and do nothing, which is neutrality. But the problem with neutrality is that there is no such thing as neutrality with human beings. You're either getting better or getting worse every day. You're getting closer to dying. So there is no such thing as being neutral when you're a human being. It is impossible. You are always building or destroying.

So when you create the expectation by being successful in yourself and in others to maintain success, if you doubt your ability, you might say, well, I might as well not even try consciously or unconsciously. You might decide to just stay where you are and never become successful so that you've never set yourself up for any form of failure and any form of disappointment of yourself or others. Because again, you may have others depending on you if you go perform at a level 12. Now they're like, oh, well Mikey's going to do a level 12 every day. Alright, now we can depend on Mikey to do a level 12. Alright? Now you have expectations. You don't want to do that. So let me not raise these expectations by being successful. Lemme just stay average. This is how people think and this is how you end up blocking your own success. This is self-sabotage.

In short, some people would rather be consistently average rather than be wildly successful and then risk falling to a lower level of success after that. It's not that you are going to fall to a lower level of success than me, what's stopping you from just staying up there? Once you get up there, it's nothing that says you have to fall back down. But some people are so afraid of what would happen if and when they fall back down that they don't want to get up in the first place. You don't want to go up. And I talked about this metaphor a long time ago, which is that you can't dunk the basketball without jumping. Or even the tallest basketball players in the world got to jump in order to dunk the basketball. And some people don't want to jump to dunk the basketball because they're afraid that they have to come back down to the ground after the dunk so they never try to dunk in the first place.

So you have to leave your feet. It's an extended metaphor for basketball, but all of you can get it just from what I said before. That is that if you are afraid of falling off before you even get to a point, you are basically predicting your failure before it even happens. Why are you doing it? Worry is a down payment on future failure. That's what it is. You're making a down payment. You are investing in your failure in the future by worrying. You're making an investment. It's like you went and bought some stocks and bonds instead of buying stocks and bonds, you just buy failure. Let me just buy some failures now so that they will mature and I'll have more failures in the future. Why would you want to do that? And see, putting it that way makes it sound more silly. It makes it sound silly, right?

And I want you to think that it's silly because I want you to stop doing it. If you've been guilty of this recapping reasons why you fear success, we're picking up on point number four, attention and criticism. When you achieve success, you will get more attention. And when you draw more attention in life, you will get more criticism. Even if you're not trying to get attention, success draws attention naturally. And just like food draws ants and you are going to get criticism because the more people look at you, the more they're going to see what you're doing and they're going to have something to say. And there's just negative people out there who think negative things. They're going to say negative things about you. This is a natural progression when you draw more attention in life. So be ready for it. It is coming. Number five, judgment.

Not just judgment from other people who will judge you because they will find ways to mentally pull you down in their own minds so they can reconcile why you are successful and they're not. But also judgment from yourself. Because again, as we talked about in yesterday's opening to the series, if you haven't achieved the self image that is a reflection of the performance that you want to get to or that you have already gotten to, then you'll be judging yourself. And also you'll be judging yourself about, hey, these loser and average ideas that you've been taught your entire life from school, from the average people in your neighborhood and your family at your job. If you haven't uprooted that negative nonsense that you've gotten from these losers and average people and there are many of them all over the world, you can't avoid them for the most part.

Once you live in a bubble, you have to get those out of your brain because those negative thoughts will start to pop up in your mind as soon as you start to look like you want to be successful. And this is why the bulletproof mindset is the first thing we teach inside of work at your game university. And number six, future failure. This is the down payment that you're putting on your failure in the future. So let me not even try to get to a higher level now because I'm not sure I'll be able to maintain it. So why don't I just stay where I'm at? So this is where I'm going to end up anyway. Alright? This is a loser mindset and this is a symptom of you having as the root cause these loser and average thinking mindsets that have been embedded in you again, by your family, by your school teachers, by your peers, by your friends, and by your coworkers, and just by average people, period.

All over the world, all of your life. This is why the bulletproof mindset is the first and most important piece of what we do in work at your game university. I know you want to make more money. I know you want to run ads. I know you want to launch your book. I know you want to put your course together, but without the right mindset, alright? Nothing you do to achieve success is going to sustain you, will self-sabotage it yourself without even knowing that you're doing it because you've been dealing with a bunch of losers all your life. I'm not saying that the people around you personally are losers. I'm saying that the world is filled with losers and you cannot avoid them. It's impossible. If you go outside, you're around losers. Alright? Just look around. Alright? There's some losers out there and you can't avoid these people and their thoughts have been embedded in your brain over the last 30 or 27 or 42 years.

And unless you do something consciously and intentionally get rid of it, those loser thoughts will bring you back to average V. This is why most people are average. Alright? It is not luck. It's not a magic trick.

#2845: Why You Fear Success [Part 3 of 10]

Let's get right into it. I don't have to give you any intro to this. So let's pick up right where we left off at point number seven and the first two episodes of the series, we covered points one through three, then fourth through sixth. Now we're on point number seven, why you may be in Fear of success. So these may be conscious or unconscious things that are stopping you from taking the steps that will get you to the success that you have been telling yourself that you want but you don't yet have.

Number seven raised expectations. This concept connects directly to the last point that we talked about in the previous installment of this series. When you become successful, and again, success is relative to where you are now. So when I say use the word successful in this series, it just means relative to where you are now, you are doing significantly better and you determine what significantly better means for you. When you become successful, both you and others around you who have seen this success will begin to expect that you will remain successful and continue to build on that success. In other words, people are going to expect upward movement from you because they have seen upward movement from you. People tend to expect you to do the same stuff that you've done before. Human beings are creatures of habit, so when you see someone doing something, they expect you to do it again. And anything that you show to people, they're going to expect you to do it over and over. And the more people who see you doing a certain thing, the more

People, let's just say, will have the expectation of you doing it again. So when you create success and only a few people know about it, then only a few people are going to have the expectation of you repeating that success. But if a lot of people know about it now you're going to have a lot of people having that expectation on you to create that success. And when a lot of people are expecting you to be successful, again, a lot being a relative term that may create pressure for you and that pressure on you could cause some people to rise to the occasion or it could cause you to crumble under what you perceive as pressure. And this is just how a lot of human beings look at things in life, but you know all these people are looking at you and expecting something. It's harder to perform than if nobody was expecting anything or nobody was watching you in the first place.

This is one of the reasons why in basketball, back in my days as an athlete, a lot of basketball players would follow my training material and I would teach them how to practice basketball and get better at playing basketball, but then when it came time to actually translate those practice skills into live game action, it was a challenge for many athletes. They would get performance anxiety or just not perform as well. Maybe it wasn't anxiety, they just weren't performing as well in front of everybody because it's a whole different ball game when you're practicing something and no one's watching and then you do the same thing. There's a whole bunch of people watching. So for example, when I record episodes of this show, it's just me here. There's nobody else in the room listening to me right now while I'm talking and I'm only speaking to a camera and into a microphone, but not to live human beings.

I don't feel the thousands of human beings who are actually going to hear this episode. I can only imagine it, but I don't feel your presence right now while I'm recording this and I'm going to have it already recorded by the time you hear it. And at the same time, I'm comparing that to even though I have a lot of stage experience, I have plenty of experience being on stages as a physical performer like in sports and also as a speaker, as a professional speaker, Ted Talks, et cetera, things like that, sales presentations and things like that. If I was to record episodes of this show in front of a live studio audience, the first few times I did it, it would feel a little bit different than it feels for me to record this show right here by myself with nobody else in the room, even though I have the experience simply because it's a different type of thing and I have those eyeballs on me, I feel those eyeballs, I don't feel any eyeballs on me right now because there aren't any.

So those raised expectations, the fact that people are just watching you can make a difference in the way that we perform in life. And any of you who's ever gone from a position of nobody knowing who you are to having some people, it doesn't have to be a million people. It could be five people watching you from zero, that's a big difference. And sometimes people can't perform as well when they know that they're being observed. So this can take the shape of, as I said, pressure because now you have to perform at a higher level all the time. Once you show that you can create success and it's no longer a surprise to other people when you're successful, it becomes a standard almost to the point that it is so normalized that people, they're not even excited when you do something that is so great. It's just normal for you to have

This level of performance to where people don't even appreciate it as much because they get so used to it that again, they almost feel entitled to that level of performance. This is something that I've talked about when you heard me talk about performing at a high level, being a superstar, what you do, you take someone like LeBron James these days in basketball or Michael Jordan if you are a little bit older, these guys normalized greatness. They normalized having a great game 97% of the time that they had a game to where having a great game was not something to get excited about. It was like this is what this person does, they just do it all the time and it's normal. If they didn't have a great game, that was a surprise. Whereas most people and their line of work, they have a great game.

Everybody's all excited because their great games are so few and far between. Whereas the superstar level people in any line of work, you having a great game is so normal that no one's excited anymore. When you have a great game is almost, not almost, but we can say for sure people come to take it for granted because it's so used to you doing it. And this is something that again becomes a mental challenge for a higher level performer because you gotta keep finding ways to get yourself mentally locked in to perform at that higher level even though everyone's already expecting it, everyone expects it from you and nobody's going to be excited when you do it, but you still have to do it anyway. That's a challenge. It is not as easy as it sounds. So when you get to that level, it's no longer a surprise.

Again, it becomes a standard, an expectation of others going along for you. And again, this sounds like a good idea from the outside looking in, it feels a whole lot different when you're the one who everyone is looking to solve every problem, codes every deal and do what nobody else has been able to do. It is much easier to just be a member of the crowd, have no expectations on you. It's much easier to do that because nobody's expecting anything. So anything you do is extra, it's gravy. But what about you doing that extra level and that's just the normal, and again, you don't even get a handshake for doing it. This is why most people are average. This is one of the reasons why most people are average. It's not because most people are incapable of success and it's not because most people don't want success.

It's because most people don't want to deal with the expectation that comes with being a known successful individual. Most people don't want to deal with the expectation that comes with success because there will be expectations in the book, relentlessly written by Tim Grover who, speaking to Michael Jordan, was Michael Jordan's trainer for a lot of his career. Tim talked about how many people in basketball, for example as a metaphor, don't want take that last shot in the game because if you make the last shot, now next game when somebody needs to make the last shot, now they're going to be looking at you to do it again and now it becomes an expectation because you've done it before. And that's exactly what I mean that people fall into human beings again as creatures of habit. We see someone doing something even one time and we start to expect that that's just what they do all the time.

We're going to expect them to do it, especially if they're doing something that we don't want to do or that we can't do. We will gladly get behind that person and let them do it instead of you doing it yourself. So again, it's not that people don't want to do something great, it's that they don't want to be expected to do something great. And that's the difference. Doing something great is one thing, but doing something great when everyone is looking at you like, all right, hey, do something great, we need you to do something great, do it right now and you just got to do it on call. That's a whole different ball game than when you're doing something great and you came out of nowhere and everybody's like, wait, who's that? We never heard of this person, but look at them. Look at this great thing that they're doing.

It's a whole other thing when everybody shows up expecting you to do a great thing and now you gotta do it with everybody looking. It is way different when the expectation is on you. And this may be a thing that holds people back, not holds people back, but causes people to hold themselves back from being successful because this is the trade off. This is what happens afterwards. Point number eight, we're talking today about why you may be in fear of success consciously or unconsciously. Number eight, less support. So this one can go both ways. I give you both sides of this when I say less support, when you become more successful, the support level may go down. So on one hand, it is true that once you start creating momentum and success for yourself, more people may want to come around and help you or stand next to you or do anything to be around you now that you really don't need it as much as you needed it before.

It's a paradoxical thing when it comes to help and assistance is that the more you help yourself and the more success you create on your own momentum, the less you need it, but the more people want to give it to you. This is how we get things like the rich get richer and the poor get poor. When you have a lot of money and people know you have a lot of money, you often don't have to pay for stuff, even stuff that is relatively expensive and when you're poor and you don't have any money, you have to pay for everything. You don't get anything for free when you're poor. So it's just funny how that works in life and this is why the gap continues to widen between the people who are at the high levels of performance and people at low levels of performance.

Because when you're at the high level, people just give you stuff and you don't even have to work for it. Not everything, but I'm just saying it's metaphorically. You get the spirit of the point that I'm saying. And when you are more successful, again, sometimes you just get more help now that you don't really need it now everybody wants to help you. It's just funny like that. Where were all these people when I actually needed some help, now everybody wants to help me. So in one way you will have more support that you don't actually need or even want. It may not even be useful support when you're already successful. People just want to be around you again because they want to just have the FRI of having that success rub off on them and offering support is their way of getting around you if you allow it.

On the other hand though, fewer people will, fewer people in some areas will want to be around or support you simply because you are doing something that they haven't done and or do not understand. Again. So this is like the third time this concept has come up in this series already. As a general rule, people avoid things that they don't understand. So it depends on how your success has come about, where you did it at and how other people can relate to how you got to where you got to and what type of people maybe more attracted or less attracted to you based on the fact that you are successful. On top of the fact that as I already told you, when you create success that other people have not created, your success can be to certain people

A reflection of their lack thereof. So you can still have support, but it may be fewer in number than when you were a less successful individual. It's funny that it can happen this way sometimes it doesn't happen exactly this way, but often it can. So this is a real fear, but at the same time, let's remember that fear is not actually a real thing. Fear is just a feeling. It's something that we conjure up in our minds. It's not something that actually happens to you. Similar to embarrassment, similar to confidence. These things don't happen to you. They're choices. They're just states of mind. They're ways of thinking because you have created a certain level of success that means you'll be able to help yourself even when others are not willing to help you. That's one of the reasons why having less support may not even matter that much, but again, you have to get your mind around accepting what I just said.

It is one thing for me to say it, and you logically get it. It is another thing for you to accept it and actually go out and live it, that the more successful you become, okay, well these people aren't going to hang around me anymore. They won't want to help me anymore. That's okay because with the success that I've created, not only have I shown myself that I can do it, I now have the resources to do it on my own. Everything that they were doing, I can do myself and I don't need them or I can replace them because I have the resources to do so. This is part of what creating success can do for you. It gives you the confidence and the mental toughness to understand that the people who left, I'm still going to do what I'm going to do, whether you're going to be around or not, we're still going to make this work one way or another.

Give you an example here, speaking of Michael Jordan, who I already mentioned in the last carnation of the Chicago Bulls dynasty, which was 19 from 1996 through 1998. The last three years they won the championships when Michael Jordan was the main guy. They had this guy on the team named Dennis Robin. If you're a basketball fan about Dennis Rodman, you might know about him even if you don't watch basketball. And Dennis was a, we can say he was a free spirited, eccentric type of guy, but he was a very good basketball player, damn good player. He is, I believe, in the basketball hall of fame to this day. And Dennis was a kind of guy who he didn't keep, he wasn't a guy who kept normal discipline, professional type of schedule that a Michael Jordan or a Scottie Pippen would've kept, but he still did his job when it was time to get on the court.

And there was a time when Dennis while playing with the Bulls, I believe it was his first year with the Chicago Bulls, he got suspended because he had kicked a cameraman on the sideline during a game, intentionally kicked a cameraman. I remember when this happened back in the nineties and Dennis got suspended for maybe 10 or 11 games. And according to the stories, the Chicago Bulls during those 10 or 11 games, Dennis Rodman was a big piece of their team. They needed what Dennis brought to the table. They had, that was a hole in their roster before he got there. At least the year before Michael Jordan and Scottie Pippen, the two leaders of the team, according to reports, they decided that they were going to play as, they didn't say this out loud, but they played as hard as possible during the games that Dennis Rodman missed. And they played as if it was for the championship because they wanted to win as many games as they

Could always. But with Dennis out, they wanted to make a point of winning games without him to prove to him that, hey, the shit you did on the other teams you've been on where when you don't play, the team loses and the team gets worse when you're not around. That's not going to work over here. We're going to win with or without you. And according to, I think Tim Grover says this in his book, he told Dennis, Robin, look, we're going to win whether you're here or not, so you might as well get on board. And that's the kind of mindset that I would want you to have. Once you understand that creating success makes you a more empowered individual regardless of your tangible resources. This is a mental resource. Point number nine, today's topic, once again, we're on part three of our series, part three of our series, why you may be in Fear of Success.

Number nine, burnout, burnout, that creating success may just make you tired from doing so much stuff to create and maintain that success. This is the person who's worried about how they will cross a bridge before they have even gotten to the bridge. Well, I don't want to become successful because then I got to do all this work, then I got to carry the load, then I'm going to have all these expectations, then people are going to want me to do this. And they won't only do that and everybody's going to be coming at me. And you haven't even created the first level of success. You ain't even taking the first step to get success yet, but you're already worried about what's going to happen once you get there. Alright, this is again, putting a down payment on failure. And a lot of people tend to do this as a rationalization for their inaction in the moment.

I want to make sure you don't fall victim to this because a lot of people do this. It is like an automatic, I'll call these ants, ANTS automatic negative thoughts. I wrote about this in my book, Work on Your Game, which you can get by going to work on your game book.com, telling yourself about all the negative things that could happen before you have even taken the first step to making anything happen. Let alone a negative thing, let alone a positive thing. You haven't done anything, you're just telling yourself all the bad stuff that could happen. And before you know it, when you allow these ants to accumulate, because if you see one ant, there's usually a bunch of ants. What happens is by the time you allow 'me to accumulate, you have thought yourself out of doing anything. You haven't taken even one action step because you thought yourself out of how bad it may be in the future.

If you do this, then this, then this, then this. Alright? They call this the chain reaction fallacy. Chain reaction fallacy is, if I do this, then that means this is going to happen, then this will happen, then this will happen and this will happen. And you take it all the way to the cognitive dissonance discussion, they call this the absurd absolute, the furthest possible extent of this. It doesn't necessarily have to be absurd, but you get to the point that you basically psych yourself out of it, psych yourself out of doing anything because you're thinking about how bad it could end up. And again, nothing's even happened yet. So people say that they don't want to create success because you don't want to burn yourself out by doing too much work or giving too much effort that you believe success requires. How about we just get the success first and then solve our problems after we get there?

Handle your problems as they come and make sure that it's an actual problem, not one that you've just conjured up in your mind. It doesn't even exist. I remember a female friend once asked me years ago to show her how to do some workouts in the gym. She had never really worked out before and she just wanted some guidance on things she could do on her own by herself in the gym. So I said, all, we'll go to the gym and I'll show you how all the machines work. I'll explain to you how they work. You tell me what parts of your body you want to work out and I'll show you how they work and then you can go do the stuff. And before we even got around to doing this, here's what she said in the same conversation we were talking about, this was not in the gym.

We're having this conversation and she says, well, Dre, let me warn you of something. I just want to get in shape. I want to get toned. I want to tone my body up. This is the kind of language that women use and they talk about the gym. I want to tone my body up, but I don't want to look like some big muscular female. I want to be one of those gym females who's like the bodybuilder females who looks like a man. This is her language that she's saying, I don't want to be looking like a man with all these muscles and all that stuff. I just want to get toned up and get my body in shape. And mind you, this woman who's talking to me, she had never done any type of consistent exercise or workout routine in her entire life up to this point.

She was worried that I don't want to have big muscles like one of those bikini competitor women. I told her that we need to focus on you actually showing up to the facility maybe three times in a row before we worry about you having too many muscles. Your problem with having too many muscles probably is not going to happen. And I stayed in contact with this woman for many years after. I haven't seen her in a while, but the last I solved, she still didn't have the problem of having too many muscles. I think she still has a problem with actually going to the gym, at least the last that I checked. Hopefully she fixed that problem at least. But this is the same thing I'm going to tell you. Alright? Don't start putting down payments on problems that you don't even have yet and problems that are based on actions that you haven't even taken yet.

That's a waste of energy, is a waste of time. And again, you're talking yourself out of success that you haven't even gotten yet. Don't do that. And this is one of the things that stops people from getting to where they want to get to. And you'll notice throughout this series that a lot of these things that keep people from success, these fears of success. Let's be clear again what a fear is. A fear is false evidence appearing real. That's how people break down the four letters of fear, false evidence appearing real. Fear is something that you create in your mind. It's not a real thing. You may have a real feeling about fear, but the fear itself is not a real thing. It is only existing in your mind and you can make it poof, disappear, just as easily as you brought it in. And a lot of the things that cause people to fear success again, are just things that you have conjured up and created in your mind that do not actually tangibly exist.

That said, recapping the next three points in this series. Number seven, raise the expectations. We're talking about why you fear success. Raise expectations. You believe that there will be more people expecting more of you because you have created success and that will happen and you are afraid or you are wanting to avoid it. Those raised expectations may cause you to sabotage your own success. Number eight, let's support. This can go both ways. You may get more support from people who just want to be around you simply because you're successful and less support from people who just don't understand how you got your success or may be a bit envious or confused about or buy your

And they may go away so you could get more or less, but more may not even be the more that you want. Number nine, burnout you are concerned about. Maybe I'll burn myself out doing too much work or having too much expectations on my shoulders or have too much to do if and when I become successful. Therefore, you sabotage your own success before you even get there. I would suggest you not make that mistake again, just like my friend who didn't want to have too many muscles but had never worked out in her life. And again, that wasn't the problem that we needed to deal with. The problem was, let's just make sure you know how to get into the gym in the first place and pick up a weight before we worry about you having too many muscles.

#2846: Why You Fear Success [Part 4 of 10]

Let's get right into it and pick up where we left off in our series of why you fear success. This is part four of what we are projecting to be a 10 part series. So part point number 10, loss of identity. No human being can perform for an extended period of time in a manner that is inconsistent with his or her self-image.

One challenge with becoming successful, especially if you have been less than successful for a long time, is that now you must step into a new identity and a new way of seeing yourself in the mirror if you want that success to sustain. So if you have been less than successful for a while now by your own estimation, by your own measure of what success means and then you become successful, the first thing that needs to change is your self-image. The way that you see yourself, the way you personally see the individual in the mirror. If that does not change but your success has changed, what's going to happen is your self image is going to pull your tangible success right back to the level of your self image. You will always perform at a level that is commensurate with how you see yourself. So if you see yourself as an average level performer but your outcomes right now are way above average, eventually those above average outcomes will pull themselves back.

You will regress to the mean as we say, and you will come back to the average level person that you see yourself as. Your results will be reflective of how you see yourself. If on the other hand you see yourself as a wildly successful individual and you are not that right now, as long as you can maintain that self image, you will then be moved to take actions that will get you to have your success measured up to the way that you see yourself. You always end up getting what you expect of yourself and you always end up living out how you personally see yourself. So one challenge with becoming successful, especially again if you haven't been successful, is that you must step into this new identity to match up to the outcomes that you have. And this is very uncomfortable for people, not because they don't want to be successful but because you are stepping outside of your comfort zone of who you have always known yourself to be.

If you've been the same type of person for the last 10 or 20 or 30 years and now you want to get a whole new level of success, understanding your self image must change as well as your outcomes. They both have to change. Now all of a sudden after 20 years of being the same type of person, now you're going to become this whole new individual all of a sudden just overnight just like that. Usually it doesn't happen that way.

I'm not saying it's impossible, but it's highly improbable and that's difficult for people because they would rather not most people, and it may seem ironic, but it is true, it's a paradox most people would rather not become successful just so they can stay in the comfort zone of being the person that they've always been rather than becoming successful and get out of their comfort zone and step into a new self-image.

Most people would rather stay the same, even if that means staying average because it's comfortable than change, even if the change means being 10 times better than they were before because the change is so uncomfortable that they'd rather not deal with it. And this is the reason why you've heard me say over and over and over again on this show, people do not change and the reason people don't change is not because they don't consciously want to is because it's very uncomfortable to change and it takes a significant amount of resources to make real change in life. It takes no resources to just stay the same even though you're not technically staying the same, you're actually slowly regressing, but it feels to most people like they're staying the same. It's much easier to do that. Most people rather stay in their comfort zones and this is a real thing and it's a serious identity challenge for people when the circumstances of your life changes.

The good news about this is that this often happens when someone gets to having or doing before they change the being. So if you get to having an outcome or you suddenly have a change in behaviors forced upon you before your self image has changed, then it is thrust upon you that you have to adjust your self image or you're not going to be able to maintain what you have or what you've been doing. For example, when a person wins the lottery, let's say a person's been making $40,000 a year all their life and they're 50 years old and then they win a lottery, now they have $10 million in cash that they never had before. The most important thing this person needs to do is not hire an accountant or not get somebody to help 'em with their taxes or a money manager they don't need.

That's not the first thing you need to do. First thing this person needs to do is invest in their mindset and in some personal development because if they don't adjust who they see themselves as, they have to adjust from being that $40,000 a year person to being a $10 million person. If they don't make that adjustment, eventually their mindset will pull their actions and their outcomes back down to that $40,000 a year person. This is why any of you have heard these stories. You hear that a lot of people who win the lottery, they eventually end up going broke or going right back to the state financially that they were in before they won the lottery simply because their self image never changed, their outcomes change. We know we have the B do in half, and I'll tell you that you achieve in that order. You have the B first, then you do, then you have.

But if someone jumps the line and they just go from being do, to have one way, then all of a sudden they're just changing and they haven't done much and they haven't changed who they are. Winning the lottery, you don't have to do anything. All you had to do was buy a lottery ticket for $2 and now all of a sudden you got all this outcome that you didn't really do any work for and you didn't do anything to work on yourself or you got a problem. There's a conflict there. One of those has to change. Either your being has to change to match what you now have or you're having to change to match who you still are. And usually it happens in the second way. You're having changes, IE you lose all the money so you can go back to being the person that you've always seen yourself as.

This is the reason why. So when you hear people talk about people winning the lottery and they end up going broke or a pro athlete makes a lot of money as an athlete, then a few years later they don't have any money left. It's not because of what they did, it's because of who they are. It's because of their mindset. Your mindset never changed. You never do any work on your mindset. You're going to go right back to the same place. This is how an athlete, let's say an athlete comes from a poor or middle class or a lower middle class background, they go become a professional athlete and make a whole lot of money is publicly noted how much money they make. It's usually these stories that happen with athletes where you know exactly how much money they make, you can look it up and you Google people's salaries and all that.

So they made all this money, say an athlete makes $50 million in their entire sporting career, which is a lot of money by any measure, and then their career ends and five years later they barely have any money left. And people are like, how the hell did this person lose all this money? And what you'll hear a lot of people saying, especially people who work in the finance space, they'll say, well, this person didn't invest or they were over leveraged or they bought all these houses, they bought all these depreciating assets and they were taking care of too many family members and they lived this lavish lifestyle that was too big for their after athlete life. And all of those things are true, but notice what all those things are. Those are all actions. Those are all doing things that caused that outcome according to what many people will tell you.

They just did all these things or they didn't do certain things that led to those outcomes. But where do actions come from folks? Where do actions come from? They come from the way that we think. You can't take an action without somehow having some thought in your mind that leads to it. There has to be some notion in your head that leads to any action that you've ever taken. Think about that almost every action you've ever taken in life, there was some thought that crossed your mind before you did it, whether it was conscious or subconscious, there was some kind of thought that crossed your mind before you did every action. So it's really the mindset that needs to change. You get an athlete, let's say an athlete goes from being in the hood and his family makes $50,000 a year per household and a whole household and now he's making $10 million a year for the next 10 years.

The first thing he needs to do is go invest in some personal development. And even if the first thing he actually does is go get himself a money manager or a financial advisor or whatever that hopefully that money manager or financial advisor says, Hey, listen to what Dre Baldwin said and go get yourself some books. Go to the library, I'll give you a $500 allowance and buy yourself some books or invest in your mind because that will last a lot longer than your ability to dunk a basketball or catch a football or hit a baseball. That's the main thing that needs to change for any of you when you're having all of a sudden changes in ways that maybe your being has not caught up to. Everybody follows what I'm saying here. So if you're going to become successful, usually you have to do it in the normal order, which is B, then do then half.

But if somehow things get out of whack, you need to as an emergency measure, make sure that your mindset catches up to the changes in having even though you haven't actually done all the other work yet. Point number 11, today's topic once again is why you may fear success. Number 11, lost connections. Now this is one that we've touched on a few times already in this series, and as you become a more successful person, and again, success is relative. So however you measure success, as your success grows and increases, you will lose touch with some people for multiple reasons. One reason is it's the natural progression of life where some people choose to consciously and intentionally make themselves better while others choose to stay in the same place and simply not improve. This just happens in life sometimes. Some people like you who listen to a show like this one, you are consciously and intentionally doing things to make yourself better, whereas most people are not going to do that.

They're not interested in that. They'd rather do something that's entertaining or something that's more of a stress relieving activity like watching TV or hanging out or going to the movies. Whereas you're doing things that are growth inducing such as listening to a masterclass or reading a book or taking a course or joining a coaching program. Those things are growth inducing, but they're not easy to do. You can't put your brain on autopilot and do those things you got to actually think. Whereas most people would rather turn their brain completely off and do something that is mindless, IE watching tv, scrolling, social media, playing video games, et cetera. So if you're going in one direction, growth inducing and other people are going in the other direction, stress relieving, well, what do you think is going to happen over time? You and that person are going to grow apart.

Y'all are doing two different things. You're on two different paths that are going in divergent directions. So this is one of the reasons why you lose connections as you create more success. Not everybody else is willing to do the things necessary to create success like you're doing again, consciously and intentionally. Two phrases you'll hear me use a lot here on the show, and so naturally you and those people have less in common. Another reason why you may lose connections is because as you become more successful, some people may not be able to see life through the same lens through which you see life because again, they don't have the experiences that you have. They're not living the life that you have. They're not doing the stuff that you're doing, so they just can't understand what you understand. This is how any of you out there who has children and you have friends who you had kids before them and maybe your kids are growing up and getting older, your kids are now five years old, 10 years old, they're going, they're in high school, they maybe going to college.

And the friends that you had when you first had children, they didn't have kids then and they still don't have kids now. They can't relate to your situation because anytime that you talk to them, you're probably telling them about something's going on with the kids. Because when you have kids, for the most part, that's one of the biggest things. A lot of your attention and focus is on what's going on with the kids for the next 18 years at least until they get out of the house and they're on their own. And that other person can't relate to that because they don't have the same experience. So not like that person stops being your friend completely, but they may not be able to relate to you as well and the connection may get weaker just because y'all can't talk about the same things, you can't do the same things or they're going and doing stuff that a single person can do or a person with no kids can do.

Let's say you as a person with kids can't do those same things. You got kids now. You can't make the same decisions, you can't go to the same places, you can't stay out as late and you have to think about the kids before you think about anything else, even yourself. So this is one example that I'm giving you here of how two people can have divergent experiences, life experiences, and it causes the connection to weaken simply because they're just not doing the same things. So also some people may be only able to live vicariously through you because maybe they just want to watch what you're doing. I remember when I first went over a seizure to play basketball, I would write a lot of the first iteration of my writing. I would write blog posts on my Facebook profile and I would just write little basic articles, my Facebook profiles just about my experiences playing overseas and stuff like that.

And a lot of my friends from back home would read those posts because it was interesting. What was interesting about it was I was doing something that most of them would never do and they were able to live that life vicariously through me. So in some ways that can create more connections depending on your style and depending on who those people are. But in other ways somebody might see that and they may shun the idea of you simply because what you're doing is a reflection of what they're not doing. Again, you've heard me say that three or four times already in the series, so that allows them to stay comfortable in their identity to just completely block out anything that you have going on because it's so different from what they have going on. Point number 12, today's topic once again is we are talking about why you fear success.

Point number 12 is vulnerability. This is another thing that may be causing you to fear success and want to stay away from it. As we have established already in this series, success makes you more visible than you previously were. You are more seen, you are more known. Even people who already knew who you were are now more aware of your presence simply because of your success, your presence has enlarged. You have an enlarged presence simply because you're doing more than you were doing before. So because of this and also on top of the fact that the more successful you become, there are fewer people on your same level, the higher up the success ladder you go. It's not like you all of a sudden are by yourself. There will always be other people on the ladder, but there are fewer people on the ladder. There's more elbow room.

The higher up the success ladder you go. And because of that, you are more visible simply because there's less of a crowd around you. So there may be a crowd of a million people at level one of success. Level two, there's only 800,000. Level three is only 500,000. Level 10, there might only be 20,000 people up there. So you're more easily seen, more easily known, and more easily identified simply because, so you have relatively fewer peers than who you had before. So because of this, the attention that you're drawing could possibly cause you to feel vulnerable simply because you are so visible. Now you don't have to feel vulnerable, but this is a possibility, which is why I'm including it in this list, in this series. I've heard many people who have not yet created, let's say, financial success. This is a good example and I've heard this from multiple people.

They haven't yet created a certain level of financial success, but they will say something like, well, maybe I don't want to be so financially successful because they are projecting in their minds all the attention that comes with financial success and how they believe that when they have financial success, especially the success that is publicly noted, meaning people know that you have a certain amount of money, it will draw too much stress on them, such as somebody trying to sue you, somebody trying to steal money from you or somebody trying to get money out of you, dishonestly stealing from you, people asking you for money, and you got to deal with the requests and other maladies that come with having financial success. And again, this is similar to my friend who was worried about having too many muscles before they started lifting weights. So let's first of all get you some money, some money period is to make sure all your bills are paid first for you worried about having too much money and everybody wanting to take some from you, alright?

Again, you're making down payments on problems that you don't even have and then using those down payments as an excuse for not doing anything to get to success. And this is how again, many people think themselves out of success based on things that have never even occurred just based on their imagination. Literally, this is imagination. I would suggest that any of you who's thinking about a future problem that will come with increased success, accomplishment or achievement, I would suggest you get the problem and deal with it as it is. Go get the success, get the problems that come with it because remember, everything in life has a trade-off episode 2174, I told you that there are no perfect scenarios. Only trade-offs. Get the scenario of success. See the trade-offs and learn to deal with them. That's it. Just learn to deal with them because understand, since I just told you, everything in life has a trade off.

Being average has a trade off too. If you do nothing and stay in the same space as you are in life right now for the next 10, 20, 30 years, there's a trade off to that too. In other words, there's a penalty for that. The same way there's a penalty, if you get 10 times more successful, there is no perfect scenario you could be in where nothing's going to happen. Only scenario you could be in where nothing's going to happen and you don't have to deal with anything. It's called death, alright? Other than that, you are always going to have to deal with something, alright? That's what we call life. That said, let's recap today's class, which is again, we are on part four of what's going to be a 10 part series on why you fear success. Number 10, point number 10, loss of identity.

Your identity must change when your success levels go up. Actually, your identity must change before your success levels go up. 99% of the time, you must change who you see yourself as and how you see you in the mirror before you can change your actions or change the effect of your actions before you can change your outcomes. If you happen to do this out of order, IE, you win the lottery before you have changed your mindset, you better change your mindset quickly or your financial level is going to go right back down to where it was and meet your mindset where you were before. Number 11, lost connections. Sometimes you lose connections because you are going in a growth direction where other people are basically receding because they're not trying to grow. If you're not growing, you're dying. It's one of the others, you may lose connections that way.

And also as you create more success, people just can't relate to your life the same way simply because you're living a way that they're not living and these connections can be lost and some people fear losing those connections. These are people like and trust and love. You don't want to get disconnected from them, so you'd rather stay average so you can stay connected to those people. And number 12, vulnerability. Alright? As you become more successful, you become more seen, you are more known, you may feel like you are becoming more of a target and you may even hear people who are successful talk about these things and it calls you to psych yourself out and think, well, maybe I shouldn't become successful because then I'll be vulnerable and somebody might want to sue me or attack me, or I might need security or somebody's going to be stalking me or I'm going to get all these haters on the internet.

How about you just get to the success first and worry about the problems later? How about that? Instead of putting a down payment on problems that you do not yet have because you don't even have the success that would bring those problems, how about you go get the success and let's see what those problems actually look like and deal with them as they come. I bet you'll be able to deal with them if for you to become successful, you got to build yourself up so much that I guarantee you'll be able to deal with things like whatever problems come with being successful and you'll be much better off dealing with the problems as a success than dealing with the problems of being average.

#2847: Why You Fear Success [Part 5 of 10]

Let's get into this topic. We are again picking up on our series of why you fear success and what are the things that we are afraid of that lead us to being afraid of success. So kind of where, taking two steps here. So point number 13 is where we are picking up here. Again, this is part five of our projected 10 part series.

Number 13, standing out, standing out similar to the prior point. Standing out means you are making yourself visible. And often this is because you are doing something intentionally that draws attention to you. And this could, doesn't always, but it could make you a target simply because you are so much more visible than you were before. The more visible you come, the more of a target you become. This is just how it works. Again, the more people can see you, the more likely someone's going to take aim at you just because you are there, not because there's anything specifically wrong with you, not because they really have any issue with you personally, it's just because you are available. So they're just going to use you because you're there. This is just how it works. Any of you who's on social media, the more your stuff gets seen on social media, the more likely you're going to get trolls and haters and negative people in your comments.

Why? Because your stuff is visible. That's the reason why it happens, not because of anything specifically that you did or said, and it doesn't even matter what topic you talk about. The more you're seen, the more negativity you are bound to get just compared to when you're arrested. It doesn't mean that everything you get is going to be negative, but you're just going to get more of it simply because you're available to be viewed. And again, being a target doesn't just mean a target from a people who want to take things from you, but a target in that you will get, as I said, negativity, hate critiques, more people looking for flaws and weaknesses in you simply because your success is a reflection of their lack of success. This is one of the reasons why people look for flaws and people who are well known simply because they're out there, alright, how is this person doing so much better than I am is the way that they're thinking and they have to find a way to either catch up to you, which will be very hard to do.

That requires work and effort and intentionality and consciousness. Or here's an easier way, lemme just find a flaw in them so I can reconcile that they're better than me in this, but they're not better than me. And these other things are areas where I found flaws. So now we're actually equal. And again, this is all happening in their mind. This is all rationalization that they happen. That happens in people's minds. Not a real thing, but this is exactly what people do. These are the two choices you have when you see someone who is clearly outperforming. You can either A, use it as motivation and inspiration to move yourself up to that level of performance. You actually got three options. Option B is you can say, well, forget about them, I don't care about them and just pay it. No mind. A, it didn't happen. Or C, you can find a way to negatively pull them down in your mind, not in fact, but in your mind such that their outperformance of you isn't really a real thing because you balance it out with some negative flaw that you found in them that you created in your mind.

Those are your three choices anytime someone's outperforming you and you know about it. So you'll notice that we come back to this point over and over again already in this series about when someone else sees you performing at a level higher than them, and we're only halfway through the series, and this is one of the biggest things that holds people back from moving towards success and that you are afraid of the negative feedback and the criticism that could come from other people who have not reached the same level of success that you have. You just don't want to deal with the negative feedback and the criticism that might result from it. Napoleon Hill laid this out almost a hundred years ago when he noted the six basic fears in his book, think and Grow Rich. And one of the six basic fears was the fear of criticism.

And I actually did a series on the six basic fears in episode number 18, 16. Now what I did was reorganize the six basic fears. So he had them laid out in a certain order. I changed that order and I'll get to that in one second. And the fear of criticism is one of those fears that Napoleon Hill laid out, and this was way back almost a hundred years ago that he wrote this book that people sometimes don't do things in life because they are afraid of negative feedback that they will get from their circle. Whether it's your social circle, your professional circle, your community circle, your family circle, the world around us, depending on what you're doing and how many people know about it, so many people are afraid of negative backlash and negative feedback that they don't do anything just to avoid having anybody talk about you.

And that's the formula. If you don't want anybody to talk negatively about you, just do nothing and be nothing and nobody will ever talk negatively about you. Maybe if you become something and you do something, people are going to talk bad about you. It is inevitable, it will happen. It always happens. So when I reorganized the six basic fears, again, that was episode number 1 8 1 6, episode 1816. You can listen to any episode by going to one of two places. You can go to work on your game podcast.com where you see every episode listed audio version, or you can go to dre all day.com/blog and then slash and then put the number of the episode and make sure you put the www there. We haven't found a way to let people just type it without the W. So you have to put the www.dreallday.com/blog/then put the number and then you can see every episode in history.

The show also weighed out in basically blog posts slash article format. So when I reorganized the six basic fears, I moved the fear of criticism to the number one of the six basic fears. Now what Napoleon Hill had when he wrote Think and Go Rich, his number one basic fear was the fear of poverty. And I'll see if I can remember the other six. Now again, I did this whole episode so I don't have to have this memorized, but it was the fear of poverty is one, fear of criticism is two. The fear of loss of love is another one. This is not in any particular order. Fear of loss of love is number three, fear of old age is number four. The fear of ill health is number five. And there was one more, and I don't even remember what it was, so I remember five of the six, but there's another one that I'm not remembering right now.

Good news is we record stuff over here so you ain't gotta remember it. So again, listen to episode 1816 and read the book, think and Grow Rich by Napoleon Hill. If you have not already, if you have read it again. So I moved the fear of criticism to the top of the list where Napoleon Hill had the fear of poverty and the reason he had the fear of poverty at the top of his list is because he wrote his book during the Great Depression. Those of you not familiar with the Great Depression, it was a period of austerity where there was not a lot of money moving. The money existed, but it wasn't moving around. Nobody was spending any money. Everyone was very depressed around the concept of money. The word depression is a good term for it. And when no money is moving in the economy, they call it a recession.

And if it lasts for a certain amount of time, they call it depression. So during the Great Depression, no money was moving in the economy. Everybody was pinching onto their pennies and afraid that they would never have money ever again. So it made sense that the number one of the six basic fears was the fear of poverty because so many people were actually experiencing it and so many people felt like they were dangerously close to it. So that was number one fear. These days there are still people in poverty, but we're not in a depression right now. So the number one fear that people have shifted their focus to is the fear of being critiqued, criticized, and had negative things said about you. And why is that? It makes perfect sense. You think about the world that we live in now, where do people spend a lot of their time?

Social media, what happens on social media? You and a bunch of other people who you have never met and probably never will meet, and a bunch of people who might not even fucking exist are making comments and saying stuff back and forth to each other and about other people and just saying things just to try to get attention. You get trolls, you get negative people, you get haters, you get people leaving stuff in the comments. And again, a good percentage of these people, you can't even tell if they're a real human being, right? They talk as if they're a human being, but you look at their profile, there's no picture, there's no real name. You don't even know these people are real. But what do they do? There's a lot of criticism happening, there's a lot of backlash, a lot of negative stuff that people just throw out there just because it could possibly draw some attention.

This is what people do these days. So it makes sense that the number one fear these days should be as I put in order when I redid the six basic fears, is the fear of criticism. People don't want to be criticized and they don't want to deal with any kind of backlash that comes from criticism. So remember what I've always told you, the opportunity folks are in what the opposites looking at what most people are afraid of. If you can make yourself unafraid of the thing that most people are afraid of, you create an opportunity for yourself. Everybody follow me here? So if everybody's afraid of criticism, one thing you should do is make yourself immune to criticism. Now, that doesn't mean all criticism. There's some criticism that you should actually accept because if you have, let's say someone, if you have a coach around you, you play a sport, you have a coach, or you have some people in your life who have the authority to hold you accountable and they have a critique for you or something that you did or didn't do, you should accept that criticism because that criticism can make you better as long as you're going to listen to it.

You don't have to take criticism from everyone, but you should listen to criticism from the right people and you should have some people in your life who have the leverage, the leeway to criticize you and accept it when they give it to you. I talked about criticism in episode number 13, 16. Correction is not criticism. Someone corrects you, they're not criticizing you again depending on who they are. Episode number 1240, stop trying to avoid criticism. Episode number seven 20, how to handle criticism. Episode number 18, dealing with criticism and episode number. Well, I flipped it around and when I talked about episode number 2375, a stupid criticism of people throughout there is that someone's just trying to get attention as if that's a bad thing. Getting attention is actually a smart thing. Anyway, those are some episodes where I've talked about attention. If any of you wanted to go over a few of those.

So these days more people are afraid of being criticized, as I said, more than they're afraid of an actual tangible, bad outcome. Poverty is a real tangible thing you can tell when you're in poverty because you can count how much money you got when you're being criticized. It's just people talking. It's just words. The words don't actually do anything to you when you're in poverty, you don't have money, maybe you can't pay your bills, you can't pay your rent, you can't put gas in your car, you can't feed your family. That's a real tangible thing that you can feel and see. Criticism is just words and words really can mean a lot. They can mean absolutely nothing depends on how you decide to look at it. So this is what happens with a lot of people: they sabotage or avoid creating any level of success just so they avoid the criticism that they believe will come with it.

Point number 14, today's topic once again, we are on to the next part of our series, is part five of why you fear success. Number five, rejection. So what I mean by rejection, if you're successful, Dre, why are you talking about rejection? Why would somebody be rejected? They're successful. Well, let's be clear and let's be honest about this. When you are aiming to be more successful than you are right now, again, I told you the definition of success in this series means you are doing significantly better than what you've done up to this point. So when you do that and you aim for that, I don't guarantee you're going to get it. So when you decide that you're going to aim to be way more successful than you are now, you are not guaranteed to actually get there. So maybe you will aim for a height that you simply fail to reach.

So in such a case, you have been effectively rejected by the height that you're trying to reach. So you're used to living at level three. You say, all right, I'm going to get up to a level 10, and you aim for a level 10, but when you get up there, you don't make it. You don't make it to a level 10, you come up short of a level 10. So you have been effectively rejected by level 10. And because you're trying to reach that height that many people will not even attempt to get to, your failure will be very public and it could cause you to feel embarrassed because again, this is you trying to do something that most people don't even try to do. So when you tried it, you had a lot of people who saw you try because again ain't like they're all trying at the same time.

So they're all watching you because they ain't doing anything and you came up short. So I say public failure that you might go through and this could cause you to feel embarrassed. And again, notice two key words in that sentence. Cause and feel could cause, could and feel extra, should be the two words could and feel because embarrassment, just like confidence, just like it was another word that I used there earlier here. Fear is another one. Let's just use fear, confidence, embarrassment. All of these things are states of mind. They are not real things. Confidence is not tangible, you can't touch confidence, you can't hold it in your hands. You cannot hold fear in your hands, you can't touch it. Embarrassment, you cannot hold it in your hand. You cannot feel it. And confidence, fear and embarrassment. These are another thing I want to tell you about these three feelings and others who are of their ilk.

No one can force these upon you. No one can force you to be afraid. No one can force you to be confident and no one can force you to feel embarrassed. Someone might say, Hey, if I was you, I would be afraid. That doesn't mean you need to be afraid. Somebody could say, well, if that happened to me, I would be embarrassed. What the hell does that have to do with you? If someone says, Hey, do this and you'll feel confident and it doesn't work for you, then hey, it doesn't work for you. So these are feelings that you create in your own mind and there are tools that can help you. I have a program called Bulletproof Mindset that helps you with all of these. And I have another course called ASAP Confidence that'll help you all out with that confidence part. And a book right there called the Super You.

If you're watching the video, it's a bright yellow cover. It's part of my bulletproof bundle. If you get the mirror motivation@mirrorofmotivation.com, check the box on that page to get the Bulletproof Bundle Super You is one of those four books that is all about confidence. There are tools that can help you develop confidence, but these exist in your mind. They're not tangible things. I can't give you confidence that you can't buy it on Amazon and get it in a package in two days or less with Amazon Prime. You have to develop these in your mind. Fear, confidence, embarrassment, alies, these are mental choices. Again, they cannot happen to you. You allow them to occur in your mind. You can go your whole life and never feel embarrassed if you want to. What embarrasses one person does not have to embarrass you. So this happens in your mind.

So if you come up short of a big goal, you can just brush it off and say, that's completely fine, or you can allow it to destroy you for the rest of your life. Okay, so it's literally a choice. Many people would rather avoid the possible rejection of going after a big goal and failing because they want to avoid the criticism that comes with it or the ridicule that comes with it. Ridicule is a form of criticism. Just people using satire in order to criticize it was the same thing. And instead what people do instead, they go after mediocre goals and succeed at reaching them just so they can feel like they did something. So they don't want to fucking complete idiot. So let's go off there mediocre, go and reach it instead of going for a big goal and failing because I don't want to get ridiculed or laughed at or criticized.

And again, this is sad, but it's true. And if you look around in life, and some of you who are listening to me right now, you need to look in the mirror because I'm talking about you. You notice that people do this all the time. This won't be hard to find. If you look around, this is actually pretty easy to find. People do it all the time and they come up with very, very, very astute rationalizations for why they're going after mediocre goals instead of big ones. I remember once I was training this basketball player, he was in high school and his thing was, this is back in my basketball playing days. His thing was shooting. He was a good outside shooter. He didn't really have much skill in any other aspect of the game. He wasn't a very good ball handler. He played no defense whatsoever.

He didn't have very good athleticism. He didn't really contribute on the court in any way other than shooting the basketball. No defense, he couldn't guard anybody. He didn't grab any rebounds. He wasn't a good passer, not a good ball handler, but he was good at shooting the outside shot. And I remember I was training him once and he wanted to work on his outside shot all the time. Every time I trained him, he just wanted to do some outside shooting stuff and we're doing it, doing it, doing it. And one day I said, well, why don't we work on the rest of your game? And he bristled at the idea a little bit. He didn't want to work on anything else and he just wanted to work on the shot, just shoot, shoot, shoot. And the last that I heard of him and saw him, his shooting took him, he went and played college basketball and he was an outside shooter, that was his thing, designated outside shooter.

But he never developed the rest of his game. And he was the same player by the time he was 22, 23 graduating college that he was when he was 16, 17, he didn't develop at all. Only thing is that he got older. That's it. You got a little bit more facial hair. That's pretty much all that happened to him. And this is what happens with a lot of people. They would rather stay in the same spot and be comfortable than go after anything different. For him to work on his ball handling would require him to get uncomfortable because he wasn't that good at ball handling, which meant he wouldn't have looked as good in his workouts. And again, it was not like it was an audience of people watching us, it was just me and him on the court and nobody else was there. He would've felt uncomfortable though working on his ball handling because it wasn't that good or working on rebounding or defense or anything other than shooting because that was the only thing he was comfortable with.

And he pretty much stayed there. And his game never evolved past being that same player that he was in high school by the time he graduated from college because he didn't want to work on the rest of his game. And again, it doesn't make him a bad person. I mean he played in college. I mean he can say he did it, but as far as evolution, he didn't go too far. And this is the same thing that happens with a lot of people. They would rather just keep doing the same things that they're comfortable with rather than force themselves into the discomfort that comes with possibly doing something new. And you want to make sure that's not you. Alright? That's the whole point of this point. Number 15, we're talking here today, point number, we're on part five of our what will be a 10 part series.

Why do you fear success number 15, is it unsustainable? This is a question, can I sustain my success? And some people fear that they won't be able to sustain their success. So they decide, they rationalize well, I might as well not even get it because I can't keep it. See, this is the question of whether or not you can maintain success once you get it. And it goes along with the expectations. We talked about expectations earlier in this series. This goes right along with it. And those expectations are real, even though expectations, again, they're not a tangible thing, you can't touch them. But do people expect certain things from you when you're a successful person? Any of you here who is successful? Any of you who is a leader of a team, any of you here who's a head of a household, any of you has people who follow you and listen to you and they're under your care or supervision or anything like that, do they have expectations of you?

Absolutely they do. They have expectations and that's real. So when you become a successful person, others who are less successful than you would rather get behind you and hope that you can keep things going rather than try to join you and do what you did to get there. So they don't want to join you and be up in the front and line with you. Now they want to get behind you and let you weed the way why? Because most humans would rather be led than to weed. Even though you might think everybody wants to lead and there's just a big competition amongst everybody who's going to be the leader. No, that's not really the case. Most people want to be led, they don't want to lead.

So once you become successful, you will be expected to remain successful. Why? Because you got a bunch of people who just got in line behind you naturally and they're just following you, alright, lead us. Show us where to go. Which means you may now start to feel the pressure of knowing that you must sustain your success not only for yourself because you want to be successful just with you, right? Forget about everybody else. You want to be successful because you want to be successful. So not only do you have to maintain the success to serve you, but now you also have to serve the people who decided to stop playing the game of getting to your level. And they decided, let me just follow this guy. Lemme just follow this girl. I'll just get behind them. They're already successful. Why don't I just follow them?

So now you got people following you and you didn't even ask him to and they're just watching you. And now you got to deal with that. I told you this, I mentioned this story a long time ago. I'll tell it again. So there was this Nike basketball commercial. This was probably, man, this had to be, this was close to maybe 20 years ago, maybe 2000 7, 6, 7, something like that. There was two players who were signing to Nike at the time. It was Paul Pierce and Jermaine O'Neill, and you don't need to know who those guys are to understand the story. They were playing pickup basketball. And this is just a commercial. So Paul Pierce was on one team. He was playing for the Boston Celtics at the time. Jermaine O'Neill was an all-star and he was an all-star. Jermaine O'Neill was an all star playing for the Indiana Pacers at the time.

So they're both Nike and Dorsey. So in his pickup game, Paul was on one team, Jermaine's on another team, and Paul's making all kinds of crazy moves and dunks and Jermaine's doing the same thing. And then they would show somebody on Paul Pierce's team would make a mistake and you could see Paul getting disgusted with his teammate for messing up. And then the same thing happened on Jermaine O'Neill's team. His teammate would make a mistake and Jermaine would get discussed with his teammate. And eventually Paul and Jermaine just decided to stop giving the ball to their teammates and they just started doing everything on their own. So they just took over the game and they're just scoring. Paul Pierce is scoring, then Jermaine O'Neill's dunking, and they're just doing stuff back to back, just scoring all the points and dominating the game to the point that the rest of the guys on the court are pretty much bystanders to these two dudes who are essentially playing one-on-one in a five on five basketball game.

So what happens over the course of the commercial is that players from Paul Pierce's team, they just stop playing in the game. They just go sit on bleach, sit in the bleachers and watch Paul because he's doing everything anyway. And then players on Jermaine O'Neill's team, they do the same thing. They stop playing, they go sit in the bleachers and watch Jermaine because he's doing everything. And eventually you got eight guys sitting in the bleachers who were playing in the game. They're all sitting there watching while Paul Pierce and Jermaine O'Neill are just playing one-on-one. So five on five becomes a one-on-one because the other guys on the court were not involved anyway, and they weren't on the level of these two guys. And what I just explained to you from that commercial is a metaphor for what I'm telling you. What happens in life when you achieve a high level of success, eventually other people stop trying to compete with you and they just sit on the bleachers.

They just sit in the bleachers and watch you because they ain't going to compete with you Anyway, lemme just sit in the bleachers and watch this guy. I am a non-factor in this game anyway, so let me just watch the game because I'm just running up and down the court for nothing. And that commercial and this commercial, this commercial didn't even pop off too much. I only remember seeing it maybe once or twice, but I always remember it because it's a great metaphor for what happens in life when you become a high level performer. Eventually people stop trying to compete with you and they just get behind you, alright? And now everybody's watching you. So ain't nobody to pass the ball to now. Now you have to do everything now. You literally have to do everything because ain't nobody to pass the ball to when you're playing one-on-one, you can't take a playoff now you got to do everything.

So it's a great metaphor for all of life. That right there that I pulled from basketball. So knowing that you got to sustain the success again, not just for yourself, but for the people who are watching. You. Notice that when you go to a concert or a sporting match, there are many more people sitting in the stands watching than there are people on the stage who are on the court or on the field, right? You go to a football game, there's what, 11 guys on both sides. So you got 22 guys on the field and 30,000 people on the stands. This is a metaphor for life folks. There is an expectation of people who are on stage. And again, a stage doesn't have to be a concert. A stage just means you have assumed an elevated position based on your performance. There are people on stages, there's an expectation on them to do things that people on the stands either cannot do or are not willing to even try doing.

The expectation is all on you. I remember seeing a movie called The Kings of Comedy. Y'all remember this movie that came out probably about 20 years ago, maybe 20 plus. And one of the comedians who did a set on the Kings of Comedy was a guy named Steve Harvey, who many of you know, and Steve Harvey in his set, he was telling a joke about going to concerts. He said, I don't like going to rap concerts because the rappers are having the fans do all the work. And Steve was like, no, I'm not standing up. I'm not young and I'm not throwing my hands in the air. I paid a hundred dollars for this ticket.

317

You throw your hands in the air, you jump up and down and all this stuff. It was funny the way that he framed it. So you can probably find a joke on YouTube, but the whole point is that when there's a bunch of people in the stands watching, you can't expect them to do the work.

They expect you to do the work. That's why they paid for the ticket. That's why they came and paid with their attention. So they're expecting you to perform. You got to perform again. That's the expectation once you assume a stage position, and this is the trade off of being successful everybody. So this question of whether or not you can sustain your success is a real question. It is real and it is a legitimate question. So let's recap today's points number 13. We're talking again. This whole episode is part five of why you fear success. Number 13, standing out, you're drawing attention. It's going to draw eyeballs. And a lot of people don't want to stand out because they don't want to deal with the possible criticism that comes with standing out the inevitable, rather criticism that comes with standing out. You will be criticized when you stand out.

The fear of criticism, I believe, is the greatest human fear that exists in the world today. It is leapfrogging the fear of poverty. And number 14, rejection, you going after big goals doesn't mean you're going to actually reach big goals, which means you may be rejected and in the process, ridiculed and criticized for even going after them in the first place. Because when you go after a big goal, the people who didn't have the courage to go after that big goal will feel relieved and satisfied that you failed because it justifies the fact that they never tried. Ching Nchu talked about this in a book called Thick Face Black Hearts. If you have not read that book again, it's called Thick Face. Black Heart is a great book. I've gifted this book to many coaching clients and members working on your game, university of mine.

So if you haven't read that book, I suggest you go buy it and read it. Because Of the fear of rejection, a lot of people don't want to be rejected, so they'd rather just try mediocre things so that they can at least succeed at it rather than going after big things and giving themselves the possibility of winning. And number 15, is it a sustainable question of whether or not you can sustain your success goes along with the expectations to come with success. When you become a successful person, people will start expecting you to be successful again, just like that Nike commercial I just described to you. They will get off the court and stop playing. They'll go sit in the bleachers and happily watch you do everything to the point that you have no one to pass the ball to. You got to do everything yourself and everybody's sitting there watching and waiting for you to do it because they ain't got nothing else to do.

They want to watch you because they're not going to be on your level. So they're going to rather watch you buy a ticket and watch you than participate in the game and compete against you. And now you have to deliver. Can you sustain that? That is a question and it's a real one.

Get Dre's #MondayMotivation Text {▮}

Dre sends out a FREE text message every Monday that's guaranteed to have you focused, sharp and on-point to start your week.

Text now to join the community: 305.384.6894. Normal texting rates apply.

Received This From a Friend?

Subscribe and get the **Bulletproof Bulletin + Black Book** to your PHYSICAL mailbox every month: http://www.BulletproofBulletin.com

Not A University Member Yet?

Join **Work On Your Game University** and get access to all of our programs that address the 5 biggest challenges we see every time with our members –

1. Mindset
2. Money
3. Discipline
4. Strategy
5. Time

– And we have courses (and are continually adding training) for EACH of these challenges.

Get access to them all NOW in Work On Your Game University here: http://www.WorkOnYourGameUniversity.com/

WORK ON YOUR GAME

Work On Your Game Inc.

Made in the USA
Columbia, SC
08 April 2024

33963559R00176